Soviet Politics

Soviet Politics
An introduction

Richard Sakwa

First published 1989
by Routledge
11 New Fetter Lane, London EC4P 4EE
29 West 35th Street, New York, NY 10001

© 1989 Richard Sakwa

British Library Cataloguing in Publication Data

Sakwa, Richard, 1953–
Soviet politics : an introduction.
1. Soviet Union. Politics
I. Title
320.947

ISBN 0-415-00506-1
ISBN 0-415-00507-X

Library of Congress Cataloging in Publication Data

Sakwa, Richard.
Soviet politics : an introduction / Richard Sakwa.
p.   cm.
Bibliography: p.
Includes index.
ISBN 0-415-00506-1. ISBN 0-415-00507-X (pbk.)
1. Soviet Union—Politics and government—1917– I. Title.
JN6515.S249 1989
320.947—dc20   88-31223
                                                       CIP

ROUTLEDGE
London and New York

First published 1989
by Routledge
11 New Fetter Lane, London EC4P 4EE
29 West 35th Street, New York, NY 10001

© 1989 Richard Sakwa

Phototypeset in 10pt Times by
Mews Photosetting, Beckenham, Kent
Printed and bound in Great Britain by Mackays of Chatham PLC, Kent

British Library Cataloguing in Publication Data

Sakwa, Richard, *1953– .*
    Soviet politics: an introduction.
    1. Soviet Union. Politics
    I. Title
    320.947

    ISBN 0-415-00505-1
    ISBN 0-415-00506-X

Library of Congress Cataloging in Publication Data

Sakwa, Richard.
        Soviet politics : an introduction / Richard Sakwa.
            p.   cm.
        Bibliography: p.
        Includes index.
        ISBN 0-415-00505-1. ISBN 0-415-00506-X (pbk.)
        1. Soviet Union — Politics and government — 1917– I. Title.
    DK266.S236   1989
    947.084 – dc19   88-30273
                                                                          CIP

Contents

Contents

Figures

Tables

Figure 1 USSR: administrative divisions

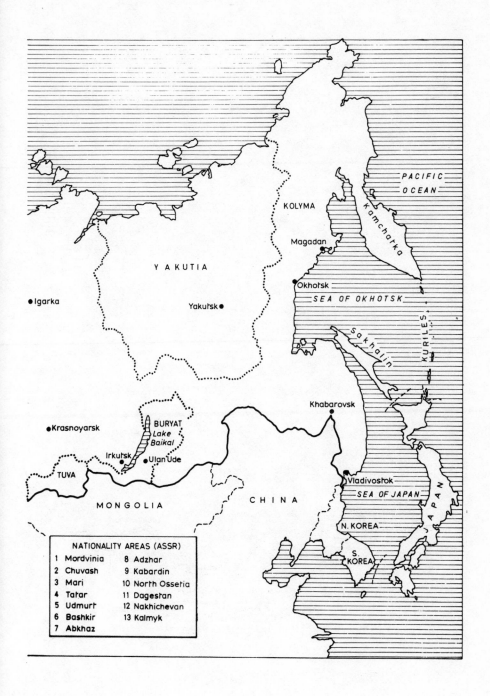

PACIFIC OCEAN

Kamchatka

KOLYMA

• Magadan

Y A K U T I A

• Igarka

Yakutsk •

• Okhotsk

SEA OF OKHOTSK

Sakhalin

KURILES

• Khabarovsk

• Krasnoyarsk

BURYAT
Lake
Baikal

Irkutsk •   • Ulan Ude

TUVA

Vladivostok

SEA OF JAPAN

JAPAN

MONGOLIA

C H I N A

N. KOREA

S. KOREA

NATIONALITY AREAS (ASSR)	
1 Mordvinia	8 Adzhar
2 Chuvash	9 Kabardin
3 Mari	10 North Ossetia
4 Tatar	11 Dagestan
5 Udmurt	12 Nakhichevan
6 Bashkir	13 Kalmyk
7 Abkhaz	

Preface

The Bolshevik revolution of October 1917 was one of the most important events of the twentieth century. The Russian revolution was not confined to a faraway country of little concern but took place in a nation straddling the two continents of Europe and Asia. The world shaped by the revolution is the one in which we live today. The revolution drew its inspiration from the legacy of Western political thought as interpreted by Marx and Engels, and its intellectual context to this day remains firmly wedded to the concerns of what is loosely called Western political discourse. But the revolution also reflected concerns peculiar to Russia itself, and its development represents the energy of Russia as harnessed by Lenin. For good or ill, changes in the Soviet Union ultimately have an impact on the lives of all the citizens of the world.

This book is designed for the general reader and for students of Soviet politics with a *penchant* for history. The aim is to provide an accessible introduction to the history and institutions of the Soviet Union accompanied by an analysis of how the system works in practice. The book falls into three broad sections. Chapters 1 to 5 provide the historical context, with the focus on major political themes rather than on detailed historical analysis. Chapters 6 to 10, the heart of the book, deal with the institutions and major formal and informal political and social processes. Chapters 11 to 15 tie together and apply the previous analysis in a series of case studies of major policy issues. The afterword briefly discusses the prospects and nature of change in the Soviet system. Shortage of space has meant that some important issues, such as social welfare, have not been discussed at the length they deserve.

The purpose is to provide a general framework through which we can understand the course of Soviet development. A major theme is the relationship between change and continuity. The Soviet Union has changed from being a relatively underdeveloped country to becoming the second most powerful industrial nation in the world. Industrialization has been accompanied by massive social changes that have transformed a primarily peasant society into an urbanized and modern nation. In political and military terms the Soviet Union has become one of the two superpowers with interests that span the globe. At the same time social and economic changes have been accompanied by a high degree of continuity in the basic structures of the political system. A second theme is the tension between ideology and practice. The Bolsheviks came to power with certain ideas about socialism, and yet while utopian in inspiration they were far from possessing any blueprint that they could simply proceed to implement. The policies of the Soviet government have always emerged out of a complex interaction of beliefs and practical necessities. A third theme is the relationship between the political system and society. As the system has matured the needs of society itself have come to the fore to join the more abstract needs of the state such as industrialization or defence. The themes of this book — the relationship between continuity and change, between ideology and circumstances, and the interaction of politics and society — are reflected in the tension between periods of reform and periods of relative political stagnation. Concepts and institutions are simultaneously drained of their old meaning and charged with a new content. The challenge facing Stalin's successors is whether a new basis can be found to develop socialist economic relations and socialist democracy.

We are all children of our times, and having come to know the Soviet Union not during the exciting years of Khrushchev but while it languished in what has now come to be called the 'era of stagnation' under Brezhnev, the inevitable tendency for me has been to stress the elements of continuity and the absence of transformations in Soviet politics. However, the onset of a period of reform under Gorbachev has once again brought the element of change to the forefront. This book has tried to reflect the changes while placing them in the context of the development of the Soviet system as a whole.

In a work of this nature the intellectual debts to generations of scholars who have laboured in the vineyard of Soviet studies are far too numerous for all to be individually acknowledged. Footnotes have been kept to a minimum in order to avoid interrupting the flow of the text. At the end of each chapter there is a list of works with the key texts marked out, and at the end of the book a bibliography of the major general works on Soviet politics. The near absence of Russian texts is not intended to disparage them or to suggest that they have not been consulted; they have been cut to permit more space for more broadly accessible works. I am grateful to colleagues who have read all or parts of various drafts: Howard White, Greg Andrusz, Lyn Mally, Peter Kenez, Peter Shearman, and an anonymous reviewer. Many thanks to them all. I would like to thank all those involved in the progress of this work at what was once Croom Helm but is now Routledge, and in particular Andrew Lockett and Jennifer Binnie, whose support, patience and efficiency were much appreciated. I owe a great debt to students I have taught, and learnt from, including those at Cheltenham and Worcester colleges of higher education, the Polytechnic of Central London, the University of Essex at Colchester, the University of California at Santa Cruz, and the University of Kent at Canterbury. It is to generations past and generations to come of students of Soviet politics that this book is dedicated.

Chapter one

The Russian legacy

The old regime

Revolutions destroy the old and yet are forced to build on the foundations established by their predecessors. The rhythms of time, of geography, and of peoples have stamped the mark of the old regime on to the new one that came to power in October 1917.

The adoption of what was to become the Orthodox form of Christianity by Prince Vladimir in Kiev, then the centre of the Russian lands, in 988 stamped Russia with a Byzantine form of religiosity which stood in sharp contrast to that of the Roman Catholic countries of Europe. The capture of Constantinople in 1453 by the Ottoman empire isolated Russia from its religious roots, and the Mongol occupation for 250 years from about 1240 further estranged Russia from the West and contributed to the creation of a unique culture. The struggle against the Mongols contributed to the emergence of a centralized state focused on Moscow. Religious and political isolation encouraged ideas of Russia's unique mission in the world, manifested in the concept of Moscow as the 'third Rome', to supplant Constantinople and Rome itself. Under Ivan the Terrible (1533–84) the power of the monarch was extended in a system termed an 'autocracy' to emphasize the personalized system of rule. These two themes came together to create 'caesaropopism', the fusion of temporal and secular power in the person of the emperor as head of both church and state, avoiding the conflicts between the two typical of Europe.

The dominance of the state was to remain and gave rise to another distinctive feature of Russian history: expansionism. Russia's geopolitical location on the vast Eurasian land mass, with few natural frontiers other than the Volga river and and the Ural mountains, encouraged a preoccupation with defence and the mainten-ance of a powerful army. Russian history was marked by national consolidation and the colonization of adjacent territories. From the conquest of the Khanates of Kazan and Astrakhan in 1552 and 1556, Russia expanded at the astonishing rate of about fifty square miles a day across Siberia as far as the Pacific Ocean in the east, into Central Asia, and pushed back the borders of the Turkish Ottoman empire to reach the Black Sea and the Balkans to the south and west. European fears of Russian expansionism provoked the Crimean War of 1854–6. At the close of the Second World War in 1945 Soviet territories were further consolidated to the west and north. There is no way of knowing whether the process has yet ended. The present Soviet state covers 8.6 million square miles, or one-sixth of the earth's land surface, extending over eleven time zones, stretching 5,600 miles from east to west.

The Mongol occupation turned Russia on to a divergent path of development from that pursued in the rest of Europe. In economic and administrative terms Russia lagged behind the more developed countries. As if to compensate, Russian history was punctuated by periodic attempts to catch up. Peter the Great (1682–1725) launched a development programme designed to graft on to Russia the latest technological developments of England and Holland. Peter established a precedent for furious state-sponsored modernization imposed on a battered society which in effect (as Lenin put it later) tried 'to defeat barbarism by barbaric means'. The pattern was established of a Russia selectively borrowing from the outside world while jealously defending its independence and uniqueness. The West was, on the one hand, a model of development and a source of ideas and, on the other, a warning and a potential threat to the Russian state. The receptivity of Catherine the Great (1762–96) to the ideas of the Enlightenment can be understood in these terms. The concept of enlightened despotism in particular combined Russian hopes of social development while preserving the powers of the monarch and the state. The republican and democratic ideas which contributed to the revolution in France from 1789, however, posed a much more formidable threat. Victory over Napoleon in 1812 boosted the monarchy's self-confidence but unleashed forces that the autocracy ultimately could not contain. The nineteenth century for Russia was a period of great achievements, especially in the industrial and cultural fields, but also one of accumulating tensions that were ultimately to destroy the old regime.

The dominance of the state was accompanied by the weakness of social estates. Western feudal ideas of the rights and duties of monarchs as well as of subjects made little headway in Russia. Max Weber talked of certain countries where there was a patrimonial relationship between the state and society in which the rights of sovereignty and the rights of property became indistinguishable. The land and the people were treated as the property of the monarch, or, in modern parlance, the property of the state. The Russian patrimonial state stood in sharp contrast to the Western system, where feudalism stressed a sharp demarcation between the state and society, expressed in conflicts between the monarch and the aristocracy and the church. The counterpart of the dominance of the Russian state was the weakness of representative institutions. Their development was stifled by the Mongol invasions, and in their place the cruel tyrannies typified by Ivan the Terrible emerged. The germs of Russian representative institutions, such as the Duma of Boyars, the Veche, and the broader body, the Zemskii Sobor (Assembly of the Land), had disappeared by the seventeenth century. The rapid advance of serfdom further undermined the roots of popular representation.

A ubiquitous state bureaucracy was created which tried to run society as the general staff runs an army. Peter the Great had systematized the Russian scheme of government into an elaborate Table of Ranks, with carefully defined gradations for government officials, at whose head stood the autocratic monarch. The centralized Tsarist bureaucracy exerted a powerful influence on the country's social, political, and economic life. The Russian nobility were never able to establish a degree of autonomy based on independent land ownership or administrative authority but instead were bound to the monarch. From the time of Peter the Great the Orthodox church was thoroughly subordinate to the crown. According to Richard Pipes the patrimonial state was converted into a 'bureaucratic-police state' from the reign of Nicholas I (1825–55).[1] The dominance of the Russian state hampered the development of civil society, the social arena of autonomous economic activity and social movements guaranteed by law and independent of the state. Furthermore, the state stifled the emergence of an indigenous mercantile bourgeoisie by relying on state monopolies. The distinctive pattern of Russian development also hindered the emergence of a middle class, or indeed of a politically aware bourgeoisie, that could effectively challenge the state. There was little tradition of autonomous group activity, including trade union activity. The conduct of politics, defined as the attempt to influence the distribution of power, was forced into oblique if not into outright subversive forms. The bureaucracy itself became the major arena of acceptable politics. The intelligentsia — a typically Russian term denoting the intellectuals as a class — were effectively excluded from the mainstream of political life.

Alexis de Tocqueville pointed out in *The Old Regime and the Revolution* the continuities in French political culture after the revolution of 1789. Similarly, seven features of Russian political culture — a distinctive religion, isolation and invasion, a strong state, an expansionist drive, the dialectic between backwardness and modernization further stimulating the dominance of the state, the weak development of representative institutions and society, and the bureaucratic attempt to replace politics by administration — to varying degrees link Tsarism with its Soviet successor. As we shall see, however, 1917 marked a sharp break in continuity, and the roots of the contemporary Soviet system are to be found as much in the ideological and organizational principles of Marxism-Leninism as in the patterns of history or of a distinctively Russian political culture.

Not least of the differences were the strict limits to autocratic power. Tsarist authoritarianism was limited by private property, foreign travel, and the inhibitions of the government itself. The great Russian historian V.O. Klyuchevskii pointed out that the Tsars of Moscow may well have been all-powerful with regard to the people but they had no power to modify social relations. The Bolsheviks, on the other hand, set themselves precisely the task of remoulding all of society. Furthermore, the traditional picture of the 'peculiarities of Russian history' was changing rapidly in the half-century before the revolutions of 1917. The judicial reforms of Alexander II (1855–81) of 1864 established an equitable system of courts and a Bar, and provided for independent judges and a twelve-person jury, although the peasantry retained their customary law. In the same year Alexander II reformed the system of local government with the creation of the *zemstva* (councils) in rural areas. However, the era of the great reforms under Alexander II were limited, and in some cases were rolled back in his later years and by his successors, Alexander III (1881–94) and the last Tsar, Nicholas II (1894–1917). In political trials there were major violations of the principles of the 1864 reform, prompted in part by the terrorism launched by sections of the radical intelligentsia. In nationality policy the earlier even-handed 'imperial' approach to the non-Russian nationalities in 1880 changed to a narrower 'Great Russia' policy of Russification. The Poles, Finns, Balts, Jews, Moslems and Armenians were especially harshly treated.

Not all was lost of the great reforms. Alexander III came into sharp conflict with his own officials when he attempted to reverse them. The bureaucracy and the government were able to resist the monarch's authority because of respect for established traditions and the monarch's need for professional expertise. The *zemstva* and municipal authorities survived the reaction, though not unscathed, and were responsible for a wide range of medical and social improvements by the eve of the revolution. An educated and critical public opinion emerged, symbolized by the spread of 'thick journals' (*tolstye zhurnaly*), read throughout the empire by concerned citizens. The last years of Tsarism were marked by a religious renaissance and a cultural 'silver age' whose luminaries included Andrei Bely, Alexander Blok, Anna Akhmatova, and Marina Tsvetaeva. The system of orders was disintegrating, to be replaced by the emergence of distinct social classes. Russian society was looking more and more modern on the eve of the revolution.

Social and economic developments

The Crimean War starkly revealed the disparity between Russia's great-power pretensions and its actual military and economic capacities when faced with more modern armies. Russia's defeat demonstrated that its great-power status could not be sustained without the modernization of the economy, and in a sense this has been the theme of Russian and Soviet history ever since. However, the options open to a country on the verge of reform are never so clear-cut as they appear to posterity. Three times in modern Russian and Soviet history the government and intelligentsia have been wracked by a debate about the means and paths of economic modernization. The first was in the second half of the nineteenth century, the second was in the 1920s, and the third debate has been rumbling on since the death of Stalin in 1953.

The basic questions facing society in the nineteenth century were a combination of economic and political issues: the degree of capitalist development in Russia; the nature of the Russian state and its role in economic development; whether Russia had to undergo the transitional phase of a bourgeois system or could pass directly to socialism; what role could the peasant commune play in this transition to socialism; and could the peasantry, rather than the working class, act as the major revolutionary class. Underlying our present understanding of these debates is the question of the prospects for an evolutionary outcome to Russia's development. Would Russia have been able to settle down to a path of capitalist development and bourgeois dominance if the country had not entered the First World War in August 1914? The contemporary debates over the nature of the Tsarist economy and over appropriate economic policies have a continuing relevance as the peasant societies of the 'Third World' seek viable patterns of development.

Russia in the nineteenth century was balanced between capitalist development and traditional patterns. The chief feature of her economic retardation was the large and unproductive agricultural sector. Serfdom, long a symbol of Russia's backwardness, had been consolidated by the state in the seventeenth century as a military and civil measure rather than as a privilege granted to the nobility. The peasant emancipation of 1861, introduced in response to the shock of defeat in the Crimean War, was only partial and did not bring into being a prosperous peasantry which could have stimulated economic development. Its economic effects were largely negative. Either the peasant received too little land or he was burdened by redemption payments on a larger parcel. The peasantry received only about half the land that they had cultivated before. The emancipation depressed the peasant's purchasing power and hence undermined the basis of a domestic market for manufactured goods. It failed to provide a cheap mobile labour force for the factories. A key anomaly of the emancipation was the retention of the peasant commune, the *obshchina*, organized in the form of a collective unit called the *mir*. Most peasant land was held collectively and periodically redistributed. The communal structure discouraged the development of modern farming methods and depressed productivity. By the turn of the century the shortage of land, caused by a rapidly expanding population, had generated enormous social discontent.

The pattern of industrialization which followed the Crimean War was designed, in part, to enhance Russia's military potential. The involvement of the state in the industrialization process was a legacy of the Russian tradition of state prominence, but it was also a sign of backwardness. The only way for Russia to catch up with the advancing economies of Western Europe, and indeed for many developing countries today, was for the state to take a leading role. There was considerable economic development from the 1830s, with the construction of the railways, designed primarily to export grain. In a programme devised by the Minister of Finance, Sergei Witte, in the 1890s Russia embarked on a vigorous attempt to stimulate industrial expansion by liberalizing credit facilities, allowing expanding state budget deficits, taking foreign loans (especially from France), and imposing protectionist tariff barriers. The casualty of industrial expansion was, as usual, the peasantry, as they were 'squeezed' ever harder through heavy taxes and sustained grain exports, even when famine struck the villages in 1891 and 1896, to service the debt and loans and maintain Russia's creditworthiness. A massive state-sponsored industrialization was grafted on to a peasant economy, causing untold social strains. The economic results, however, were impressive, with an average annual growth rate of over 8 per cent in the 1890s.

Economic and social developments began to change the old pattern of autocracy to allow the emergence of a quasi-capitalist state. An essential feature of modernization theory is the stress on the links between self-sustaining economic growth, reforms favouring social mobility, and political modernization incorporating the aspirations of all groups in society. These conditions were developing, if only slowly, in Tsarist Russia. Private initiative played an important and often underrated part in economic development. The role of the state was balanced by a strong autonomous domestic contribution to economic development. Paul Gregory has provided higher estimates of the independent contribution of agriculture to the industrialization process. Olga Crisp has shown that from the eighteenth century there was a spontaneous stream of industrialization, notably in the textile and food industries. Furthermore, the degree to which Witte's industrialization drive was consciously state-sponsored has often been exaggerated. There is much evidence of bitter conflict in the government, and the industrialization-inducing measures were not so much part of a consciously planned programme as the result of bureaucratic in-fighting. The state played a key role, but the pattern of industrialization differed markedly from that established by Stalin in the late 1920s. The consumer goods industries developed together with heavy industry, and the municipalities took an increasingly important role. By 1914 only 8.3 per cent of total estimated wealth was in the state sector, whereas over a quarter was in the public co-operative sector. Alexander Gerschenkron argues that after the state-sponsored industrialization drive of the 1890s the state could afford to take a less prominent role. Reforms from 1907 permitted the peasant to move out of the communes and hence become more dynamic and to create an expanding domestic market to stimulate manufacturing industry. The emerging commercial banking network could take over from the state the financing of investment. For Gerschenkron, the outbreak of the First World War interrupted an otherwise successful process of economic modernization. This schema shares some features with Walt Rostow's modernization theory, where economies pass through five stages: traditional; preconditions for take-off; the economic take-off phase itself; the drive to maturity; and finally the onset of the age of mass consumption. The take-off period, according to Rostow, lasts about twenty years and in Russia took place between 1890–1914.

In *The Development of Capitalism in Russia* (1899) Vladimir Ilich Ulyanov, known to posterity as Lenin, argued that capitalism had made major inroads into the Russian economy and agriculture. The country, he asserted, was acquiring the economic preconditions for socialism, and in addition the social strains generated by industrialization created the political conditions for revolution. A large class of peasants were losing their land and being forced to become wage labourers who he expected to ally with the urban workers. Economic development saw the emergence of a significant working class, although the common practice of locating factories in the countryside blurred the distinction between peasants and workers. By 1913 3.5 million were in the factories out of a total population of 150 million. Most retained some contact with the village and kept their land within the communal system. The pattern of Russian industrialization has been called uneven development, a pattern in which backward countries skip several stages to catch up with the more advanced. This leads to the insertion of advanced capitalism into agrarian societies, and to a high degree of concentration of the labour force. In Petrograd, for example, huge factories such as the Putilov iron and steel works employed about 50,000 workers in 1914. Despite vigorous attempts by the municipal authorities to improve living conditions, often provoked by scathing reports by the government factory inspectorate, workers' living conditions, especially for the unskilled, remained appalling and marked by long hours, crude barrack-type housing, poor hygiene, low wages, and an exceptionally high accident rate.

Despite major economic and social advances prior to the First World War, Russia's 'backwardness' still consisted of two key features: a large peasantry only loosely integrated into a national market and culture; and a weak entrepreneurial class which was still stifled by state tutelage. The patrimonial legacy of the Russian state became modernized in the form of state paternalism designed to restrain the bitter class conflicts and contestatory politics typical of Western European and American industrialization. Following the eruption of the first major workers' strikes in the 1880s the autocracy was unable to develop an effective response which could have secured the loyalty of the working class to the monarchy and capitalism. The autocratic state clung to the bureaucratic image of itself as being above contending social forces and the ultimate arbiter of all social affairs. The state tried to protect the interests of both the employer and the employed. Its policies veered between the repressive and the paternalistic. Police trade unions were formed under Sergei Zubatov, a former revolutionary who came to head the Moscow Okhrana (secret police) from 1896 to 1902, who pioneered brilliant counter-insurgency techniques designed to convert socialists into monarchist trade unionists.

The ten years from 1905 were marked by astonishing economic progress, with extensions to the railway system and the doubling of its traffic and revenue. Consumption statistics show great improvements in the standard of living, and the production of consumer goods was higher than in Germany. The industrial sector was not an enclave, as is common in developing countries, but organically linked to the rest of the economy through market and financial ties. By 1914 the vigorous social and economic developments of the past half-century had closed the gap between Russia and the more developed countries and had elevated it to fifth place in the league of industrial powers. However, while socio-economic progress was encouraged the autocracy tried to retain its political pre-eminence. Powerful social and political conflicts remained unresolved.

Revolutionary movements and Bolshevism

During the nineteenth century the crown's claim to a monopoly of power was increasingly challenged. Only with decreasing justification could Russia fulfil Weber's definition of a state as 'a community that (successfully) claims the monopoly of the legitimate use of physical force within a given territory'.[2] Against a background of continuing nationalist unrest, the old regime came to be challenged by three major social philosophies: liberalism, populism, and what came to be known as Marxism-Leninism. These political challenges were interwoven with contrasting economic programmes.

French revolutionary ideas were transmitted back to Russia by the officers of the imperial army who had helped defeat Napoleon in 1814. A period of revolutionary debate and plotting climaxed with a rising, sometimes called the first Russian revolution, on Senate Square in St Petersburg on 14 December 1825 against Nicholas I. The Decembrists, as the movement became known, aimed to establish a democratic 'republic'. The quality of their thought, the emphasis on establishing a constitutional system, and their qualms over spilling blood mark them out as imaginative, if hesitant, revolutionaries. The uprising signalled the onset of a century of revolutionary activity in Russia.

The liberal view of development took England as its model, in which economic and political advances reinforced each other. Economic modernization, the development of a capitalist agriculture, and industrialization, liberals hoped, would promote and sustain a democratic governmental system. The reforms of the 1860s buoyed their hopes of such an evolution, but their spirits were dampened by the reaction that set in under Alexander III in the 1880s. The liberals were particularly active in the *zemstva*, where they were able to achieve 'small deeds' in education, welfare, and administration. Nicholas II's inaugural speech of 17 January 1895, however, dampened hopes of reform by talking of the 'senseless dreams' of liberals who hoped to raise their perspectives from local to national concerns. The torch of liberalism gradually passed from gentry activists to the intelligentsia, and in the process took on a more challenging guise which George Fischer dubbed 'have-not' liberalism typical of underdeveloped countries. This was increasingly willing to challenge the existing regime and to demand a constitutional government bounded by laws and institutional liberties. Deprived of effective political and institutional channels to advance their cause, liberals turned to the press to argue their case. Only in 1905 were they able to create the natural vehicle for liberalism, a political party. The weakness of liberalism in Russia, moreover, reflected the underdeveloped tradition of autonomous group movements.

A marked feature of the democratic intelligentsia born of the gentry was that it tended towards illiberality from the outset. The democratic movement in Russia was consistently anti-capitalist and anti-bourgeois, perhaps because it began as a movement of nobles, and their philosophy was opposed to Western individualism and materialism. Alexander Herzen, the finest example of this tendency, forged the strivings and hopes of the intellectuals into an effective anti-government political ideology in which they would lead the people to a better future. The radical intelligentsia held to abstract ideals that became ever more suffused with the spirit of grandiose social engineering rather than with the liberal principles of freedom and democracy. This spirit was taken to the extreme by Lenin, who came from a rising intelligentsia family in Simbirsk (now Ulyanovsk). Lenin always displayed a profound contempt for liberalism and all its works.

Russian and Soviet history is marked by a profound ambiguity over Russia's Europeanness. Echoes of the controversy in the 1830s between the Slavophiles and the Westernizers can be heard throughout later debates to this day. The Slavophiles contended that each country should follow its historic mission and that Russia's path diverged from that of the West. The Westernizers insisted that Russia was a European country and that its uniqueness represented backwardness, and hence the major task was to modernize on the Western pattern. The Slavophiles condemned Peter the Great for having undermined traditional Russian life, for having humbled the Orthodox church and for having imposed an alien Western culture on the upper classes, whereas the Westernizers praised him for attempting to modernize the country. The Westernizers lauded the rationalism, individualism, and legal formalism of the West, whereas the Slavophiles extolled the mystic inner truth of the Russian people and the Orthodox religion. Their social ideal focused on a paternalistic government, communal land-holding and the peasant collectivist tradition of self-government.

After the failure of the 1848 revolutions throughout Europe, sections of the Russian intelligentsia abandoned hopes of liberalism and representative democracy and placed its hopes on the peasantry. This vast mass, who comprised 90 per cent of the population, seemed to represent a dormant power which only needed to be roused in order to shatter the autocracy. It was from this point that the intelligentsia adopted an increasingly authoritarian tone. Its passion for justice took precedence over liberty, and it was increasingly willing to use violence to achieve its aims. The Russian Populists (or *Narodniki*) were a diffuse tendency whose programme found a ready response among the intelligentsia. They echoed Herzen's suggestion that Russia represented a special case and could escape the capitalist phase of development. They rejected the need for capitalist industrialization in Russia and instead placed their hopes on consolidating the land commune (*mir*) and its collective way of life. Russia could evolve its own form of socialism without having to undergo the preliminary capitalist phase of exploitation and wage slavery. They shared with the Slavophiles a contempt for European constitutionalism and stressed the moral duty of the intelligentsia to enlighten the people.

The Land and Freedom (*Zemlya i Volya*) movement from the 1860s represented a back-to-the-land movement expressed through good works and urban benevolence to the exploited peasant. The programme was as fundamentally misconceived as it was clumsily executed. In summer 1874 the Populists tried to 'go to the people': an army of young people dressed up as peasants went to live in the villages to absorb popular wisdom and instruct the peasants. In some places the villagers were bemused; in others they contacted the police, leading to the arrest of over 800 activists. In 1876 a new Land and Freedom Party demanded that land be given to the peasants and that the state be destroyed in the name of collectivism. The weakness of the programme was compensated by a growing reliance on strong organization. For the first time a revolutionary party no longer based itself on the mass of the people and began a programme of terrorism. In 1878 Vera Zasulich shot and wounded the governor of Petersburg, General Trepov. In 1879 a secret organization called 'People's Will' (*Narodnay a Volya*) was created to fight for political freedom. The campaign of bomb-throwing and assassination culminated in March 1881 in the death of Alexander II, the 'Tsar liberator'. The foundation of the Socialist Revolutionary (SR) party in 1900 represented a fusion of terroristic principle with the practice of mass agitation. The party's leader, Victor Chernov, insisted that the solution to peasant grievances lay in the redistribution of state and gentry land to the peasants, and not so much in the abolition of the commune or industrialization. The party was essentially a loose coalition of anti-bourgeois forces, and, though it renounced utopian socialism in favour of so-called 'scientific socialism', it remained resolutely opposed to Marxism .

The evolution of Russian Populism illustrates a major theme in the development of the revolutionary movement: the increasing emphasis on conspiracy and the principle of the small number exerting leverage at the crucial spot to effect major changes. S.G. Nechaev in the late 1860s advocated terror and was the first to use cells and conspiracy. A much more sophisticated version was developed by Peter Tkachev, a follower of the French revolutionary August Blanqui, and one of the leaders of the People's Will party. He insisted that only a tightly knit group of professional underground revolutionaries could evade the police. Nechaev and Tkachev represented a shift not only in organizational tactics but also in theoretical principle. They required the absolute subordination of the individual to the revolution, a belief in the conscious minority who would remould the world, and argued that in the service of the cause the end always justified the means. The terror campaign, however, succeeded only in making the autocracy more obdurate and repressive. The accession of Alexander III in 1881 saw a more mystical if no less vigorous assertion of the power of the throne, summed up by the slogan developed by Count Sergei Uvarov in the 1820s of 'Autocracy, Orthodoxy, and Nationality', a policy continued by his successor, Nicholas II. He was supported by the Union of Russian People, organized in 'Black Hundreds', who used Jews and foreigners as scapegoats for what they saw as the declining cohesion of Russian society. The blockage of reforms 'from above' only intensified the struggle for change 'from below'.

The third major challenge to the autocracy came from the Marxists. Marx argued that 'the more developed society shows to the less developed the image of its own future', yet even he was willing to countenance the Populist belief that Russia could avoid the Western path of capitalist development and move directly to socialism on the basis of peasant collective traditions. In 1878 he wrote that 'if Russia continues along the road she has followed since 1861, she will forego the finest opportunity that history has ever placed before a nation and will undergo all the fateful misfortune of capitalist development'.[3] In a series of draft letters to Vera Zasulich in 1881 he explored the possibility that under certain conditions the commune might became the kernel of a regenerated Russia.[4]

Marx's followers in Russia, however, insisted that capitalism was as much an essential stage of development for Russia as it was for the West. Marx's late thoughts on the communal option were ignored, or not known. George Plekhanov, the 'father' of Russian social democracy and one of the founders of the Emancipation of Labour group in Geneva in 1883, together with Pavel Axelrod and Vera Zasulich, insisted that the immediate future belonged to capitalism. Plekhanov argued that the peasant commune was no more than a fiscal device used by the government to obtain taxes, and Lenin and Plekhanov ridiculed the Populist belief that the *mir* could form the basis of socialism in Russia. The Marxists supported the efforts of the Tsarist government to industrialize, since it was creating the economic base for socialism. Moreover, according to their theory of class conflict the government was nurturing its own gravedigger, the proletariat. From the 1890s a number of 'Legal Marxists', most notably Peter Struve, used the legal press to agitate for the accelerated economic development of capitalism as being in the long-term interests of the labour movement. Such 'economism' emphasized that Russia would have to go through the economic stages outlined by Marx, and yet the question remained whether it would have to go through the same political stages: the ascendance of the bourgeoisie and only then the socialist revolution carried out by the proletariat.

In a process that has often been seen as the assimilation of Marxism to Russian traditions Lenin tried to weld the Russian Social Democratic Labour Party (RSDLP), founded in 1898, into a coherent organization. He attacked the economist argument that the working class should wait for the economy to develop and in the meantime restrict its struggles to economic rather than political issues. The newspaper *Iskra* (*The Spark*), founded by Lenin, Julius Martov, Plekhanov, and others in 1900, helped bridge the gap between the workers and the intelligentsia, but served to divide the social democratic movement. In 1902 Lenin published his crucial pamphlet *What is to be Done?* which outlined his concept of a tightly knit organization of dedicated revolutionaries who would lead the class struggle of the proletariat. Somewhat reminiscent of the Tkachev principle of the small number, Lenin wrote, 'Give us a revolutionary organization and we will turn Russia upside down.' At the second congress of the RSDLP in 1903, in London, Martov defended a broader definition of party membership. The division was over Lenin's wording in the party programme of 'personal participation', in contrast to Martov's looser 'personal support'. The actual vote on the party statutes was lost by Lenin, but his group achieved a majority of two in the elections to the editorial board of *Iskra* and hence adopted the name Bolsheviks ('the majority') and Martov's group was left with the inglorious name of 'the minority' (Mensheviks).

The focus of Lenin's political thinking was opposition to passivity and wishful hopes for the spontaneous development of the revolution. Lenin argued that on its own the working class could develop only a trade-union consciousness (i.e. would concern only itself with wages, conditions, and so on, and not with changing the fundamental structure of society) and hence needed to be guided from outside by the revolutionary party. The critical role of the intelligentsia in devising the revolutionary programme and leading the masses was clearly reminiscent of the Populists, and indeed Lenin drew many of his ideas, including some of his thoughts on party organization, from them. Lenin modified Marx's thinking about revolutionary organization, which had stressed that the liberation of the working class would be achieved by the working class itself. In Lenin's theory, as Lev Davidovich Trotsky (who was not yet a Bolshevik) prophetically pointed out, there was the danger of the party substituting for the working class, and the process would not stop there: 'The party is replaced by the organization of the party, the organization by the Central Committee, and finally the Central Committee by the dictator.'

The problem still remained of how to make the revolution in Russia. The theory of autocratic power increasingly came into conflict with the modernizing impulse of the Russian state. There was a fundamental incompatibility between imperial ambitions and the existing structure of power in a world undergoing a technological transformation. Could this transformation be grafted on to the autocratic system? Russian defeats in the Russo-Japanese war of 1904–5 confirmed the lessons of the Crimean War half a century earlier: substantial reforms were required in society for the Russian state to meet the heavy demands of modern warfare. The Japanese were themselves a good example of how this grafting could be achieved, and Germany as well. But could Russia emulate their achievements in assimilating technological modernization and economic change to a conservative social and political framework?

For a number of reasons Russia was not able to achieve this in time, and in the short term failures in war abroad led to social revolution at home. On 9 January 1905 a demonstration led by Father Gapon, an Orthodox priest and labour organizer, demanded food and workers' rights. It was gunned down outside the Winter Palace by Cossacks, thus precipitating widespread worker and peasant unrest. In the October Manifesto of that year the monarchy was forced to concede a State Duma (parliament), unions, and elements of the rule of law. Juridically a constitutional monarchy came into being. The year also witnessed the formation of soviets, organizations which began as workers' strike committees but which were to evolve into the constitutional basis of the communist state. Peasant discontent erupted in uprisings that dragged on into 1907. The monarchy was saved by the fact that the army as a whole remained loyal, yet the revolution was a clear warning that the survival of the autocracy was at stake. As Lenin put it, 1905 was a 'dress rehearsal' for 1917.

The 1905 revolution focused on a liberal programme of political demands, but already it was clear that the dynamism of the revolution would be mass action. The revolution demonstrated that the Tsar was no longer an acceptable source of authority for large sections of the population and that society was capable of making and sustaining demands on the crown. As yet, the organization of these demands was weak. The parties played little role in 1905, and the differences between the Bolsheviks and the Mensheviks were little understood and their rivalry was unpopular among workers. Events seemed to show that, contrary to Lenin's inclinations, spontaneity did indeed have a role to play in the Russian revolution.

For a brief period following the 1905 revolution it appeared that a path could be found between the demands of the revolutionaries and the resistance of the autocracy in a Russian form of constitutionalism represented by the State Duma. However, the Russian constitution (or Organic Laws) of 1906 placed few restrictions on the powers of the monarch, and failed to provide for a broad suffrage and a parliament to which governments would be responsible. The First Duma met in the spring of 1906 and saw the crystallization of a number of parties. On the right the Octobrists, named after the Tsar's manifesto, were a loose grouping of business interests, conservative noble landowners, and *zemstvo* gentry moderates. The Constitutional Democrats (Kadets), formed in 1905, were the major standard-bearers of the liberals, representing the more progressive intelligentsia of the capitals, the *zemstvo* gentry constitutionalists, and the moderate intelligentsia in the provinces. They held the single largest bloc of seats in the First Duma, 196 seats out of 478. The Duma was boycotted by the SRs and the Social Democrats. The Duma lasted two and a half months before it was dissolved on 20 July 1906, the government considering it too radical. The Second Duma, however, proved little less oppositional, and while the Kadet total fell to ninety-two, the socialists, having given up their boycott, gained the impressive total of 113 seats. The Second Duma survived barely three months, from March to June 1907.

Gradually the Tsar restored order and could take back his concessions. In June 1907 Nicholas' most able Prime Minister, Peter Stolypin, manipulated the electoral system by reducing the number eligible to vote, to allow the gentry, whose economic power had been declining, to dominate the legislature. The Third Duma from 1907 to 1912, the 'landowners' Duma', proved amenable to the Tsar. The government, however, did not restrict itself to a policy of repression. The Stolypin reforms in the countryside tried to buttress the Tsarist social system by the creation of an independent peasantry. Stolypin argued that the peasantry could be used to defeat the revolution, and to this end the government must free them from the commune and permit them to acquire private property. The principles of economic liberalism were introduced into peasant agriculture. This 'wager on the strong' only made the weak even more aware of the shortage of land, and in the short run did not markedly improve the technological level of Russian agriculture. Only a small minority of peasants by 1914 had established the Western-style farm (*khutor*). At the same time the regime shed some of its paternalistic ethos and took the first steps towards the liberal approach to labour. A law of March 1906 permitted the creation of trade unions to defend workers' interests. The monarchy tried to remove some of the causes of unrest by enacting some social legislation, as in the rather modest Social Insurance Laws of June 1912.

The reforms fell short of the German social insurance laws promoted by Bismarck or the British or French full legalization of the labour movement. The development of a peculiarly Russian labour policy lacked sufficient vision and energy to divert the working class from its increasingly revolutionary path.

The Tsar alienated most of his sources of support. His relationship with the growing industrial middle class, for example, was not, as Soviet historiography tends to suggest, an easy one. The industrialists were unable to get their way in 1913 in their plans to replace the system of indirect taxation, which disadvantaged the industrial sector, in favour of a single progressive income tax. The alliance between the government, the landed classes, and the bourgeoisie was strong enough to neutralize the forces of change but not strong enough to develop a programme of positive development. Liberal forces, it appeared, were simply too weak to sustain the constitutional experiment. The major paradox is that as Russia modernized, the retention of a monarchical form of personalized rule inhibited the development of effective political institutions worthy of a modern state. The incompatibility of the two created an almost permanent governmental crisis in the last years of the autocracy.

Lenin's view that the Russian middle class was not strong enough to sustain a 'bourgeois revolution' on the British or French model was confirmed by the failure of the 1905 revolution. He came to the conclusion that the working class, in alliance with the peasantry, would have to take the lead. Following the onset of severe repression in 1907 the Bolsheviks conducted both legal and illegal activity. This was the period of the spectacular 'expropriations', some of which were organized by Joseph Vissarionovich Djugashvili, who was to enter history under the name of Stalin. Lenin insisted that the Bolsheviks should take advantage of the opportunities allowed by the law and defeated 'recallism', the movement to withdraw deputies from the Duma and other bodies. In January 1912 at the Prague Congress the Bolsheviks constituted themselves as a separate party. They were just in time to take advantage of the massive upsurge in the workers' movement provoked by the shooting of unarmed workers in the Lena River goldfields on 4 April 1912. The incident provided the spark for a wave of labour unrest that lasted until the outbreak of the war in August 1914. The strikes gradually became 'political' in character, to which the employers responded with lock-outs, fines, and closures. Whether Russia entered the war in part to divert attention from the strikes is a moot point, although it appears that by the eve of hostilities the strikes were waning.

Russian constitutionalism was dealt a fatal blow by the Great War. The Russian leaders, motivated by considerations of national prestige and trapped in the system of international diplomacy, entered the war on the side of Britain and France. They had failed to learn that military adventures placed Russia's political system under intolerable strain and exacerbated the discontents smouldering in Russian society. An extensive moderate liberal opposition emerged. In the Fourth Duma (1912–17) opposition to the monarchy coalesced in August 1915 in a 'Progressive Bloc' of liberals who urged the creation of a responsible government, one accountable to parliament. The Kadet leader Paul Milyukov is a classic example of a liberal who virulently condemned the abuses of the monarchical system and yet defended the monarchical principle to the end. The inability of the monarch to work with the legislature ultimately provoked even his natural allies, the Octobrists, to join forces with the Progressive Bloc in demanding a responsible ministry. Outside the Duma liberal hopes focused on the national association of town and *zemstvo* unions. The *zemstvo* union was formed during the Russo-Japanese war of 1904–5, and the union of towns in 1914, to assist the Tsar in prosecuting his wars. By 1916 they had on the whole become more hostile to the autocratic regime, which they increasingly saw as a major obstacle to victory. Another centre of opposition focused on the War Industry Committees, consisting more narrowly of industrialists who sought to assist the war effort. A debate continues over whether these three forces together made up the kernel of a 'bourgeois revolution', or whether, as Lenin and the Bolsheviks insisted, their own fear of popular movements ultimately transformed their temerity into cowardice, and hence undermined attempts at moderate reform.

During the war the Bolsheviks were isolated and persecuted. The party was mostly abroad and maintained only a vestigial presence underground in Russia. Severe repression destroyed internal organization and sent worker activists to the front. In 1914 the majority of parties in the Second International, the grouping of European social democratic parties, put nation over class and voted for war credits, with the notable exception of the Russians and the Serbs. From the first Lenin insisted on a policy of 'defeatism' and called for the transformation of the 'imperialist' war into a civil war which he hoped would lead on to revolution. Despite the signs of political and social crisis, however, as late as January 1917 Lenin admitted that it was unlikely that he would see the revolution in his lifetime and left it as a bequest to the younger generation. A few weeks later the revolution broke out in Petrograd.

Notes

1 R. Pipes, *Russia under the Old Regime* (Pelican, Harmondsworth, 1974), p. xvii.
2 Max Weber, 'Politics as a Vocation', in H.H. Gerth and C.W. Mills (eds.), *From Max Weber: Essays in Sociology* (Oxford University Press, New York, 1956), p. 77.
3 Letter from Marx to Danielson, 15 November 1878, quoted in Haruki Wada, 'Marx and Revolutionary Russia', in T. Shanin (ed.), *Late Marx and the Russian Road: Marx and the 'Peripheries of Capitalism'* (Routledge and Kegan Paul, London, 1984), p. 58.
4 ibid., pp. 98–126.

Key texts

Carr, E.H., *The Bolshevik Revolution, 1917–1923*, 1 (Pelican, Harmondsworth, 1966)
Kochan, L., *The Making of Modern Russia*, 2nd edn (Macmillan, London, 1983)
Pipes, R., *Russia under the Old Regime* (Pelican, Harmondsworth, 1974)
Raeff, Marc, *Understanding Imperial Russia: State and Society in the Old Regime*, trans. Arthur Goldhammer, (Columbia University Press, New York, 1984)

Riasanovsky, Nicholas V., *A History of Russia*, 4th edn (Oxford University Press, Oxford, 1984)

White, Stephen, 'The USSR: Patterns of Autocracy and Industrialism', in Archie Brown and Jack Gray (eds.) *Political Culture and Political Change in Communist States* (Macmillan, London, 1979), pp. 25–63

Select bibliography

The old regime

Auty, R., and D. Obolensky (eds.), *An Introduction to Russian History* (Cambridge University Press, Cambridge, 1976)

Black, C.E. (ed.), *The Transformation of Russian Society* (Harvard University Press, Cambridge, Mass., 1960)

Emmons, T., and W. Vucinich (eds.), *The Zemstvo in Russia: an Experiment in Local Self-government* (Cambridge University Press, Cambridge, 1982)

Emmons, T., *The Formation of Political Parties and the first National Elections in Russia* (Harvard University Press, Cambridge, Mass., 1983)

Haimson, L.H. (ed.), *The Politics of Rural Russia, 1905–1914* (Indiana University Press, Bloomington, 1979)

Hosking, Geoffrey, *The Russian Constitutional Experiment: Government and Duma, 1907–1914* (Cambridge University Press, Cambridge, 1973)

Lieven, D.C.B., *Russia and the Origins of the First World War* (Macmillan, London, 1983)

Lincoln, W. Bruce, *In the Vanguard of Reform: Russia's Enlightened Bureaucrats, 1825–1861* (Northern Illinois University Press, DeKalb, Ill., 1982)

McCauley, Martin, and Peter Waldron, *Octobrists to Bolsheviks: Imperial Russia, 1905–17* (Edward Arnold, London, 1984)

Manning, Roberta T., *The Crisis of the Old Order in Russia: Gentry and Government* (Princeton University Press, Princeton, N.J., 1982)

Nichols, R.L., and T.G. Stavrou (eds.), *Russian Orthodoxy under the Old Regime* (University of Minnesota Press, Minneapolis, 1978)

Orlovsky, Daniel, *The Limits to Reform: the Ministry of Internal Affairs in Imperial Russia, 1801–1881* (Harvard University Press, Cambridge, Mass., 1981)

Raeff, M., *The Decembrist Movement* (Prentice-Hall, Englewood Cliffs, N.J., 1966)

Rogger, Hans, *Russia in the Age of Modernization and Revolutuion, 1881–1917* (Longman, London, 1983)

Seton-Watson, Hugh, *The Russian Empire, 1801–1917* (Clarendon, Oxford, 1967)

Seton-Watson, Hugh, *The Decline of Imperial Russia* (Westview, Boulder, Colo. 1985)

Weissman, N.B., *Reform in Tsarist Russia: the State Bureaucracy and Local Government, 1900–1914* (Rutgers University Press, New Brunswick, N.J., 1981)

Wortman, R.S., *The Development of a Russian Legal Consciousness* (University of Chicago Press, Chicago, 1976)

Yaney, George L., *The Systematisation of Russian Government: Social Evolution in the Domestic Administration of Imperial Russia, 1711–1905* (University of Illinois Press, Urbana, 1973)

Social and economic developments

Atkinson, Dorothy, *The End of the Russian Land Commune, 1905–1930* (Stanford University Press, Stanford, Cal., 1983)

Bidelux, Robert, *Communism and Development* (Methuen, London, 1985)

Blackwell, W.L. (ed.), *Russian Economic Development from Peter the Great to Stalin* (New Viewpoints, New York, 1974)

Bonnell, V.E., *Roots of Rebellion: Workers' Politics and Organization in St. Petersburg and Moscow, 1900–1914* (University of California Press, Berkeley, 1983)

Crisp, Olga, *Studies in the Russian Economy before 1914* (Macmillan, London, 1976)

Emmons, T., *The Russian Landed Gentry and the Peasant Emancipation of 1861* (Cambridge University Press, Cambridge, 1968)

Falkus, M.E., *The Industrialisation of Russia, 1700–1914* (Macmillan, London, 1972)

Gatrell, Peter, *The Tsarist Economy, 1850–1917* (Batsford, London, 1986)

Gerschenkron, A., *Economic Backwardness in Historical Perspective* (Harvard University Press, Cambridge, Mass., 1962)

Gregory, P.R., *Russian National Income, 1885–1913* (Cambridge University Press, Cambridge, 1982)

Haimson, L., 'The Problem of Social Stability in Urban Russia, 1905–1917', *Slavic Review*, 23 (1964), pp. 619–42; 24 (1965), pp. 1–23

Johnson, R.E., *Peasant and Proletarian: the Working Class of Moscow in the late Nineteenth Century* (Leicester University Press, Leicester, 1979)

Kitching, G., *Development and Underdevelopment in Historical Perspective: Populism, Nationalism and Industrialisation* (Methuen, London, 1982)

Laue, T.H. von, *Sergei Witte and the Industrialisation of Russia* (Columbia University Press, New York, 1963)

Rostow, W.W., *The Stages of Economic Growth: a Non-communist Manifesto* (Cambridge University Press, Cambridge, 1960)

Schneiderman, Jeremiah, *Sergei Zubatov and Revolutionary Marxism: the Struggle for the Working Class in Tsarist Russia* (Cornell University Press, London and Ithaca, N.Y., 1976)

Shanin, Teodor, *The Roots of Otherness: Russia's Turn of the Century*, 1, *Russia as a 'Developing Society'*; II, *Russia, 1905–1907: Revolution as a Moment of Truth* (Macmillan, London, 1985/6).

Thurston, Robert W., *Liberal City, Conservative State: Moscow and Russia's Urban Crisis, 1906–1914* Oxford University Press, Oxford and New York, 1987)

Vucinich, W. (ed.), *The Peasant in Nineteenth-Century Russia* (Stanford University Press, Stanford, Cal., 1968)

Yaney, G.L., *The Urge to Mobilise: Agrarian Reform in Russia, 1861–1930* (University of Illinois Press, Urbana, 1982)

Zelnik, Reginald E., *Labor and Society in Tsarist Russia: the Factory Workers of St. Petersburg, 1855–1870* (Stanford University Press, Stanford, Cal., 1971)

Revolutionary movements and Bolshevism

Ascher, A., *Pavel Axelrod and the Development of Menshevism* (Harvard University Press, Cambridge, Mass., 1972)

Baron, S.H., *Plekhanov: the Father of Russian Marxism* (Stanford University Press, Stanford, Cal., 1963)

Berdyaev, Nicolas, *The Origin of Russian Communism* (Bles, London, 1937)

Berlin, Isaiah, *Russian Thinkers* (Penguin, Harmondsworth, 1979)

Besancon, A., *The Rise of the Gulag: the Intellectual Origins of Leninism* (Continuum, New York, 1981)

Fischer, George, *Russian Liberalism: from Gentry to Intelligentsia* (Harvard University Press, Harvard, Mass., 1958)

Getzler, I., *Martov: a Political Biography of a Russian Social Democrat* (Oxford University Press, Oxford, 1967)

Haimson, Leopold H., *The Russian Marxists and the Origins of Bolshevism* (Beacon, Boston, Mass., 1966)

Harding, Neil, *Lenin's Political Thought*, 2 vols. (Macmillan, London, 1981)

Harding, Neil (ed.). *Marxism in Russia: Key Documents, 1879–1906*, trans. Richard Taylor (Cambridge University Press, Cambridge, 1983)

Herzen, Alexander, *My Past and Thoughts* (Knopf, New York, 1973)

Keep, J., *The Rise of Social Democracy in Russia* (Clarendon, Oxford, 1963)

Kingston-Mann, Esther, *Lenin and the Problem of Marxist Peasant Revolution* (Oxford University Press, New York, 1983)

Lane, David, *The Roots of Russian Communism* (van Gorcum, Assen, 1969/75)

Lane, David, *Leninism: a Sociological Interpretation* (Cambridge University Press, Cambridge, 1981)

Lenin, V.I., key writings include *What is to be Done?; Two Tactics of Social Democracy; Imperialism, the Highest Stage of Capitalism; The State and Revolution*

Malia, M., *Alexander Herzen and the Birth of Russian Socialism* (Harvard University Press, Cambridge, Mass, 1961)

Meyer, Alfred G., *Leninism* (Praeger, New York, 1957)

Perrie, M., *The Agrarian Policy of the Russian Socialist Revolutionary Party, 1905–1907* (Cambridge University Press, Cambridge, 1976)

Pipes, R., *Struve: Liberal on the Left, 1870–1905* (Harvard University Press, Cambridge, Mass., 1970)

Pipes, R., *Struve: Liberal on the Right, 1905–1944* (Harvard University Press, Cambridge, Mass., 1980)

Shub, David, *Lenin* (Pelican, Harmondsworth, 1966)

Swain, Geoffrey, *Russian Social Democracy and the Legal Labour Movement, 1906–1914* (Macmillan, London, 1983)

Szamuely, Tibor, *The Russian Tradition* (Secker & Warburg, London, 1974)

Tucker, Robert C., *The Marxian Revolutionary Idea* (Allen & Unwin, London, 1970)

Ulam, Adam, *The Bolsheviks: the Intellectual and Political History of the Triumph of Communism in Russia* (Macmillan, New York, 1965)

Venturi, F., *Roots of Revolution: a History of the Populist and Socialist Movements in Nineteenth-Century Russia* (Weidenfeld & Nicolson, London, 1961)

Walicki, Andrez, *A History of Russian Thought: from the Enlightenment to Marxism* (Oxford University Press, Oxford, 1988)

Chapter two

The creation of the Soviet state

The revolutions of 1917

Tsarism fell because of military reverses and war-weariness, social strains sharpened by economic dislocation and incompetance, and the failure to create a government in which the Duma and the people could have faith. The influence of the drunken debauchee Grigorii Rasputin on the court further discredited the monarchy. The war acted as a catalyst, bringing out the underlying social and political tensions. Nicholas II's weak and vacillating character only exacerbated the constitutional crisis at the heart of the Russian polity and thwarted the development of rational administration.

From 23 February 1917 strikes in St Petersburg protesting against food shortages gradually developed into widespread disturbances. The fate of the monarchy was sealed once mutinies broke out in the garrison as soldiers joined the demonstrators. On 3 March Nicholas II abdicated, bringing an end to the Romanov dynasty after 304 years. The revolutionaries had played little part in its fall. Power passed to a 'Provisional Committee' of the Duma which became the first Provisional Government, headed by Prince G.E. Lvov, head of the union of *zemstva* and towns, and based on the Kadet party. At the same time, power was shared with a hastily formed 'Provisional Executive Committee of the Petrograd Soviet', meeting in the Duma building, which energetically set about organizing the revolution. The age of mass politics was thrust upon Russia in February 1917 with little ceremony. The problem was how to reconstitute central authority in a society riven by class divisions and national jealousies while trying to conduct a war against a powerful protagonist. Ultimately the task proved impossible for the Provisional Government.

For most of 1917 Russia in effect had two governments, sustained by antagonistic though not necessarily mutually exclusive ideologies. For the liberals and the bourgeoisie, and indeed for a large segment of the socialist leadership of the Mensheviks and Social Revolutionaries, the February events represented primarily a political revolution. Its tasks were seen as establishing a constitutional parliamentary system on the principles of universal suffrage, equality before the law, and private property. A so-called bourgeois democratic republic was

19

established amid scenes of national rejoicing in the days after the overthrow of the monarchy. The Provisional Government promised general elections to a Constituent Assembly which would adopt a new constitution for the democratic republic. By April Lenin was able to declare that Russia was 'the freest country in the world'. There was a tremendous explosion of social organizations and popular political activity. These months showed that despite Russia's relatively backward socio-economic development and the restrictions imposed by the Tsarist regime on political life there was a great capacity for the development of a vigorous public sphere. Everywhere one looked a committee was being formed and people drawn into struggles of one form or another. A distinctively Russian form of liberalism was struggling to emerge which could combine social justice with political rights.

The second view of the revolution stressed its social and class character, an interpretation taken to the extreme by the Bolsheviks. The Provisional Government remained fundamentally out of step with the popular forces that had generated the revolution and which continued to propel it to the left until the *dénouement* in October that year. From the first the political revolution of February 1917 had the capacity for being transformed into a socialist revolution. The system of 'dual power' inaugurated in February meant that the government had to share power with the resurgent soviets, which were being formed the length and breadth of the country. The famous Order No. 1 of 1 March of the Petrograd soviet called for the election of committees in all military units in the Petrograd garrison, though it was seized upon by soldiers elsewhere and contributed massively to the disintegration of the Russian army. The order deprived the government of control over troop dispositions. The soviets in 1917 were organized loosely, but fairly quickly their executive committees, composed of socialist politicians and intellectuals, came to dominate the rank-and-file delegates in the plenary meetings.

The Provisional Government was broken over a number of policy failures. Above all, the first Provisional Government considered the February revolution a protest against the inept conduct of the war by the Tsarist regime and not directed against the war itself. Foreign Minister Milyukov's note to the Allies in April, promising to fight until 'decisive victory', led to the fall of the government and the creation of the first coalition government, still under Lvov, which lasted from May to July. The new government included liberals and socialists, with the SR Alexander Kerensky as War Minister. The moderate socialists took a 'defensist' position in the war: insisting on the defence of Russian territory but rejecting any annexations or indemnities from the defeated powers. In June Kerensky hoped to take advantage of the expected revolutionary enthusiasm and launched an ill-fated offensive. He soon discovered that the concept of national defence was losing its meaning to hungry and exhausted soldiers and workers. Kerensky fatally misinterpreted the French revolution, where, as has often been pointed out, the revolutionary war was launched three years after the revolution. In Russia the revolution took place three years into a disastrous war. Lenin understood that war-weariness was at the root of the revolution, and Bolshevik anti-war agitation found a receptive audience. The failure of the offensive undermined the government's authority and led to the fall of the first coalition government. On 15 July tensions betwee the moderate socialists and the bourgeois parties led to the resignation of Lvov and four Kadet ministers, and a second coalition government was formed, headed by Kerensky.

The integrity of the multinational empire was weakened by the revolution, and a number of peoples took advantage of the temporary weakness of central authority to demand independence. Poland was occupied by Germany, so the Provisional Government's promise of independence cost it little, but over Finland the government temporized. The Ukrainians set up their own embryonic government in the form of the Rada. Disagreements over recognizing the autonomy of the Ukraine led to the fall of the Lvov government. Moslem national movements developed rapidly during the course of 1917, while in the Caucasus the foundations were laid of an independent Georgia and Armenia. Nationalist demands within a multinational empire, in which Russians made up barely half the population, were to remain a constant source of tensions for the Provisional Government and its successor.

The decline of Russia as a military force was hastened by the agrarian crisis. From May 1917 soldiers left the fronts to participate in a spontaneous wave of land seizure. The peasant communes in conjuction with the newly elected district land committees became the *de facto* rulers of the countryside. Victor Chernov, head of the SR party and minister of agriculture, was in a unique position to implement his party's land programme. This called for the socialization of land, its transfer to the peasant communes to be distributed equally for personal use, and the banning of hired labour. However, wary of encouraging further desertions from the army by peasants eager to take part in land redistribution, and intimidated by the complexity of land reform, the government made the fatal mistake of refusing to implement the programme in its entirety until the convocation of the Constituent Assembly. The government thereby failed to gain the support of the peasantry, who ultimately simply took the land.

In industry workers began to organize factory committees to defend themselves and to keep the enterprises open in the face of economic disruption and lockouts. The principle of private property and the power of the industrialists was challenged. The government, as in other areas, temporized in the face of the workers' control movement organized by factory committees, and thus forfeited the trust of the business community, who demanded the unequivocal defence of the rights of private property. The Bolshevik party supported the workers' control movement but did not control what in effect constituted a revolution within the revolution. It is important to realize that the workers' movement in 1917 was not a homogeneous movement manipulated by a tightly organized Bolshevik party. There were major divisions within the working class, especially between skilled and unskilled, hereditary and new workers. The worsening economic crisis of 1917 was accompanied by a deepening radicalization of the working class to which the Bolshevik party responded. The relationship between the party and the

21

working class is not easy to conceptualize, but at the local level the party was not external to developments. Large numbers of activists joined the Bolshevik party and encourged worker radicalism. By October 1917 the Bolsheviks appeared to be the only party offering a viable economic and social alternative to economic catastrophe. The simple and basic issue of food shortages in the towns came to fuel the political struggle.

The rivalry between the two sources of authority represented by the Provisional Government and the Bolsheviks, with the Soviets swinging towards the latter as part of an increasingly polarized political atmosphere, was a contest between two philosophies and by October 1917 was transformed into a second revolution. On a range of issues the Provisional Government found itself not flowing with the current of demands and social pressures but attempting to obstruct, divert, or suppress them. The cumulative nature of these problems ultimately overwhelmed the government. The Kadets strove for a constitutional system and looked to the West for models, but they failed to tackle the key problems facing the country. These were accurately reflected by the Bolshevik slogan 'Peace, bread, land'. Lenin himself returned from exile in Switzerland in a sealed carriage with the help of the Germans in April 1917. The Bolsheviks were by no means united over policy and Lenin was forced to wage a vigorous struggle to obstruct the natural inclinations of many moderate Bolsheviks to enter into coalition with other socialists like the Mensheviks or to give critical support to the government. In his 'April Theses' Lenin sharply condemned the moderation of the leaders in Russia such as Stalin and L.B. Kamenev who prior to his return had been carried away by the general rejoicing at the fall of the autocracy. The theses vigorously rejected the othodox social democratic advocacy (to which the Mensheviks remained loyal) of a two-stage revolution. The 'bourgeois' revolution would have to be completed before socialism could be considered. Lenin insisted that a socialist revolution was on the agenda in Russia on the grounds that (1) alliance with the peasantry would give the working class strength to overthrow the old system and (2) the theory of imperialism saw the revolution as only the first step in the world revolution, which then would come to the assistance of backward Russia. The legal first all-Russian conference of Bolsheviks (7–12 May 1917) adopted, though against considerable opposition, Lenin's views on the transfer of power to the soviets, the immediate giving of land to the peasants, workers' control in industry, and the end of the war by spreading the revolution. Lenin preached irreconcilable opposition to the Provisional Government.

On 3–5 July demonstrations of exasperated workers and soldiers broke out in Petrograd. Bolshevik activists at the grass roots were heavily involved in transforming them into a challenge to the government itself, a step which the Bolshevik leadership only reluctantly endorsed and which Lenin considered premature. The moderate socialist leadership of the soviets categorically refused to take power. The government suppressed the disturbances at the cost of some 400 killed or wounded. In the aftermath of the 'July days' Lenin and his colleague G.E. Zinoviev were forced to go into hiding, Kamenev was arrested and *Pravda* banned.

In late August 1917 the military high command under General L.G. Kornilov moved to restore order by establishing a military dictatorship. The attempt met with no more success than Russian arms at the front and was repulsed by the Petrograd soviet and the city's workers organized in Red Guard units. The Bolsheviks took the credit, however, and were rescued from the crisis in which they had languished since the July days. In September they gained majorities in the Petrograd and Moscow city soviets. Kerensky's attempts to broaden the base of the regime by forming a third coalition government in late September failed to overcome the alienation of the left and right. Driven by Lenin's urgings, and against the warnings of Kamenev and Zinoviev, on 24 October the Bolsheviks, organized by Trotsky, moved to take power. Against weak resistance, and with the majority of the population passive, they took control of Petrograd and the Winter Palace. On the night of 24–5 October they presented the second congress of soviets with a *fait accompli*: power belonged to the Bolsheviks and the soviets. An exclusively Bolshevik government headed by Lenin called the Council of People's Commissars (*Sovnarkom*) was formed. The Bolsheviks in October 1917 were the beneficiaries of a broad coalition united only in despair at the ineffectiveness of the Provisional Government.

The nature of the October revolution has been hotly debated. Only a relatively tiny number of people were involved in the fighting; the rest of the population looked on passively. The revolution was not against a fully fledged capitalist state. The Provisional Government lacked the time to develop the institutions of political democracy, and its popular support was still weak. An effective administrative machine was only gradually emerging and the government was reduced to the voluntary co-operation of various agencies. In other words, the Bolsheviks struck not against a liberal democratic capitalist system but against one in the act of creation.

The failure of the Provisional Government was as much the responsibility of the moderate socialist parties, the Mensheviks and the SRs, as it was of the liberal parties, primarily the Kadets. All were increasingly tainted with the government's inability to deal with the problems facing the country. The moderate socialists failed to seize the initiative in policies. Their ideological dogmatism confined them to the prearranged scenario that capitalist development and the bourgeois revolution must precede socialism. The liberals failed to define an adequate response to the fact that the Russian revolution was as much a social as a political revolution. Given a different set of circumstances — an end to the war, some economic stability, a unified moderate socialist movement — then the February revolution might have survived. In the event the problems that had overwhelmed the Tsarist government engulfed the Provisional Government as well.

Neither the February nor the October revolution was caused by rising social classes bursting into prominence (the Marxist view); rather, a specific set of conjunctural factors was abetted by long-term social and political strains. The weakness of the Provisional Government might not have mattered so much if it had not had the misfortune of having its own resolute executioner to hand, the Bolsheviks.

Only they offered a clear political and social alternative. The demand to transfer power to the soviets offered the prospect of a break with capitalism and the fulfilment of worker and peasant aspirations. It appeared to present an opportunity of improving their economic conditions and status. Only Lenin was willing to use the power of the social struggles unleashed in Russia. In October 1917 the aims of the social movements and that of the Bolsheviks coincided; together they swept away the old government and took the destiny of Russia into their hands.

The formation of the Soviet state, 1918–21

The dictatorship of the proletariat and commune democracy

The revolution was tactically brilliant. Lenin admitted that an attempt a few days earlier might well have failed; a few days later, and it would have been crushed. Theoretically, the revolution was justified by the theory of imperialism. Capitalism had become a world system and would not be able to survive once its weakest link, in this case Russia, was broken. In an early version of the domino theory, for Lenin the Russian revolution was only the beginning of the world revolution. It would set all the developed world alight, and Russia's own backwardness would be compensated by foreign assistance. As it turned out, there was no successful general European revolution and Russia was forced to rely on its own resources.

The Bolshevik seizure of power was not so much a *coup d'état* as a revolution with a clear social and political logic of its own. The social demands reflected the fact that what had taken place was not simply a workers' revolution but a peasant one also. The Bolshevik decree 'On Land' of 26 October 1917 implemented the SR land programme, giving legal status to the wholesale redivision of land on egalitarian principles carried out by the village commune. The Bolsheviks were forced to compromise on their aim of introducing what they considered more modern forms of large agricultural holdings. The size and productivity of peasant allotments fell sharply but the neutrality, if not the loyalty, of the peasants had been secured, one of the essential conditions for Bolshevik victory in the civil war.

The social demands of the workers focused on the defence of employment and ensuring food supplies. In the first months the regime conducted a 'red guard attack against capital'. The factory committees were given formal power by a decree of 14 November 1917 to 'control' (supervise) the capitalist managements. The run-down in war orders in late 1917 compounded the earlier general economic collapse and increased unemployment. The factory system came to be maintained only through state support and subsidies. In the short term at least, rather than solving the economic crisis the revolution only made things worse, and by the spring of 1918 the capital cities were on the verge of starvation.

The political concerns of the revolution were focused on the integration of the soviets into a new system of state power and an end to the war. The Bolsheviks on coming to power had no political blueprint which they proceeded to implement. As the first successful Marxist revolution they were forced to adapt their ideas to circumstances. The new government never pretended to favour generalized (liberal) freedom, but insisted that freedom was only for the working class and its allies. According to Marx, the period after the revolution was to be the dictatorship of the proletariat, a phase in which the working class were to maximize the use of state power in order to crush their enemies. Since the revolution would in principle be supported by the majority, this period was expected to last but a short time as they completed the unpleasant task, and then the socialist state could begin to wither away.

The key point in this theory was that the bourgeois state was to be smashed, and with it all the alleged left-overs from the past such as the rule of law, courts, and the separation of powers. Power was to be consolidated on the model of the Paris Commune of 1871, extolled by Marx in his *Civil War in France*. The central features of commune democracy were the fusion of executive and legislative functions, the conversion of deputies from representatives to delegates who could be recalled by the electorate at any time, and a thoroughgoing egalitarianism in which no delegate was to be paid more than workmen's wages. Lenin took up these ideas in his *State and Revolution*, completed in September 1917, maintaining that in the post-revolutionary system there would be a great simplification of administrative functions so that a cook would be able ultimately to manage the affairs of state. The soviets were to act as the basis of this new system. Liberal democracy was to be replaced by a commune democracy which promised to end the division between state and society and to permit the broad participation of the people in public affairs.

The model, however, was flawed. Instead of becoming simpler, as society develops administration becomes more complex and the division of labour intensifies. Little was said about who would do the managing in these circumstances. The fundamental problem was that no mechanism was established to ensure popular control over executive bodies. The commune model was an inclusive rather than a contestatory type of democracy which despised competitive politics and independent associations in society. The absence of checks and balances allowed an enormous concentration of power, which when combined with the Bolsheviks' definition of themselves as 'doers' encouraged the growth of an unchecked *dirigisme* (commandism or leaderism). In 1916 Nikolai Bukharin had warned Lenin of the massive authoritarian potential of the modern state. Lenin preferred to believe that the destruction of the bourgeois state and the creation of the proletarian dictatorship based on commune democracy would solve the problems. It was an act of faith that was to have momentous consequences.

The Bolshevik party itself was not a united body on coming to power. It had grown from a small group of about 25,000 in February 1917 to something around 300,000 in October. Part of the perennial fascination of the early years of Bolshevik rule is the interaction between Bolshevik ideological principles and the realities of power. The collision gave rise to a series of vigorous controversies over policy and organization.

The first major debate was over the organization of Soviet power. The creation of an exclusively Bolshevik government in the *Sovnarkom* headed by Lenin on 25 October shocked and disappointed many radicals. The formation of *Sovnarkom* took power away from the Central Executive Committee (CEC) of the soviets in whose name the revolution had been made. Power was transferred to a body responsible to no one but the Bolshevik party itself. A group including Kamenev, Zinoviev, and A.I. Rykov insisted on the formation of a coalition government with some of the anti-war moderate socialists and envisaged a role for some organizations in addition to the soviets in the new system. Some of the coalitionists felt so strongly over the issue that they resigned from the new government, warning that Lenin's policies would lead to civil war. Lenin, inspired by the idea of commune democracy, insisted that power was to be based on the soviets alone, now dominated in the major cities by the Bolsheviks. Only a month later Lenin agreed to share power with the Left SRs, a group which constituted itself as a separate party in November. After a bitter struggle the coalitionists were defeated. They had envisaged a far broader coalition than one with the Left SRs alone. This was the first instance of a major debate in a revolutionary party in power.

Their defeat opened the way for the destruction of the long-awaited representative assembly. In the elections to the Constituent Assembly in November 1917 the Bolsheviks maintained their hold on the cities of Petrograd and Moscow and gained almost a quarter of the total seats (147), but in the country as a whole the peasant-based Socialist Revolutionaries gained a large majority (410 delegates). It is difficult to gauge how different the results might have been if the elections had been held a month later after the formal split of the SRs and when the Bolshevik land decree had become better known. The Assembly met on 5 January 1918, only to be dissolved that same day. Bukharin read a declaration stating that the Bolsheviks 'declare war without mercy against the bourgeois parliamentary republic'. Soviet Russia's constitutional experiment had come to an end before it had begun. Lenin claimed that a far higher form of democracy had been instated in Russia, commune democracy and the dictatorship of the proletariat. The shooting of workers demonstrating in favour of the assembly illustrated the country's slide into civil war and gave notice that the coincidence of the social and political revolutions of October was beginning to unravel.

Armed peace and civil war

Soviet Russia's attempt to withdraw from the Great War nearly tore the Bolshevik party apart. Negotiations were begun at the border town of Brest-Litovsk in November 1917. Trotsky hoped to force concessions by threatening revolution behind the German and Austrian lines, yet the Central Powers proved stubborn. With the Russian army disintegrating, due in part to the success of their earlier propaganda, the Bolsheviks were forced to concede vast territories containing some of the most valuable industries. The Treaty of Brest-Litovsk in March 1918 was bitterly opposed by a group of Left Communists, led by Bukharin, who asserted that a revolutionary war should be waged to defend Russia and take the revolution to the 'imperialists'. The peace did not entail a rejection of the Bolshevik commitment to internationalism but it did represent a shift of emphasis to communist nationalism. The defence of the solid achievement of the Soviet revolution was regarded as the priority rather than the intangible benefits of trying to spread the revolution militarily. A by-product of the peace was the resignation of the Left SRs from the government, leaving the Bolsheviks to rule alone.

In the 'breathing space' following the Brest-Litovsk peace Lenin developed a strategy for Russia's development based on what he called state capitalism. Aware that the revolution had taken place in a relatively underdeveloped country and not in a mature capitalist society as expected by Marx, Lenin argued that the socialist state should compromise with elements of capitalism in order to further economic development. He sought to emulate the successes of the German war economy based on the emergence of gigantic cartels but stripped of the bourgeois political system — the Krupp empire without the Krupps. Lenin negotiated with certain capitalists to form trusts through which, he hoped, the enormous potential of modern industrial organization could be harnessed to serve the socialist state. The compromise was to be with capitalism, not with the bourgeoisie or with liberal democracy.

The state capitalist period of April-May 1918 was accompanied by attempts to restore labour discipline and raise labour productivity in the factories, attended by enthusiasm for Frederick Taylor's time-and-motion studies on Ford production lines. For the first time a socialist state was forced to face up to the problem that egalitarianism in an industrial society tends to undermine labour productivity. The factory committees were incorporated into the trade unions as the party sought to weaken their independence. Lenin's policies enraged the Left Communists. They insisted that the peace of Brest-Litovsk was economically disastrous, that the compromise with capitalists represented a betrayal of the interests of the working class, and that any labour discipline should begin with the workers themselves. The debate was cut short by the onset of full-scale civil war from May 1918. On 28 June 1918 the majority of Russian industry was nationalized, putting an end to state capitalism and compromises with capitalists.

The civil war from 1918 to 1920 was not an elemental disaster visited upon the Bolshevik state but a logical consequence of Bolshevik policies, as the coalitionists had warned. The Bolsheviks never denied that their seizure of power represented an act of war against the 'exploiting' classes and the 'imperialist' nations. Fourteen countries intervened in the conflict, but in most respects it was a real civil war. The 'whites' were hampered by Bolshevik control of the centralized railway network focused on Moscow, by a divided command structure, relegation to the peripheries of the empire, the absence of a single inspiring alternative to the Bolsheviks, and the lack of support from the peasants accompanied by the hostility of the working class. They were unable even to harness the discontent of the nationalities to their cause, since they were in favour of reconstituting the Russian empire.[1]

In military affairs the Bolsheviks rapidly sloughed off utopian visions of collective decision-making and reconciled themselves to the use of former Tsarist officers, known euphemistically as 'military specialists', thousands of whom were drafted to provide military expertise as commanders under the supervision of Bolshevik commissars. The war was fought by the Bolsheviks largely as a traditional war, with centralization and military discipline. A regular army was recreated by Trotsky which was very different from the militia army long hoped for by Marxists, and indeed very different from the egalitarianism of the People's Liberation Army during the Chinese civil war. Opposition to traditional standing armies, however, was very much a Marxist conviction. The idea of a militia army lingered on into the 1920s as a way of integrating the army into society. Trotsky's attempt to militarize labour in 1920 was designed to redeploy the by then massive Red Army of 5 million to reconstruct the civilian economy. Instead of integrating the army into society, Trotsky sought to remodel society on the pattern of an army. The legacy of the civil war was a militaristic approach to social and political administration.

War communism

The civil war was accompanied by war communism, which lasted from mid-1918 to March 1921. War communism represented the massive consolidation of state power and the extension of the revolution to all spheres of the economy and society in the belief that a rapid transition to socialism could be achieved. The concentration of national resources in the hands of central authority and their military disposition can be called a mobilization regime, the attempt by government to rule all aspects of social life.[2] It represented the apogee of nineteenth-century sociology, with its utopian belief that a direct leap could be made into socialism by enacting social measures. The politics of this transition was left vague. The degree to which war communist policies can be attributed to the pressures of fighting a war or to the intrinsic ideological convictions of the Bolshevik regime has been the subject of sharp controversy. In practice the civil war acted as the catalyst which brought out the most radical features of Bolshevik ideology. War communism was a distinctive blend of revolutionary enthusiasm and pragmatism. Some war communist policies were not destined to outlive the civil war, but others were to become a permanent part of Bolshevism in power.

In the countryside war communism represented a system of transferring grain from the peasantry to the hungry urban working class. Armed detachments left the cities to take the alleged 'surpluses' from the peasantry, and at the same time to foment class war against the richer peasants, the kulaks. From May 1918 committees of the poor (*kombedy*) were established which attacked not only the kulaks but the middle peasants as well. By late 1918 the excesses and negative impact of such policies on the amount of grain available to the regime, accompanied by peasant uprisings, forced Lenin to modify the policy and make peace with the middle peasants, a foretaste of the compromise made with the peasantry as a whole in 1921. The requisitions were the characteristic feature of war communism and continued until March 1921. Lenin called them a 'loan' from the peasantry to the working class, who were in no position to supply the countryside with much-needed manufactured goods. Relations between the Soviet government and the peasantry were to remain uneasy.

In industry war communism was marked by the gradual elimination of private property and enthusiasm for such schemes as the abolition of money. Nationalization not only covered large plants but was extended to encompass even the smaller ones, culminating in a decree of November 1920 which brought the remaining small enterprises into state ownership. The management of nationalized enterprises was not vested in the workers' collectives or the trade unions, but in special economic councils (*sovnarkhozy*), rising in a pyramidal structure to the Supreme Economic Council (*Vesenkha*) in Moscow. This system in effect represented a giant corporation divided into an ever-increasing number of branches (*glavki*). It held the whole economic life of the country in its hands but was not able to organize even the smallest plants effectively. The rights of workers' organizations, the trade unions and workers' control bodies, were limited. In the chaotic circumstances of 1917 and early 1918 the workers' control commissions played a vital part in maintaining industry, but the role of workers' control was ambiguous from the start. After the October revolution there had been high hopes that the trade unions, incorporating the workers' control movement, would take over as the managers of the economy. The eighth party congress in March 1919 resolved that such would indeed ultimately be the case, but as the years passed this goal receded ever further into the future. The factory committees were gradually divested of any major supervisory role and were restricted to agitational functions. The tripartite system of factory management established in the first period after full-scale nationalization, in which power was shared by the economic councils, the trade unions, and the technical and managerial staff of plants, gave way by late 1920 to the imposition of one-person management.

This was a period of terrible economic decline. By 1920 industrial output had fallen to only 20 per cent of the 1913 level, while the harvest of 1921 was only 43 per cent of that of 1913. The working class were drained by military mobilizations, and weakened by hunger and cold in the grim, unlit cities. Unemployment gave way to labour shortages and a system of compulsory labour conscription.

In the political sphere war communism saw the consolidation of power in the hands of the communist party. The Kadet and other 'bourgeois' parties were outlawed in the days following the revolution. The press was from the first heavily controlled by the Bolsheviks. The Right SRs moved into open opposition, and following an abortive uprising in July 1918 the Left SRs were outlawed. The position of the Mensheviks was more ambiguous, since they refused to declare themselves in outright opposition to the Bolsheviks. They retained a lingering presence in the soviets until their destruction in the early 1920s.

The role of the Bolshevik party following the victorious revolution was ambivalent. In principle, once it had helped organize the revolution, power could be transferred to the working class, organized in the soviets. But how was this to work in practice? As far as the Bolsheviks were concerned the soviets were unreliable, since not only did they contain (a few) non-Bolshevik deputies, primarily Mensheviks, but they also represented the peasantry. Only the Bolshevik party represented the proletariat alone and hence were entitled to primacy. They were the repository of the higher revolutionary consciousness. This was the theoretical basis for the emergence of the one-party state and party control over the soviets. However, the practical implementation of these relations between the party and the state was a contentious one from the start. How could the party's 'leading role' be reconciled with a meaningful role for the soviets? In a major debate over this issue a group of Bolsheviks known as the Democratic Centralists from late 1918 insisted that the relationship should be based on a division of labour: the party would provide the ideological leadership; but the soviets should be respected as institutions representing the working class. The eighth party congress agreed that the party should 'guide' the soviets, and not 'replace' them, though this formulation left the details vague, and the problem of substitutionalism (*podmena*) remains to this day. In effect a novel form of dual power was established which in principle retained revolutionary implications. A revived network of soviets challenging party control could form the basis of a regenerated Soviet democracy.

After the revolution the party sent its best activists, or cadres, to work in the soviets and the commissariats, and as an organization began to 'wither away' while the state expanded. The party committees, however, remained the kernel of the new political system. In 1918 Central Committee Secretary Sverdlov had begun to restore organizational coherence to the party, and these attempts were intensified during war communism. By March 1921 a uniform network of party committees had emerged under the central party secretariat in Moscow. The principle of democratic centralism, with the subordination of lower to the higher bodies, was established as earlier federal forms of organization were undermined. The party cells in the factories and the army lost their earlier direct control over their respective institutions. War communism saw the elimination of the mass of independent groupings in society and they were replaced by special groups like the Komsomol (Communist League of Youth). All organizations were to be imbued with the 'party spirit' (*partiinost*), a fundamental principle of Soviet political life. The system was not yet quite like the totalitarianism of Stalin's rule, but the trend towards the suffocation of civil society was clear.

The war communist political system was not internally coherent. On the organizational level not only was it riven by divisions and overlapping competencies between the party, on the one hand, and the soviets and the state mechanism in general, on the other, but the state organizations themselves were locked in struggle with each other. This was a period of massive institution-building: the economic ministries expanded their ambit; other commissariats, such as those of the interior and justice, sought to establish unchallenged authority in their sphere. These two commissariats in particular were challenged by the security police, the Cheka, established in December 1917, one of the most ambitious and uncontrollable bodies spawned in the early period of Soviet power. The Cheka represented a force to establish not only organizational unity but — and this was its original feature — ideological conformity as well. Attempts to establish effective party control over the Cheka failed.

While bureaucratic conflict between various institutions was rife, the whole problem of rampant bureaucracy was an obsession of the period. Its manifestations were legion: red tape, corruption, and inefficiency. As the functions of the state expanded, so the bureaucracy mushroomed. Lenin's optimism in *State and Revolution* about the possibilities of eliminating bureaucracy under socialism proved ill founded, or, at the least, premature. Everywhere new committees and commissions were born, regulating ever smaller segments of life. The fact that the whole vast apparatus did not work very well was usually attributed to 'minor inadequacies of the mechanism', and just one more reorganization, it was asserted, would improve matters no end. The numbers employed in bureaucratic administrations swelled to make up over a third of the labour force. The Bolsheviks were at a loss to comprehend the omnipotence of bureaucracy, all the more so since the theory of commune democracy held that bureaucracy would disappear entirely. Lenin insisted it was a social problem and reflected the lack of culture of Russia. Others insisted that it was a legacy of the Tsarist regime that would be overcome in time. Such responses were rejected as inadequate by the perceptive Moscow Bolshevik E.N. Ignatov and the Democratic Centralists, who insisted that structural factors were at work. The very fact that the Bolsheviks were trying to run the whole life of the country from Moscow gave rise to the bureaucracy, they argued. The responses to the emergence of a native Soviet bureaucracy merged with the ideological debates of the period.

The oppositions

Bureaucratic conflicts were paralleled by ideological rifts. The coalitionists have already been mentioned, and the Left Communist critique of Bolshevik centralization without adequate worker representation was to give rise to a series of oppositional groupings. Trotsky later insisted that during the civil war the political culture of the Bolsheviks had become militarized, but it should be noted that there were powerful anti-militarization forces in such oppositions as the Democratic Centralists and the Workers' Opposition. This was a period of profound ideological restructuring as Marxist abstractions and Leninist organizational nostrums encountered the harsh realities of building socialism in a war-torn country. The Democratic Centralists, as we have seen, fought for a partnership between the party and the soviets. The first Soviet constitution of July 1918 was long on declarations of principle but left the institutional arrangements for the actual organization of power extremely vague. The Democratic Centralists hoped to remedy the situation by revising the constitution to safeguard the rights of lower-level bodies from the encroachments of the centre. By 1920 they were arguing that the temporary infringements of lower-level rights, which they had been willing to tolerate during the civil war, now had a tendency to become permanent.

In 1920–1 two interrelated but separate debates challenged the whole structure of power as it had taken shape during war communism. The first issue focused on inner-party democracy and can be labelled the party debate. This covered such issues as free speech within the party, the rights of party cells, the functions of the committees, and the role of leadership. The polarization of society in 1917 between the *verkhi* (upper classes) and the *nizy* (lower classes) was by the end of the civil war thoroughly internalized within the Bolshevik party, but now the *verkhi* were represented by higher party officials, and the *nizy* by the party's rank and file. The second debate focused on the trade unions. The Workers' Opposition, led by Alexander Shlyapnikov and Alexandra Kollontai, insisted that more rights should be vested in workers' organizations. The stifling of worker initiative in the economy should be replaced by a national congress of producers. Kollontai criticized the bureaucratic regulation of all aspects of social existence, which included the attempt to instil *partiinost* in dog lovers' clubs! Trotsky, on the other hand, took war communist practices to their logical conclusion and insisted that the unions should be incorporated into the economic apparatus. Lenin ultimately took a middle path: the unions should remain independent and act as educators of the working class rather than the organizers of production.

By early 1921 war communism was in crisis. Peasant revolts in the countryside, notably in Tambov, against the forced requisitioning were compounded by urban unrest. The protests climaxed in March 1921 with the revolt of workers and sailors at the Kronstadt naval fortress in the Gulf of Finland, earlier one of the strongholds of Bolshevism. The insurgents rallied under the slogan of 'Soviets without Bolsheviks', denouncing the Bolshevik usurpation of the rights of the soviets. At the tenth party congress that month economic concessions were balanced by the intensification of war communist political processes. The first measures that were to lead to the New Economic Policy were launched, and in particular forced requisitioning from the peasantry was replaced by a fixed tax in kind. Lenin admitted that the attempt to continue the organization of the economy by wartime means had been a mistake. War communism, he insisted, had been necessitated by the war and dislocation but it was not a viable long term policy. Lenin hoped to justify both the necessity of war communism and its repeal.

The party debate as such was never resolved. A cosmetic programme of reform under the label of workers' democracy was instituted, but its effect was only to consolidate the powers of the committees and the party leadership in a process which first saw the use of the term *perestroika* (restructuring) in the Soviet context. The challenge to war communist political relationships was met not by compromise but by repression. At the congress two decrees condemned the oppositional groupings and imposed a 'ban on factions', a 'temporary' measure which long remained a cardinal principle of Soviet rule.

The eight brief months of the Provisional Government proved to be a mere interregnum between two *dirigiste* systems. By 1921 a powerful new state had emerged in Russia following the virtual collapse of authority in 1917. Its grip on political life was almost total, even though its ability to govern the country had yet to be proved. All intermediary organizations in society, including working-class and non-Bolshevik socialist ones, were subordinated to the new authorities. Organized opposition within the party was no longer tolerated. A system based on hierarchy and coercion had become consolidated. This outcome was not an inevitable result of the pattern of Russian history with the veneration for the Tsar simply shifted to the Bolsheviks, and the ideology of absolutism drummed into the people over the ages transferred from one subject to another. Some of the problems faced by the Bolsheviks were similar to those of the Tsars, such as governing a vast territory, but their responses were very different. Tsarist authoritarianism cannot be held responsible for Bolshevik *dirigisme*, since the Bolsheviks had come to power with the idea of achieving a certain programme, however much the precise speed and details of that programme were open to discussion. The new regime's own social base was weak, the political relationship between the party and the working class was ambiguous, and the institutional arrangements of the dictatorship of the proletariat and commune democracy made no provision for institutional or ideological bulwarks against authoritarianism. There was a tendency to reduce every sign of opposition to class contradictions. No distinction was made between opposition *within* the revolution and opposition *to* the revolution.[3] Political debates were not integrated into the structure of Soviet power, though of necessity tolerated in the early years. The result was a particularly Leninist definition of socialism. The defeat of the oppositions in 1921 meant the end of the chance of the emergence of social bodies independent of the state under Soviet socialism. It is not so much Tsarist political culture as the new regime's own contradictions and ideological convictions that help explain these developments.

The Leninist revolution had a double — and contradictory — objective. The first concentrated on overthrowing the Europeanized elite and the destruction of Westernizing social and political processes, a project justified by the attempt to smash the bourgeois state and to extirpate alienating capitalist relations. The second objective, however, ran counter to the first. In attempting to transform Soviet Russia into a modern industrial state the Bolsheviks required the technological sophistication of the West, a scientific rationality, and political modernity. The West was both a model and an anti-model: its productive capacities were to be emulated but its political system was to be decried. Like Peter the Great and other Russian modernizers, the Bolsheviks hoped to take Western technology without Western values.

The various oppositions of the civil war years tried to answer the fundamental conundrum of why there was such a discrepancy between Marxist expectations of socialism and the realities of the Soviet republic. One approach was to lay responsibility on the fact that the revolution lacked the conditions laid down by Marx and instead took place in a relatively underdeveloped country with a small proletariat. The military demands of the civil war and economic collapse further eroded the social basis of the regime. This led to the party-state massively expanding and ultimately acting as a substitute for the social movement that should have made and sustained the revolution. A second approach, favoured by Trotsky, held the absence of a world revolution responsible for domestic distortions. Isolation added force to later arguments in favour of accelerated industrialization to provide a defensive base for the regime. A third view holds the Bolshevik ideology itself responsible. The critical dynamic between a relatively backward country and the distinctive ideology and mentality of the Bolshevik party was to have momentous consequences for the country and the revolution.

Notes

1 Evan Mawdsley, *The Russian Civil War* (Allen & Unwin, London, 1987).
2 See, for example, Thomas Remington, *Building Socialism in Bolshevik Russia: Ideology and Industrial Organisation, 1917-21* (University of Pittsburgh Press, Pittsburgh, Pa., 1984).
3 David W. Lovell, *From Marx to Lenin: an Evaluation of Marx's Responsibility for Soviet Authoritarianism* (Cambridge University Press, Cambridge, 1984); see also Steven Lukes, *Marxism and Morality* (Oxford University Press, Oxford and New York, 1987).

Key texts

Carr, E.H., *The Russian Revolution from Lenin to Stalin, 1917-1929* (Macmillan, London, 1979)
Carrère d'Encausse, H., *Lenin: Revolution and Power* (Longman, London, 1982)
Fitzpatrick, Sheila, *The Russian Revolution, 1917-1932* (Oxford University Press, Oxford and New York, 1982)
Kaiser, Daniel (ed.), *The Workers' Revolution in Russia: the View from Below* (Cambridge University Press, Cambridge, 1987)
Keep, John L.H., *The Russian Revolution: a Study in Mass Mobilisation* (Weidenfeld & Nicolson, London, 1976)
Kochan, Lionel, *Russia in Revolution* (Paladin, London, 1970)
Liebman, Marcel, *Leninism under Lenin* (Merlin, London, 1975)
Sakwa, Richard, *Soviet Communists in Power: a Study of Moscow during the Civil War, 1918-21* (Macmillan, London, 1988)
Service, Robert, *The Bolshevik Party in Revolution: a Study in Organisational Change, 1917-1923* (Macmillan, London, 1979)
Suny, Ronald G., 'Towards a Social History of the October Revolution', *American Historical Review*, 88, 1 (February 1983), pp. 31-52
Von Laue, Theodore H., *Why Lenin? Why Stalin?* 2nd edn (Lippincott, Philadelphia, Pa., 1971)

Select bibliography

The revolutions of 1917

Abraham, Richard, *Alexander Kerensky: the First Love of the Revolution* (Sidgwick & Jackson, London, 1987)

Anweiler, O., *The Soviets: the Russian Workers', Peasants', and Soldiers' Councils* (Pantheon, New York, 1974)

Avrich, Paul, *The Russian Anarchists* (Princeton University Press, Princeton, N.J., 1967)

Brinton, Crane, *The Anatomy of Revolution* (Vintage, New York, 1952)

Carr, E.H., *The Bolshevik Revolution*, 3 vols. (Pelican, Harmondsworth, 1966)

Daniels, Robert V., *Red October: the Bolshevik Revolution of 1917* (New York, 1967)

Dukes, Paul, *October and the World* (Macmillan, London, 1979)

Elwood, Ralph Carter (ed.), *Reconsiderations on the Russian Revolution* (Slavica, Cambridge, Mass., 1976)

Ferro, Marc, *The Russian Revolution of February 1917* (Routledge and Kegan Paul, London, 1972)

Ferro, Marc, *The Bolshevik Revolution: a Social History of the Russian Revolution* (Routledge and Kegan Paul, London, 1985)

Gill, G., *Peasants and Government in the Russian Revolution* (Macmillan, London, 1979)

Haimson, Leopold H. (ed.), *The Mensheviks: from the Revolution of 1917 to the Second World War* (Chicago University Press, Chicago and London, 1974)

Hasegawa, Tsuyoshi, *The February Revolution: Petrograd 1917* (University of Washington Press, Seattle, 1980)

Katkov, George, *Russia 1917: the February Revolution* (Collins, London and New York, 1967)

Koenker, D., *Moscow Workers and the 1917 Revolution* (Princeton University Press, Princeton, N.J., 1981)

Mandel, David, *The Petrograd Workers and the Fall of the Old Regime: from the February Revolution to the July Days, 1917* (Macmillan, London, 1983)

Mandel, David, *Petrograd Workers and the Soviet Seizure of Power (July 1917–June 1918)* (Macmillan, London, 1984)

Medvedev, Roy, *The October Revolution*, (Constable, London, 1979)

Pearson, R., *The Russian Moderates and the Crisis of Tsardom* (Macmillan, London, 1977)

Pipes, R. (ed.), *Revolutionary Russia: a Symposium* (Harvard University Press, Cambridge, Mass., 1968)

Rabinowitch, Alexander, *Prelude to Revolution: the Petrograd Bolsheviks and the July 1917 Uprising* (Indiana University Press, Bloomington, 1968)

Rabinowitch, Alexander, *The Bolsheviks Come to Power: the Revolution of 1917 in Petrograd* (Norton, New York and London, 1976)

Radkey, Oliver, *The Agrarian Foes of Bolshevism: Promise and Default of the Russian Socialist Revolutionaries, February to October 1917* (Columbia University Press, New York, 1958)

Radkey, Oliver, *The Sickle under the Hammer: the Russian Socialist Revolutionaries in the early Months of Soviet Rule* (Columbia University Press, New York, 1963)

Raleigh, Donald J., *Revolution on the Volga: 1917 in Saratov* (Cornell University Press, Ithaca, N.Y., and London, 1986)

Reed, John, *Ten Days that Shook the World* (Vintage, New York, 1960)

Rosenberg, William G., *Liberals in the Russian Revolution: the Constitutional Democratic Party, 1917–1921* (Princeton University Press, Princeton, N.J., 1974)

Schapiro, Leonard, *The Russian Revolutions of 1917: the Origins of Modern Communism* (Basic Books, New York, 1984)

Service, Robert, *The Russian Revolution: Culminations, Beginnings, Disruptions* (Macmillan, London, 1986)

Smith, S.A., *Red Petrograd: Revolution in the Factories, 1917–1918* (Cambridge University Press, Cambridge, 1983)

Suny, Ronald G., *The Baku Commune, 1917–1918: Class and Nationality in the Russian Revolution* (Princeton University Press, Princeton, N.J., 1972)

Trotsky, Leon, *The History of the Russian Revolution*, trans. Max Eastman (Gollancz, London, 1934)

Wade, Rex A., *Red Guards and Workers' Militias: Spontaneity and Leadership in the Russian Revolution* (Stanford University Press, Stanford, Cal., 1983)

Wildman, Allen K., *The End of the Russian Imperial Army, I, The old Army and the Soldiers' Revolt (March-April 1917)* (Princeton University Press, Princeton, N.J., 1980); II, *The Road to Soviet Power and Peace* (Princeton University Press, Princeton, N.J., 1988).

Wilson, Edmund, *To the Finland Station* (Collins, London, 1960)

Wolfe, Bertram, *Three who Made a Revolution* 4th edn (Penguin, Harmondsworth, 1966)

The formation of the Soviet state, 1918–21

Bettelheim, Charles, *Class Struggles in the USSR: First Period, 1917–1923* (Harvester, Brighton, 1976)

Bradley, John, *Civil War in Russia, 1917–1920* (Batsford, London, 1975)

Broido, Vera, *Lenin and the Mensheviks: the Persecution of Socialists under Bolshevism* (Gower, Aldershot, 1987)

Bukharin, N.I., and E.A. Preobrazhensky, *The ABC of Communism*, ed. E.H. Carr (Penguin, Harmondsworth, 1969)

Chamberlin, W.H., *The Russian Revolution, 1917–1921* (Macmillan, London, 1935)

Daniels, R.V., *The Conscience of the Revolution: Communist Opposition in Soviet Russia* (Oxford University Press, Oxford, 1960)

Gleason, Abbott, Peter Kenez, and Richard Stites (eds.), *Bolshevik Culture: Experiment and Order in the Russian Revolution* (Indiana University Press, Bloomington, 1985)

Ilyin-Zhenevsky, A.F., *The Bolsheviks in Power: Reminiscences of the Year 1918 of the Petrograd Military Commissariat* (New Park, London, 1984)

McCauley, Martin (ed.), *The Russian Revolution and the Soviet State, 1917–1921: Documents* (Macmillan, London, 1975)

Malle, Silvana, *The Economic Organisation of War Communism, 1918–1921* (Cambridge University Press, Cambridge, 1985)

Mawdsley, Evan, *The Russian Civil War* (Allen & Unwin, London, 1987)

Remington, Thomas, *Building Socialism in Bolshevik Russia* (University of Pittsburgh Press, Pittsburgh, Pa., 1984)

Rigby, T.H., *Lenin's Government: Sovnarkom, 1917–1922* (Cambridge University Press, Cambridge, 1979)

Rosenberg, W.G. (ed.), *Bolshevik Visions: First Phase of the Cultural Revolution in Soviet Russia* (Ardis, Ann Arbor, Mich., 1985)

Schapiro, L., *The Origin of the Communist Autocracy: Political Opposition in the Soviet State, 1917–1922* (Bell, London, 1955)

Sirianni, Carmen, *Workers' Control and Socialist Democracy: the Soviet Experience* (Verso/NLB, London, 1982)

Chapter three

Stalin and Stalinism

The NEP compromise

The New Economic Policy (NEP) was introduced in March 1921 in response to peasant hostility, worker unrest, and political fragmentation within the communist party. The NEP was a concession but it soon gained adherents, who argued that it was a system which could lay the basis of the transition to socialism in Russia. The NEP represented another version of Soviet politics in contrast to the harshness of war communism, and in some ways it took up the ideas of the state capitalist period of early 1918. Lenin personally was not long to preside over the new system. He suffered a stroke in May 1922 and after two more in late 1922 and March 1923 he died on 21 January 1924. The fate of the NEP became bound up with the succession struggle.

In 1921 the Bolsheviks found themselves in the position forecast by Plekhanov in 1883 when he argued that a socialist party would find itself in enormous difficulties if it took control in the absence of the necessary economic conditions for the realization of its programme. Given such a premature revolution, the party would be obliged either to rule by terror or to grant concessions to the very forces that socialism was pledged to eliminate. The Soviet government at first chose the second option. The enormous central economic monopolies were broken up, market relations were restored between the peasant villages and the urban economy, and free exchange and private enterprise were tolerated. Underlying the NEP was a compromise with the peasantry justified by the idea of a link (*smychka*) between them and the proletariat. The peasants were allowed to sell their surpluses on the market after having paid their tax in kind, usually grain, to the state. This was converted to a monetary tax in 1925.

The New Economic Policy was not accompanied by a new political policy, and indeed Lenin insisted that during a retreat discipline was at a premium to avoid a rout. In the early 1920s the vestiges of non-Bolshevik parties were effectively eliminated. The trial of a group of leading Socialist Revolutionaries in mid-1922 presaged the show trials of the 1930s. To compensate for the real and imaginary threats to Bolshevik rule the mystique and power of the party were enhanced all the more. The introduction of the NEP was accompanied by what was called a 'restructuring' (*perestroika*) of the party. The Bolshevik committees tightened their administrative control over local party organizations. Centralization and conformity within the party were intensified just as they were being relaxed in the economy. In April 1922 Stalin became General Secretary of the party, a post regarded at the time as a key administrative rather than political job. In a consummate manner he consolidated the party machine and his own power over that machine. His ability to appoint, dismiss, and transfer party officials prefigured the ubiquitous *nomenklatura* personnel placement mechanism of later years and gave him a powerful weapon in the inner-party debates. A 'circular flow of power' (R.V. Daniels) was established whereby Stalin's appointments became beholden to him for their positions. Stalin became the beneficiary of a process of restructuring that had begun quite independently of him.

The struggle for Lenin's succession took the form of a personalized contest between Stalin, Trotsky, and other leaders. At first Stalin cloaked his ambitions behind the triumvirate of Zinoviev, Kamenev, and himself, which assumed the leadership at Lenin's request in late 1921, but gradually Stalin was able to dispense with subterfuge. The Lenin succession was complicated by the fact that no one knew what formal post constituted the leadership. As the Democratic Centralists had earlier charged, the system of government under Lenin lacked the formal delineation of functions. Lenin himself was head of the government (*Sovnarkom*) and held no official party post, although dominating the party through his immense personal prestige.

In December 1922 Lenin, recovering from his first illness, dictated his 'Testament', which characterized the leading contenders. Bukharin's intellectuality was criticized, while the hesitations of Kamenev and Zinoviev in October 1917 were branded as not having been 'accidental'. Trotsky was accused of 'excessive self-assurance' and a 'preoccupation with the purely administrative side of work'. Lenin had long held a high opinion of Stalin's ability, and he was elevated as Trotsky's equal. But, Lenin noted, 'comrade Stalin, having become General Secretary, has concentrated enormous power in his hands, and I am not sure whether he will always be capable of using that authority with sufficient caution'.[1] Lenin was dismayed by Stalin's rudeness at this time towards the Georgian communists, reflecting his lack of respect for nationalities, which reminded Lenin of the worst traditions of Russian chauvinism. The Testament maximized personal conflicts by drawing attention to the weaknesses of all the major leaders. Hearing of a personal affront to his wife, Krupskaya, Lenin dropped his even-handed approach. In a postscript of 4 January 1923 he accused Stalin of intolerable rudeness and urged his colleagues 'to think of removing Stalin from that post'. Trotsky's failure to make known Lenin's condemnation of Stalin's behaviour over the nationality question at the twelfth party congress in 1923 destroyed one of the best chances of suffocating Stalinism at birth. Lenin's failure to nominate his own successor or a replacement for Stalin was understandable but did not help matters.

The *perestroika* of the party following war communism prompted forty-six leading party members in October 1923 to write a letter protesting against the suppression of party democracy. Trotsky took the opportunity to write his famous letter, known as *The New Course*, to the Central Committee, warning against the consolidation of the party bureaucracy spawned during the civil war. Tactlessly, he spoke slightingly of most of the Bolshevik leaders of 1917. Stalin's fellow triumvars, Zinoviev and Kamenev, launched a ferocious attack, and both Trotsky and the forty-six were condemned by the thirteenth party congress in May 1924. Trotsky not only accepted the congress decision but went so far as to support the assault against the Left Opposition. Trotsky's behaviour between 1923 and his expulsion from the party in 1927 was contradictory, torn as he was between loyalty to the party and opposition to Stalin. His vacillations and appeasement actually disarmed and confused the anti-Stalin opposition by such statements at the thirteenth congress as 'the party is always right . . . We can only be right with and by the party.'[2]

Lenin's last year was taken up with concern over the succession and the formation of the USSR (see pp. 297–9), but above all by the problem of bureaucracy. His last article, 'Better fewer, but better' was a bitter denunciation of the morass of bureaucratism in which the Soviet government found itself, but could suggest no effective solution. The great expansion in the Lenin Enrolment following his death and the continued recruitment swept a mass of new, untested communists into the party. Between 1924 and 1928 party membership nearly trebled, from 472,000 to 1,304,471, swamping the old generation of Bolsheviks. Trotsky later insisted that the mass recruitment of this time rendered the party machine, dominated by Stalin, almost completely independent of the rank and file.[3]

In late 1924 Trotsky's *The Lessons of October* was attacked by Zinoviev and Kamenev. Stalin in the guise of the moderate accused them of going too far: 'The policy of cutting off heads is fraught with dangers for the party.' In January 1925 Trotsky was deprived of his post as Commissar of War, and 'Trotskyism' was officially condemned. At the fourteenth party congress in December 1925 Stalin appeared for the first time as reporter of the Central Committee, on which he now enjoyed a majority. Stalin's policies were endorsed by the congress, which had been packed with his supporters. Alarmed, Stalin's erstwhile co-leaders Zinoviev and Kamenev, who had been hopelessly outmanoeuvred, were even prepared to attack the NEP as part of their campaign against him. They joined forces with Trotsky in a United Opposition which did little to enhance their reputation for integrity. Bukharin, the key supporter of the NEP, rallied to Stalin in defence of moderate economic policies. The opposition's appeal to the party's rank and file contravened the rules on party discipline, and they were easily crushed by the Stalinist machine. In July 1926 Zinoviev was expelled from the Politburo, followed by Trotsky and Kamenev in October. In November 1927 the opposition in desperation took to the streets, and thus played into Stalin's hands. They were expelled from the party on 15 November 1927 and denounced by Bukharin at the fifteenth party congress in December 1927. Having defeated the United Opposition with Bukharin's assistance, Stalin moved to defeat Bukharin and what he called the Right Deviation. The succession struggle entered its final phase.

The NEP has often been seen as a golden age, a period of communist liberalism coming between the harshness of war communism and the brutality of Stalinism in the 1930s. The NEP did indeed see an effervescence of cultural life, with a brilliant age of film-making by the likes of Sergei Eisenstein and Dziga Vertov. The *Smenavekh* (Change of Landmarks) movement from 1922 was an attempt by various intellectuals to act as a mediating force between the regime and cultural interests, a project which met with little success. Compared to what came later it was a period of cultural diversity, but already the empire-building of Soviet institutions that had begun during war communism was being extended to the cultural sphere. The suicide of Sergei Esenin in 1925 prefigured the despair that led to the death by his own hand of Vladimir Mayakovskii in 1930. Nadezhda Mandelshtam has dismissed the myth of the 'happy 'twenties' as serving to dissociate contemporaries from the rise of Stalin, who alone is blamed for putting an end to the flowering of the arts, sciences, and literature.[4]

The great industrialization debate

The tensions generated by the conflict between political concentration and economic liberalization provided the context for the rise of Stalinism. The debate in the 1920s over the means to achieve the industrialization of the Soviet Union represented the second phase of a controversy that had begun in the nineteenth century. At issue was the question of whether the NEP was a temporary expedient to allow the Soviet regime and economy to recuperate from the travails of the civil war before launching a new offensive, or whether it was a more permanent attempt at establishing a system that might approximate to that required for the long-term development of socialism. Like his evaluation of war communism, Lenin's position on this question was open to conflicting interpretations. At first he insisted that it would last for a long time 'but not for ever', but by the end of his life he appears to have changed his mind. Instead of viewing the NEP as a tactical retreat, Lenin began to see it as lasting a considerable period and acting as a 'bridge into socialism'. He hoped that by entering into co-operatives and other joint endeavours the peasantry would gradually be won over to socialism. Had he lived his views might well have changed yet again, but he died convinced of the value of gradualism in Soviet economic policy.

The NEP had many achievements to its credit. In 1923–4 financial stability was restored following the hyper-inflation of the civil war. By 1926–7 pre-war levels of agricultural and industrial production were achieved, although the urban economy lacked dynamism. The restoration of market relations in the countryside allowed the peasant economy to strengthen. However, the NEP was accompanied by major social problems such as unemployment and gross inequalities symbolized by the NEPmen, who were regarded as 'speculators' peddling wares at inflated prices.

In foreign affairs the Soviet revolution remained isolated. During the 1920s the world revolutionary movement suffered a series of reverses. The conclusive defeat of the German revolution in autumn 1923 alarmed the Bolshevik leadership, while the massacre of Chinese communists in 1927 by the nationalist Guomingdang illustrated the pitfalls of alliances with bourgeois revolutionary forces. The international revolution, on which the Bolsheviks had staked so much, was clearly delayed and therefore help would not be immediately forthcoming from abroad. Capitalism, it appeared, had entered upon a period of stabilization. Indeed, by May 1927 a scare of war with Britain suggested that capitalism was prepared to launch a new offensive.

A mood bordering on panic circulated among the leadership. Several times Trotsky related that the Soviet government was hanging by a thread. Trotsky's views on the precariousness of the Soviet regime were coloured by the slow advance of the collective farms (*kolkhozy*), which the Soviet government neglected. Furthermore, the weakness of state rural administration (rural soviets) was notorious, and for most of the 1920s communist influence over the countryside was minimal. The relationship between the peasant soviets and the state can be characterized by Robert Redfield's terms 'the little community' and the 'big community'.[5] The majority of the population lived in the little community in the villages, with its own rituals and patterns. Even after the launching in 1925 of a vigorous 'Face to the countryside' campaign to strengthen the rural party the number of communists in the villages rose from 153,000 (31 per cent of total membership) to only 333,000 (25 per cent) in 1929. The quality of the new recruits left much to be desired.

Stalin offered an alternative to alarmist and gloomy prognoses. From 1924 he challenged the pessimists and declared that it would be possible to build 'socialism in one country' with or without foreign assistance. Underlying the debate over the economy were political issues which became bound up with the factional in-fighting for the succession. Yet Stalin's victory was assured by more than his mastery of the Bolshevik political machine. His policies had a broad political appeal. Stalin's concept of socialism in one country held that Russia could not only *begin* the building of socialism, but could on its own resources go on and *complete* the process. The theory of socialism in one country, as opposed to its *de facto* practice since the establishment of the Bolshevik regime, constituted a major revision of Marxist theory and made a virtue of necessity. Socialism gradually became identified with the national interests of the Soviet Union. In contrast, Trotsky while agreeing that Russia could begin to build socialism, from his theory of permanent revolution argued that the process could be completed only after the revolution had spread to other countries. It implied that the Russian revolution was dependent, and in a sense hostage, to the revolutionary process elsewhere.

The NEP stabilized the Soviet regime but the question remained of how to build socialism in a relatively backward country. The Soviet regime became a 'modernizing' one (as most Marxist regimes have), but the commitment to industrialization was above all vexed by the 'peasant contradiction'. The free market in agricultural products seemed to stymie the Soviet government's urge to industrialize. The Bolsheviks had come to power and established the political system of socialism, but in the countryside the capitalist system in effect still reigned. Bukharin stressed reformist gradualism, an agrarian co-operative socialism whereby socialism would be reached on the 'peasant nag', eschewing social conflict and securing marketable surpluses by allowing the kulaks, who were more efficient, to expand their holdings. One of the major problems of the NEP, however, was illustrated by the 'scissors crisis' of summer 1923, a term used to show the discrepancy between agricultural and industrial prices. The 'scissors' were never completely closed, meaning that the terms of trade remained skewed against the countryside. Bukharin's strategy called for low industrial prices, to increase demand, which could be taxed for further development. He admitted that this would be a long path. Once again, as with Stolypin, it was a 'wager on the strong' which increased inequality in the countryside.

Bolshevik activists increasingly perceived the peasants as an obstacle to their hopes of rapid industrialization. For many the NEP could be tolerated as no more than a temporary expedient. The left accused it of betraying working-class interests in favour of the 'petty-bourgeois' peasantry. The NEP was unadventurous, and to those nurtured on the revolutionary enthusiasm of the fight against Tsarism and the heroism of war communism it appeared a decidedly poor substitute for the vision of the socialist society to which they had devoted their lives. The NEP's emphasis on educational work, long-term cultural improvement, and gradualism contrasted with the Bolsheviks' image of themselves as the masters of social and political forces. The institutional tensions inherited from war communism also played their role in undermining the consensus over the continuation of NEP. Above all, this centred on the state bureaucracy, which thrived under the NEP in the towns. This powerful bureaucracy, Trotskyists argue, was irked by the existence of spheres beyond its immediate control, above all by market relations among the peasantry and parts of the economy. For the leftist oppositions the NEP itself was responsible for providing an atmosphere conducive to the growth of the bureaucracy as revolutionary methods gave way to routine administration. Lenin's position was sufficiently ambiguous to allow the view to flourish among Bolsheviks that the NEP was a 'retreat', and that as soon as the state became strong enough the advance would continue.

Opposition to the NEP focused on the danger of the restoration of capitalism through the allegedly nefarious activities of the NEPmen and the kulaks. Trotsky and the United Opposition condemned the idea of socialism in one country and feared the moment when the bastions of the nationalized economy would be swept away by the petty-capitalist tide led by the peasants. The strategy, they argued, should be to build up the state-run industrial economy as fast as possible. But where would the necessary funds be found? The answer was provided by Evgenii Preobrazhenskii in his concept of primitive socialist accumulation, a 'feudal exploitation of the peasantry' mimicking the process, described by Marx, of capital formation in Britain. The state was to accumulate the resources for accelerated industrial investment at the expense of the peasantry by demanding high prices for industrial products and by high taxes. The market was to be suppressed in the industrial sector and relations with agriculture were to be highly controlled. This programme relied on a series of fiscal measures, and not on direct coercion. Condemned at the time by Bukharin and Stalin, it was this programme, stripped of its subtleties, that Stalin later implemented.

Stalin's position, which in the period after Lenin's death seemed to coincide with that of Bukharin, gained the support of the majority of party leaders. Rejecting Trotsky's views on the necessity of a combined strategy of intensifying the class struggle between workers and peasants while simultaneously pressing for world revolution, Stalin argued that the peasants could be won over to socialism by expanding the private market and improving supplies of industrial goods. Yet Stalin increasingly revealed an enthusiasm for accelerated industrialization incompatible with the maintenance of NEP. The sixteenth party conference in November 1926 resolved on 'catching up and then overtaking the level of industrial development of the advanced capitalist countries in a relatively short historical period'. At the fifteenth party congress in December 1927 even Bukharin was willing to accept an ambitious programme of industrial investment and the voluntary collectivization of agriculture.

The congress met against the background of a threatening international climate. There were growing food shortages in the cities. Peasants were reluctant to part with their grain, since prices were low, and in any case there was a scarcity of industrial goods for them to purchase as a result of Bukharin's policy of low industrial prices. Stalin identified the 'kulak hoarder' as responsible for the shortfall in procurements, and he reacted by launching a series of 'extraordinary measures'. In one of his rare departures from Moscow he travelled to the Urals and Siberia in January 1928 to obtain the planned amounts of grain through coercion, bypassing the regular procurement agencies. The 'Urals-Siberian' method of grain requisitioning signalled the breakdown of the will to keep the NEP in operation.

Bukharin accepted the necessity for more rapid industrialization but urged that it should be kept within the bounds of a balanced economic programme. In his *Notes of an Economist* he insisted that sustained industrial growth could best be achieved within the framework of the NEP and with the balanced development of agriculture.[6] His condemnation of the leftists' arguments for super-industrialization as constituting a 'feudal-military exploitation of the peasantry' was an oblique attack on Stalin himself. Defeat of Bukharin now signalled the end of the NEP as Stalin adopted the arguments for rapid industrialization from Preobrazhenskii, though not the means.

The revolution from above

Between 1929 and 1932 the NEP was reversed as the Soviet Union witnessed a veritable 'revolution from above', consisting of three main aspects: accelerated industrialization, rapid compulsory collectivization, and cultural revolution.

The state took a leading role in the industrialization process, but the contrast with the 1890s was marked. In the earlier period state intervention to obtain foreign loans and to promote the capital goods sector had been accompanied by the vigorous development of commercially based capitalism and consumer goods. Stalin's industrialization, on the other hand, was accompanied by the elimination of the capitalist sector in its entirety and by a great concentration on heavy industry (known as sector A) as opposed to consumer goods (sector B). As if to echo Stalin's own name (which means 'man of steel'), this was an epoch of 'metal-eating' industries. Consumption was reduced to an absolute minimum to permit greater investment in heavy and associated defence industries. The Stalinist definition of 'industrialization' was a narrow one, aimed at maximizing development through national programmes of economies of scale. This super-industrialization represented a complete rupture with Bukharin's gradualism.

The key to the whole period was the idea of planning. The State Planning Bureau (Gosplan) had been established in 1921 and by 1925 was issuing 'control' figures for industries which in 1929 were to become the plan target figures. In 1928 the first five-year plan was introduced, which substantially raised the tempos hitherto achieved for industrial development. Within a few weeks of its adoption the key targets were revised substantially upwards to begin a headlong spiral of ever-rising goals. The establishment of targets became not so much a function of planning as a way of accelerating growth. There was chaos within the plans, since, as Nove points out, any plan which aims towards overfulfilment under-mines the very notion of planning. The plans were determined by considerations other than the rational attempt to harmonize economic targets with resources. This 'wilful' planning system, G. Grossman argues, was not so much a planned economy as a 'command economy'.[7] The first five-year-plan engendered the massive expansion of the administrative apparatus. A system of ministries respon-sible for branches of Soviet industry was born which survives to this day. Ministries controlled not only plants but also housing and various ancillary networks. The management of industrial plants was strictly centralized under one person responsible to the relevant ministry.

The speeded-up industrialization was accompanied by intensified pressure on the peasantry. The *smychka* between the peasantry and the proletariat was a fragile one, marked by suspicion on the side of the party authorities, afraid of the luxuriant capitalism in the countryside. Above all, hostility was directed against the kulaks. Economic means of obtaining grain gave way to direct political and administrative coercion reminiscent of war communism. Food shortages in the towns led to the tightening of rationing in February 1929, and the 'Urals-Siberian' method of compulsory grain requisitioning was intensified. Wholesale collectivization became increasingly attractive to a section of the party to solve the problem of grain supplies once and for all. Stalin took advantage of the frustrations at the discrep-ancy between Bolshevik ideology and the peasant realities of the countryside. The urban-based Bolsheviks were no longer prepared to accept a situation in which the peasants could apparently hold the revolution hostage through the operation of the market in grain. We cannot really know whether Stalin shared or manipulated the party mood to his advantage. Bukharin's moderate line gained much support, and the views of the party on developing the economy were far from unanimous. At the least we can say that most Bolsheviks shared the Marxist contempt for the peasant and were convinced that collective agriculture was preferable to individual peasant farming.

Of more immediate concern were Bolshevik views about the class structure of the countryside. During the early years of the revolution there had been a profound levelling process in the countryside as the large farms were divided and the poorer peasants gained land. Little had changed during the NEP, and the Bolshevik class analysis of the countryside as divided into kulaks, middle peasants, and poor peasants (and a group of itinerant workers, *batraki*) was artificial. Of the Soviet Union's 125 million peasants no more than 2.3 million were farmhands (poor peasants), and the kulaks owned no more than 750,000, or 3.4 per cent of all farms. Most kulaks employed nobody, and even the most prosperous peasant in 1927 had no more than three cows and three working animals, with about ten hectares of sowing area to support an average family of seven.[8] The Bolshevik definition of the kulak was imprecise and transformed a statistical category into a social class.

Bukharin had argued that the process of collectivizing agriculture should be voluntary, extend over a long period, and be based on the gradual mechanization of agriculture. Attempts during the NEP to encourage peasants to join the collective farms (*kolkhozy*) and state farms (*sovkhozy*) were half-hearted. By 1928 97.3 per cent of total sown area was still being farmed by individual peasant cultivation. The voluntary collectivization of the peasantry gradually gave way to coercion as armed detachments were sent into the countryside. It was suddenly discovered that even without mechanization the small and medium peasants were ready to join. In November 1929 Bukharin was removed from the Politburo, opening the way for Stalin to decree on 27 December 'the liquidation of the kulaks as a class'. The dekulakization programme was to provide the other peasants with the kulaks' land, animals, and tools in the absence of machines. Violent social conflict was unleashed as the poorer sections of the village community were set against the kulaks and old scores were settled.

War was declared against the private peasants as they began to be forced off their 25 million family holdings on to the collective farms. A desperate civil war broke out in the countryside as kulaks and other sections of the rural population, notably peasant women in the so-called 'women's riots' (*bab'i bunty*), resisted wholesale collectivization. Particularly detested were the 'twenty-five-thousanders', an urban invasion of factory workers and urban party activists sent to organize the *kolkhozy* even though they knew little about agriculture.[9] By March 1930 over 55 per cent of the peasantry had been collectivized. In that month Stalin called a temporary halt to the bloodletting in his speech 'Dizzy with success', which held the overenthusiasm of the activists responsible for the 'excesses'. By the end of the year about half the recently collectivized peasants had drifted back into private production. But the pressure was sustained, and by 1936 90 per cent of all farms were collectivized. According to official statistics 115,200 kulak families were deported in 1930 and 265,800 in 1931. Unofficial statistics suggest that 15 million were left homeless by collectivization, a million of whom were sent to labour camps and some 12 million deported to Siberia.[10] A large proportion perished in the north. Rather than donating their livestock to the collective farms peasants preferred to kill their animals. The results were catastrophic. Between 1928 and 1934 the number of horses declined from 32 million to 15 million, cattle from 60 million to 34 million, pigs from 22 million to 11.5 million and sheep from 97.3 million to 32.9 million. Heavy compulsory deliveries coupled with the slaughter of animals led to a famine in 1932–3 over the south Ukraine, the north Caucasus and other traditional grain-producing regions. About 7 million died in what is now bluntly called the 'murder famine', and throughout the land there was unimaginable misery.[11]

Collectivization and industrialization were accompanied by a cultural revolution which owed as much to dynamism from below as initiatives from above. The cultural revolution was not simply imposed by the party but represented the partial resolution of tensions within the society of the NEP period. The pressure came from sections of the party, the youth movement (Komsomol), and the working class for more radical policies. The targets of the cultural revolutionaries were bureaucratic administration and the old intelligentsia. In their place they propounded utopian visions of collective life, with new approaches to education, architecture, law, and social relations in general. The elements of utopianism in effect represented a cultural purge, as the social and natural sciences were bent towards a dogmatic leftism. Experimentation in literature, for example, was ended as the Russian Association of Proletarian Writers (RAPP), founded in 1928, sought to destroy various bourgeois and other cultural organizations in order to establish its dominance in the literary field. David Joravsky speaks of a 'great break' in 1928–9 as the old intelligentsia lost out to a new generation who had been emerging in various professions during the NEP.[12] However, by mid-1931 Stalin had begun to repudiate some of the excesses of the cultural revolution and began what Timashev has labelled the 'great retreat' of the 1930s towards more conservative cultural and social attitudes.[13]

The fundamental question in understanding the end of NEP is whether there were real economic alternatives to the policies adopted by Stalin. The Bukharin approach has been held up as a viable alternative which would have achieved strong economic results while avoiding the political brutalization of the Stalin years.[14] As a mechanism the NEP might well have survived with some fine tuning of the exchange mechanisms between town and country, such as in setting industrial prices and the level of the agricultural tax, and with more far-sighted investment to provide the peasants with the means of production. Rather than any fundamental inherent flaws it was distrust between the party leadership and the peasants, ideological hostility to the market and co-operatives, political manoeuvring to succeed Lenin, and the lack of political will to maintain the NEP which caused its demise. The debate, however, was not concerned with the development of the socialist economy only but with the definition of socialism itself.

Were forced collectivization and rapid industrialization the only options open to the Soviet regime in 1929? The cornerstone of the government's strategy was for agriculture to finance industrial development. Yet the search for a steady supply of grain or more efficient farming barely figured in the collectivization process. If there was not a direct economic logic to the process, then one has to look at political reasons. Mass collectivization had always been an integral component of the Bolshevik programme, in line with Marx's bias against peasant individualism. When combined with Bolshevik political culture, which encouraged a lack of restraint when dealing with social forces, the scene was set for conflict. War communism left a legacy of Bolshevik enthusiasm and maximalism that was not satisfied by the gradualist programmes of the NEP.

The arguments of Bukharin and the right were defeated not on rational grounds but as part of the political struggle. The revolution from above was a way of consolidating Stalin's own position and destroying the bases of opposition influence. Stalin himself justified his policies on nationalistic grounds in terms of the need to make up the lag compared to the advanced countries and to secure Soviet defences. Political competition with the West was now transformed into an economic race, but one whose standards and measure of achievement were set in the West. Furthermore, the Bolshevik leadership was increasingly dissatisfied at having to 'bribe' the peasants to part with their grain. There was a fundamental contradiction between a socialist political 'superstructure' sitting uncomfortably on top of the peasant economic 'base'. The second revolution was a way of integrating the two and of securing the social foundations of the Bolshevik regime.

Command economy and society

The central question of the 1920s had been how agriculture could contribute to industrialization. There was no essential economic connection between forced collectivization and rapid industrialization, contrary to the views of advocates of the latter, although without collectivization the industrial growth rate of that period might not have been quite so high.[15] Collectivization freed the government from having to placate the peasant producer and allowed resources to be concentrated in industrial investment. The harvest in 1931, at 65 million tonnes, was slightly less than in 1929, but the state's share had doubled to some 32 million tonnes, some of it being exported for hard currency to purchase machinery for the first five-year-plan. Cheap food for the expanding labour force in the towns allowed wages to be kept low. Gains were offset, however, by the need to divert resources into accelerated tractor-building to make up for the huge losses of livestock and horses.

The *kolkhozy* were forced to fulfil extremely high delivery quotas at low prices in a state-directed system of peasant exploitation. In addition, prices for industrial goods were set so high that they amounted to a further onerous tax on the peasantry. As Khrushchev later admitted, for long periods the peasantry were unable even to cover production costs. They descended into a 'state of semi-serfdom'[16] and were forced to fulfil high labour norms in return for a share of the usually non-existent profits. Personal plots of land were legalized in 1932 as a measure to stave off generalized famine and perhaps as a concession to defuse the unrest in the countryside. The *kolkhozy* did not own the machinery but had to hire it from machine tractor stations (MTS), which acted as both economic and political centres of control. The result of such policies was the sustained impoverishment of the peasantry and the extended debilitation of the agricultural sector of the economy.

Despite the catastrophic losses sustained by the agricultural sector, industry was able to maintain impressive development. By the time of the German invasion of 22 June 1941 the Soviet Union was one of the world's major industrial powers and the foundations had been laid on which to fight the war. Accompanying the industrial expansion there were massive changes in society (see Table 1). This was the 'quicksand society', as Moshe Lewin has dubbed it. To escape from the poverty and violence of the countryside in 1931 4·1 million peasants moved to the cities, a total which by 1935 had grown to 17·7 million. Between 1926 and 1939 the cities gained some 30 million people. Urban dwellers as a proportion of the total population increased from 18 to 24 per cent. During the first five-year-plan the salaried labour force (workers and officials) doubled, from 10·8 million to 20·6 million, with the bulk of the growth coming from the peasantry. By 1940 the number had increased to 31·2 million.[17]

Table 1 Class composition of the population (%)

	1913	1928	1939	1959	1970	1979	1986
Workers and employees	17·0	17·6	50·2	68·3	79·5	85·1	87·9
Manual workers	14·6	12·4	33·7	50·2	57·4	60·0	61·7
Employees	2·4	5·2	16·5	18·1	22·1	25·1	26·2
Collective farmers	—	2·9	47·2	31·4	20·5	14·9	12·1
Individual peasants	66·7	74·9	2·6	0·3	—	—	—
Property owners	16·3	—	—	—	—	—	—

Sources: *SSSR v tsifrakh v 1985 godu* (Moscow, 1986), p. 13; *SSSR v tsifrakh v 1986 godu* (Moscow, 1987), p. 6.

The first five-year-plans were marked by enormous upward social mobility as peasants moved to join the industrial working class, and skilled workers were promoted into white-collar and managerial positions. One of the major aims of the cultural revolution was to replace the old intelligentsia by new cadres. This was achieved through a massive programme of 'proletarian advancement' (*vydvizhenie*) whereby workers and working-class communists were promoted to fill the expanding ranks of engineers and administrators. The educational system was reformed to allow workers maximum access to the expanded courses in technical subjects. Universities were opened to adults even if they had not completed a full secondary education. A generation stamped by the crash industrialization programme were rapidly trained and promoted under the auspices of the party (the 'thousanders'), a total of about 110,000 communist adult workers and 40,000 non-communist ones. This cohort of 'red specialists' formed a generation of economic and political leaders which is only now being replaced.

The vast intake of new factory workers experienced massive labour turnover. The free market in goods had been abolished but the labour market remained. Industrial discipline and productivity were low. In response the authorities introduced a system of internal passports in December 1932 in an attempt to decrease mobility, and in 1938 labour books were issued, recording an individual's work record. The urban work force was incapable of any but the most inchoate resistance against state and factory authorities. After collectivization standards of living fell sharply. Real wages had fallen by at least half by 1932, and workers were sustained only by general rationing, in force from 1928 to 1935. The housing stock lagged far behind the tripled urban population, which rose from 22 million in 1922 to 63 million in 1940. The meat consumption of urban and country dwellers alike declined to only a third of the 1928 level in 1932. The peasantry were denied the benefits of social security and were not issued with internal passports. They responded by working badly and devoting their energies to their personal plots.

The end of the cultural revolution in 1932 was marked by the great retreat which permitted the consolidation of a conservative society. The educational system took on a more traditional look, and from 1931 engineers and other sections of the old intelligentsia were once again in favour. Experimentation in the arts gave way to the stifling orthodoxies of 'socialist realism'. The beneficiaries of the crash educational programme, the worker *vydvizhentsy*, consolidated their gains in 1937 as the great purge carried off the old managerial and administrative elite. The stress was increasingly on conservative marriage laws, restrictions on divorce, and the banning of abortion except on medical grounds. Under Stalin a new hierarchy of inequality emerged, together with an overbearing officialdom, but the position of this group, dubbed by Djilas a 'new class', was insecure. They could never be sure that the early-morning knock would not one day sound on their door. Even under Stalin social laws operated with a degree of independence, but individuals remained at the mercy of the political system. At the base of Stalinism were those who profited from it in one way or another. Vera Dunham has identified a post-war 'Big Deal' between the Stalinist system and the rising middle class of Soviet functionaries. In return for loyalty and labour they were rewarded with privileges, responsibility, and the opportunity to pass on their advantages to their children. The *mores* of the new Soviet middle class simulated those of the West but stripped of any entrepreneurial dynamism in contributing to economic development. The price of the Stalinist model of industrialization was a parasitic 'new class', inefficiency, and low labour productivity. As radical economic reformers later admitted, only so much could be achieved through planning, commanding and storming. Above all, the creation of a massive state and party bureaucracy to run the economy was to have a baleful effect on the quality of Soviet political life for several decades.

The great purges

The concept of the purge (*chistka*) was familiar to the Soviet citizen from the periodic campaigns within the party to expel so-called careerists, hangers-on, and other undesirables. The civil war had been accompanied by annual re-registrations of communists to screen the party, but the campaign of 1921 was the first occasion on which the term 'purge' was used to describe the process. The rapid recruitment of 1924 following Lenin's death continued into the early 1930s and raised new concern about the quality of party membership. A purge in 1930 saw over 100,000 communists expelled, and this was repeated in 1933–4, when over a million were expelled. In the exchange of party cards in 1935 about half a million members were expelled. According to Brzezinski, the ruling party requires a permament purge to maintain its own internal discipline and to prevent its degeneration into a corrupt, self-serving body. However, in the 1930s the idea of the purge was extended to the rest of society, and the cleansing of the party was no longer restricted to the expulsion of undesirables but meant their elimination.

Stalin's fiftieth birthday in 1929 was celebrated by the inflation of his personality cult. The powers of the secret police, the OGPU (as the Cheka was now known), headed by V.R. Menzhinskii and later G.G. Yagoda, had been steadily increasing. A series of trials selectively attacked important groups. In June 1928 the trial of fifty-three engineers and technicians in the Shakhty district of the Donetsk basin set the pattern for the trial in late 1930 of eight high economic officials who had allegedly formed an Industrial Party. The whole technical intelligentsia inherited from Tsarist times came under threat. Accounts were settled with the Mensheviks in a trial of March 1931. The brutality of collectivization infected the whole political system and allowed any criticism to be identified with the sabotage of class enemies.

Despite the risks there were attempts to limit Stalin's powers. In late 1930 two leading party figures, S.I. Syrtsov and B. Lominadze, were demoted for privately criticizing the harm done by crash industrialization and collectivization. In 1932 M. Ryutin in Moscow went further and called for a change in priorities from industry to agriculture and consumer goods, demands which prefigured the concerns of the post-Stalin leadership. Stalin personally was severely criticized. Apparently S.M. Kirov, the head of the Leningrad party organization, led the group in the leadership who resisted Stalin's demands for Ryutin's death. They were unwilling to set the precedent of executing leading party figures, and Ryutin was merely exiled. The discontent reportedly culminated at the seventeenth party congress in January 1934, dubbed the 'congress of victors'. The abasement of defeated oppositionists like Bukharin, Zinoviev, and Kamenev can be interpreted as an attempt to remain in the party and resist Stalin from within. The desire for a relaxation now that the foundations of the socialist economy had been laid focused, apparently, on Kirov. He seemed to represent a reaffirmation of the leading role of the party as opposed to the dominance of the informal structures focusing on Stalin personally, compromises with the intelligentsia, and a relaxation of terror and exploitation in the countryside. According to Anastas Mikoyan 300 votes were cast against Stalin out of 1,225 voting delegates and only three against Kirov.[18]

Alarmed by Kirov's popularity and the tactics of the Old Bolsheviks, Stalin struck first in a brilliant double blow that eliminated the one and brought down the others. The assassination of Kirov in Leningrad on 1 December 1934 was blamed on a conspiracy by Trotsky and, in time, Zinoviev, Kamenev, and others. Khrushchev and Roy Medvedev, the unofficial historian, claim that Stalin was behind the murder, and much circumstantial evidence points in that direction.[19] The assassin, L. Nikolaev, had been released in suspicious circumstances by the NKVD (the new name for the OGPU) after earlier trying to approach Kirov with a pistol. On that very day Stalin launched a wave of terror with the implementation of legislation that had obviously been prepared beforehand. A system of closed hearings was introduced which routinely applied the death penalty. After a brief hiatus in 1935, from 1936 there was a steady escalation of the great terror which culminated in the *Ezhovshchina* (named after the head of the secret police, Ezhov, who replaced Yagoda in 1937). With the partial exception of the war there was barely a pause of the mincing machine up to Stalin's death in 1953.

The purges were remarkable for several reasons. In the first place, their scale was unprecedented. The precise figures have been the subject of vituperative exchanges between historians whose main result has been less to establish precise numbers than to force a thorough review of the available evidence. Steven Rosefielde argues that the average gulag forced labour population in 1929–53 was about 8.8 million, and that the total adult losses attributable to forced labour, collectivization, and the purges was over 20 million.[20] There was a shortfall in the Soviet population from various causes, including dekulakization, famine and a decline in the birth rate, from 1930 to 1937 of about 15 to 16 million. Medvedev estimates that up to 1937 Stalin's policies had claimed some 18 million victims, of whom 10 million died. The 'great terror' of 1937–8 itself saw some 5 to 7 million arrested, most of whom went to the gulag but about a million may have been shot. Some 10 to 12 million suffered deportation or arrest during and after the war.[21] It is estimated that there were some 12 million deaths between 1936 and 1950 attributable to persecution.[22] In Kolyma, where the gulag was particularly dense, there are so many burial grounds that geologists find drilling for minerals today a difficult task.

A further notable feature was the use of show trials. There were three main ones presided over by Andrei Vyshinsky. The first, in August 1936, starred Zinoviev and Kamenev and saw their names joined in death as in life. The second, in January-February 1937, featured Radek and Pyatakov, and the third, in March 1938, put an end to Bukharin, Rykov, and Yagoda. Vyshinsky, a former

Menshevik who in Moscow in 1917 had called for Lenin's arrest, considered the confession 'the queen of evidence'. He ended the prosecution cases with the words 'Shoot the mad dogs', which became the catch phrase of the purges. No more than seventy people were involved in the trials and they acted, as foreign observers put it, as latter-day witch hunts. They were literally 'shows' directed at the population and were apparently masterminded by Stalin personally. They were designed to illustrate the penalties of deviation from Stalinist orthodoxy and demonstrated that enemies could be found in the very highest circles. Their crude populism sought to drive home the lesson that unceasing vigilance was required and that justice could strike down even the great. A striking aspect of the terror, displayed during the show trials, was the forcing of 'confessions' from the victims. Moral debasement was added to physical destruction. The torture and confessions lent credence to another feature of the terror, the forging of great chains of conspiracy. The friends, relatives, and workmates of a victim were often caught up in the whirlwind.

An astonishing feature was the secrecy surrounding the whole process. A few show trials were publicized, but behind them the machine of terror claimed millions of victims. The scale of the purges was unknown within the USSR, let alone abroad. Most contemporaries believed the confessions and in the existence of the conspiracies. Gradually information did filter to the West through such publications as Trotsky's *Bulletin of the Opposition* but it had little impact. The publications of eye-witnesses went largely ignored. Western socialists argued that such 'rumours' were slanders against the Soviet system; right-wingers had been talking about the atrocities of the Soviet regime for so long that their warnings came as yet another cry of 'wolf'. Stalin's purges were particularly unsettling since they took place at a time of peace. The Bolshevik Red Terror of 1918 or the Jacobin terror of 1793 in France could at least be justified on the grounds of military emergency. Like the Jacobin terror, however, the operation of revolutionary justice focused on social and class factors rather than on any proof of having committed an offence. Such attitudes were not born under Stalin but had typified Lenin's dealings with recalcitrant social groups from the first days of Soviet power. However, the dekulakization campaign had so brutalized Soviet life that justifications could be found even for the scale of Stalin's purges.

Successive waves of 'fifty-eighters' (those convicted under Article 58 of the Criminal Code, covering political offences) filled the 'labour-extermination camps', as Solzhenitsyn terms them. The police powers that had previously been employed against people outside the party were now turned against Bolsheviks themselves. Some 60 per cent of the party activists of 1931 had been purged by 1937. The purges destroyed the majority of the 'Old Bolsheviks', those who had been Lenin's comrades. Of the 139 members of the Central Committee elected by the seventeenth congress in 1934, 110 (79 per cent) had been arrested before the next congress in 1939; and 1,108 (56 per cent) of its 1,966 delegates. Rank-and-file communists were not immune: members of previous oppositions were swept up together with thousands of ordinary party members. The leaders of the national republics were purged almost in their entirety, amid accusations of bourgeois nationalism and other crimes. The purges led to the wholesale destruction of the old managers who had led the first phase of Soviet industrialization. Exhausted, they were replaced by a vigorous younger generation trained in the school of Stalinism. Following the cultural revolution the old intelligentsia and technical specialists were rehabilitated and became a privileged group, but as individuals they suffered particularly badly. All the professions were hit, and in particular those who had had any contact with the outside world. Understandably, diplomats suffered a particularly high casualty rate. But one group of special significance were the military officers purged in 1937–8. On the eve of the war Stalin dealt the Soviet Union an almost mortal self-inflicted blow by striking down over three-quarters of the Soviet high command and the officer elite.[23] The victims included Marshal Tukhachevskii, one of the most talented officers. The sufferings of the mass of the population, Russians and non-Russians, should not be forgotten. The victims were random, often the object of anonymous denunciations as neighbours sought a few extra metres of living space. The chains of conspiracy and denunciation caught up relatives and friends in arbitrary patterns, with names often chosen to fulfil the local police quotas. The leadership of the NKVD itself was periodically purged: Yagoda in 1937 gave way to Ezhov, who himself fell victim in 1939, having been replaced in 1938 by Lavrenty Beria, who put an end to the first phase of the great terror.

The purges did not end with the onset of war and final victory: the only difference was that their scope now extended to the international stage. Already in the 1930s groups behind the lines in the Spanish civil war had been purged. The world war saw a certain degree of liberalization and was fought under nationalist rather than socialist slogans (see p. 276). The central political structures had their roles redefined, especially the secret police and the party, which witnessed a massive recruitment. However, victory was not accompanied by a relaxation of the terror, and the relative liberalism of the war years was reversed. The *Zhdanovshchina* (named after Andrei Zhdanov, the Leningrad party boss) of 1946–8 was an attempt to eradicate laxity in culture and the economy, and to reassert the 'party line' through discipline and central control. It was in these years that the poet Anna Akhmatova suffered internal exile, the writer Mikhail Zoshchenko was persecuted, and the outstanding Jewish actor Solomon Mikhoels murdered. This period was marked by conflicts at the top, especially between Beria and Malenkov, who together led a state faction against Zhdanov's party revivalism. The formulation and implementation of major policies were frequently the result of compromise between contending factions both inside and outside the Politburo.[24] Zhdanov's death in 1948 was followed by a purge of the Leningrad party organization. Campaigns of an antisemitic nature continued in the form of a struggle against 'cosmopolitanism'. Beria's own position came under threat in 1951, and it appears that he was due to become a victim of his own machine. At the nineteenth party congress in 1952 the Politburo and the Praesidium were united to form the Praesidium and enlarged and renewed to thirty-six members.

This seemed to imply that some of the old 'dead wood' could be cut away as soon as their replacements were ready. The so-called 'doctors' plot' in early 1953, in which a group of doctors with Jewish-sounding names were allegedly plotting to eliminate the entire Soviet leadership, presaged a new round of bloodletting. With the axe poised for yet more purges Stalin died on 5 March 1953, and only then was the terror machine stilled.

There are constant attempts to look for rationality in the purge process in general and in the great terror of 1936–8 in particular. The easiest explanations focus on Stalin's personality, his paranoid mentality, which sought to destroy all opposition to himself and the regime that he created. Out of a sense of inadequacy, it is argued, he destroyed all those who had known Lenin or could be judged his equal. Some have sought to enhance this psychological model by showing that there was a logic to the purge of Old Bolsheviks, with all those against whom he had a grudge dating back to 1917 and earlier falling victim. Moshe Lewin points out that the endless purges may have reflected Stalin's fear of becoming the prisoner of the bureaucratic machine that he had nurtured. There is no doubt that Stalin personally was the greatest beneficiary of the purges, with his opponents eliminated and his subordinates cowed. Without Stalin, it is argued, there would have been no purges.

To counter this, a second type of explanation focuses on the legacy of Leninism. From this perspective Stalinist terror was no more than the logical outcome of trends begun under Lenin. Political life since October 1917 had been marked by narrow sectarianism and intolerance of conflicting views. Even within the party the scope of debate had become limited to a narrow circle of leaders. The broad streams of Bolshevism, it could be argued, were narrowed to a harsh Leninism. Solzhenitsyn points out that the terror machine was created by Lenin and began its work under him. With collectivization the whole political elite became accustomed to routine violence. Both these types of explanation, the one which holds a single individual responsible and the other which blames the system, must be modified. Stalin's personality was important, but it could only operate in interaction with a system prone to violence.

A third set of explanations places the purges in a developmental perspective. The revolution from above was a way of concentrating all resources, human and material, on industrialisation. The destruction of the old managers and intelligentsia and their replacement by a new generation trained by Soviet power ensured a loyal managerial class. Modernization required an elite, but subordinate to the leadership and to Stalin personally. This is associated with a fourth type of explanation, which places the purges in the international context of the 1930s. All Bolsheviks were in favour of industrialization, but the frenetic pace of Stalinist development, focusing on defence heavy industry, was, it is argued, determined by the hostility of Western capitalist powers and later by the threat posed by Nazi Germany. Both these types of explanation take an unduly short-sighted view, since they leave out of the analysis, firstly, the harm inflicted on Soviet development by the extraordinarily wasteful pattern of Stalinist industrialization and, secondly, the distortions imposed on Soviet foreign policy by Stalin's vengeful, manipulative, and secretive diplomacy. Foreign-policy factors clearly played a role and could be used to justify clearing the country of all possible sources of opposition in case of war. This does not explain the destruction of the best officers, which lowered Hitler's estimation of Soviet military power and may well have hastened the war. It certainly contributed to Nazi military successes in 1941.

A fifth view sets the purges of the 1930s in the context of domestic politics and challenges some of the conventional wisdom. J. Arch Getty argues that the purges were more than a result of Stalin's megalomania, and that the centre had remarkably little say in their conduct at the local level. He insists that even in the mid-1930s there were factional conflicts among the leadership, particularly between Molotov and Ordzhonikidze. Given our knowledge of Soviet politics in other periods, this is a reasonable supposition. Getty restores the original sense of the concept of the purge by firmly locating them in the context of a cleansing of the party of undesirable elements, and sees the 1935 verification of party documents as an opportunity for officials to settle personal scores at the local level. He takes issue with the view of the party as a totalitarian monolith and stresses the liveliness of politics and debates over industrialization. Above all, he focuses on conflicts between the centre and the localities, Moscow and the regional party organizations. Stalin is exonerated from personally initiating the purges, and the link with Kirov's assassination is dismissed. The fundamental logic of the purges is seen to be less of a central bureaucratic process swallowing up the old revolutionaries than a grass-roots reaction against party bureaucracy. The consolidation of Stalin's personal rule is seen as part of the process of establishing order amidst chaos.

Getty's interpretation derives from a misreading of the course of the Bolshevik revolution from 1917. While he is undoubtedly correct in stressing the chaotic elements in Soviet administration in the early years, his characterization of party organization as inept, corrupt, badly organized, and with poor communications between the centre and the locality is exaggerated. At its worst and in many rural districts this was the case, but a feature of Soviet rule has been the coexistence of pockets of strong organization with poor integration between them. To characterize city party organizations as he does is absurd, and yet the purges were no less violent in Moscow than in the Smolensk region, his major source of information. Getty's interpretation adds much to our understanding of the dynamics of the purges but not to the processes that gave rise to them.

'Stalinism'

The ambiguities in Lenin's legacy, the tensions within the NEP and the isolation of the revolution allowed Stalin to consolidate his power. A decisive 'man of action' capable of mobilizing the revolutionary elite and drawing on the unfil-filled aspirations of the revolution was able to launch a new revolution which transformed the face of the country. However, while the term 'Stalinism' is useful for describing a particular phase of Soviet history, it is misleading if the features of that period are assigned to the doings of one man. The problem of defining Stalinism, and hence combating the legacy of the man, still haunts the Soviet system. There is much that we do not know about the period, including the precise role played by Stalin personally in policy-making, the operation of the political and economic systems at the local and national levels, the economic and political dynamics of the purges, and the social basis of the regime. Any evaluation of Stalinism depends on when it began. Khrushchev dates its beginning to 1934, after the horrors of collectivization and with industrialization in full swing. His view accepts the sacrifices of those years as emanating from party policy. Only after 1934 was Stalin able to attack the party itself and hence Bolshevism was transformed into 'Stalinism'. Others trace the origins back further, to 1929, to 1921, and even to the very act of revolution in 1917.

Was Stalinism the inevitable outcome of Soviet development as charted by Lenin and of Bolshevik ideological and organizational traditions and distinct from what preceded and succeeded it? Stalin himself never claimed that his regime differed from that of Lenin. Indeed, the basis of the legitimacy of his rule was that it was a continuation of Lenin's policies. Solzhenitsyn argues that:

> We may justifiably wonder whether 'Stalinism' is in fact a distinctive phenomenon . . . Stalin himself never tried to establish any distinctive doctrine (and given his intellectual limitations he could never have created one), nor any distinctive political system of his own . . . he was a faithful Leninist and never in any matter of consequence diverged from Lenin.[25]

Solzhenitsyn argues that the Stalinist horror, with its camps, the use of the death penalty against ideological opponents, be they of the left or right, the willingness to use coercion against sections of society, and the arbitrariness of the secret police, the ban on factions within the party (albeit as a 'temporary' measure), the accumulating power of the leadership, all began under Lenin. The only major departure, according to Solzhenitsyn, was Stalin's treatment of the party.

Trotsky tried to salvage Lenin's reputation by talking of the party as the repository of a higher democracy, and implying that society was to be held responsible for what the party brought upon it. He cultivated the myth of a 'democratic party in an undemocratic society'.[26] Trotsky's description of Stalinism as 'Marxism reflected in a samovar' emphasized the continuity with Russian political culture. Trotsky radically rejected the idea that there was any essential link between the October revolution and the emergence of Stalinism, which he saw as the outcome of social rather than political forces and stimulated by such factors as the experience of the civil war, the smallness of the working class, Russia's low level of culture, the capitalist elements released by the NEP, and the emergence of the bureaucracy. For Trotsky's biographer, Isaac Deutscher, Stalin fulfilled elements of Russia's historical destiny. The socialist revolution came about in an isolated, backward country and so forced the bureaucracy to industrialize and carry out defensive preparations. The inevitable, but fundamentally necessary, cost was the wholesale destruction of civil liberties and socialist democracy. A geopolitical and cultural determinism permeates the Trotskyist view.

Roy Medvedev argues that Stalin was only one possible route of Soviet development. Stalinism emerged because of a series of unfortunate circumstances, among which Lenin's death in 1924 was crucial.[27] R.C. Tucker supports the view that there was no causal connection between Lenin and Stalin. Stalin's own particular personality was a crucial factor. Tucker insists that the NEP course laid out by Lenin, with all its defects, was a far cry from the totalitarianism of Stalin.[28] Stephen F. Cohen's argument that Stalinism differs from Leninism because of the difference of scale, the sheer excess of Stalin, is true but does not reveal the source of excess.[29]

What are the distinguishing features of Stalin's rule? War communism was full of ideological and institutional tensions and left a disputed legacy to the next period. Those tensions increased steadily during the NEP as the debate over industrialization became bound up with the contest for the succession. Bolshevik ideology did not offer a blueprint for the government to follow, and the rise of Stalin to supremacy from 1928 brought about a significant change to the Soviet polity. It was the metamorphosis of the original Bolshevik movement into a leader-dominated 'mass-movement regime' (Tucker). It was not accompanied by any change in the regime's self-definition but it marked a shift in its ideological emphasis and institutional arrangements.

Under Stalin the teleological elements of Bolshevism were taken to the limit. The utopian belief in the rapid move to socialism ensured the dominance of the end justifying the means. In a young power the ideology was marked by a revolutionary idealism which craved the immediate creation of a secular version of the New Jerusalem. Under mature Stalinism this chiliasm was accompanied by a powerful vulgarization of the ideology and its reduction to a number of basic propositions, and the stifling of intellectual debate. This did not exclude some policy disagreements among the leadership, especially in the period following the Second World War, but for the mass of the population adherence to the single ideology and acceptance of cultural conformity were a condition of survival. The primary allegiance, however, was to the party line as interpreted by Stalin, however much it might change. Stalin intensified Lenin's habit of reducing the ideas of his antagonists to pronouncements of the class enemy. There could be only one truth, and that was the current line being put out by Stalin and the party. The Stalinist system was permeated by a hyper-rationalism which Karl Mannheim described as the ability to justify the consequences of actions taken on pragmatic grounds, however unprincipled they might be. Any action, however deplorable, could be rationalized in terms of service to the revolution. Society itself lived in a horrendous informational vacuum of the true state of affairs both within the country and beyond its borders. The lack of feedback in the political system reached such a pitch that Stalin himself apparently even began to believe his propaganda films of a well nourished and contented peasantry!

Stalinism rested on a realignment of the major institutions making up Soviet power. Lenin's legacy of a polity governed more by convention and his personal charisma than by rules was intensified. The party suffered a dramatic decline in relation to the other main institutions. The party survived as a mass movement and as a power machine, but as a functioning political organism it was gutted. No party congress was convened between 1939 and 1952, party conferences were discontinued after the eighteenth, in 1941, and the Central Committee did not meet once during the critical years of the war. From 1941 Stalin headed both the party and governmental hierarchies, and played one off against the other with the help of the secret police. His power derived less from any formal office than from his undisputed personal dominance. He ruled both through the party and over it as the party's decision-making functions were usurped by a small coterie of leaders. Even at the nadir of its fortunes, however, the party remained the principal symbol of legitimacy.

If the party was the greatest loser under Stalin, the secret police were one of the greatest beneficiaries. A powerful security police had already emerged under Lenin and now the terror consolidated its dominance over society. The theory justifying the purges was one of Stalin's few original contributions to Bolshevik ideology, namely the belief that the class struggle intensifies as society approaches socialism. The security police, however, were not allowed to achieve an independent institutional legitimacy and were always at Stalin's own command. Stalin was obviously irked by Beria's power, and it appears that the doctors' plot was directed partially at him. Rumours that Beria struck first and murdered Stalin add an element of poetic justice to the dictator's death.

There was an enormous expansion of state power and the bureaucracy, but the government itself was 'shapeless' (S. Bialer). The system was rigidly hierarchical and worked 'bureaucratically', in the sense that it was plagued by paper-pushing, buck-passing, and procrastination, but it can hardly be described as bureaucratic in the Weberian sense. It did not operate according to a binding set of rules with steady aims and targets, and, as noted, the purges prevented the system settling down into bureaucratic routine. Stalin's rise after 1922 was as the archetypal 'organization man', yet he loathed organizations that could not be bent to his service. His fears in this respect were perfectly rational in that he achieved his aim of subordinating the party-state bureaucracy that had brought him to power.

The trends of war communism concerning mass organizations were intensified. The soviets, the major instruments of popular participation, underwent a long period of stagnation. All remaining non-Bolshevik intermediary organizations in society were eliminated and in their place 'transmission belt' mass organizations mobilized the population to build the new society. For Rigby the USSR under Stalin emerged as a tyranny exercising its power over a mono-organizational society in which everything was directed from above through an organic system of control.[30] As we shall see, according to totalitarian theory society was atomized as the state expanded to become the universal employer.

The institutional framework of Stalinism was integrated by a *dirigisme* that took the leadership principle espoused by Lenin to the absolute limit. Soviet *dirigisme* was personified by Stalin himself, who was venerated as the *vozhd*, the leader or *Führer*. Stalin's charisma was like Lenin's in that it operated in a modern scientific context, i.e. the ability to understand and apply the laws of history to specific circumstances, but differed in that it was consciously cultivated in a manner which Trotsky called 'Asiatic'.[31] Stalin's charisma derived from the movement that he led, and it was the creative tension between the movement and the leader that raised both to unprecedented heights. Districts and factories were run by powerful bosses whose powers often appeared unlimited until they themselves perished in the purges. Fainsod's work on Smolensk in the 1930s has shown that arrests and deportations could be ordered at a fairly low level by these 'little Stalins'. The cult of Stalin found favour with the 'new' members of the urban working class and the rapidly advanced working-class intelligentsia who were emerging to make up the new Soviet middle class. The mass mourning at his death illustrates a high degree of veneration, and there remains a solid bedrock of support for Stalin even after the denunciation of his excesses. His extraordinary powers arose from his ability to manipulate the relationship between the emerging elite and popular forces, together with his dominance of the security police and the party.

Following Stalin's death the political system was given some stability in the abandonment of further revolutions from above, but this had already been prefigured by an increasingly conservative social ethos. The institutions that Stalin moulded in the 1930s became synonymous with the concept of communism itself. The achievements in industrialization and war laid the foundations of the Soviet Union as a 'superpower'. In the context of socialism in one country Stalinism was primarily a war machine, with the emphasis on heavy industry, a way of industrializing the country to sustain its military potential. Bukharin's view that the same ends could have been achieved at less cost has been much debated, but there is no doubt that the view of Stalin as a traditional nationalist, a ruthless modernizer in the tradition of Peter the Great, assumes a simplified notion of what modernization entails. The Stalinist legacy was a distorted modernization in which some features were highly developed whereas others, like responsiveness in the political sphere and criteria for rational decision-making, were grossly underdeveloped. Stalinism can be defined as anti-social socialism. The cost of the 'externalities' of the Stalinist command economy, the rural holocaust, the terror, the stifling of initiative, the excess losses during the war, the loss of labour power, low labour productivity, poor quality of consumer goods, and the slow uptake of new technology in production must all be weighed in the balance. The Soviet polity and economy were endowed with a legacy of inflexibility, in particular in agriculture and industrial management, that have come to haunt the present generation of leaders. Stalinism can be seen as a distinctive mutation of the Soviet system, neither inevitable nor immutable, but not necessarily avoidable either.

Notes

1 M. Lewin, *Lenin's Last Struggle* (Pluto, London, 1975), pp. 79–81.
2 For a discussion of this see C. Lefort, *The Political Forms of Modern Society: Bureaucracy, Democracy, Totalitarianism* (MIT Press, Cambridge, Mass., 1986), p. 40.
3 L. Trotsky, *The Revolution Betrayed* (New Park, London, 1973).
4 N. Mandelshtam, *Hope against Hope* (Penguin, Harmondsworth, 1970), p. 167.
5 R. Redfield, *Peasant Society and Culture* (Chicago, 1956), pp. 17–20, 40–5.
6 Bukharin's views in 'Notes of an Economist' (*Pravda*, 30 September 1928) are discussed by M. Lewin, *Political Undercurrents in Soviet Economic Debates* (Pluto, London, 1975), pp. 49–72.
7 G. Grossman, 'Notes for a Theory of the Planned Economy', *Soviet Studies*, 15 (1963), pp. 101–23.
8 Moshe Lewin, 'Society and the Stalinist State in the Period of the Five-year Plans', *Social History* (May 1976), p. 148.
9 L. Viola, '*Bab'i Bunty* and Peasant Women's Protest during Collectivization', *Russian Review*, 45, 4 (1986), pp. 23–42, and see bibliography.
10 Official statistics, cited by R. Medvedev, 'New Pages from the Political Biography of Stalin', in R.C. Tucker (ed.), *Stalinism: Essays in Historical Interpretation* (Norton, New York, 1977), p. 211; unofficial figures from Vladimir Tikhenov, *Literaturnaya gazeta*, 31, 3 August 1988.
11 See R. Conquest, *The Harvest of Sorrow* (Hutchinson, London, 1986).
12 D. Joravsky, 'The Construction of the Stalinist Psyche', in S. Fitzpatrick (ed.), *Cultural Revolution in Russia, 1928–1931* (Indiana University Press, Bloomington, 1978), pp. 105–28.
13 J.H. Hough, 'The Cultural Revolution and Western Understanding of the Soviet System', in Fitzpatrick (ed.), *Cultural Revolution*, pp. 241–53.
14 S. Cohen, *Bukharin and the Bolshevik Revolution* (Vintage Books, New York, 1975), chapter IX.
15 See S.G. Wheatcroft, R.W. Davis, and J.M. Cooper, 'Soviet Industrialization Reconsidered: some Preliminary Conclusions about Economic Development between 1926 and 1941', *Economic History Review*, 2nd series, XXXIX, 2 (1986), pp. 264–94.
16 R. and Z. Medvedev, *Khrushchev: the Years in Power* (Columbia University Press, New York, 1976), p. 28.
17 M. Lewin, 'Society and the Stalinist State', p. 15; 'Society, State and Ideology during the First Five-year Plan', in *The Making of the Soviet System* (Pantheon Books, New York, 1985), pp. 218–31.
18 *Ogonek*, 50 (December 1987), p. 6.
19 For the contrary view of the Kirov murder see J.A. Getty, *Origins of the Great Purges* (Cambridge University Press, Cambridge, 1985), pp. 207–10.
20 The major articles by S. Rosefielde are 'An Assessment of the Sources and Uses of Gulag Forced Labour, 1929–1956', *Soviet Studies*, 33, 1 (January 1981); 'Excess Mortality in the Soviet Union: a Reconsideration of the Demographic Consequences of Forced Industrialisation, 1929–1949', *Soviet Studies*, 35, 2 (July 1983); 'Incriminating Evidence: Excess Deaths and Forced Labour under Stalin: a Final Reply to my Critics', *Soviet Studies*, 39, 2 (April 1987), pp. 292–313.
21 S. Wheatcroft, 'On Assessing the Size of Forced Concentration Camp Labour in the Soviet Union, 1929–56', *Soviet Studies*, 33, 2 (April 1981), pp. 265–95; 'A Note on Steven Rosefielde's Calculations of Excess Mortality in the USSR, 1929–49', *Soviet Studies*, 34, 2 (April 1984), pp. 277–81.
22 Figures from I.G. Dyadkin, *Unnatural Deaths in the USSR, 1928–54* (Transaction Books, New Brunswick, N.J., 1983), p. 60; Conquest, *Harvest of Sorrow*, p. 229;

R. Conquest, *The Great Terror* (Pelican, Harmondsworth, 1971), pp. 699–713.
23 On numbers of party victims see A.L. Unger, 'Stalin's Renewal of the Leading Stratum', *Soviet Studies*, 20, 3 (July 1969), p. 321; on military victims see *Kommunist*, 13 (June 1987).
24 T. Dunmore, *Soviet Politics, 1945–53* (Macmillan, London, 1984), p. 2.
25 A. Solzhenitsyn, *From under the Rubble* (Fontana, London, 1976), pp. 10–11.
26 M. Hirszowicz, *The Bureaucratic Leviathan* (Martin Robertson, Oxford, 1980), p. 57.
27 R. Medvedev, *Let History Judge* (Spokesman Books, Nottingham, 1976), p. 360.
28 R.C. Tucker, *Stalin as a Revolutionary: Essays in Historical Interpretation* (Norton, New York, 1977), pp. 77–108.
29 S.F. Cohen, 'Bolshevism and Stalinism', in *Rethinking the Soviet Experience* (Oxford University Press, New York and Oxford, 1985), p. 48.
30 T.H. Rigby, 'Stalinism and the Mono-organisational Society', in Tucker (ed.), *Stalinism*, pp. 53–76.
31 A. Janos (ed.) *Authoritarian Politics in Communist Europe* (University of California Press, Berkeley, 1976), p. 9.

Key texts

Carrère d'Encausse, H., *Stalin: Order through Terror* (Longman, London, 1981)
Deutscher, I., *Stalin: a Political Biography* (Penguin, Harmondsworth, 1966)
Dunmore, Tim, *Soviet Politics, 1945–1953* (Macmillan, London, 1984)
Medvedev, Roy, *Let History Judge: the Origin and Consequences of Stalinism* (Spokesman, Nottingham, 1976)
Nove, Alec, *Economic Rationality and Soviet Politics, or Was Stalin Really Necessary?* (Allen & Unwin, London, 1964)
Tucker, R.C., *Stalinism: Essays in Historical Interpretation* (Norton, New York, 1977)
Von Laue, T.H., *Why Lenin? Why Stalin?* 2nd edn (Lippincott, Philadelphia, Pa., 1971)

Select bibliography

Ali, Tariq (ed.), *The Stalinist Legacy* (Penguin, Harmondsworth, 1984)
Alliluyeva, Svetlana, *Twenty Letters to a Friend* (Hutchinson, London, 1967)
Antonov-Ovseyenko, Anton, *The Time of Stalin: a Portrait of Tyranny* (Harper & Row, New York, 1981)
Bialer, S., *Stalin and his Generals* (London, 1970)
Brzezinski, Z. *The Permanent Purge* (Harvard University Press, Cambridge, Mass., 1956)
Campeanu, Pavel, *The Origins of Stalinism: from Leninist Revolution to Stalinist Society* (Sharpe, London, 1986)
Carr, E.H., *The Interregnum, 1923–1924* (Macmillan, London, 1954)
Carr, E.H., *Socialism in one Country, 1924–1926*, 3 vols (Macmillan, London, 1958, 1959)
Carr, E.H. (vol. 1 with R.W. Davies), *Foundations of a Planned Economy, 1926–1929*, 3 vols (Macmillan, London, 1969)
Clark, A., *Barbarossa — the Russo-German Conflict, 1941–45* (Hutchinson, London, 1965)
Cohen, Stephen, *Bukharin and the Bolshevik Revolution: a Political Biography 1888–1938* (Vintage, New York, 1975)
Conquest, Robert, *The Great Terror: Stalin's Purge of the Thirties* (Pelican, Harmondsworth, 1971)
Conquest, Robert, *Inside Stalin's Secret Police: NKVD Politics, 1936–39* (Macmillan, London, 1985)
Conquest, Robert, *The Harvest of Sorrow: Soviet Collectivisation and the Terror Famine* (Hutchinson, London, 1986)

Dallin, Alexander, and George W. Breslauer, *Political Terror in Communist Systems* (Stanford University Press, Stanford, Cal., 1970)

Daniels, R.V. (ed.), *The Stalin Revolution: Foundations of Soviet Totalitarianism*, 2nd edn (Heath, Lexington, Mass., 1972)

Danilov, Viktor, *Rural Russia under the New Regime* (Hutchinson, London, 1988)

Davies, R.W., *The Socialist Offensive: the Collectivisation of Soviet Agriculture, 1929–1930* (Macmillan, London, 1980)

Davies, R.W., *The Soviet Collective Farm, 1929–1930* (Macmillan, London, 1980)

Day, Richard, *Leon Trotsky and the Politics of Economic Isolation* (Cambridge University Press, Cambridge, 1973)

Deutscher, Isaac, *The Prophet Armed: Trotsky, 1879–1921* (Oxford University Press, London and New York, 1954)

Deutscher, Isaac, *The Prophet Unarmed: Trotsky, 1921–1929* (Oxford University Press, London and New York, 1959)

Deutscher, Isaac, *The Prophet Outcast: Trotsky, 1929–1940* (Oxford University Press, London and New York, 1963)

Deutscher, Isaac (ed.), *The Age of Permanent Revolution: a Trotsky Anthology* (Dell, New York, 1964)

Deutscher, Isaac, and David King, *The Great Purges* (Blackwell, Oxford, 1984)

Djilas, Milovan, *Conversations with Stalin* (Harmondsworth, Pelican, 1962)

Djilas, Milovan, *The New Class* (Praeger, New York, 1957)

Dunham, Vera, *In Stalin's Time* (Harvard University Press, Cambridge, Mass., 1979)

Dunmore, Tim, *The Stalinist Command Economy: the Soviet State Apparatus and Economic Policy, 1945–53* (Macmillan, London, 1980)

Ellenstein, J., *The Stalin Phenomenon* (Lawrence & Wishart, London, 1976)

Erlich, A., *The Soviet Industrialisation Debates, 1924–1928* (Harvard University Press, Cambridge, Mass., 1975)

Fainsod, Merle, *Smolensk under Soviet Rule* (Harvard University Press, Cambridge, Mass., 1958)

Filtzer, Donald, *Soviet Workers and Stalinist Industrialization* (Pluto, London, 1986)

Fitzpatrick, Sheila, (ed.), *Cultural Revolution in Russia, 1928–1931* (Indiana University Press, Bloomington and London, 1978)

Getty, J. Arch, *Origins of the Great Purges: the Soviet Communist Party Reconsidered, 1933–1938* (Cambridge University Press, Cambridge, 1985)

Ginzburg, Eugenia, *Into the Whirlwind* (Penguin, Harmondsworth, 1968)

Gouldner, Alvin W., 'Stalinism: a Study of Internal Colonialism', *Telos* 34 (winter 1977/78), pp. 5–48

Grey, Ian, *Stalin: Man of History* (Weidenfeld & Nicolson, London, 1979)

Grossman, Vasily, *Forever Flowing* (Collins Harvill, London, 1988)

Hahn, Werner G., *Postwar Soviet Politics: the Fall of Zhdanov and the Defeat of Moderation, 1946–53* (Cornell University Press, Ithaca, N.Y., and London, 1982)

Harrison, Mark, *Soviet Planning in Peace and War, 1938–1945* (Cambridge University Press, Cambridge, 1985)

Haynes, M., *Nikolai Bukharin and the Transition from Capitalism to Socialism* (Croom Helm, London, 1985)

Hingley, R., *Joseph Stalin: Man and Legend* (Hutchinson, London, 1974)

Jasny, N., *Soviet Industrialization, 1928–1952* (Chicago University Press, 1961)

Krasso, N. (ed.), *Trotsky: the Great Debate Renewed* (New Critics Press, St Louis, Mo, 1972)

Lewin, Moshe, *Russian Peasants and Soviet Power* (Northwestern University Press, Evanston, Ill., 1968)

Lewin, Moshe, *Lenin's Last Struggle* (Pluto, London, 1975)

Lewin, Moshe, *Political Undercurrents in Soviet Economic Debates: from Bukharin to *the Modern Reformers* (Pluto, London, 1975)

Lewin, Moshe, *The Making of the Soviet System: Essays in the Social History of Inter-war Russia* (Methuen, London, 1985)

McCagg, W.O., *Stalin Embattled, 1943–48* (Wayne State University Press, Detroit, 1978)

McCauley, Martin, *Stalin and Stalinism* (Longman, London, 1984)

McNeal, Robert, *Stalin: Man and Ruler* (Macmillan, London, 1988)

Mandelshtam, N., *Hope against Hope: a Memoir* and *Hope Abandoned* (Penguin, Harmondsworth, 1970)

Medvedev, Roy, *On Stalin and Stalinism* (Oxford University Press, Oxford, 1979)

Medvedev, Roy, *All Stalin's Men* (Blackwell, Oxford, 1983)

Narkiewicz, Olga, *The Making of the Soviet State Apparatus* (Manchester University Press, Manchester, 1970)

Nicolaevsky, Boris, *Power and the Soviet Elite* (Praeger, New York, 1965)

Nove, Alec, *Stalinism and After: the Road to Gorbachev*, 3rd edn (Unwin Hyman, London, 1988)

Pethybridge, Roger, *The Social Prelude to Stalinism* (Macmillan, London, 1974)

Reiman, M., *The Birth of Stalinism* (Tauris, London, 1987)

Rigby, T.H. (ed.), *Stalin* (Prentice-Hall, Englewood Cliffs, N.J., 1966)

Rosenfeldt, N.E., *Knowledge and Power: the Role of Stalin's Secret Chancellery in the Soviet System of Government* (Rosenkilde & Bagger, Copenhagen, 1978)

Salisbury, H.E., *The 900 Days: The Siege of Leningrad* (Macmillan, London, 1969)

Scott, John, *Behind the Urals: an American Worker in Russia's City of Steel* (Secker and Warburg, London, 1942)

Serge, V., *Memoirs of a Revolutionary*, trans. Peter Sedgwick (Writers and Readers, London, 1984)

Solzhenitsyn, Alexander, *The Gulag Archipelago: an Experiment in Literary Investigation*, 3 vols (Collins-Fontana, Glasgow, 1974–6)

Souvarine, Boris, *Stalin: a Critical Survey of Bolshevism* (Secker & Warburg, London, n.d.)

Trotsky, L., *Stalin* (Hollis & Carter, London, 1947)

Trotsky, L., *The Revolution Betrayed* (New Park, London, 1973)

Tucker, R.C., *The Soviet Political Mind: Stalinism and post-Stalin Change*, rev. edn (Allen & Unwin, London, 1972)

Tucker, R.C., *Stalin as a Revolutionary, 1879–1929* (Chatto & Windus, London, 1974)

Ulam, Adam B., *Stalin: the Man and his Era* (Allen Lane, London, 1974)

Urban, G.R. (ed.), *Stalinism: its Impact on Russia and the World* (Wildwood, Aldershot, 1985)

Viola, Lynne, *The Best Sons of the Fatherland: Workers in the Vanguard of Soviet Collectivisation* (Oxford University Press, New York, 1987)

Voznesensky, N., *The Economy of the Soviet Union during World War II* (Moscow, 1948).

Werth, A., *Russia at War, 1941–45* (Barrie & Rockcliff, London, 1964)

Chapter four

Khrushchev and destalinization

The Stalinist system placed enormous strains on the social and political cohesion of Soviet society. As Gorbachev put it, in Stalin's later years there arose 'a contradiction between what our society had become and the old method of leadership'.[1] Everything had to be decided at the top, and the Stalinist state became heavily overloaded through its extirpation of initiative from below. The challenge facing Stalin's successors was to find new ways of achieving the integration of the system once terror and personal dictatorship had ended.

The new course

Lenin's decline and death in the early 1920s were accompanied by vigorous policy debates, and similarly Stalin's death in March 1953 allowed suppressed policy divisions to emerge. A number of outstanding issues urgently required attention. The Korean War was dragging on into its fourth year and the Cold War confrontation with the West was at its height. The economy had been restored to pre-war levels but agriculture continued to drag out a miserable existence and there were few consumer goods in the shops. The immediate issue was the succession itself. Beria held the most effective card through his dominance of the vast security apparatus, and in the weeks following Stalin's death it was clear that he was prepared to make use of it. But his very identification with the axe ensured his downfall. His colleagues on the Politburo, united on little else, conspired to secure his arrest in June 1953 and his execution by the end of the year. The military, led by Marshals Zhukov and Konev, played a key part in Beria's demise and helped bring the KGB under party control (see p. 118).

At Stalin's death G.M. Malenkov was simultaneously both First (now General) Secretary of the party and Chair of the Council of Ministers. In other words, he held both posts at the summit of the Soviet political system. His colleagues, worried about this undue concentration of power, and with recent memories of dictatorship, insisted that he choose between them in order to install a system of collective leadership. Malenkov's decision to divest himself of the party leadership illustrates the low status of the party at the time. Nikita S. Khrushchev became party leader, and from that position was able to consolidate his own power while restoring the party to the centre of the policy-making process. The struggle between Khrushchev and Malenkov was also a conflict between two competing bureaucracies, the party and state. As in the 1920s the post of Party Secretary was the crucial one in the succession struggle because of its powers of appointment. Khrushchev nominated his supporters to key positions, especially in the republic and regional (*oblast*) levels of the party, who in turn elected delegates who voted for the top party bodies. As during Stalin's rise in the 1920s, they became beholden to the leader for their jobs and security in the process termed the circular flow of power.

The contest between Malenkov and Khrushchev was fought in terms of policy issues. The debates of Stalin's last years were no longer waged as murderous faction fights with the losers being dubbed counter-revolutionaries. With Stalin dead it would have been absurd to insist on a single line of absolute correctness. Differing ideas over such issues as industrial policy, agriculture, culture, and foreign policy now openly competed. In the cultural world a 'thaw' began to push back the icy wastes of Stalinist orthodoxy. However, the debates were conducted within the terms of the system established by Stalin. At issue was the 'fine tuning' of his mechanism, not its abolition, and hence this period differs significantly from the great debates of the 1920s when the very future of the country and society was at stake. 1953 did not represent quite such a radical break in Soviet history as Khrushchev liked to believe.[2]

The first years of the post-Stalin era witnessed remarkably open discussion of policy. Malenkov proposed what was called a New Course and called for the redirection of investment from heavy to light industry to provide the long-suffering Soviet population with consumer goods. Khrushchev called for greater investment in agriculture, and in particular proposed to plough the 'virgin lands' of Kazakhstan and south Siberia for grain. The plan would once again divert scarce resources into heavy industry to produce the necessary agricultural equipment. The debate over the sowing of an area of 30 million hectares of virgin and idle land, an area greater than that covered by Austria and Switzerland combined, acts as a famous case study of policy formation in the early post-Stalin years. The debate was launched by Khrushchev in September 1953, when he argued that there was a grain shortfall, while Malenkov insisted that the situation was not critical. The programme encountered the resistance of the Kazakhstan party organization, fearing an influx of Russians. In February 1954 the Kazakhstan first and second party secretaries, Z. Shayakhmetov and I.I. Afonov, were dismissed by the Khrushchev-dominated four-person Secretariat of the Communist Party of the Soviet Union (CPSU) and replaced by Russians, P.K. Ponomarenko and L.I. Brezhnev respectively. Brezhnev later became party leader of the republic. The programme was then adopted by the Central Committee in March 1954. The case illustrates the stages that a major policy has to go through, from initiation to adoption and implementation. The prominent role of the agriculturalists signalled the increased scope for specialist input in policy-making in the post-Stalin era. Khrushchev had been obliged to work hard to obtain approval for his policy, and the resolution of the issue in his favour revealed the power of the party secretariat.

In foreign policy Malenkov recommended lower spending on defence and a policy of peaceful coexistence. In a Stalinist manner he insisted that the changes taking place in the Soviet Union should be adopted across-the-board in Eastern Europe. Defeat over the Virgin Lands Scheme, however, sealed Malenkov's fate, and in February 1955 he was replaced as Prime Minister by N.A. Bulganin. No executions followed, and a non-bloody precedent had been set for leadership change. In keeping with tradition, however, the whole affair was kept secret. Malenkov's demotion did not remove all opposition to Khrushchev, and in the Politburo he was confronted by a phalanx of dedicated Stalinists: V.M. Molotov, L.M. Kaganovich, M.Z. Saburov, and K.E. Voroshilov.

Destalinization

Malenkov's reappraisal of Stalinist policies focused on economic issues, whereas with the passage of time Khrushchev's criticisms became more and more political. There were approximately 8 million people in the labour camps, about 15 per cent of the entire adult male population. This represented a severe drain on the economy, compensated in part by the retention of German prisoners-of-war until 1955. After Stalin's death a trickle of prisoners were released, including some relatives of leaders, such as Molotov's wife. A Central Committee commission established in 1954 under P.N. Pospelov was horrified by what it discovered during its investigation into Stalin's persecution of leading party figures. The fundamental problem was what was to be done about the crimes and how to analyse the political system that had given rise to them. How much could be revealed without undermining the stabilility of the state? If too much was made known there was a risk of an outburst of mass anger against the system which had permitted the crimes and in which all the current leaders were deeply implicated.

One option was to maintain a stolid silence, the tactic later pursued by Brezhnev for so many years. The twentieth party congress, the first since Stalin's death, meeting from 14 to 25 February 1956, at first took this course. The official party report delivered by Khrushchev concentrated on foreign and economic policy and said nothing about the purges. A new Central Committee was chosen which contained only seventy nine (63 per cent) of the 125 elected at Stalin's last party congress in 1952. Khrushchev was re-elected First Secretary, and his position was consolidated by the election of fifty four (41 per cent) new members onto the enlarged 133-person committee. With the business of the congress over, the delegates were preparing to leave when in the late evening of 24 February they were called back to attend a closed session where they were informed that Khrushchev would deliver a speech. At the time Khrushchev was 62 years old, a colourful personality all the more unique when set against the drab *apparatchiki* of the Stalin years. He had been an enthusiastic young communist in the 1920s, the head of the Moscow party organization in the 1930s and leader of the Ukrainian party in the 1940s. For over two decades he had been one of Stalin's closest colleagues and in the inner circle from 1949, so he had a unique vantage point from which to observe the inner workings of the regime.

Khrushchev addressed the gathering for four hours, until late into the night. The delegates listened in amazement to his extraordinary revelations about Stalin's crimes. There were occasional shouts of anger or ripples of laughter when he employed a particularly vivid turn of phrase. Khrushchev accused Stalin of having breached the 'Leninist' principle of collective leadership and of covering his rise by suppressing Lenin's Testament. He had developed a 'personality cult', with its attendant 'loathsome adulation', and had falsified history by claiming that he had been Lenin's main helper. Khrushchev's main indictment was that he had 'victimized' innnocent people. His condemnation on this score was mainly restricted to Stalin's attack on the party after 1934, accusing him in effect of the murder of Kirov and the majority of delegates to the seventeenth party congress. A large part of the speech was devoted to the rehabilitation of party and military people. He denounced the continuation of the purges after the war, in particular in Leningrad, and the preparations for a new purge in 1953 (the 'doctors' plot'). Moreover, Khrushchev condemned the theory behind the purges, the Stalinist principle 'that the closer we are to socialism, the more enemies we will have'. This was absurd, he argued, especially after 1934, when 'the exploiting classes were already liquidated and socialist relations were rooted in all phases of the economy, when our party was politically consolidated'. Closely linked to this was the further charge that Stalin had allowed the party to decline as a functioning institution. This was a matter particularly close to Khrushchev's heart, and not only because he used it as a vehicle in the factional in-fighting of the 1950s. Khrushchev's whole life had been sincerely devoted to the party and its ideology, and this perhaps more than anything else marked him out from those whose lip service to the party covered a primary allegiance to Stalin himself.

Stalin was accused of the misconduct of the war, especially the woeful misreading of Hitler's intentions and ignoring warnings. The lack of preparations had been compounded by the slaughter of military leaders between 1937 and 1939. Khrushchev's emotion here revealed itself in the intensely personal way he tried to destroy Stalin's reputation as a war leader. Stalin's psychological collapse in the first days of the war had been followed by the grossly wasteful use of men as Stalin planned operations on a globe. Khrushchev summed up: 'This is Stalin's military ''genius'': this is what it cost us.' Furthermore, Khrushchev condemned the wholesale deportation towards the end of the war of peoples who had been under German occupation and who were accused of collaboration — the Chechen, Ingush, Kalmyks, and others, but he notably failed to mention the Crimean Tatars: 'The Ukrainians avoided meeting this fate only because there were too many of them and there was no place to which to deport them.' Among the other charges were Stalin's mishandling of foreign policy and in particular the high-handedness which had led to the break with Yugoslavia in 1948 (see pp. 279–80). Khrushchev touched on one of his pet themes in criticizing Stalin's neglect of agriculture.

The speech was a broad attack on the personality and some of the policies of Stalin. What became known as the 'secret speech' did not remain a secret for long. It was initially circulated among party activists and then in all workplaces and thus became quickly known at home and abroad, although it was not actually published in the Soviet Union. The means of its broadcasting was as much of a compromise as its contents. Despite its limitations, owing partly to the fact that it had evidently been prepared in haste, the speech was a courageous and important event. Never before had the policies of the regime been the target of such sustained criticism by one of its leaders. However, the speech restricted itself to describing the Stalinist horror and failed to analyse how it had come about. The indictment is restricted to the years after 1934 and hence forced collectivization and industrialization were accepted, as was the way in which they were conducted. Khrushchev was careful to present the party as the victim and as somehow dissociated from Stalin's crimes. All that was positive under Stalin came from the party, all that was negative from Stalin: 'Our historical victories were attained thanks to the organizational work of the party.' Just as Khrushchev's reforms were in the main limited to adjusting the operation of the system established by Stalin, based on collective farms and enterprises responsible to state organiza-tions, so his speech was largely concerned not with the Stalinist system itself but with its excesses. Khrushchev said little about the sufferings of the peasantry and ordinary people, and he was selective in his choice of victims to rehabilitate. The losers in the power game following Lenin's death, dubbed oppositionists, such as Trotsky, Bukharin, Rykov, Zinoviev, and Kamenev, were mentioned only to be condemned. The victory of Stalin personally as well as of his policies was therefore adumbrated, but the way he misused his power was condemned.

In a perverse inversion of the Stalin cult the entire responsibility for the negative features of the Stalin years was placed on Stalin personally, whereas previously all the victories had been his own doing. As Palmiro Togliatti, the leader of the Italian communist party, pointed out, 'All that was good used to be attributed to the superhuman qualities of one man; now all that was evil is attributed to him'.[3] The responsibility of Stalin's associates, including Khrushchev himself, for the crimes was evaded, and no figures were given. Togliatti insisted that it was un-Marxist to seek the explanation of a major historical phenomenon in the evil of an individual, not in economic or social circumstances. The exposure of Stalin was partial and left many areas in the dark. If the party had retained its basic correctness, why had it, and indeed Stalin's colleagues, not resisted his reckless policies and the purges? The speech failed to provide any theoretical or his-torical explanation for the emergence of the Stalin phenomenon. There was no analysis of the legal, political, ideological, or institutional foundations of Stalinism.

The criticisms were moral rather than political. The aim was to condemn Stalin rather than to provide a political explanation of Stalinism. The speech failed to provide a structural analysis, although the system that Stalin had nurtured was forcefully distinguished from what was termed Leninist socialist legality. The 'back to Lenin' theme served important functions in the adjustment of the Soviet system but it was only a partial retreat from Stalinism. In displacing Stalin's person-ality cult on to an inflated cult of Lenin Khrushchev was guilty of a Stalinist practice. Khrushchev argued that if the matter were analysed seriously 'we may preclude any possibility of a repetition in any form whatsoever of what took place during the life of Stalin'. However, the basic apparatus created by Stalin continued to rule, and no institutional or political barriers were erected against a revival of Stalinism. The CPSU remained the dominant political institution, but the curbs on the KGB and the destalinization process itself proved to some extent reversible.

In the circumstances Khrushchev's victory of the half-truth over the unmitigated lie was a major victory. To have gone much deeper into the roots of Stalinism in an international forum attended by Mao Zedong and other international communist leaders, with Stalin's henchmen such as Molotov and Kaganovich present, might well have been bravery taken to the point of folly. The speech was undoubtedly partly motivated by the desire to discredit the Stalinist hard-liners, who earlier in 1956 had rallied against Khrushchev, though it was much more than that. Stalin's betrayal of the loyalty and idealism of his generation made Khrushchev's denunciation of Stalin a personal mission as much as an act of political calculation. From a Marxist perspective Medvedev argues that Khrushchev denounced Stalin's crimes in order to rationalize the system of bureaucratic government and to consolidate the privileges and power of the class of office-holders, the *nomenklatura*.[4] This group had developed under Stalin, and now the lifting of the terror allowed them to enjoy their rewards. Stalin's crimes and personality were dissociated from Soviet socialism. Having consolidated the rule of the party and the existence of the bureaucratic system, Khrushchev became expendable.

For many the speech came as a great shock. The idol of a generation was deposed from his pedestal. They were forced to face up to what had been suppressed for so long. In the West there were major debates in the communist parties, and by the end of the year mass desertions. A New Left, more critical of the Soviet Union began to emerge. The Italian communist party under Togliatti now publicized the idea of national roads to socialism under the term 'polycentrism'. Moscow was no longer the Rome of the world communist movement.

In Eastern Europe the shock was all the greater since the Stalin cult had been imposed together with Soviet power as an act of faith for a decade. (see pp. 280–1). In 1955 Khrushchev conceded the principle of national roads to socialism during his reconciliation with Tito's Yugoslavia. The succession struggle in Moscow and ideological divisions had a profoundly destabilizing effect. In Hungary in June 1953 the Stalinist leader Mátyás Rákosi had been replaced by Imre Nagy, who launched a series of reforms. However, angered by the pace of change, which outstripped that of the Soviet Union, the Soviet leaders engineered the fall of Nagy, whose reforms were similar to those proposed by Malenkov. Khrushchev's victory over Malenkov saw the return of Rákosi to power in April 1955. In June 1956 a Declaration on Relations between the Soviet and

Yugoslav parties was followed a week later by strikes in Poznan in western Poland. In October a potentially disastrous political confrontation between hard-liners and reformers was averted only after Khrushchev's personal intervention and by the return of Wladyslaw Gomulka to head the communist party to implement a Polish road to socialism. Divergence from the Soviet model allowed the development of forms of national communism. The Polish party was conceded a degree of autonomy in domestic policies in return for political loyalty to Moscow and the maintenance of the leading role of the party. The Soviet economic model was swiftly discarded as a wave of decollectivization swept 85 per cent of Polish agriculture back into private hands. The factory councils established in 1956 were gradually undermined, but some of the achievements of the 'Polish October' remained — in a fairly relaxed censorship, relatively free travel, and a concordat with the church.

In Hungary events took a far more explosive turn. Destalinization sparked off a challenge to the very existence of communist rule. Nationalist themes merged with factional struggles over the Hungarian road to socialism. The major difference from Poland was the greater degree of disunity at the head of the Hungarian party and the absence of a sufficiently forceful leader who might have controlled the destalinization process and facilitated an internal solution to the challenges. The Stalinist Rákosi and his supporters clung to power for too long, and once belatedly returned to power in October 1956 Nagy was always one step behind the demands for popular government, full freedom of speech and publicity, and ultimately for national independence. In the last days of October the crisis developed into a full-scale revolution. The Soviet ambassador, Yuri Andropov, lulled Nagy into a false sense of security as Soviet troops prepared to invade. From the Soviet point of view the benefits of intervention far outweighed the costs, especially since world attention was distracted by the disastrous Israeli, British, and French seizure of the Suez Canal. After several days of street fighting in early November 1956 the Hungarian revolution was crushed. The clear lesson was that destalinization would not be allowed to permit the disintegration of the Soviet bloc in Eastern Europe, though some latitude was permitted in domestic policies. The declining ideological unity and the absence of Stalin's personalized leadership were compensated by increased institutional ties through the Warsaw Treaty Organization (WTO, the Warsaw Pact), created in 1955, and by rejuvenating the Council for Mutual Economic Assistance (CMEA, or Comecon), formed in 1949. The events in Poland and Hungary illustrated that the thaw would not be allowed to bloom into spring.

Within the Soviet Union responses to the speech were more muted, as the years of suppressing independent thought had left their mark. Destalinization was at its most explosive when combined with nationalism. Only in Georgia, Stalin's homeland, did the speech lead to disturbances when in March 1956 on the anniversary of his death demonstrations protested against the debunking of the local hero, even though the republic had suffered particularly harshly during the purges. Khrushchev himself began to backtrack in the face of a conservative backlash. In June 1956 he declared that Stalin was a 'great Marxist-Leninist' and condemned the concept of 'Stalinism', which he alleged to be the invention of anti-Soviet propaganda. The main result of the speech was the creation of commissions to visit the labour camps. Between 1954 and 1958 they authorized the rehabilitation and release of over 2 million political prisoners. Throughout the summer of 1956 a wave of ragged and emaciated camp inmates struggled home, witnesses to the crimes and living testimony of the need for reform. However, those most closely responsible for the Soviet holocaust remained unpunished and still held responsible posts.

The thaw was taken furthest in the cultural sphere. The poet Alexander Tvardovsky had been appointed editor of *Novy Mir* (*New World*) in 1950, and now the journal became the forum for the best contemporary literature. Unofficial free thought blossomed in a movement that became a 'cultural opposition' as it sought to probe the origins of the Stalin phenomenon beyond the official limits. These years were a time of relative cultural and intellectual liberalism as censorship became less heavy-handed and the cultural intelligentsia began to participate more fully in political and intellectual life.

The inconsistencies of Khrushchev's speech were reflected in the sharpening of the inner-party struggle. His opponents focused on the alleged economic and political deficiencies of Khrushchev's leadership (see below), but fears of the pace of destalinization played their part. They opposed what they considered an excessive relaxation of Soviet controls over the international communist movement, especially in Yugoslavia, and condemned Khrushchev's policy of peaceful coexistence. A grouping of Malenkov, Molotov, Kaganovich, and the foreign minister D.T. Shepilov launched an attack in June 1957. They obtained a majority on the Praesidium (now called the Politburo) of seven to four and denounced the whole gamut of Khrushchev's policies. They demanded his resignation, but Khrushchev argued that only the Central Committee could dismiss him. A Central Committee plenum was hastily convened, with the assistance of Zhukov and the military. Khrushchev's earlier appointments now stood him in good stead, and he obtained an overwhelming vote in his favour, the tradition of unanimity still exercising its power. His policies in agriculture and destalinization commanded more support than the alternative put forward by the hard-liners. He followed up this victory by dismissing his opponents, dubbed the 'anti-party group'. Molotov was sent as ambassador to Mongolia and Malenkov to manage a power station in Siberia. Zhukov's support was cruelly rewarded by demotion and his replacement by Marshal Malinovskii. Zhukov's popularity and independence had weakened one of the basic principles of the Soviet Union: party control over the army. In 1958 Khrushchev further consolidated his position by replacing Bulganin as Premier, and he therefore combined the two key posts, as Stalin had done in 1941.

However, while Khrushchev's formal power continued to grow his personal popularity was in decline as his policies caused confusion. It was partly this which prompted him to raise the Stalin question again in 1961 at the twenty-second party congress. In many respects this congress represented a far more radical destalinization than the twentieth. On 17 October 1961 Khrushchev addressed an open session, naming Stalin's accomplices and launching an attack on Stalin. His scope was broader than in 1956, criticizing parts of Stalin's strategy of economic development, in particular condemning the 'steel-hungry' heavy-industry programmes. Once again the major charge against the personality cult was that it had raised itself above the party. Khrushchev's tone was much more bitter than it had been in the secret speech, though the level of analysis was not taken much further. With the congress still in session, on the night of 31 October, Stalin's body was removed from the mausoleum where it had rested next to Lenin. It was buried by the Kremlin wall, marked by a plain slab inscribed 'J.V. Stalin' and covered by tons of concrete as if the leadership feared his resurrection. Soon afterwards his name was removed from thousands of towns and streets.

The condemnation of Stalin was now conducted in the open, and the congress speeches were published in the press. A pent-up flood of revelations about the Stalin period was released. A genre known as 'camp literature' burgeoned as books and articles described Stalin's atrocities. In 1962 Khrushchev personally authorized the publication in *Novy Mir* of Alexander Solzhenitsyn's *One Day in the Life of Ivan Denisovich*, describing life in the camps. Evgenii Evtushenko's poem 'The Heirs of Stalin' warned against the survival of the spirit of Stalinism. However, as after the twentieth congress, Khrushchev became alarmed about the outpouring of this literature and began a retreat. Extremely conservative culturally, he was disturbed by the potential of the revelations to destabilize the system. One of the shortcomings of destalinization under Khrushchev was that it was partly a function of his struggle to retain the leadership. Indeed, the lack of a structural analysis of Stalinism allowed Khrushchev to develop a minor personality cult of his own. When he was ousted in October 1964 destalinization swiftly lost momentum.

Its main achievements were the termination of twenty five years of mass terror and the limitation of the powers of the security police. Millions of prison-camp survivors were released, many administrative and bureaucratic abuses were curbed, and the role of charismatic one-person rule was reduced. But the whole Stalinist phenomenon remained a festering sore in the absence of a credible official structural analysis of the phenomenon.

Economy and society

Stalin laid the foundations of the Soviet Union's modern economy. Certain sectors, however, had been woefully neglected, such as agriculture, and new technologies such as plastics had been almost completely ignored. His centralizing zeal meant that the ministries in Moscow were responsible for overseeing the smallest operational details of plants perhaps thousands of miles away. Plan targets were set in terms of quantity rather than quality. The problem now was to devise a strategy to capitalize on the achievements of the Stalinist system while inducing a new dynamism to the economy, a combination which was still being sought thirty years later. Possible solutions were as familiar to Stalin's immediate successors as they are now: greater reliance on the market, more decentralization, more and better consumer goods, greater private initiative within the collective system, and economic incentives to the introduction of new technology.

Malenkov's New Course of 1953–4 had shifted the emphasis to providing more consumer goods for Soviet citizens, though his cuts in retail prices went too far and led to shortages. Malenkov, however, was unable to gain sufficient support for his reform programme. Khrushchev led the assault but, having wrested the leadership from Malenkov, proceeded to take over the latter's economic policies. The most pressing problem was in agriculture, a sphere that Khrushchev made his own. The wartime destruction of villages and shortages of labour were exacerbated by the continued high delivery obligations and high taxes. Agricultural productivity stagnated under the authoritarian collective farm structure. Khrushchev continued Malenkov's long overdue payment of higher procurement prices for agricultural products, relaxations on the peasant's personal plot, and higher investment, which quadrupled between 1953 and 1964. Apart from these sensible reforms many of Khrushchev's policies were ludicrously overoptimistic. The Virgin Land Scheme ignored ecological factors, and after some years in which grain output increased the region began to suffer from soil erosion and duststorms. Another of Khrushchev's 'harebrained schemes' followed his visit to Iowa in 1959, when he seized on maize as a fodder crop to increase meat and dairy production. Farms were forced to grow maize irrespective of local conditions, and in general the livestock campaign was conducted in a hopelessly inept manner. His forceful methods were often reminiscent of Stalin's.

In 1958 he dissolved the machine-tractor stations which supplied the farms with machinery. Khrushchev's policy veered from one extreme to the other. Previously farms had been forbidden to own their equipment, but now they were forced to own the machinery even if they did not want to and lacked servicing facilities. The abolition of the MTSs allowed the revival of the 'link' system, introduced during the war and abolished in 1950, whereby groups were allowed to work a piece of land for extended periods and even to own machinery. It was a concession to personal agriculture, but despite much talk the system was not allowed to make the contribution it was capable of until the 1980s. After the initial easing of restrictions on the personal plot Khrushchev began to take fiscal and administrative measures against private livestock. The restrictions were imposed on ideological grounds and were designed to discourage private farming. They contributed to declining productivity as the peasants once again found themselves under attack. Agriculture did show some improvement as grain output increased, but Khrushchev's enthusiasms led to disruption. Increases in food prices in 1962 led to unprecedented riots and to workers' protests in Novocherkassk which were crushed by tanks. Bad weather in 1963 exacerbated the poor harvest, and scarce foreign currency was spent to import grain.

Khrushchev moved to tackle a problem highlighted by the anti-party group.

73

The industrial ministries were carving out empires which were becoming increasingly independent of the bodies responsible for co-ordinating economic plans. Khrushchev proposed a radical solution by abolishing the central ministries and transferring their responsibilities to over 100 regional economic councils (*sovnarkhozy*) which were to be co-ordinated by larger republican bodies and the central planning agencies. The change was accompanied by the first major economic debate since the 1920s. The reform proved flawed, since it proved well-nigh impossible to combine central planning with regional authority. The plethora of sectoral state committees established to reconcile the demands of the centre and the localities failed to prevent economic chaos. In response the number of councils was reduced, but when such measures as merging several republics to create larger economic units were proposed national sensitivities were provoked. The duplication of tasks at the local and national levels only increased the bureaucracy. Following Khrushchev's ousting the councils were abolished and the central ministries were re-established in Moscow.

In 1957 Khrushchev asserted his authority over economic policy, scrapping the sixth five-year plan and adopting an ambitious new seven-year plan which attempted simultaneously to increase consumer satisfaction and to achieve high economic growth rates. The result, inevitably, was high-handedness and centralization as agencies desperately sought to fulfil their part of the plan by applying administrative pressure. Khrushchev's enthusiasms offended many key groups and threatened to unbalance the economy. There was a marked slowing down of economic growth after 1958 as his administrative methods led to disorganization. His reforms relied more on organizational changes than on changes in economic mechanisms themselves. Khrushchev's tragedy was not that he tried to tackle the real economic problems but that his education, background, and personality did not provide him with the ability to achieve his aims.

In the summer of 1957 the USSR hosted the sixth world youth festival. Moscow had not seen so many visitors since the revolution as Soviet citizens and foreigners met and exchanged ideas in what was called 'the spirit of the twentieth congress'. It was a period of great Soviet achievements. The first sputnik circled the globe in October 1957, and a month later the dog Laika was the first animate object in space. In 1961 the Soviet Union registered yet another first with the orbiting of the earth by Yuri Gagarin. These events made a great impression on the rest of the world and signalled that the Soviet Union had come of age as a technological power. Of greater concern for the military planners of the West, it demonstrated that the USSR had the capacity to launch intercontinental ballistic missiles (ICBMs).

In social policy Khrushchev's ascendancy was marked by the extension of social security benefits. Stalin's legacy in the field of housing was years of neglect and crowded communal apartments. As workers crowded into the cities from the 1930s to work in industry Stalin concentrated resources on building yet more factories and few but grandiose housing projects. Khrushchev achieved a doubling of the housing stock between 1955 and 1964. The Khrushchev era saw a notable improvement in the standard of living, especially in the countryside. No longer did heavy industry absorb all the available resources.

Under Khrushchev the educational system witnessed a major expansion. In a reform of the system he attempted to remedy the problem of social inequality which had become such a pronounced feature of Stalin's rule. Between 1955 and 1957 Khrushchev tried to undermine educational privilege and the advantages of the elite in their access to higher education by combining education with labour. This culminated in 1958 with his plan to abolish the higher grades at school and to force all children over 15 to enter the labour force for at least two years and to learn a trade. Access to higher education would be through part-time programmes of evening or correspondence courses. It amounted to a 'polytechniza-tion' of education through work training, harking back to some of the educational experiments of the early Soviet years. The debate over the reform provides a second good example, together with the Virgin Lands Scheme, of policy formation in the post-Stalin period. The reform provides one of the clearest examples of resistance from a professional group to the policies of the government. Khrushchev's plans were not based on the advice of educational specialists or on the practical experience gained since 1955. He underestimated the value of full-time education in secondary schools and the problems youngsters of 15 faced in choosing a profession. Khrushchev was thwarted in his plans by a coalition of vested interests. After brief discussion a milder version of his plans was adopted in December 1958. Even this was never fully implemented, and the reform was quietly dropped in 1965.

In the legal sphere Khrushchev tried to establish certain basic rules and procedures. The principle that only properly constituted courts could pass sentence was enshrined in the new Criminal Code of 1958. Khrushchev, however, undermined the principles of legality that he himself had set. The code had limited the death penalty to treason alone, yet in 1961 some black-marketeers were shot after its retrospective extension, a procedure against all accepted norms of justice. The terms of the 'anti-parasite laws' of 1957 were cast so broadly against those not in official gainful employment that officials frequently used them as a catch-all statute against individuals guilty of a range of offences, including 'dissent'. The commitment to the restoration of socialist legality was undermined by the fact that Khrushchev did not renounce force to impose his will on specific issues. As Breslauer points out, Khrushchev based his authority on achieving impressive results in a short time, the politics of 'pressure', hence the tendency to resort to coercion to overcome resistance. Mass terror was ended, but coercion remained embedded in the operation of the system.

Authority and ideology

The zigzags in policy between 1953 and 1964 and the erratic style of Khrushchev's leadership reflected the enormous power vacuum left by the end of dictatorial rule and mass terror. Stalin's successors were forced to devise new patterns of power and authority. Khrushchev's economic policies had been maturing within the Stalinist shell, but in the sphere of authority patterns and ideology his approach did contain some genuinely novel features.[5] The aim was to overcome the political ossification imposed by Stalin. At the centre of Khrushchev's approach was a Leninist fundamentalism adapted to new conditions.

The novel feature of Khrushchev's rule was the attempt to revitalize political participation, which has been labelled a Soviet form of populism. Under both Lenin and Stalin mass participation had been encouraged as one of the fundamental principles of commune democracy. Participation, however, can be divided into two types. The managerial approach, adopted by Malenkov and practised by Brezhnev, channelled participation into safe paths which would not threaten the political and bureaucratic prerogatives of Soviet officials; while the populist approach challenged their autonomy and exposed bureaucrats to effective criticism. Khrushchev adopted the second type, and despite equivocations he led a deter- mined assault against elitism and bureaucratism somewhat reminiscent of the workers' inspection movement (Rabkrin) during war communism. Khrushchev tried to draw the population into the building of socialism. His populism was more than a tactic in the factional struggle but was conceived as part of a strategy to improve economic and political efficiency.[6] Khrushchev sought to supplement political controls from above by expanding the bounds of decision-making by seeking the advice of specialist groupings, such as scientists, and by extending popular participation in political processes. This was to be achieved by drawing (*privlechenie*) new social activists, known as *obshchestvenniki*, into public life by accelerated recruitment to the party, expanding the rights of the soviets and the trade unions, and transferring some state functions to public or social organiza- tions. In the factories, for example, the penal system was to be supplemented by the establishment of comrades' courts, which tried minor offences. The work of the militia was bolstered by the creation of volunteer patrols (*druzhiny*) in the streets. The creation of a centralized united Party-State Control Committee in 1963 had the potential of acting as a powerful means of control over party and state bureaucrats, giving official sanction to popular supervision. Khrushchev sought to use the masses to supervise the state and economic bureaucrats.

Khrushchev's Leninist fundamentalism was particularly apparent in religious affairs, where he revealed himself to be a 1920s type of militant atheist. He was more of a 'conviction politician' in this respect than Stalin, whose religious policy was pragmatic. Stalin's persecution of religion during the collectivization campaign had been accompanied by the closure of churches, but during the war many had been given permission to reopen. Whenever Khrushchev found himself in a strong political position he initiated an anti-religious campaign. Having consolidated his power, in December 1958 he launched an offensive which resulted in the closure of most of the churches reopened during the war, and of many more churches, mosques, and synagogues. They were converted into government stores or left to rot, thus destroying a priceless cultural heritage. His aim was to remedy the perceived ideological laxness of Stalin's last decade, and in this respect continued the tradition of 'party revivalism' pursued by Zhdanov. He placed the churches under a far more invidious system of state supervision, through the Council for Church Affairs, than Stalin ever had. For him religion was antithetical to the values of communist society and its scientific-materialist basis.[7]

Under Stalin the government bureaucracy had dominated the party and become the main institutional expression of power. Khrushchev's defeat of the anti-party group in 1957 ruined the collective leadership, and he emerged as the single most powerful figure. However, he did not attain a position above the party and state comparable to Stalin's. He governed through the party, not over its head. The party was restored to the position it had enjoyed under Lenin as the ruling political organization. Its institutional life was revived, with regular congresses, and its central and local committees functioned according to the party rules. The Praesidium (Politburo), the party's top executive body, became the central political arbiter in the Soviet Union. But Khrushchev, having raised the status of the party as an institution, did his best to ensure that it did not function as such. The decline in collective leadership after 1957 was accompanied by his strengthened personal dominance over the party machine. No party secretary or official could withstand the First Secretary's imperious will. The growing economic problems from 1960 encouraged Khrushchev to broaden his assault on the bureaucracy to encompass party officials. In the purge that followed nearly half of all provincial and territorial party first secretaries lost their jobs in the space of a year. It became clear that party officials owed their jobs to the First Secretary and not to an anonymous bureaucracy in Moscow. This was a measure of how little had changed since Stalin had used such methods to consolidate his power in the 1920s.

In addition to continuing the destalinization campaign the twenty-second party congress in 1961 adopted a new party programme to replace the 1919 one. It summed-up the party's achievements and outlined highly ambitious plans for the future. According to the programme the Soviet Union would catch up and over-take the USA economically by 1970, and within twenty years (by 1980) the USSR would 'in the main' be a communist society. The economic objectives were ludicrously optimistic, but the programme's main interest lies in its attempt to provide a theoretical restatement of the historical position of the USSR. The pro-gramme argued that the economic, social, and international achievements, the new and higher stage of the Soviet material base, necessitated corresponding theoretical developments. The programme reflected Khrushchev's own beliefs concerning the role of the party and the nature of Soviet society. The programme advanced the theory of peaceful coexistence with the West, a greater stress on equality, and foresaw the emergence of a 'new Soviet person', ideologically con-scious, skilled, and politically active.

The programme's major novelty was the assertion that socialism had already been constructed in the Soviet Union. Contradictory classes had disappeared and therefore the state was no longer the dictatorship of the proletariat: it was now viewed as a 'state of all the people' engaged in building communism. In 1936 Stalin had argued that socialism had been built, but to justify the purges had insisted that the state grew stronger as it approached its end because of the intensification of the class struggle, a theory repudiated by Khrushchev in his secret speech. The new programme was an attempt to remove Stalin's inconsistencies. Its major emphasis was on the withering away of the state, which it argued could now commence. This was to take place through the transfer of the coercive power of the state and its functions to such public organizations as the trade unions, popular militias, and comrades' courts. Bureaucratic organizations like ministries were to disappear, while the soviets were to be revitalized to stimulate communist self-government. Reflecting the usual Khrushchevian ambivalence, the programme argued that the withering away of the state would be a protracted process and that the party, as a social organization, was to expand its functions. The question of the role of the party in the future communist society had always been left vague, yet it had always been assumed, and Stalin concurred, that the party would wither away at the end of the dictatorship of the proletariat. Now Khrushchev proposed its consolidation. The ringing utopias of earlier years gave way to an image of communist society as a consensual, depoliticized, limited participatory socialist democracy dedicated to welfarist improvement in standards of living. The charge of revisionism levelled at Khrushchev by Mao Zedong and others rested on the programme's assertion of the ending of the class struggle: the Chinese declared that all states are class states until the final establishment of communism.

The twenty-second congress proceeded to implement some of the programme's doctrines. The principle of rotation of offices within the party was established: for Central Committee members four terms of four years each (a maximum of sixteen years, unless they were especially good, a flattering loophole utilized by Brezhnev); members of the Praesidium for no more than three terms; and shorter periods lower down the hierarchy. In effect, Khrushchev abolished security of tenure in the party. The shock to those used to the idea of a career in office can be imagined. It provoked widespread discontent, since party officials now faced the prospect of having to readjust to a new job at some point in their career.

Khrushchev's economic problems in this period encouraged him to look to the party, his favourite body, for a solution. He divided the party in 1962 into industrial and agricultural sectors at the provincial and lower levels. This was designed to integrate it more closely into economic administration. Separate agricultural and industrial hierarchies were established, and party officials had to decide which to join. The reform only exacerbated the chronic ambiguity over the functions of the party officials in production. To what extent was their role to be advisory, or should they rule directly, thus replacing the responsible official? Khrushchev was trying to cut the number of salaried party officials by increasing the number of voluntary and part-time staff, and to stimulate the involvement of rank-and-file party members, yet the division further expanded the bureaucracy by having two of everything.

Khrushchev's populism inevitably encountered the opposition of those with a vested interest in maintaining their position and accustomed authority. Attempts to open up administration inevitably engendered the hostility of the bureaucrats themselves. They considered themselves the masters of a narrowly defined political sphere in which they brooked no interference. Their priority was the smooth management of state and economic affairs rather than the extension of democratic self-management. They shared the bureaucrat's traditional antipathy to popular government and mass participation, which threatened their political autonomy. The underlying assumption of Khrushchev's destalinization campaign and the promulgation of the theory that the class struggle had ended in the Soviet Union was that the Soviet people could now be trusted to manage their own affairs to a greater extent than before. The strategy sought to bring administrative and political processes within the ambit of popular control.

Yet Khrushchev's populism was contradictory. The party programme had compromised on the question of popular initiative by channelling it through bureaucratic agencies. Despite the proclamation of the 'state of all the people', with the emphasis on volunteers and standing commissions, after 1961 the authority and functions of the soviets continued to decline and the government and party still maintained their 'petty tutelage' over them. It would take more than exhortation to revive the soviets. The greater respect shown to specialists was balanced by Khrushchev's support for the biologist Trofim Lysenko, whose insistence on the ability of species to assimilate rapidly to new circumstances represented the triumph of Bolshevik voluntarism over nature. Lysenkoism set the study of genetics in the USSR back by a generation. It was at this time that a campaign was launched against unofficial art and literature. Khrushchev's populism did not amount to a liberalization of the system as a whole. His attempts to achieve greater social homogeneity through his anti-corruption drive, the assault against 'parasitism', and his heavy-handed campaigns against religion and cultural nonconformity, all revealed a high degree of authoritarianism. The opposition of officialdom to his programme was bolstered by a great degree of popular resistance. It proved impossible to reconcile the contradictory aims of maintaining the centralized and directorial administrative mechanism with the attempt to expand public influence on the operation of the system. This remained a problem for post-Khrushchev reformers.

Khrushchev's fall

Khrushchev had been able to impose his policies in investment priorities, administrative reform, political participation, and foreign policy, but from 1962 his authority weakened. By October 1964 his power seemed to be at a peak but his authority, the ability to initiate and see policies through, had crumbled.[8] Problems were mounting in all fields, and Khrushchev lacked a coherent strategy for dealing with them. His colleagues in the leadership increasingly saw him as a liability. Moreover, he had gratuitously weakened his position by attacking his natural power base, the party officials. On 12 October 1964 he was summoned to a meeting of the Praesidium and the twenty-two people present were unanimous that he had to go. He was replaced by a collective leadership of Leonid Ilich

Brezhnev (First Secretary, soon after renamed General Secretary, of the party), Aleksei Kosygin (Chair of the Council of Ministers), and Nikolai Podgorny (Chair of the Praesidium of the Supreme Soviet). Khrushchev was accused of infringing the principle of collective leadership and returning to the style of the personality cult, though the very fact that he was ousted reveals the limits to his power.

The Central Committee next day confirmed his ousting and Mikhail Suslov outlined the main charges against him. They included precipitate decision-making, nepotism (his son-in-law, A.I. Adzhubai, had been appointed editor of *Izvestiya*), causing administrative confusion by splitting the party, foolish 'campaigns' in agriculture which had led to the agricultural crisis of 1963–4, and pursuing an adventurist foreign policy which had led the world to the brink of nuclear war over Cuba in October 1962. Khrushchev was stripped of his posts and retired. No punitive action was taken against him, and the peaceful nature of the transition was a measure of the changes he had wrought. It is for this reason that Mark Frankland paradoxically calls the moment of Khrushchev's humiliation his 'finest hour'.[9] After the bloodthirsty years of Stalin's rule he had restored basic civilized norms to the conduct of Soviet politics.

The accusations levelled against Khrushchev were on the whole justified, but they were not the full reason for his dismissal. On the social level his removal can be seen as an elite (and possibly bureaucratic) counter-revolution. The recruitment of specialists into the party, government, and management undermined the rough-and-ready politicians, like Khrushchev himself, drawn into the leadership in the 1920s and 1930s. Khrushchev's style jarred on the newcomers' sense of decorum and procedure. The political elite objected to the introduction of the principle of the rotation of offices. The division of the party gave Khrushchev massively expanded powers of patronage and introduced an intimidating new form of 'permanent purge'. His populist measures prevented the consolidation of managerial autonomy and production efficiency in industry. His leadership style, tempered in the various campaigns of Stalinist industrialization, was cast in the mould of 'storming' rather than settled routines. In the name of stability and order the political and economic bureaucracy rallied in October 1964 and ousted Khrushchev.

Under Khrushchev an alliance for reform was to some extent created, but it came up against the social realities of an entrenched bureaucracy which fought hard to preserve its privileges and power. His overthrow marked the end of a sustained period of reform and inaugurated two decades of conservatism. As Stephen Cohen points out, 'Change in the Soviet system, and resistance to change, have been the central features of Soviet political life since Stalin's death in 1953.'[10] It is a conflict between 'innovation' and 'tradition', or between 'reformism' and 'conservatism', a split which to some extent coincides with the division between anti-Stalinists and neo-Stalinists. The battle between the two tendencies is fought on many grounds, including the evaluation of the Stalinist past, Russia's historical role, and the potential for socialist development in the Soviet Union. The reformists insist that the system and the ideology are capable of indefinite development, whereas the conservatives focus on the defence of present achievements. Khrushchev's reforms were imposed from above, and attempts to generate a self-sustaining movement reform from below, as with the cultural opposition, were repressed. The reforms therefore lacked an institutional base to continue them once he was gone. The reformism of the Khrushchev years, Cohen argues, was a reaction to the long period of Stalin's tyranny. In other words, reform was sustained by a relatively small constituency and was permitted for a time by the revulsion against some of Stalin's excesses. Following the stabilization of the system, the end of the terror, and the restrictions on arbitrary police power, the forces of reform were left with few powerful allies. To put it another way, and from the totalitarian point of view, Khrushchev never got beyond the 'struggle for succession' phase of dictatorships. The cause of destalinization was allied to his political struggle against the conservatives and the Stalinists.

Stalinism represented the period of 'system-building', whereas Khrushchev's rule established the framework for the 'system-management' phase of the governance of the USSR. Khrushchev's aim was to achieve the maximum viability of the regime. He hoped to reduce coercion as standards of living increased, to decrease the scope of administrative agencies as the public became more involved, and to improve the efficiency of the economic system as workers became more conscious. The ideological legitimacy of the system was to be bolstered by its practical achievements in the sphere of social consumption and political interaction between regime and society. Stalin's revolution from above had laid the basis of a more educated and complex society, and it was left to Khrushchev to devise a strategy to find a means of integrating this into the political regime bequeathed by Stalin. The destalinization campaigns, administrative reforms, and populism were all responses to the problem. However, while rejecting the excesses of Stalin, he returned to the Leninist system that had provided the *milieu* for them to emerge in the first instance.

His rule was marked by a degree of continuity with the preceding period, such as the unprincipled struggle to come to power against Malenkov, his clear discomfort with the limitations of collective leadership and the emergence of a mini-personality cult of his own, the sacrifice of Imre Nagy in Hungary, and the struggle against the peasants' personal plots. His commitment to sustained social changes spoke of his refusal to allow the regime to make peace with society. His rule was distinguished by populist strategies for mobilizing the citizenry against the office-holders and by the erratic nature of policy formation and implementation. His ideological ardour represented a genuine return to Leninist fundamentalism. There was, of course, no suggestion of introducing some form of political pluralism either in the party or in society. On a very general level two basic patterns of Soviet power can be identified, the war communist and the NEP. Khrushchev's reforms represented no more than the modification of the war communist model restored by Stalin in 1929, marked by state domination of the economy and permeated by a high level of ideological and social coercion but stripped of some of its more violent characteristics. Khrushchev represented not so much an alternative to the long-term pattern of Soviet politics as an attempt to infuse the existing practices with some life.

The Stalinist regime, with its purges and wars against its own people, its economic storms, and social catastrophes, could not continue for ever. Khrushchev's major achievement was to accept the need for change and to set the mould for post-Stalinist governance. The net effect of his policies was to alienate most of his former bases of support, since the reforms threatened the power and privileges of the very people he was forced to rely on to implement the changes. Khrushchev was ousted not because of any fundamental policy disagreements, but over the manner of their implementation and the challenge that his methods posed to officialdom. Under Khrushchev the heroic but terrible storms of the early Soviet years were ended and he began the task, completed by Brezhnev, of putting post-Stalinist administration and its relationship to society onto a more coherent basis.

Notes

1 M.S. Gorbachev, 2 November 1987 speech for seventieth anniversary of the October revolution, *Soviet News*, 4 November 1987.
2 Dunmore, *Soviet Politics, 1945–53*, p. 158.
3 Quoted by Conquest, *Great Terror*, p. 685.
4 R. Medvedev, *Khrushchev* (Blackwell, Oxford, 1982), p. 89.
5 For a discussion of the 'Khrushchev alternative' see M. McAuley, *Politics and the Soviet Union* (Penguin, Harmondsworth, 1977), chapter 7.
6 G.W. Breslauer, 'Khrushchev Reconsidered', in S.F. Cohen, A. Rabinowitch, and R. Sharlet (eds.), *The Soviet Union since Stalin* (Macmillan, London, 1980), pp. 51–2.
7 J.D. Grossman, 'Khrushchev's Anti-religious Policy', *Soviet Studies*, 24, 3 (1972–3), pp. 374–86.
8 G.W. Breslauer, *Khrushchev and Brezhnev as Leaders* (Allen & Unwin, London, 1982), pp. 114–17, 133.
9 Quoted by Medvedev, *Khrushchev*, p. 245.
10 S.F. Cohen, 'The Friends and Foes of Change', in E.P. Hoffmann and R.F. Laird (eds.), *The Soviet Polity in the Modern Era* (Aldine, New York, 1984), p. 85.

Key texts

Breslauer, G., 'Khrushchev Reconsidered', *Problems of Communism*, 25, 5 (September-October 1976), pp. 18–33; also in S.F. Cohen, A. Rabinowich, and R. Sharlet (eds.), *The Soviet Union since Stalin* (Macmillan, London, 1980)
Cohen, S.F., 'The Friends and Foes of Change: Reformism and Conservatism in the Soviet Union', first published in S.F. Cohen *et al* (eds.), *The Soviet Union since Stalin* (Macmillan, London, 1980); also in E.P. Hoffmann and R.F. Laird (eds.), *The Soviet Polity in the Modern Era* (Aldine, New York, 1984); revised version in *Rethinking the Soviet Experience* (Oxford University Press, New York, 1985), pp. 128–57
McCauley, Martin (ed.), *Khrushchev and Khrushchevism* (Macmillan, London, 1987)
Medvedev, Roy, *Khrushchev*, trans. Brian Pearce (Blackwell, Oxford, 1982)

Select bibliography

Breslauer, G., *Khrushchev and Brezhnev as Leaders: Building Authority in Soviet Politics* (Allen & Unwin, London, 1982)

Brinkley, George A., 'Khrushchev Remembered: on the Theory of Soviet Statehood', *Soviet Studies*, 3, (1972–3), pp. 387–401

Brumberg, Abraham (ed.), *Russia under Khrushchev* (Methuen, London, 1982)

Chotiner, B.A., *Khrushchev's Party Reform: Coalition Building and Institutional Innovation* (Greenwood Press, Westport, Conn., 1984)

Crankshaw, Edward, *Khrushchev's Russia* (Penguin, Harmondsworth, 1959)

Frankland, Mark, *Khrushchev* (Penguin, Harmondsworth, 1966)

Johnson, Priscilla, and Leo Labedz, *Khrushchev and the Arts, 1962–64* (MIT Press, Cambridge, Mass., 1965)

Grossman, Joan Delaney, 'Khrushchev's Anti-religious Policy and the Campaign of 1954', *Soviet Studies*, 24, 3 (1972–3), pp. 374–86

Khrushchev, Nikita, *Khrushchev Remembers*, includes the 'secret speech', introduced by Edward Crankshaw (Little Brown, London, 1971)

Leonhard, Wolfgang, *The Kremlin since Stalin* (Praeger, New York, 1962)

Linden, Carl A., *Khrushchev and the Soviet Leadership, 1957–1964* (Johns Hopkins University Press, Baltimore, Md, 1966)

McCauley, Martin, *Khrushchev and the Development of Soviet Agriculture: the Debate on the Virgin Lands, 1953–64* (Macmillan, London, 1976)

McCauley, Martin, *Khrushchev and Khrushchevism* (Macmillan, London, 1987)

Medvedev, R., and Z. Medvedev, *Khrushchev: the Years in Power* (Oxford University Press, Oxford, 1977)

Miller, R.F., and F. Feher (eds.), *Khrushchev and the Communist World* (Croom Helm, London, 1984)

Pethybridge, R.W., *A Key to Soviet Politics: the Crisis of the Anti-party Group* (Praeger, New York, 1962)

Pethybridge, R.W., *A History of Post-war Russia* (Allen & Unwin, London, 1966)

Schapiro, L. (ed.), *The USSR and the Future: an Analysis of the New Programme of the CPSU* (Praeger, New York, 1963)

Tatu, M., *Power in the Kremlin: from Khrushchev's Decline to Collective Leadership* (Collins, London, 1969)

Werth, Alexander, *The Khrushchev Phase* (Hale, London, 1961)

Wolfe, B. (ed.), *Khrushchev and Stalin's Ghost* (Greenwood Press, London, 1983)

Chapter five

From Brezhnev to Gorbachev

Corporatism and compromise

Khrushchev was overthrown by an alliance of interests threatened by his erratic behaviour and populist impulses. By contrast, the Brezhnev years were marked by a stability which imperceptibly degenerated into stagnation. An unprecedented degree of security of tenure for office-holders was established, known as the policy of 'stability of cadres', whereby an increasingly stable elite could enjoy the fruits of office. The new leadership consolidated the pattern of post-Stalinist politics developed by Khrushchev but shorn of his populism. The Brezhnev approach was marked by a limited and pragmatic view of social engineering, an end to revolutions from above, continued restraints on mass terror, and a commitment to improved social welfare. The corporatist elements of his rule were reflected in a broadening of consultation with specialist groupings, the political elite, certain powerful interests, represented above all by the ministries, and regional authorities. Brezhnev decisively rejected tempestuous mass mobilizations or the encouragement of mass initiatives from below. The period was the Soviet equivalent of a modest version of the 'Great Society' of the United States. The utopian vision of communism was pushed into the distant future and domesticated to suit the regime's mediocre tastes.

The Brezhnev period was based on a type of social compromise, a social compact or contract. Its fundamental principle was that if the state did not make excessive demands on the population, provided a steadily improving standard of living, and conceded a degree of private autonomy, then the population should not make excessive demands of the state such as calling for political involvement, self-governance, or other aspects of Khrushchev's populism. Victor Zaslavsky characterized the system as a neo-Stalinist compromise based on organized consensus, since the essentials of a modified Stalinism were retained without the personality cult.[1] Breslauer denoted the compromise as welfare-state authoritarianism, marked by a distinctive approach to political participation, social transformation, and material welfare. It was based on a 'contract', not in the classical political philosophy sense of an agreement between bargaining equals, but as a *quid pro quo*.[2] The grand compromise of the Brezhnev period represented a major development, since for the first time the regime established a degree of peace with society. Janos Kadar, the party leader in Hungary installed by the Soviet invasion in 1956, formulated the compromise in 1962 as 'He who is not against us is for us'. Political conformity ensured physical security. However, by the late 1970s the compromise had given rise to complacency, decay, and corruption. The fallacy of the assumption that economic development could be achieved without modifying the social and political system endowed the Brezhnev era with an increasing air of unreality. The bargain was undermined by faltering economic performance and social alienation.

Khrushchev's ousting was not followed by any dramatic changes in policy or personnel. The majority (83 per cent) of the members of Khrushchev's 1961 Central Committee remained on the one elected in 1966, and of the latter 80 per cent were again re-elected in 1971. The provisions of the 1961 party programme for the rotation of offices were repealed at the twenty-third party congress in 1966 and its ambitious targets were ignored. The division of the party into industrial and agricultural wings was abolished in November 1964. Khrushchev's spate of reorganization was now followed by a lengthy period of administrative stability. Almost for the first time since the formation of the Soviet state periods of emergency gave way to settled routines and procedures. The requirements made of officials were known and not too demanding. Officials were able to enjoy the physical security achieved under Khrushchev with the job security established under Brezhnev. The stability of cadres policy, however, endowed the Brezhnev leadership with an increasingly geriatric tone. By 1982 the average age of the Politburo was over 70. Hough notes that the period cannot quite be called petrification, since there remained fairly extensive turnover at intermediate and lower levels. Nevertheless, the political system under Brezhnev became transformed into a relatively stable oligarchy marked by a form of corrupt pluralism as ministries and regions carved out petty fiefdoms.

The consolidation of Brezhnev's personal dominance took several years as the collective leadership established in 1964 died a lingering death. Brezhnev brought in personal associates such as K.U. Chernenko to buttress his position. In May 1977 he replaced Podgorny as President, and in October 1980 the last of the triumvirate that had come to power in 1964, the ailing Kosygin, was replaced as Premier by the octogenarian N. Tikhonov. Elements of the old collective leadership did not altogether disappear, as Suslov retained his stifling guardianship of Soviet ideological orthodoxy. His death in January 1982 presaged the end of the Brezhnev era.

The role of leadership underwent a change. Even more than under Khrushchev the leader's authority was based on his administrative ability and success as an economic manager. The heroic image gave way to a more practical exercise of leadership. In this respect Khrushchev represented a transitional period. His personality and schooling in the shadow of Stalin encouraged elements of charismatic leadership, giving rise to 'harebrained schemes' and lack of consultation with colleagues. Brezhnev acted as a political broker rather than as a charismatic leader. He ruled with his colleagues and did not appeal to the masses over their heads as Stalin and Khrushchev had done.[3] Both, however, shared a belief in the party as the ideal instrument of rule.

Having consolidated his position, Brezhnev enjoyed considerable power over policy. In contrast to Khrushchev's confrontational style, Brezhnev preferred to rule in a consensual manner by coalition-building. Since he never challenged the establishment, the limits to his personal power over policy are unknown. His policy priorities, such as agriculture, defence, and *détente* were for the most part those of the majority. However, his actual method of implementing policy was his own. It amounted to an expensive capitulation to a multitude of demands, placing a heavy strain on financial resources. Brezhnev's policies included many of the major planks of the reformers' economic and social programmes, such as a commitment to consumerism and light industry, high investment in agriculture, the espousal of increased social spending and improved standards of living, scientific management, and legal proceduralism. These policies, moreover, were politically expedient, since they helped consolidate the new leadership in power.

The major economic question of the Brezhnev years was not the general direction of policy, over which there was a large degree of consensus, but the means of achieving the goals. Economic reform figured largely in official debate from 1964 but in practice it came to be stripped of the essential elements of any genuine reform, an increased role for the market and decentralization. The reforms favoured by Brezhnev focused on institutional reorganization and exhortation rather than on structural change. He worked within the terms of the basic Stalinist economic model, marked by a high degree of centralization, tight and detailed planning, the stress on quantitative outputs, the absence of autonomy for lower economic tiers or managers combined with the dominance of the ministries, and the lack of any self-regulating on self-generating mechanisms. Various attempts at economic reform (see Chapter 12) failed to alter the system substantially. More rational economic and administrative policies did expand the scope of consultation with interested groups and specialists before decisions were taken. Nevertheless, the Brezhnev era never capitulated to a technocratic ethos of depoliticized decision-making.

In the 1970s Khrushchev's peaceful coexistence policy was transformed into a period of agreements with the West denoted by the term *détente*. *Détente* had major economic implications as foreign and domestic policy became entwined. The failure of earlier optimism that administrative reorganization could substitute for more thoroughgoing economic reform created a unique situation in the early 1970s. Like American presidents, Brezhnev became increasingly conservative at home while innovative abroad. The strategy of satisfying major economic and political interests through an expanding welfare state has been seen as a Soviet type of corporatism. The main ideological concept of the Brezhnev era was 'developed socialism'. It represented 'a corporate vision of a consensual society, in which conflict would be managed by deals struck between the state and functionally based interests'.[4] The high level of defence expenditure, the enormous drain of agriculture, the highly centralized administrative system, the slow rise in productivity, and the massive and inefficient economic apparatus all placed excessive demands on the system and heavy burdens on the domestic consumer. Brezhnev sought to pay for these 'deals' by improving foreign ties to provide a rapid transfusion of technological know-how, consumer goods, and credits. For the first time the Soviet Union became closely associated with foreign economic and political systems as Brezhnev went abroad to finance the corporatist deal.[5] Instead of engaging in effective economic reforms, which might have threatened the sovereignty of the party and the planners, the viability of the domestic *impasse* was to be maintained by Western assistance. Brezhnev broadened support for *détente* in 1973 by co-opting key figures on to the Politburo; the foreign minister Andrei Gromyko, the defence minister Marshal Grechko (on his death in 1976 replaced by Dmitrii Ustinov), and the head of the KGB, Yuri Andropov.

Brezhnev's ascendancy marked an elite reaction and the triumph of the bureaucracy. It was not a return to Lenin or Stalin but represented a new pattern. Khrushchev's populism was not abandoned but redefined as it became attuned to the managerial approach to political participation. There was little attempt to redefine authority relations as trust in society gave way to trust in cadres. Order and discipline became the watchwords of the regime. The world of politics became very much the preserve of elite groups and their trusted allies, and only routine matters were delegated. Non-political forms of participation were encouraged, but the choice of what was political and what was routine, not surprisingly, was kept firmly in the hands of the leadership.[6]

The conservatism of the Brezhnev years manifested itself in the consolidation of due process rather than in challenges to the entrenched elites. Participation in policy debates within the government was broadened as the authority of specialist groupings rose.[7] Contrary to the long-standing ideal of Soviet policy-making, interest groups began to assert their own 'departmental' interests over those of an 'objective' national interest. The implementation of policy became increasingly difficult. A secure class of *apparatchiki* was consolidated as political officials became relatively autonomous.[8] Appeals over the heads of the elite to the people were discouraged. The dismantling of the joint Party-State Control Committee in December 1965 removed an important channel of popular supervision. Much weaker separate control commissions for the party, state, and people were established. The concept of the state of all the people, and with it the idea of ever-increasing mass involvement which would ultimately lead to the withering away of the state, was played down, though it was revived in a weaker form in the 1970s. Discussion of the theoretical distinction between state and society was discouraged. Lenin's fulminations against bureaucracy in *State and Revolution* and in his later works such as *Better Fewer, but Better* were ignored. The inculcation of civic pride and Soviet nationalism were to compensate for the absence of democratization. The Soviet victory in the Second World War, and Brezhnev's own modest role in that victory, became obsessive themes of the agit-prop apparatus. The period appealed not to a sense of dynamism but to the yearning for stability and savouring of past victories.

There was no full-scale return to Stalinism, but the conservatism of the period was marked by a partial restalinization. In 1965 a movement began for the reconsideration of the two destalinization congresses. On the eve of the twenty-third party congress in 1966 a letter of twenty-five leading intellectuals protested against the creeping rehabilitation of Stalin. The leadership clearly realized that the political costs of rehabilitation would be high, and the issue was left vague at the congress. By 1968 the neo-Stalinists were gaining ground, and sensed victory with the military intervention in Czechoslovakia in August to crush the democratizing reforms introduced by party leader Alexander Dubček. In 1969 the conservatives planned to erect a statue on Stalin's grave and to celebrate his birthday on 21 December with a laudatory article in *Pravda*. Only the warnings of the Polish and Hungarian communist parties, and — it was rumoured — the personal visits of Gomulka and Kadar to argue against rehabilitating Stalin, led to the last-minute cancellation of the article — but too late to prevent it being published in Ulan Bator. Western communist parties would undoubtedly have protested. The episode highlights the international context of destalinization and illustrates what effect association with other socialist countries might have had during Stalin's rise in the 1920s. After 1969 Brezhnev checked those in favour of a complete rehabilitation of Stalin, but the battle between the two forces continued. Brezhnev's rule became increasingly heavy-handed as he permitted a series of trials against dissenters, even though it undermined his own *détente* policy. Social scientists — particularly historians dealing with sensitive episodes in the USSR's past — were subject to increasing restrictions. There were, however, major novelties in style. Greater individual autonomy was permitted as long as it did not pass beyond the bounds and become an open challenge to the regime. The Brezhnevite compromise was reflected in the muted celebration of Stalin's centenary on 21 December 1979, with *Pravda* praising Stalin's leadership during the war but noting the excesses of the personality cult. There was no mention of the purges, and indeed the very existence of the labour camps was officially ignored.

The decline of the regime

The Brezhnev era is now fated to pass into history as the 'era of stagnation', yet it was a time of great successes for the country. The Soviet Union achieved strategic parity with the United States, it rose from being a regional to a global superpower, and the *détente* process culminated in the Conference on Security and Co-operation in Europe in Helsinki in 1975 which ratified the Soviet Union's wartime territorial gains and its status in Eastern Europe. Agricultural output, the standard of living, and housing all improved significantly. Under Brezhnev it appeared that the Soviet polity had finally achieved a rational approach to policy-making and had made peace with its own society. Brezhnev's rule marked a period of tranquillity after decades of turbulence. But, while the stability was based on solid achievements, the fundamental structural reforms needed to deal with the accumulating problems of the economy and society were deferred. Already in 1976 Hough had pointed out that Brezhnev was emulating Louis XIV with his attitude of 'after me the deluge'.[9] Policy conflicts were not resolved but smoothed over, and so the problems were bequeathed to his successors. The administration was increasingly unable to achieve even relatively simple goals. Brezhnev's last years were marked by political stagnation and leadership immobility. It was not clear whether this reflected the top leadership's own particular failings or a more general shortcoming of the system. Was the twenty-year stagnation a personal, social, economic, or political phenomenon, or a combination of all four? Brezhnev was aware of the problems but could find no solution. His gradual political death between 1979 and 1982 in some ways parallels Lenin's between 1921 and 1924, and reflects the general rule that in the absence of constitutional limitations leaders are unlikely voluntarily to resign. Brezhnev loved the trappings of power but reconciled himself to his inability to exercise that power.

The historic failure of the Brezhnev era consisted of several related aspects. The prestige of the Soviet model of development in the world at large was eroded. The apparent inability to move beyond a stiflingly self-satisfied appraisal of political performance and coercive social integration undermined the ideological and moral cohesion of society. This was made all the more acute by the declining vigour of Soviet economic performance. Growth rates fell as capital investments and inputs gave a declining rate of return. The introduction of new technology remained partial and industrial productivity stubbornly refused to increase as rapidly as planned. The sense of stagnation was exacerbated by the decay of Soviet ideology to dogmatic utterance. The Brezhnev period increasingly lived on the political capital accumulated during earlier periods of Soviet power.

The compromises of the social compact between the regime and society were mirrored by a number of unresolved contradictions within the polity itself. Among them was the balance to be struck between traditional party interventionism in economic and social life and the technocratic demand for a depoliticized sphere of administrative competence. Similarly, the balance between the use of material incentives and ideological exhortations to stimulate performance under developed socialism remained unclear. What was to be the relationship between participation from below and orders from above? Economic reform was left hanging in the air as an unfinished item on the agenda for nearly twenty years. Even the direction of change was not clear as in some spheres the market emerged while the economic and planning organs lost few of their powers. Would managers finally be allowed to encroach on the job security of their employees in order to attain economic efficiency? To what extent would the *de facto* corporatist devolution of power to the ministries and a range of monopolies, dubbed by Hough a type of 'feudalistic socialism', be allowed to continue? The social costs of the stability of cadres policy were becoming increasingly glaring. Corruption was rife, with leaders beginning to act as petty princelings within their fiefdoms. The political role of the party was undermined as informal and unofficial contacts between officials increased. Systemic integration was beginning to take place through social rather than political mechanisms.

Brezhnev himself was well aware of the shortcomings and tried to deal with them in so far as he knew how. From 1972, coinciding with the golden period of *détente*, new acts were passed enforcing social discipline and tightening censorship. A sustained campaign was waged to impose labour discipline through legal measures, social pressure, and exhortation. This was accompanied by a renewed stress on social conformity. Brezhnev's twilight years were attended by his increasingly bitter but impotent denunciations of ministerial officials. He was unable to move beyond an analysis which contrasted the failings of individuals with the basic soundness of the system itself.

By the late 1970s it was clear that Brezhnev's compromise would not work. A combination of foreign and domestic problems saw the disintegration of the corporatist deal. What had made corporatism possible in the first instance, *détente*, with which Brezhnev was so closely identified, appeared to be running into terminal difficulties (see pp. 282–3). The level of assistance from abroad was not as extensive as Brezhnev had hoped, and he was forced to consider domestic solutions to economic problems. This necessarily entailed challenging some of the entrenched corporate interests. From 1976 Brezhnev's health rapidly deteriorated and the succession issue became all the more pronounced. The jockeying for power, the building of alliances, and the undermining of opponents began in earnest. Furthermore, the Soviet economy's poor performance after 1978 became critical after a series of poor harvests and harsh winters. The social manifestations of the long stability became increasingly alarming to the leadership. There was a general sense that Soviet society was suffering from an unspecified malaise marked by the rapid growth of official corruption, a perceived decline in labour discipline, and youth rebelliousness.

Under the superficial tranquillity of the Brezhnev integument (to borrow a word favoured by Marx), it increasingly became clear that a new style of politics was being born. A new approach was maturing which proposed alternative solutions to Soviet problems. Leaders since the death of Brezhnev have reflected various facets of this new approach.

One of the major elements in the new Soviet politics was a long-term process which can be labelled Andropovism, the emphasis on enforcing social discipline through authoritarianism and KGB activism. This approach began to be applied from 1969 in Azerbaidzhan. As part of a drive against corruption Geidar Aliev, the former chief of the KGB in the republic, came to head the party organization. In 1972 in Georgia the corrupt Brezhnev protégé V.P. Mzhavanadze was replaced by the republic's MVD chief, Eduard Shevardnadze. These two leaders revived the 'permanent purge', though with a minimum of bloodshed, as key figures were dismissed, some of whom were tried for corruption and other offences. Lacking the ability to introduce substantive political reforms, the political and economic elites in the two republics were purged and purged again. The process revealed the limits of reform under the Brezhnev system, with its emphasis on the quality of cadres within immutable structures.

The anti-corruption campaign became prominent nationally in September 1978, when the involvement of the deputy fishing industry minister, Rytov, in a great 'caviar scandal' led to his disgrace and execution. It became clear that hundreds were involved in the spectacular economic crime of exporting caviar in cans labelled herring. The investigation, led by the KGB, implicated such high party figures as S. Medunov, Brezhnev's associate and first secretary in the Krasnodar region. The 'fish case' strengthened the hand of those in favour of greater discipline and probably prompted the August 1979 Central Committee decree on the need to strengthen law and order. Brezhnev paid lip service to the campaign, but he was well aware that it threatened his own position. Just as with the party purges from 1920, there were attempts to make the anti-corruption campaign a public movement, though it does not appear to have got very far. Solutions were being sought to the problem of informal practices weakening the party's ability to act as the leading force in society. The party's bureaucratic procedures and personnel prerogatives were being undermined by corruption, clientelism, and the abuse of power.

By 1979 Brezhnev's political position had been much weakened under the impact of cumulative policy failures. The year in many ways represents the real end of the Brezhnev era. Stable leadership patterns and policies gave way to a series of major initiatives. We do not know what Brezhnev's personal view was of the invasion of Afghanistan in December 1979, but the leadership as a whole clearly felt that they had little to lose, since *détente* lay in shreds. Similarly, the decision to step up the pressure on nonconformity and ultimately to eliminate dissent was precipitated by the forthcoming 1980 Olympic Games, to be held in Moscow. Brezhnev acquiesced in the law-and-order campaign, and from late 1981 to the anti-corruption campaign, which struck at the very roots of his personal and political power. A politically astute campaign masterminded by Andropov exposed the sordid underside of Brezhnevite stability. Brezhnev's own daughter, Galina, was harassed by the KGB, and his ally Medunov was demoted amidst a political scandal. Brezhnev outlived the 'Brezhnev era' by two to three years. A change in the political terms of reference had taken place that comes about but once a generation.

The new Soviet politics

Andropov: the struggle for discipline

The Brezhnev era began with the slogans of stability and order but ended in intrigues and crisis. The absence of a clear succession mechanism and the jostling for power revived the Kremlinological approach to Soviet politics, the detailed and necessarily elliptical analysis of power struggles within the leadership. It was an extraordinary finale to the Brezhnev years. His death in November 1982 was followed by a rapid sequence of leadership changes. However, contrary to the expectations of some, the long-awaited succession was not accompanied by a new 'time of troubles'. The interregnum was relatively brief and ended peacefully.

A new style in Soviet politics had emerged to accompany the decline of Brezhnev. One of its major expressions was the enhanced role of the KGB, headed since 1967 by Andropov. The basic principle of Andropov's policing was to achieve the maximum effect with the minimum of violence. Although the KGB was restrained by the rules established at Stalin's death and remained under party control, under Brezhnev its influence and prestige had risen. Andropov's accession to the Politburo in 1973 marked the first occasion when a KGB chief had sat on that body since the death of Beria in 1953. From 1974 there were increasing numbers of KGB personnel on the Central Committee, and in February 1981 Brezhnev paid elaborate though not necessarily sincere compliments to the KGB at the twenty-sixth party congress. In May 1982 Andropov replaced the deceased Suslov in the party secretariat in charge of ideological affairs and thus distanced himself from the KGB. As a member of the Politburo and Central Committee Secretariat Andropov was ideally placed to succeed Brezhnev as General Secretary. The interests supporting Andropov are not precisely known, but it is clear that in addition to being the choice of the police and the army he carried the hopes of certain economic reformers. Andropov's bid was aided by the brilliant cultivation of his image, projecting himself as dynamic, and indeed as a man of culture, enjoying jazz, whisky and novels by Jacqueline Susanne. His experience in foreign and domestic politics was stressed, as was his reputation for being uncorrupted and blameless for the failings of the Brezhnev years.

Andropov's appointment was greeted, on the one side, with hopes that some major economic, or even political, reforms would be carried out by someone who appeared a pragmatist and in favour of greater debate; on the other, by those who with much greater vehemence condemned Andropov as the redoubtable police chief and the representative of the rising tide of KGB influence and authoritarianism. In fact Andropov combined these images, as he broke with Brezhnev's consensual politics and established a distinctive style of rule which sought to integrate the reformist and conservative strands in Soviet political life. His short tenure seemed to establish him as a bureaucratic authoritarian reformer rather than a reformer in the sense of a decentralizer and liberalizer. As during the transition to the NEP, economic reforms were to be balanced by political consolidation.

Not surprisingly, given his background, Andropov turned first to an extensive anti-corruption campaign whose roots went back at least to the early 1970s. The programme was presented as coming as much from below as from above. Some of the reputed thousands of letters complaining about corruption were now featured in the press and on television. Early 1983 was marked by a spate of dismissals of corrupt, and usually elderly, officials who had benefited from the lax political and moral atmosphere of the Brezhnev years. Brezhnev's close associate Nikolai Shchelokov was dismissed as police chief and the Ministry of

Internal Affairs (MVD) itself came under the influence of the KGB with the appointment of V.V. Fedorchuk, the former head of the KGB. The campaign succeeded in discrediting the Brezhnev elite and achieved a significant consolidation of the KGB's institutional position. It alone emerged unscathed, and even in the post-Andropov period the KGB escaped with remarkably little criticism.

Along with the battle against corruption came a new emphasis on discipline, both in political and in social life. After 1961 Khrushchev had dropped the stress on discipline, in line with his idea of the state of all the people. Discipline allowed officials broad discretion to exercise their powers, whereas Khrushchev's populism stymied their rights in this respect. The term was revived in 1965 by Brezhnev and signalled the decreased emphasis on changing patterns of authority.[10] Under Andropov the concept of discipline was expanded to become the cornerstone of his rule. Khrushchev-type social controls were intensified, accompanied by the more scientific application of discipline by the government. As a harbinger of the *glasnost*, or openness, to come, the tone of the press changed, with fewer eulogies and more straightforward criticism of shortcomings. The reins of the party over institutional interests were tightened. A programme of labour discipline tried to reverse the habits of a labour force that had become used to slackness, moonlighting, and an easy-going attitude to plan fulfilment. The Andropov period opened amid extraordinary scenes of people being pulled out of bath houses and snatched from queues during working hours and charged with absenteeism. In August 1983 harsh new penalties for labour indiscipline were announced which cut a day off holidays for every day absent from work, penalized late arrival, and introduced the concept of compensation for loss of production resulting from absenteeism. The campaign launched in 1979 to eliminate the vestiges of dissent was continued with great vigour and was extended to the cultural sphere.

Like all new Soviet leaders Andropov had to consolidate his own position through a series of personnel changes in the party and state apparatuses. Brezhnev's close group of colleagues, known as the 'Dnepropetrovsk mafia', was broken up. By June 1983 Andropov felt strong enough to take on the post of President in addition to that of General Secretary and thus continued the Brezhnev tradition of combining both posts. Andropov's changes focused on strengthening his team concerned with economic affairs. Egor Ligachev was brought on to the Politburo and Secretariat, in charge of personnel affairs, and Nikolai Ryzhkov, a former director of Uralmash (one of the largest engineering complexes in the Soviet Union) was appointed to the Secretariat and later replaced Tikhonov as Premier. Both represented the new technocratic bias of appointments, favouring people who had risen through economic lines rather than through party appointments. M.S. Gorbachev, Central Committee secretary in charge of agriculture since 1978, was given overall responsibility for the economy.

Andropov's economic programme did not change Brezhnev's basic priorities, retaining the emphasis on agriculture and accepting the need to maintain the output of high-quality consumer items, but it did try to come to terms with the challenges posed by a mature economy. A limited experiment launched in July

1983 aimed to encourage greater managerial autonomy by reducing the number of instructions from the central ministries. The limited decentralization permitted a greater proportion of profits to remain in the plant, to be used at the discretion of the manager. The aim was to encourage the introduction of new technology and to improve productivity by shedding surplus labour within the framework of an improved planning mechanism. Andropov did not put forward any far-reaching solutions or any major structural changes. The problem remained of introducing real incentives to genuine improvements in labour productivity. This was tackled in July 1983 by a law on labour collectives, promoting a limited form of self-management which extended the scope for organized groups of workers to discuss questions concerning their work. The law encouraged the use of the brigade system whereby groups of workers themselves decide on the allocation of tasks and distribute the pay, though workers were unable to appoint their own leaders or encroach on the rights of managers. It was an attempt to introduce self-policing mechanisms on the shop floor by instilling a greater sense of responsibility. In agriculture there was a renewed emphasis on the 'link' system, now known as the 'collective contract', in which a group of 50–100 agricultural workers are offered a piece of land, equipment, seeds, and so on, and are paid by results. They were allowed to keep any profit on crops produced over and above the plan, although this was hedged in to prevent the emergence of a class of rich peasants (kulaks). The plan's greatest proponent was Gorbachev, who saw greater local initiative and decentralization as an alternative to Brezhnev's wasteful investment strategy for improving agricultural productivity.

In foreign policy Andropov's rule coincided with the second Cold War, following the decline of *détente*, the imposition of martial law in Poland, the continuing war in Afghanistan and the imminent deployment of Cruise and Pershing II missiles in Western Europe to counter the Soviet SS20s. The shooting down of the civilian South Korean airliner KAL 007 in September 1983 saw East-West relations at their lowest for twenty years. The mismanagement of that affair was partly due to Andropov's poor health. He suffered kidney failure in February 1983, and his increasing absence from public view from August 1983 meant that his period tailed off into a period of drift, rather like Brezhnev's, brought to a close by his death on 9 February 1984.

Andropov's period in office signalled a reversion to the tradition of authoritarian reform that had emerged victorious in 1921 over the trend of 'democratic reform' proposed by the various oppositional groupings of that time. His policies were a combination of martial law and economic reform. He began to curtail the expanded privileges of the elite and to limit corruption, and promised to clip the powers of the institutions and interest groups. His rule witnessed an institutional shift of emphasis away from the party to operating other levers of power. This does not mean, however, that he accepted that power should be more diffuse. The increased role of the KGB was designed to buttress, not to supplant, the party's leading role.

Chernenko: the struggle for conformity

The remarkable feature of Chernenko's rule is that he was chosen to be General Secretary at all. Aged 73 and suffering from emphysema, his appointment at a time when the country faced critical challenges seemed a singularly short-sighted act by his peers. They appeared more intent on saving themselves than the country, a desperate attempt to hold back the tide of biological decay and political change. Chernenko's accession can be seen in terms of a backlash of the party old guard, threatened by the Andropov discipline and anti-corruption campaigns and worried about his economic reforms. They were forced, however, to concede certain powers to the representative of the new politics, Gorbachev, who acted as an unofficial deputy General Secretary.

Chernenko's appointment revealed the strength of the Brezhnev approach in Soviet politics. Brezhnevism cannot be simply equated with the resistance of entrenched office-holders to the encroachments of political and economic reform. The Brezhnev system satisfied a range of concerns, including officialdom, and gave them a powerful vested interest in the maintenance of a relatively *laissez-faire* approach to social and political management. Reform not only challenges the privileges of the powerful but exposes the thousand little stratagems devised by individuals to survive under Soviet conditions. Overt dissent was crushed under Brezhnev, only to reappear in a myriad acts of social nonconformity. The new Soviet politics associated with Andropov threatened not only the excessive privileges of the powerful but also the tiny exigencies of the weak.

Chernenko's rise under Brezhnev's patronage revealed the worst features of Brezhnevite political cronyism. Chernenko continued the anti-corruption drive but deflected some of its force to social deviance and nonconformity, and relieved the pressure against political corruption. Coming to power at a time when relations with the West were extremely poor, he concentrated on imposing ideological conformity through such petty acts as banning the import of foreign pop music and unlicensed videos. His thought was imbued with notions of ideological pollution and noxious Western influences that harked back to the worst features of the Cold War under Stalin. Chernenko became the guardian of dogma: 'There are some truths that are not subject to revision, problems that were solved long ago and once and for all. The basic principles of dialectical materialism cannot be forgotten.'[11] The second Cold War as far as Soviet domestic policies were concerned was indeed a farcical re-run of the tragedy of the first. Only Gorbachev's intervention prevented Chernenko restoring the name of Stalingrad to the city that Khrushchev had renamed Volvograd. He did, however, make some gestures towards reviving *détente* and obtaining an arms control agreement. An article by Chernenko in September 1981 insisted on the need to avoid antagonizing any social groups and to obviate social tension.[12] This blast against the politics of discipline, judging from his performance in office, appears to have been an attempt to establish his 'liberal' credentials in opposition to Andropov in the struggle for power. Chernenko's assumption of the presidency together with the post of party

General Secretary may have given him the illusion of great power but it certainly did not endow his leadership with authority. There is insufficient evidence to establish the direction that Chernenko might have taken, given better health and a longer period in office. It is probable that he would have tried to combine the Brezhnev approach with some of Andropov's initiatives in the economic and social spheres. His long-expected death on 10 March 1985 brought an end to the interregnum between Brezhnev and Gorbachev.

Gorbachev: the struggle for change

While Chernenko was clearly an interim leader, the selection of Gorbachev as General Secretary looks set to break the mould of Soviet politics and establish the tone of Soviet leadership for the rest of the century. Economic and political factors propelled Gorbachev to challenge the social contract policies of the neo-Stalinist compromise in order to stimulate the economy and to tackle the country's grave social problems. Gorbachev argued that the later Brezhnev years were marked by a 'pre-crisis' which would have become a full-scale crisis had timely action not been taken. Brezhnev's comfortable corporatism was rejected as the powers of the ministries, republican party bosses, and other vested interests, were challenged. In addition Gorbachev rejected Andropov's authoritarian approach to reform and returned to the traditions, so sharply truncated in 1921, of democratic and even liberal reform. Gorbachev joins the long Russian tradition of reformers from above, but at the same time the novelty of his reforms is that they offer some real scope for initiative from below.

Mikhail Sergeevich Gorbachev was born of peasant stock on 2 March 1931 in the agricultural Stavropol region (*krai*) of south Russia. He graduated with a degree in law from Moscow State University in 1955, and in 1967 he passed a correspondence degree in agronomy. At Moscow University he met his wife, Raisa, who holds a doctorate in Marxist-Leninist philosophy. He spent most of his early career in his native Stavropol *krai*, rising from Komsomol chief to the leadership. His career was that of a typical party official. It was advanced by his association with Fedor Kulakov, the first secretary of the party in the region, and with Suslov, the guardian of Brezhnevite ideological orthodoxy, who acted as Gorbachev's patrons. When Kulakov was appointed minister of agriculture in 1970 Gorbachev replaced him and the next year became a full member of the Central Committee. He achieved significant successes with his policies of agricultural innovation and support for greater individual initiative. On Kulakov's death in 1978 Gorbachev, at the youthful age of 47, replaced him as Central Committee secretary responsible for agriculture. Gorbachev's reputation emerged remarkably unscathed from the series of poor harvests from 1979; he rose to become a candidate member of the Politburo in November 1979 and a full member in October 1980. Promoted by Andropov, and in effect sharing power with Chernenko, his election as General Secretary was nevertheless no foregone conclusion. He was opposed by the Brezhnevites V. Grishin and G. Romanov, and a large number of the Central Committee apparently had misgivings. His support from the relatively conservative E. Ligachev, A. Gromyko, and M. Solomentsev was to limit his freedom of manoeuvre in later years. On coming to power in March 1985 Gorbachev was 54 years old, the youngest Soviet leader since Malenkov (51 in 1953). His experience was mostly of the post-war era, and for him the traumas of collectivization, purges, and war were history. Comparisons were drawn between him and President Kennedy, sharpened by persistent rumours about Gorbachev's personal safety.

Gorbachev came to power when there was an unprecedented desire for change in the Soviet Union. There was a sense that the country faced a mounting and intolerable 'lack of order' (*bezporyadok*), as manifested by alcoholism, corruption, and less effective party and police mechanisms. The political climate was more conducive to reform than at any time since the early years of Khrushchev. And it appeared that Gorbachev was the man to face up to these challenges. His relative youth, his education, and his lively, enquiring mind all marked him out from his predecessors. The accession of Gorbachev as a reform-minded leader has seemed to confirm the hopes of those, like Roy Medvedev, who have long argued that the most realistic perspective for change in the Soviet Union would come from within the system itself, a new leader supported by reforming officials and sections of society.[13] Gorbachev is not alone in demanding change, but he has been able to stamp his personality on the reform coalition to a degree that would make it fair to talk of a Gorbachev reform process. Gorbachev has revived the revisionist approach of inner-party renewal last practised in the USSR by Khrushchev and thought to have died with the crushing of the Prague Spring in Czechoslovakia in 1968.

He signalled his intentions straight away at the April 1985 plenum of the Central Committee, which advanced a critique of 'Brezhnevism' that was to become the hallmark of his rule. The launching of the policies of restructuring (*perestroika*) of the economy, of acceleration (*uskorenie*) and of *glasnost* all indicated the advent of a serious reformer. The Andropov leadership shared the belief in the need for economic reform, but this was to be based on greater discipline. Under Gorbachev a realization increasingly came to the fore that the technocratic approach was inadequate and that economic reform could not be achieved by administrative measures alone. The reform process would have to tackle the roots of the problem by 'democratization'. A link was forged between further economic development and political modernization. Otherwise the Soviet Union was in danger of sinking in the world economy to the economic status of a Third World primary materials exporter. No longer were the legacy of Tsarist backwardness and the destruction of the Second World War convincing excuses to explain the USSR's continued relative backwardness in most spheres other than the military. Gorbachev argued that *perestroika* was placed on the agenda by the entire course of social development, and minor repairs were no longer enough. His maiden speech to the Central Committee in April 1985 stressed the objective need for reform, since there was 'no other way'.

Gorbachev's ambitious early programme was geared to the year 2000, by which time he hoped the economy would have been successfully restructured and society democratized. He defined *perestroika* at the twenty-seventh congress of the CPSU as not only raising the rate of economic growth but as a qualitatively different type of growth: the intensification of production on the basis of scientific and technological progress, the structural reorganization of the economy, improved management, and better incentives for labour. He had no illusions about the magnitude of the task. The nineteenth party conference in June-July 1988 accepted his argument that the entire system needed overhauling. In a break with the Andropov approach political *glasnost*, criticism, and democracy were seen as essential facets of economic *perestroika*. At the conference Gorbachev called for the creation of a 'society of socialist self-management by the people, of profound and consistent democracy, in which the rule of law, openness, and *glasnost* will prevail'. He has also talked about the need for a 'psychological restructuring' entailing a spiritual reformation away from Stalinist authoritarianism towards individual initiative and the 'human factor', operating within effective structures. *Glasnost* was designed to permit the greater democratization of society and the extension of socialist self-management and popular initiative. As Gorbachev insisted at the June 1987 Central Committee plenum, the command and administrative approach to managing society put a brake on development and could be remedied only by promoting democracy.

The leadership changes of the early 1980s were remarkable for the almost complete absence, at least explicitly, of the issue of destalinization. With the leadership question settled by the accession of Gorbachev, *glasnost* permitted a re-examination not only of the person of Stalin but of the policies as well. This was no longer part of a destalinization campaign from above but was accompanied by a reappraisal from below. At the Writers' Union congress of the Russian republic in December 1985 Evgenii Evtushenko returned to the theme that had made him famous under Khrushchev: the problem of Stalin's crimes. The debate was taken up in literary journals, and once again the 'blank pages' in Soviet history were examined. The film *Repentance* by Tengiz Abuladze exposed the character of Stalin, Beria, and the Stalinist period. Anatolii Rybakov's *Children of the Arbat* painfully revealed the reality of life and suffering in the 1930s. In February 1988 the Supreme Court cleared Bukharin of criminal charges and in July 1988 he was at last rehabilitated, signalling that the NEP alternative to war communist policies could now be openly discussed. Not only the human but also the economic costs of Stalin's policies were now exposed. Typical of the falsity of many of the alleged achievements of Stalinism was the revelation that the prodigious, and much emulated, achievement of the Donbas miner Alexei Stakhanov in lifting 102 tonnes of coal in a single shift in 1935 had been rigged from start to finish. The nineteenth party conference at last agreed to the proposal, raised by Khrushchev at the twenty-second party congress in 1962, to erect a memorial to Stalin's victims. The scale of rehabilitations is an accurate indicator of the degree to which party policy has changed, but it has nothing to do with redressing injustice until law exists independently of party policy. The third wave of destalinization, where Stalin's hangmen are called to account, is only just beginning. Destalinization entails a political challenge for the Soviet regime to face up to its own past. The controversy over Stalin's legacy continues.

In certain respects Gorbachev's reform programme represents a return to the themes of Khrushchev's rule, such as the need for popular initiative, the stress on a return to original Leninism, an understanding of the past, and a new approach to economic and political organization. However, whereas Khrushchev's reforms were predicated on overcoming the baleful consequences of the doings of one man, Joseph Stalin, *perestroika* suggests that the problems go much deeper. The sources of Brezhnevite 'stagnation' now also have to be explained. The problems and achievements of Gorbachev's struggle for change will be dealt with in the following chapters.

Notes

1 V. Zaslavsky, *The Neo-Stalinist State: Class, Ethnicity and Consensus in Soviet Society* (Harvester Press, Brighton, 1982), pp. vii–x.
2 G.W. Breslauer, 'On the Adaptability of Soviet Welfare-State Authoritarianism', in Hoffmann and Laird (eds.), *The Soviet Polity*, p. 221.
3 Breslauer, *Khrushchev and Brezhnev as Leaders*, pp. 12–13.
4 V. Bunce, 'The Political Economy of the Brezhnev Era', *British Journal of Political Science*, 13 (April 1983), p. 134.
5 ibid., p. 145.
6 G.W. Breslauer, 'Khrushchev Reconsidered', *Problems of Communism*, 25, 5 (September-October 1976), p. 30.
7 J. Hough, 'The Brezhnev Era', *Problems of Communism*, 25, 2 (March-April 1976), p. 10.
8 Breslauer, 'Khrushchev Reconsidered', pp. 31–2.
9 Hough, 'The Brezhnev Era', p. 17.
10 Breslauer, 'Khrushchev Reconsidered', in S.F. Cohen *et al.* (eds.), *The Soviet Union since Stalin* (Macmillan, London, 1980), p. 60.
11 Speech to the June 1983 plenum of the Central Committee. For a discussion see D. Sturman, 'Chernenko and Andropov: Ideological Perspectives', *Survey*, 28, 1 (spring 1984), p. 17.
12 W.G. Hyland, 'Kto Kogo in the Kremlin', *Problems of Communism*, 31, 1 (January-February 1982), p. 24.
13 The perspective of 'evolution from above' was discussed by G.W. Breslauer, *Five Images of the Soviet Future: a Critical Review and Synthesis* (Berkeley, Institute of International Studies, University of California, 1978), p. 75.

Key texts

Bialer, Seweryn, *Stalin's Successors: Leadership, Stability and Change in the Soviet Union* (Cambridge University Press, Cambridge, 1980)
Brown, A. and M. Kaser (eds.), *Soviet Policy for the 1980s* (Macmillan, London, 1982)
Bunce, V., 'The Political Economy of the Brezhnev Era', *British Journal of Political Science*, 13 (April 1983), pp. 129–58

McCauley, Martin (ed.), *The Soviet Union after Brezhnev* (Heinemann, London, 1983)
McCauley, Martin (ed.), *The Soviet Union under Gorbachev* (Macmillan, London, 1987)
Shtromas, A., *The Soviet Union in the 1980s* (Wheatsheaf, Brighton, 1987)
Veen, Hans-Joachim (ed.), *From Brezhnev to Gorbachev: Domestic Affairs and Soviet Foreign Policy*, (Berg, Leamington Spa, 1987)

Select bibliography

Brezhnev

Brown, A., and M. Kaser (eds.), *The Soviet Union since the Fall of Khrushchev*, 2nd edn (Macmillan, London, 1982)
Brzezinski, Z., 'The Soviet Political System: Transformation or Degeneration', *Problems of Communism*, 15, 1 (January-February 1966), pp. 1–15; also in Z. Brzezinski (ed.), *Dilemmas of Change in Soviet Politics* (Columbia University Press, New York and London, 1969), pp. 1–34.
Bunce, V., and J. Echols, 'Soviet Politics in the Brezhnev Era: "Pluralism" or "Corporatism"?', in D. Kelley (ed.), *Soviet Politics in the Brezhnev Era* (Praeger, New York, 1980)
Evans, A., 'Developed Socialism in Soviet Ideology', *Soviet Studies*, 26, 3 (July 1977), pp. 409–28
Hazan, Baruch A., *From Brezhnev to Gorbachev: Infighting in the Kremlin* (Westview, Boulder, Colo., 1987)
Hough, J., 'The Soviet Union: Petrification or Pluralism?', *Problems of Communism*, 21, 2 (March-April 1972), pp. 25–45
Hough, J., 'The Brezhnev Era: the Man and the System', in *Problems of Communism*, 25, 2 (March-April 1976), pp. 1–17
Millar, James R., 'The Little Deal: Brezhnev's Contribution to Acquisitive Socialism, *Slavic Review* (winter 1985), pp. 694–706
Strong, J.W. (ed.), *The Soviet Union under Brezhnev and Kosygin* (Van Nostrand Reinhold, New York, 1971)

Andropov and Chernenko

Andropov, Yuri V., *Speeches and Writings*, 2nd edn (Pergamon, Oxford, 1983)
Beichman, Arnold, and Mikhail S. Bernshtam, *Andropov: New Challenge to the West* (Stein & Day, New York, 1983)
Besancon, Alain, 'Andropov and his Soviet Union', *Policy Review* (summer 1983)
Brown, Archie, 'Andropov: Discipline and Reform', *Problems of Communism*, 32, 1 (January-February 1983), pp. 18–31
Ebon, Martin, *The Andropov File* (McGraw-Hill, New York, 1983)
Elliot, Iain, 'Andropov Scrutinised' *Survey*, 28, 1 (spring 1984), pp. 61–67
Goodman, Elliot, R., 'The Brezhnev-Andropov Legacy', *Survey*, 28, 2 (1984)
Heller, M., 'Andropov: a Retrospective View', *Survey*, 28, 1 (spring 1984), pp. 46–60
Hough, J.F., 'Andropov's First Year', *Problems of Communism*, 32, 6 (November-December 1983), pp. 49–64
Medvedev, Zhores, *Andropov: his Life and Death* (Blackwell, Oxford, 1984)
Meissner, Boris, 'The Transition in the Kremlin' *Problems of Communism*, 32, 1 (January-February 1983), pp. 8–17
Odom, W.E., 'Choice and Change in Soviet Politics', *Problems of Communism*, 32, 3 (May-June 1983), pp. 1–21
Steele, J., and E. Abraham, *Andropov in Power* (Blackwell, Oxford, 1983)

Sturman, D., 'Chernenko and Andropov: Ideological Perspectives', *Survey*, 28, 1 (spring 1984), pp. 9–21

Zlotnik, Mark D., 'Chernenko's Platform', *Problems of Communism*, 31, 6 (November-December 1982), pp. 70–80

Zlotnik, Mark D., 'Chernenko Succeeds', *Problems of Communism*, 33, 2 (March-April 1984), pp. 17–31

Gorbachev

Brown, Archie, 'Gorbachev: New Man in the Kremlin', *Problems of Communism*, 34, 3 (May-June 1985), pp. 1–23

Brown, Archie, 'Gorbachev and the Reform of the Soviet System', *Political Quarterly*, 58, 2 (April-June 1987), pp. 139–51

Dellenbrant, Jan Ake and Ronald J. Hill (eds.), *Gorbachev and Perestroika* (Elgar Publishing, Aldershot, 1989)

Dyker, David A. (ed.), *The Soviet Union under Gorbachev: Prospects for Reform* (Croom Helm, London, 1987)

Feher, Ferenc, and Andrew Arato, *Gorbachev* (Polity, Oxford, 1988)

Friedberg, Maurice, *Soviet Society under Gorbachev: Current Trends and the Prospect for Reform* (Sharpe, London, 1988)

Gorbachev, M.S., *Perestroika: New Thinking for our Country and the World* (Collins, London, 1987)

Gunlicks, A.B. and J.D. Treadway (eds.) *The Soviet Union under Gorbachev: Assessing the First Year* (Praeger, New York and London, 1987)

Gustafson, Thane and Dawn Mann, 'Gorbachev's First Year; Building Power and Authority', *Problems of Communism*, 35, 3 (May–June 1986), pp. 1–19

Gustafson, Thane and Dawn Mann, 'Gorbachev's Next Gamble', *Problems of Communism*, 36, 4 (July–August 1987), pp. 1–20

Hazan, Baruch A., *From Brezhnev to Gorbachev: Infighting in the Kremlin* (Westview/Praeger, Boulder, Colo., 1987)

Hough, J.F., 'Gorbachev's Strategy', *Foreign Affairs*, 64, 1 (fall 1985), pp. 33–55

Hough, Jerry H., 'Gorbachev Consolidating Power', *Problems of Communism*, 36, 4 (July–August 1987), pp. 21–43

Kagarlitsky, Boris, 'The Intelligentsia and the Changes', *New Left Review*, 164 (July–August 1987), pp. 5–26

Kagarlitsky, Boris, '*Perestroika*: The Dialectics of Change', *New Left Review*, 169 (May–June 1988), pp. 63–83

Lewin, Moshe, *The Gorbachev Phenomenon: a Historical Interpretation* (University of California Press, Berkeley, 1988)

McCauley, Martin (ed.), *The Soviet Union Under Gorbachev* (Macmillan, London, 1987)

Mandel, Ernest, *Beyond Perestroika* (Verso, London, 1988)

Medvedev, Zhores, *Gorbachev* (Blackwell, Oxford, 1986)

Miller, R.F., *et al.* (eds.), *Gorbachev at the Helm: a new Era in Soviet Politics* (Croom Helm, London, 1987)

Ploss, S.L., 'A New Soviet Era?', *Foreign Policy*, 62 (spring 1986), pp. 46–60

Sakwa, Richard, *Gorbachev and His Reforms* (Philip Allan, Oxford, 1990)

Schmidt-Hauer, Christian, *Gorbachev: the Path to Power* (Tauris, London, 1986)

Simes, Dimitri K., 'Gorbachev: a New Foreign Policy?', *Foreign Affairs*, 65, 3 (1987), pp. 477–500

Weickhardt, G.G., 'Gorbachev's Record on Economic Reform', *Soviet Union/Union Soviétique*, 12, 3 (1985), pp. 251–76

Chapter six

The structure of power

The Soviet polity is made up of a unique blend of institutions and procedures which have been adopted in about sixteen countries that proclaim themselves to be Marxist-Leninist states on the road to communism. There are three interlocking hierarchies of power: the Communist Party of the Soviet Union; the state structure of soviets, crowned by the Supreme Soviet; and the governmental system of ministries, headed by the Council of Ministers. The state and governmental hierarchies are two aspects of what is conventionally termed the state system, but for clarity they have been separated throughout this book. They operate in a markedly different way from the practices of liberal democracies but confusion was often caused by the use of similar terminology. Hence, for convenience, the Chair of the Praesidium of the Supreme Soviet was often called 'President', and the Chair of the Council of Ministers is called 'Prime Minister', though until 1988 neither office officially existed in the Soviet Union. The nineteenth party conference in 1988 opened the way for the appointment of a powerful new executive presidency. The apparent clarity of the threefold division between party, state, and government in fact covers a highly complex power structure in which a series of institutions compete for influence.

The military and the security police play an important part in Soviet politics, reflecting the relative youth of this power born in revolution less than a century ago, while the judiciary has traditionally played a smaller role than in liberal democratic states. The party, the economic apparatus, the secret police, the military, the economic and political bureaucracy, and the leaders of the various Soviet republics make up a delicate balance of power. These forces act directly and indirectly to constrain the powers of the central leadership. At various times one or other of them, either singly or in concert, has dominated. Under Lenin the party apparatus presided over the soviets but never really gained a hold over the secret police or the vast economic commissariats spawned by war communist centralization. Under Stalin the major coalition was the economic apparatus, the security police, and his personal apparatus of power in the Kremlin. With Khrushchev the party once again dominated, but its rule was tempered by an element of populism and headstrong leadership. Brezhnev's rule saw the emergence of a broad coalition comprised of the party apparatus, the administrative bureaucracy, the economic ministries, the military, and increasingly the security apparatus. During Andropov's brief ascendancy the security apparatus was more prominent than at any time since the death of Stalin. Under Gorbachev the military's influence has waned and specialist groupings have been encouraged within the context of revived political activism inspired by the leader. These shifts have given Soviet politics its dynamism and allowed each successive leader to stamp a period with his name. Overall, it must be stressed, it is the communist party that acts as the source of legitimacy but within the context of a fragmented politics. The fundamental political relationship between the power centre and the mass of the population was subject only to slow modification as the society and the system matured. Society was unable to establish direct legal or political restraints on the exercise of power.

Constitutions and power

The Soviet constitution says little about the relationship between the party, soviet, and governmental hierarchies. Neither does it give precise details on the relative powers of the centre and the republics in the federal framework of the USSR. Soviet constitutionalism differs significantly from that in the West. The aim of the four Soviet constitutions, promulgated in 1918, 1924, 1936, and 1977 (amended in 1988), is less to define the functions of political institutions or the relations between them than to act as a general ideological statement. They reflect the Marxist-Leninist approach to popular sovereignty and the scope of politics in socialist society. The rights granted to individuals are limited by catch-all general phrases such as the 'interests of the people' and are defined primarily in social rather than in political terms. The constitutions reflect the collectivism of the Soviet system in stressing that the interests of the individual are subordinate to those of society as a whole, and in the emphasis that individual rights are inseparable from duties. Until the creation of the Committee of Constitutional Review in 1989 there was no higher court of appeal against infringements of constitutional rights. The constitutions have only hesitantly moved away from the view that the need for 'politics' itself has been transcended, with no contestatory political parties, hence no open competition for power, and no overt conflicting social or national interests. For long periods the tautology that the state can do no wrong in a people's state dominated.

Up to 1989 there was no formal separation of powers either between the three main structures of power or within the soviets, where executive and legislative powers were merged. The American constitutional concept of checks and balances is alien to Soviet practice and there is little of the Madisonian attempt to restrain the exercise of power. The Supreme Soviet itself, the highest state body according to the constitution, has no independent legislative powers and its political role is dependent on decisions taken elsewhere. The constitution does not set limits to state power and above all there is little attempt to define the powers of the communist party. The operation of the political system has always been more a matter of convention and informal practices than the strict definition of prerogatives. Power in the Soviet Union is not defined and is therefore not limited, although informal restraints, as in Britain, have increasingly come to the fore.

The Soviet constitution can be changed by the Supreme Soviet much more easily than Americans can change the US constitution. Each of the four to date has marked a new stage in the development of the Soviet political system: the foundation of the Soviet republic in 1918; the creation of the USSR in 1924; the achievement of socialism in 1936; and the onset of developed socialism in 1977. They reflect the regime's own assessment of the achievements and perspectives of the system at the time. They ratify the gains and establish a programme of further developments rather than give details of the operation of the political system. They have a declaratory rather than a defining function.

Constitutionalism is foreign to the Russian political tradition. The Decembrists in 1825 failed to achieve the creation of a constitutional system, and no popular movement ever managed to force Tsarism to concede limits to its authority or to ensure the rights of citizens. Only after the revolution of 1905 was a Fundamental Law (constitution) adopted in 1906, but Nicholas II insisted that Russia was still an autocracy. The powers of the State Duma (parliament) were limited and ministers remained responsible solely to the autocrat.

The first Soviet constitution of 10 July 1918 established the pattern for the future. It summed up the experience of the first eight months of Bolshevik power but left the details of government uncertain. The document reflected commune democratic concepts of state organization: no separation of powers; the fusion of executive and legislative functions; a bias in favour of working people; the right of recall of deputies to soviets; and the use of open rather than secret voting. The first part consisted of a 'Declaration of the Rights of Toiling and Exploited Peoples', rather like the French Declaration of the Rights of Man. The communist party was not mentioned and its role was unclear. The constitution applied the principles of the dictatorship of the proletariat in its open class discrimination against property owners and in the differential voting for workers and peasants. There was no attempt to establish a framework for the defence of individual rights against the state. Laws were to serve the interests of class justice. The absence of a delineation of functions led the Democratic Centralist group within the Bolshevik party from late 1918 to demand revisions to the constitution to define the powers of the party, soviets, and other bodies. The group alleged that decisions were being taken by small coteries of people in *ad hoc* groups. The Central Executive Committee (CEC) of the soviets was nominally the highest body, yet it was being undermined by the Council of People's Commissars (*Sovnarkom*), the forerunner of today's Council of Ministers, which was permitted at a time of war to enact 'measures of extreme urgency' without reference to the CEC, to which it was constitutionally responsible. Once again, as in the last years of the autocracy, the opposition demanded a responsible ministry. The defeat of the group in early 1921 and its dissolution marked the end of attempts to define the powers of the constituent elements of the Soviet state. The tradition of constitutional chaos was thus perpetuated.

In January 1924 the second Soviet constitution was adopted to mark the creation of the Union of Soviet Socialist Republics (USSR) in December 1922. With victory in the civil war and Soviet power consolidated over the greater part of the old Tsarist empire, the shape of the new multinational Soviet state had to be decided. The Bolsheviks had always proclaimed the rights of nations to self-determination (see Chapter 14). However, from the first there were powerful pressures in favour of extreme centralization, and the independence of Russia's peoples was made conditional on the class struggle. The 1924 constitution defined the Soviet system as federal yet said little about the highly centralized power system in the country, dominated by the unitary communist party. It allowed each republic to maintain the trappings of nationhood and permitted some variations in legal practices but, as with the internal governmental arrangements, the precise rights of the national republics were left vague. The Central Executive Committee elected at a Congress of Soviets was now to be bicameral. One chamber was to be elected on the basis of population representation alone; the other was to be based on representation from each nationality group in the USSR. This concession to the nationalities reflected the belief that the revolution would soon spread to other countries which would be incorporated into the Soviet constitutional framework.

The so-called 'Stalin constitution' of 5 December 1936 remained in force for over forty years. It consolidated what had been achieved rather than striking out in new directions: its ethos was conservative rather than revolutionary. A commission had been established in February 1935, in the hiatus between the assassination of Kirov in December 1934 and the onset of the great terror in 1936, to draft a new constitution which would register the progress made since the industrialization and collectivization drives of 1929, and which through its humanistic and progressive principles would stand in stark contrast to the fascist order that had come to power in Germany in 1933. Bukharin played a leading role in drafting the document and sought to enshrine legality to restrain the Stalinist terror. For the first time the constitution mentioned the party as uniting the 'leading forces' in the country, but its role remained vague. The constitution registered that socialism had been built in the USSR and that antagonistic classes had been eliminated. Private property had been abolished, in particular that in land, and a socialist economic system had been established. The constitution was extremely democratic in its provisions, although Bukharin knew better than anyone that no legal recourse was available to ensure their fulfilment. The whole population was enfranchised and the legal distinctions between workers and peasants were dropped. The old system of elections through the pyramidal structure of the soviets gave way to universal, direct, equal, and secret voting for delegates to the new bicameral Supreme Soviet. The drafting commission claimed to be adapting the Soviet political structure to the successful construction of the socialist base. However, political relations were marked by a thoroughly statist conception of socialism, and the absence of legal guarantees for citizens against the state reached its tragic *dénouement* in the purges.

The 1977 'Brezhnev constitution' underwent a long period of gestation. The idea of a new constitution had first been mooted in 1959 to reflect the state of all the people and Khrushchev's ambitious plans for the 'full-scale construction of communism'. Brezhnev's proposal for a new constitution to mark the fiftieth anniversary of the October revolution in 1967 fell by the wayside, and only in 1972 was the project taken up. In June 1977 a draft appeared, followed by a four-month nationwide discussion (see p. 169). The campaign was a typical Brezhnev exercise to demonstrate the legitimacy of the new constitution and its provisions.

The new constitution's long preparation indicated disagreements over the formulation of ideological and institutional programmes, yet when it appeared it did not differ in any fundamental way from the 1936 constitution. The introduction once again summed up the stage through which the country was passing. It called the Soviet Union a 'developed socialist society' and argued that a 'state of all the people' had been created, with no antagonistic classes. There was more on the role of the party (Article 6), but as usual the details of governmental relationships were kept vague and did not place any constitutional limitations on the party's freedom. The constitution made explicit the party's leading role in Soviet society and therefore implied less of an emphasis on Khrushchev's long-term aim of creating a self-managed society. The concept of the withering away of the state was quietly shelved. The state, and with it political conformity, was rehabilitated. A new section discussed foreign policy and combined the stress on peaceful coexistence with declarations of support for wars of national liberation. There was a slight shift of power from the constituent republics to the centre. This constitution, as with the three others, once again illustrated that while constitutions are ubiquitous in communist states, the actual operation of these systems is more often governed by an 'unwritten constitution' of informal rules and convention than by statute.

The nineteenth party conference in June-July 1988 vowed to remedy the unclear definition of powers and confused competencies. Several constitutional amendments were adopted in December 1988 that sought to make the Soviet Union a 'socialist legal state' where rights would be protected and authority defined. Constitutional reform lies at the heart of Gorbachev's long-term goal of making the USSR a modern democratic socialist state.

The Congress of People's Deputies and the Supreme Soviet

According to the constitution the soviets (literally meaning 'councils') are formally sovereign, yet their role is severely constrained by the powers of the two other networks of power, the party and the ministries. The system is now in a state of considerable flux as the Gorbachevite reformers try to revive the soviets.

The Supreme Soviet was created by the 1936 constitution and is the highest body of state power in the USSR. It is the legislative authority, and as a representative institution endows the system with formal legitimacy. Until 1989 the Supreme Soviet was made up of two chambers with an equal number of deputies (750) in each. The Soviet of the Union was elected directly from the people by universal suffrage, with about 300,000 electors per constituency. The Soviet of

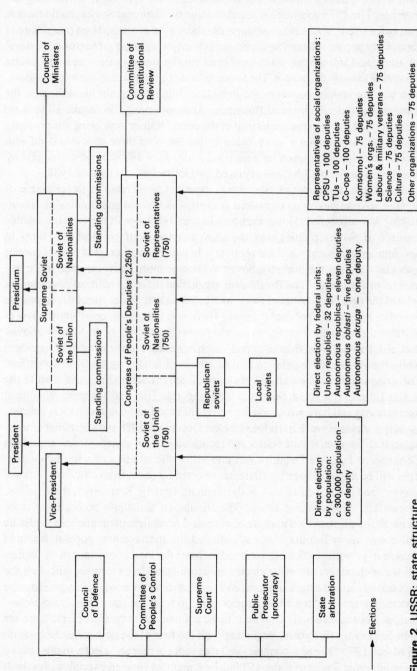

Figure 2 USSR: state structure

Council of Ministers

Committee of Constitutional Review

Presidium

Supreme Soviet

Soviet of the Union

Soviet of Nationalities

Standing commissions

Soviet of Representatives (750)

Soviet of Nationalities (750)

Soviet of the Union (750)

Congress of People's Deputies (2,250)

Standing commissions

President

Vice-President

Council of Defence

Committee of People's Control

Supreme Court

Public Prosecutor (procuracy)

State arbitration

Republican soviets

Local soviets

Representatives of social organizations:
CPSU – 100 deputies
TUs – 100 deputies
Co-ops – 100 deputies
Komsomol – 75 deputies
Women's orgs. – 75 deputies
Labour & military veterans – 75 deputies
Science – 75 deputies
Culture – 75 deputies
Other organizations – 75 deputies

Direct election by federal units:
Union republics – 32 deputies
Autonomous republics – eleven deputies
Autonomous *oblasti* – five deputies
Autonomous *okruga* – one deputy

Direct election by population:
c. 300,000 population – one deputy

⟶ Elections

Nationalities was elected from the various federal and national units with a fixed number of deputies from each. The two chambers had equal rights and usually met together. The 1977 constitution stipulated that the Supreme Soviet should meet at least twice a year, and between sessions its affairs were conducted by a praesidium of about forty people. Plenary sessions were usually very short, of two or three days' duration, and infrequent, often no more than the stated twice a year, including December to ratify the budget. The Supreme Soviet elected a chair for its praesidium, who was commonly known as the President. Mikhail Kalinin filled the post for many years under Stalin, and Brezhnev, Andropov, and Chernenko all took on the post in addition to the leadership of the party. Rather than being simply party leaders, the assumption of the presidency for the latter three endowed them with greater prestige, if not greater authority. From June 1985 the post was held by Andrei Gromyko until he was replaced by Gorbachev in October 1988.

The role of the Supreme Soviet was expected to increase as the principle of popular sovereignty in a communist context was revived and political decision-making was broadened. However, up to the mid-1980s one of the most remarkable features of Soviet politics was the slow adaptation of political structures to developments in society and the economy. In particular, there was no evidence of a secular trend for the Supreme Soviet to become more active, to meet more frequently or for longer. The Brezhnevite stagnation in Soviet political development refuted the optimistic hopes of those who believed that Soviet social developments would be reflected in political changes. There was little evidence of an 'iron law of pluralism' and on the contrary on several counts the activity of the Supreme Soviet declined, such as in the frequency and length of sessions or the number of speeches, while the volume of legislation passed remained fairly constant.[1] In some East European countries the parliaments were already much more active than in the Soviet Union. The Polish Sejm and the Hungarian Diet make important political interventions and have witnessed the revival of broad-ranging and critical debates.

Major changes were introduced by the December 1988 constitutional amendments both for central state bodies and replicated in local soviets. A new tricameral Congress of People's Deputies was created by the addition of a third chamber. This will be a type of social parliament, selected by quota from all-union sectional interests and public bodies such as the communist party, Komsomol, trade unions, women's committees and so on. The stipulation that these bodies have to be national organizations led to protests in several republics, particularly in the Baltic and above all in Estonia, since it excluded the massive new popular fronts in support of *perestroika* that had emerged to dwarf the local communist party parties. All three chambers are to be elected by multi-candidate elections, although the necessarily limited nature of elections for deputies to the Soviet of Representative undermines the trend towards more open elections for the other two chambers, and ensures a guaranteed number of seats to the communist party. General elections are to be held every five years, beginning with the first of the new-style elections on 26 March 1989. The new congress will meet once a year and elect a smaller permanent Supreme Soviet of some 450 full-time members and an executive president.

The congress is the highest body of state power in the USSR. It retains responsibility for electing the new Committee of Constitutional Review which is 'independent and subordinate only to the constitution' (Article 125). It is responsible for ensuring the implementation of the new constitutionalism and the emergence of a law-governed state. The committee is elected for ten years and is made up of a chair, a deputy chair, and twenty-one committee members, including one from each republic, all of whom should be specialists in the fields of law and politics.

The Supreme Soviet will meet annually for two sessions of three to four months each and will thus be able to fulfil its slated functions of parliamentary scrutiny much more effectively than the old body. The soviet is made up of two chambers, one-fifth of which is replaced annually by the Congress of People's Deputies. The Soviet of the Union is responsible for social and economic questions, the organization of government and general questions concerning the rights, freedoms and duties of Soviet citizens, and foreign, defence and state security issues. The Soviet of Nationalities is concerned with ensuring national equality and the rights of the various Soviet peoples and with regulating relations between these peoples (Article 116).

The Supreme Soviet appoints the chair of the Council of Ministers (the prime minister), and then confirms his or her appointments to the government. Soviet government therefore has the appearance of a classic parliamentary system with the principle of ministerial responsibility to a legislative body. The old principle of commune democracy that executive and legislative power should be fused has been rejected at all levels of the Soviet system. The Supreme Soviet appoints the Council of Defence (headed by the president) and the leading military figures, the Committee of People's Control, and the members of the state arbitration service. The Supreme Soviet interprets the laws of the USSR, oversees the planning process, ratifies international treaties, and has the power to order military mobilizations, declare war, and send troops abroad. Legislation can be initiated by any deputy or any of the legislative agencies, and indeed any all-union body and the USSR Academy of Sciences. In the Supreme Soviet laws are passed by a simple majority of both houses and, in case of disagreement, the matter is passed to a commission.

The Supreme Soviet elects a praesidium made up of the president, the vice-president, fifteen deputy chairs of the Supreme Soviet, the fifteen chairs of the union-republic Supreme Soviets, the chairs of the Soviets of the Union and Nationalities, the chair of the Committee of People's Control, and the chairs of the standing commissions of the Supreme Soviet. The praesidium's powers are carefully limited and while remaining the supreme power between sessions it is strictly accountable to the Supreme Soviet for its actions. The constitutional amendments tried to ensure that there would be no repetition of the mistakes of the past that allowed various praesidiums and executive bodies to dominate the plenums and organizations to which they were formally responsible. In the same spirit, the powers of the executive president were carefully defined in the attempt to ensure that the reforms themselves did not spawn a new *Moloch* of the Stalin type.

The standing commissions of both houses of the Supreme Soviet are also renewed by one fifth every year. They review legislation and scrutinise the various appointments in the Supreme Soviet's competency. Their oversight function is bolstered by the fact that Supreme Soviet deputies are now allowed to concentrate full-time on their parliamentary duties. The rights of individual deputies have been much strengthened in order to ensure that there is no return to the grey monolithicity of earlier years. The new spirit was already evoked by the fact that five deputies voted against, and twenty-seven abstained, in the vote of 1 December 1988 that saw the old rubber stamp Supreme Soviet vote itself out of existence.

The communist party retains a guiding role in the Supreme Soviet, with many Politburo and Central Committee members holding key positions, and the president simultaneously holding the position of General Secretary of the Party. A fundamental issue is whether an expansion of Supreme Soviet power will lead to a diminution of party power. This is necessarily the case, since a gain by one does not automatically imply a loss on the part of the other, and indeed might mean an enhanced status for both. One of the major thrusts of the Gorbachevite reforms is to revive the soviets in general and the Supreme Soviet in particular. Gorbachev is rousing deputies from their long political hibernation, and through organizational changes hopes to achieve a permanent awakening.

The government

The governmental system as Stalin left it was an enormous bureaucratic complex, responsible for the planning and administration of the whole economy and society, from the farms, shops, and factories to the armed forces and the education system. Every ministry was an administrative empire, a vast realm of bureaucracy. The ministry of one of the heavy industries such as steel was like a giant monopolistic concern, with its own housing, transport, and shops, down to the actual steel mills. The common Soviet quip was that the ministries were the equivalent of giant Western multinationals, with the difference that the ministries provided housing, a political focus, holidays, and much more not usually catered for by Western companies. Alfred Meyer wrote of 'USSR Incorporated' to highlight the integrated bureaucratic system of economic and political power. The source of the inertia of the Soviet system lies in the ministries, and the harsh condemnations of all post-Stalin leaders reflected their frustration with the system. Each ministry represents an island of power stretching across the land. Khrushchev's deconcentration of the ministries to the regions was a brave but poorly executed attempt to tackle the problem. Brezhnev's consensual style of politics once again allowed the ministries to consolidate their power.

The number of ministries and state committees changes, with a rising trend following the recentralization of the ministries in 1965 until the accession of Gorbachev in 1985. In 1984 there were fifty-nine ministries and twenty-two state committees, and some other committees responsible for sport, religious affairs, state prizes, and so on. A ministry is usually responsible for one vertically organized branch such as agriculture or defence, while a state committee often cuts across several branches, such as prices, planning, or science and technology.

A typical ministry was fairly small, with about 1,000 officials, but under Gorbachev there has been some merging to create so-called 'super-ministries'. The five ministries and two state committees concerned with agriculture and its equipment were united to form an agro-industrial (Gosagroprom) state committee. The ministerial network in total employs hundreds of thousands of trained officials, although staff are selected not according to strict civil service criteria but largely through informal networks. Elements of competitive entry appear to have evolved but are still rudimentary. Most of the senior officials are trained in their fields, and even the ministers themselves are not usually politicians but specialists who tend to remain in their jobs for extended periods. The creation of super-ministries and the relaxation of central economic management has been accompanied by the vigorous shedding of staff.

It should be stressed that Soviet governmental practice does not distinguish between the permanent bureaucracy, responsible for the implementation of policies, and the politicians who establish the policies. The concept of a permanent civil service that survives changes of government is anathema to commune democracy principles. The Soviet system is a single bureaucratic chain with no constitutional divisions between the Politburo or ministerial policy-makers and the lower officials who execute them.

The ministerial system comes to a head in the USSR Council of Ministers, made up of a chair, eight deputy chairs, over fifty ministers, the head of the state committees and the chairs of the councils of ministers of the union republics, a total of about 120 people in 1987, over half of whom were involved with managing the economy. According to the 1977 constitution it is 'the highest executive and administrative organ of state power' (Article 128) and is responsible to the Supreme Soviet. It deals with a large volume of legislative activity and is still the source of the majority of decrees in the country. It is not clear how often it meets but its sheer size prevents it becoming an effective cabinet. The 1977 constitution (Article 132) for the first time identified a praesidium which probably acts as an inner cabinet, but little is known about this body. In late 1985 the aged Tikhonov was replaced as chair of the Council of Ministers by the more reform-minded Nikolai Ryzhkov. Under Gorbachev the Council of Ministers has increased in political weight, but it still does not by any means outweigh the Politburo or the Central Committee Secretariat. The Council of Ministers and its executive bodies are responsible for the day-to-day running of the country and represent the executive branch of the government. They have traditionally been more involved with policy implementation than policy origination.

The state committees and ministries themselves fall into three categories: all-union, union-republic, and republican. The all-union ministries are responsible for all aspects of their brief throughout the country. Defence, transport and most heavy industrial concerns come into this category. The union-republican group, which includes education, culture, finance, health, justice, and internal affairs (MVD), directs its subordinate units through affiliate ministries of the same name in the capitals of the union republics. There is a tendency for union-republican ministries, such as coal and geology, to be reorganized into all-union ministries. The

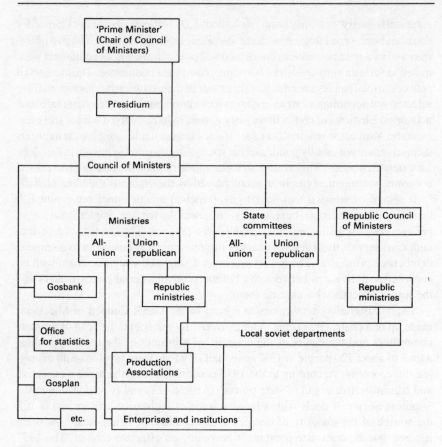

Figure 3 USSR: governmental structure

affiliated ministries operate according to the principle of 'dual subordination': subordinate both to their local council of ministers and to the Moscow ministry.

Each of the fifteen union republics has its own local council of ministers and its own supreme soviet. The governmental institutions of a union republic and an autonomous republic duplicate on a smaller scale those of the national government. The republican supreme soviets, as nationally, act as the legislative arm, and have their own praesidiums to serve as legislative organs between plenary sessions. The republican executive branch, as at the national level, is represented by a council of ministers which oversees the ministries of local significance and includes the top officials in the republican government. The republican ministries work under the direct control of the local council of ministers.

Under Stalin there was extreme centralization of power in Moscow. Official jargon represented Moscow as the 'centre' and all the rest of the country as the 'periphery' or the 'localities'. The reality of Soviet federalism was an extremely centralized political system with little authority vested in the republican capitals. In the soviets, the ministries, and the party actual authority was consolidated to a large extent in small and interlinked praesidiums: the Praesidium of the Supreme Soviet, the Praesidium of the Council of Ministers, and the Politburo of the CPSU Central Committee. In practice the three hierarchies combine to form a unified power structure, but it would be misleading to call it a party-state monolith because of the tensions engendered by the element of fragmentation. The departments and commissions of the Central Committee Secretariat, for example, have an ambiguous relationship to the ministries. They are supervisory and policy-making and yet no doubt, as in the United States, the regulatory bodies have a tendency to coalesce into policy communities with the organization they supervise. The Council of Ministers has several commissions overlapping with the departments of the party Secretariat, giving scope for conflicts. Brezhnev's relaxed administrative style put a premium on formal unity, but behind the scenes it permitted departmental interests to coalesce. The system, however, tries to ensure the primacy of the general interest as defined by the party. The unified structure emerges out of the centralized system of appointments and the integrating role of the party. However, the structure of power is in a condition of tense equilibrium, profoundly stable in normal circumstances but possibly brittle in a crisis. The inertia of the ministerial system is what makes reforming the Soviet Union such a gargantuan task, one which even the party might fail to achieve.

The military and Soviet politics

Born in revolution and war, the Soviet regime has always placed a strong emphasis on its armed forces. The Red Army was formed in the spring of 1918 to defend the infant Soviet regime from foreign intervention and domestic enemies. It was moulded by the military genius of Leon Trotsky, the military commissar, during the civil war of 1918–21. The system of dual control whereby military officers were supervised by political commissars survives in a modified form to this day. Despite the traditional Marxist antipathy to standing armies, the failure of the revolution to spread undermined hopes after the civil war that a militia army could be created. Paradoxically, a system born in hostility to standing armies has become one of the most militarized in the world. This in part explains why the party leadership has been haunted by the ghost of 'Bonapartism', the military strong man coming to power and ousting the civilian leadership. The spectre has taken a new turn, and instead of the general appearing on horseback he emerges as the staff officer intent on maintaining the dominance of the 'metal-eating' industries which supply the armed forces with military hardware. Bonapartism with a briefcase poses no less of a challenge than the horseback version to Gorbachev as he tries to reform the economy.

The party has established an elaborate mechanism to forestall any Napoleonic urges within the military. The fear that Trotsky might play that role as head of the army in the early 1920s significantly weakened his position in the struggle against Stalin, and his own misgivings that he might fulfil such a destiny paralysed his will. Once in power Stalin was careful to insure against a military challenge to his rule, culminating in the bloody purge of the military officers in 1937. The destruction of the army high command led to the USSR's poor performance against the Finns in the Winter War of 1939–40, and to the initial defeats following the German invasion of 22 June 1941. The struggle was accompanied by a relaxation of the system of dual command, allowing officers a degree of operational autonomy. The military emerged from the war with their prestige greatly enhanced. This alone was enough to unsettle Stalin, and soon after he pointedly demoted Marshal Zhukov, the captor of Berlin. Zhukov fared little better under Khrushchev despite his assistance in defeating Beria in 1953 and the anti-party group in 1957. Khrushchev was intent that no rival would emerge to challenge the party. Furthermore, his belief that nuclear weapons made ground forces obsolete led to cuts in the conventional military budget. Khrushchev's overthrow in 1964 was therefore welcomed by the military.

Brezhnev removed the challenge to the ground forces' budget while maintaining the strategic missile programme and thus enabled the military to become one of the main supports of his rule. The elevation of Marshal Grechko to full membership of the Politburo in 1973, to consolidate support for *détente*, underlined the importance of the military as an interest group. The defence budget grew steadily, with a sustained 4–5 per cent annual increment in the decade up to 1976, falling off to about 2 per cent since then. The figures have been disputed, but about 15 per cent of gross national product is devoted to military expenditure, double that of the USA in an economy that is 40 per cent larger. There are an estimated 5 million men under arms (excluding KGB and MVD troops) in a large conscript army, compared with 2.2 million in the US armed forces, although many are employed in labour battalions and suchlike rather than in directly military concerns. The most visible result of the spending was the development of the Soviet navy under Admiral S.G. Gorshkov from a fairly modest coastal defence force to a powerful strategic, submarine and high-seas fleet capable of projecting Soviet power worldwide.

The principle of party leadership over the armed forces is the central one in Soviet civil-military relations. Party control was ensured through the Defence Council, whose existence was acknowledged only in 1976 when Brezhnev was chair, and its position was formalized by the 1977 constitution (Article 121). The Defence Council is now chaired by the President, and includes the Premier and the defence and foreign ministers, though its full membership is not known. The Defence Council is one of the most important decision-making bodies in the fields of foreign policy, military affairs, and the domestic economy through the defence industries. Party influence over the military is directed by the Main Political Administration of the Armed Forces. It parallels the military command structure with a network responsible for political affairs. Its role has changed from the civil war years, when the loyalty of officers was in doubt, and it is now mainly concerned with political education and socialization. Since the overwhelming majority of top officers are party members, the residual system of dual control is rather anachronistic. The actual management of the Soviet military is the responsibility of the General Staff, which oversees the running of the five services

(Ground Forces, Strategic Rocket Forces, Navy, Air Forces and Air Defence Forces) as well as the intelligence directorate, the GRU.

There has been a steady rise in military professionalism. More and more the premium in modern warfare is on scientific skills, and no army can afford to lag behind its adversaries, especially in micro-electronics and communications. In some areas the technological sophistication of the Soviet forces is second to none, yet the problems here are the same as in the economy as a whole: the lack of initiative in routine matters, slow rate of innovation, the shortage of technicians, and poor maintenance in a system which has stressed political reliability rather than technical ability. This might well induce some of the more forward-looking among the military staffs to support the modernization of the economy to provide the technological basis for an advanced defence industry. The poor performance of Soviet weaponry in the June 1982 fighting in the Lebanon highlighted the fact that today's wars are won as much in the scientist's laboratory as on the field of battle. One of the challenges of Reagan's Strategic Defence Initiative (Star Wars) lay in its exploitation of American technological advances.

The new generation of officers has less personal experience of the Second World War, but many have been tested in the Horn of Africa and Afghanistan. The professional military are becoming an increasingly distinctive caste in society, with recruitment coming largely from within their own circles. Some no doubt strive to defend the privileges gained under Brezhnev. There is a sharp contrast between the officer elite and the mass of the Soviet army, raw and often ill-educated conscripts from villages and factories. The military ethos is part of the political culture of the Soviet Union, with all men at the age of 18 having to serve two years in the army; three in the navy. The demographic shift to Central Asia means that every year a growing proportion of recruits do not have Russian as their primary language. The time spent in the army is designed to inculcate Soviet youth with patriotic and party values, yet the military are not insulated from the problems facing Soviet society. Alienation and indiscipline are as rife in the forces as in the factories.

The Soviet military is the cornerstone of the Warsaw Pact, established in 1955 to integrate the command structures of the Soviet Union and its allies in Eastern Europe. Until the withdrawals announced in 1988 the USSR had thirty-one divisions based in Eastern Europe (twenty in the German Democratic Republic, five in Czechoslovakia, four in Hungary, and two in Poland). The supreme commander is always Soviet. The Warsaw Pact is as much responsible for maintaining Soviet power in the area, as in Czechoslovakia in 1968, as it is for countering NATO. The army has a dual role in Soviet-type systems: defence against external aggression, and to act as the ultimate domestic arbiter. Eastern European armies are national institutions yet act, as Jaruzelski did in December 1981 in imposing martial law in Poland, in the Soviet interest. The sight of generals in power in Poland clearly evoked shades of the Bonapartist nightmare as party governance gave way to military rule. Further developments, however, illustrated that the military had intervened not to usurp the role of the party but to consolidate it.

The growing power of the military in Soviet domestic affairs up to 1985 was seen as posing a challenge to the hegemony of the party. Despite the elaborate mechanisms of party control Roman Kolkowicz argues that under Brezhnev the military as an interest group gained prominence at the expense of civilian party leaders. The increased routinization of government allowed the military to consolidate their position in leading bodies, and the Soviet Union's growing global ambitions frequently took on a military form. Both Brezhnev in his last speech and Andropov in his first assented to the vigorous demands being put forward at the time by Marshal Nikolai Ogarkov, the Chief of the General Staff from 1977 to 1984, for further expenditure on conventional forces. The military play an important part in foreign-policy formation and foreign relations, with a broad military assistance programme. The high level of arms sales, has carried the USSR to become the runaway world leader in arms exports. Flushed by their successes in the Horn of Africa, the military allowed the political leadership to exaggerate their capacities, leading to the invasion of Afghanistan in December 1979. The baleful consequences of military influence on Soviet foreign-policy formation committed the USSR to its longest war.

Stalinist industrialization focused on heavy industry in order to create a powerful defence sector. By Brezhnev's time the defence industry had achieved a rare degree of privilege in the Soviet economy, even though it was not only responsible for supplying weaponry but also provided some consumer durables for the domestic economy. This distorted pattern of development has led to claims that the Soviet Union has a military industrial complex which dominates the political system. To this Bialer retorted that the Soviet Union *is* a military industrial complex.[2] Quincy Wright observed long ago that socialism had proved to be 'the war organization of capitalism'.[3] Gerner calls it a 'militarized industrial state'.[4] While highlighting an important facet of Soviet politics, the concept of a military industrial complex is somewhat too narrow to describe the complex interpenetration of Soviet military, political, and economic concerns.

It would be an exaggeration to talk of a struggle between the military and the party. With 96 per cent of senior Soviet officers belonging to the communist party, the military are thoroughly imbued with the party spirit (*partiinost*). The party and the military share a common ethos and both were for long imbued with a military perspective on decision-making. The shared values include a respect for hierarchy and discipline, a strong sense of Soviet patriotism and Russian nationalism, and a compaigning and 'storming' mentality. The civilian and military elites are barely distinguishable and shared a common militaristic perception of global affairs. The career of the former defence minister Dmitrii Ustinov, who had enjoyed a long period as a civilian administrator in the defence industries before becoming the party's choice as military leader, illustrates the close relationship between sectors. The long absence of a department of military affairs in the Secretariat of the Central Committee meant that the party was forced to rely on the advice of the professional military in debates over Soviet military policy. The traditional premium on secrecy gave the General Staff broad discretion in shaping the policy options. The Soviet slogan of the 'unity of the party and the army' reflects the reality.

This is not to suggest that the relationship is always a smooth one. Gorbachev was well aware that the military represented one of the most significant drains on investment and hoped to divert some of these resources to his programme of domestic restructuring. The conventional Soviet view that technological developments and production innovations would somehow spill over to invigorate the domestic economy palpably failed to materialize. Apart from investment priorities, another issue on which he found himself at odds with them was over military doctrine. The Soviet military until the mid-1980s had never fully accepted the doctrine of Mutually Assured Destruction (MAD) and retained belief in the concept of limited war. In 1977 in Tula Brezhnev accepted that this was not the case, and yet the military fought a long rearguard action to sustain the belief that a nuclear confrontation could be fought and won.[5] Clearly, such arguments ran counter to Gorbachev's deeply held beliefs on disarmament and the lunacy of nuclear war. Gorbachev conducted his bold arms control initiatives in the face of military misgivings. Gradually the military came round to accepting the proposition that there could be no victors in a nuclear exchange and accepted the elimination of whole categories of nuclear weapons. This places the emphases all the more on conventional arms, where the Warsaw Pact is believed to have the advantage over NATO.

There has been a noticeable decline in the status of the military. Gorbachev has all but removed them from the mausoleum on ceremonial occasions. Following Ustinov's death in December 1984 his successor, nominated by Chernenko, Marshal Sergei Sokolov, a man in his 70s, obtained only consultative (non-voting) status on the Politburo. The flight of the young West German Mathias Rust in a light aircraft to Red Square enabled Gorbachev to change key figures in the military, including the replacement of Sokolov by General Dmitrii Yazov. The military, however, are still well represented on the Central Committee. Gorbachev's references to the military have usually been pointedly short. Military reform is aided by the generational revolution in progress, since the leaders of the armed forces are mostly veterans of the Second World War who are destined to pass from the stage. Military power will remain a high priority under Gorbachev, but he has begun the arduous task of reconstructing the Soviet military away from its traditional belief that the *only* way to maintain peace is to prepare for war.

The KGB

Shortly after the Bolshevik revolution Lenin placed the battle against 'counter-revolution' on a firm footing. Since then the establishment of a secret police apparatus has been one of the first acts of a Marxist-Leninist revolution. On 20 December 1917 the All-Russian Commission for the Fight against Counter-revolution, Sabotage, and Speculation was created, known by the acronym Cheka. The Cheka's first leader, F.E. Dzerzhinskii, gained for his organization the right not only to hold prisoners but also to judge and execute sentences. The Red Terror of September 1918, following the attempted assassination of Lenin, saw the powers used to such an extent that even many Bolshevik leaders, such as Lev Kamenev, were horrified and sought to bind the actions of the Cheka in some form of legality. This was the intent of the reforms after the civil war, with the creation in February 1922 of the State Political Directorate (GPU). Soon after, in November 1923, this name was restricted to local organizations, and the central body became officially the Unified Political Directorate of the USSR, the OGPU. In 1934 the security police were further restructured into a centralized People's Commissariat of Internal Affairs, the NKVD, which Conquest interprets as part of Stalin's planning for power. The changes certainly signified no effective reduction in police powers. Following the assassination of Kirov on 1 December 1934, special enabling legislation forged the NKVD into the potent weapon of the great purges. Stalin's power came to rest on his personal dominance of the police apparatus.

Following the death of Stalin the Politburo sought to restrain the security police and thus remove the danger to themselves. The police system was split into two parts so that the one would be able to restrain the other, a primitive version of checks and balances. The security police were demoted in status from a ministry to a state committee, becoming the Committee for State Security (KGB). The various ministries took over the old NKVD's economic functions, and its legal functions such as the Special Boards and the running of the labour camps went to the Ministry of Justice. The other part of the balance, the MVD (Ministry of Internal Affairs) was responsible for the militia, which conducts routine police business against crime, traffic control, and administers the internal passport system. The principle of 'socialist legality' was established, and normal judicial proceedings replaced secret trials. The KGB was brought under strict party control and loyal communists were appointed to run it: Ivan Serov (1953–8), followed by two men from the Komsomol, A.N. Shelepin (1958–61) and V.E. Semichastny (1961–7), then Y.V. Andropov (1967–82), and V.V. Fedorchuk (1982). The appointment of Viktor Chebrikov by Andropov in 1982 marked a break in post-Stalinist tradition, since he was a career officer in the service. His replacement in 1988, General Vladimir Kryuchkov, was also a serving officer but not a member of the Politburo. The KGB is part of the governmental network but in addition it is thought to be subordinate to the General Department of the Central Committee Secretariat.

For the first years the division of power held. However, the reversal of destalinization under Brezhnev was accompanied by a growing role for the KGB in Soviet society. Under Andropov's leadership the KGB became a much more professional organization and its prestige rose. The KGB reasserted itself as a relatively independent centre of political power, a position it had lost with the death of Stalin. Andropov was ultimately able to use this power base to launch his bid for the party leadership in November 1982. His accession was accompanied by the promotion of KGB personnel to top party and government posts. In 1982 Fedorchuk, head of the Ukrainian KGB, was brought in to replace Andropov and then to lead the corrupt MVD. The division between the MVD and the KGB was in effect undermined. The KGB took the lead in the anti-corruption campaign, putting political leaders once again at the mercy of the security police. The KGB consolidated its hold on the OBKhSS, the Bureau for the Prevention of the Pilfering of Socialist Property. In the midst of a sea of corruption, only the KGB appeared to stand as an island of incorruptibility.

The Soviet Union is a controlled society and hence the role of the security apparatus is inevitably prominent. The KGB is structured into a number of Chief Directorates, the main ones being the First, which conducts foreign operations; the Second, responsible for domestic political control, the Fourth, responsible for border controls and several categories of forces including the border guards and internal security troops, while the Fifth deals with internal subversion. It has offices throughout the country, with a staff of about 700,000 and at least an equal number of informers. The KGB is represented on the bureaus of all the republican party committees, and its former leader, Chebrikov, had full membership of the Politburo. The republican heads of the KGB are usually Russian, and hence they act as a powerful force of unity in the polity. The personnel office in an enterprise usually has a special department run by the KGB to maintain surveillance over the work force. The secret police are not restricted to malevolent tasks but, in line with Lenin's initial idea, have an important part to play in maintaining the civilian economy through the battle against corruption and enforcing labour discipline.

The KGB is an influential political actor in its own right and represents an important interest group in both foreign and domestic policy. It has its own sources of power relatively independent of the party and state structures. The KGB operates as a vast bureaucratic organization, with files on everything and almost everybody. The reality of the neo-Stalinist compromise was of a sustained low-level terror practised in the context of a culture of informers and betrayal. The lesson of Jaruzelski's *coup* in Poland seemed to be that the party is dispensable but the security apparatus is not. However, in the Soviet Union the police remain under strict party control and Andropov was always careful to present himself as a loyal party official rather than as a policeman. The KGB provides an alternative source of information to the party leadership and, as witnessed during Andropov's rule, can be an important means of implementing policies beyond its immediate sphere of concern, such as the anti-corruption campaign. In a sense the modern KGB stands in relation to the party as the party stands to the state apparatus. It places its operatives at all levels of the party and maintains extensive files on party officials, although (with memories of Stalin) it is not able to act against them directly. It acts as an important pillar complementing the state and party hierarchies.

The KGB clearly has an important part to play in the reform process initiated by Gorbachev. While it appears to support moderate economic *perestroika*, it clearly has major reservations about political *glasnost*. Chebrikov appeared to have joined forces with Ligachev to blunt the radicalism of Gorbachev's reforms. The KGB was one of the few organizations to escape criticism at the twenty-seventh party congress, yet, after a long period when it appeared to be the only organization in the Soviet Union above criticism, in January 1987 Chebrikov was forced to apologize in *Pravda* for the unlawful persecution of the editor of *Soviet Miner* for his exposé of poor safety conditions for miners. Chebrikov promised that 'the organs of state security will act in complete accordance with the law',[6] yet the delay in investigating the case, in which the editor, V. Verkhin, later died, revealed the limits of *glasnost*. The incident showed not only that under Gorbachev no organization could consider itself immune from criticism, but also that the road to Canossa was reversible.

Justice

Soviet constitutional practice recognizes no role for an independent judiciary. The ambiguous role of law in the Soviet state derived from the belief that both the 'state' and 'law' would wither away with the development of a self-governing and self-regulating communist society. At first the system was defined as a 'dictatorship of the proletariat' in which the proletarian state would have to consolidate itself for a short time while it carried out the unpleasant task of eliminating bourgeois and capitalist opposition. This would entail a massive consolidation of the state and necessarily makc any laws regarding personal inviolability redundant. The institutions of the class dictatorship were unregulated, since they were destined to disappear, and were considered mere epiphenomena to the overriding struggle between the proletariat and its enemies. As a Soviet text put it in 1928:

> The undisguised and deliberate use of state institutions as an instrument in the class struggle is fully in accord with the Marxian doctrine of the State, namely, that it is a class organisation. In this case it is an instrument of the ruling proletarian class.[7]

Justice was dependent on the nature of the case, and in class terms objective guilt or innocence was meaningless. The state could wither away once the exploiting classes had been eliminated. However, contrary to expectations, the state remained the basic form of socialist society and hence gradually there came the recognition that its practices would have to be defined by laws and some sort of balance struck between state power and the rights of society.

In the first years of Soviet power there was no theoretical or practical role for law and lawyers: they simply did not fit into the political project of the Bolshevik revolution. The leading exponent of this 'legal nihilism' was E.B. Pashukanis, who argued in favour of the rapid withering away of traditional civil and criminal law. With the onset of the NEP law was partially rehabilitated, including the restoration of the Defence Bar, a reform regarded with hostility by communist ideologues, since most lawyers had been trained by the Tsarist regime. A renewed offensive against law accompanied the cultural revolution of 1928–32. However, from 1932 Vyshinskii led the theoretical re-evaluation that led to official recognition that a stable legal framework was essential for the operation of government. The 1936 constitution restored the concept of law in socialist society, perhaps in part owing to Bukharin's desperate attempt to avert the purges. It is ironic that this re-evaluation coincided with the mass lawlessness of the great terror. It reflected the dualism of a legal system comprised of what has been called 'prerogative law', used against dissidents, and the 'due process of law' approach applied to judging ordinary criminality and regulating economic and social affairs. The restoration of law in the 1930s was not simply a facade for terror but an attempt to constitute a centrally directed legal system that could operate in parallel to the terror. Due process, of course, could not be totally insulated from prerogative law.

The introduction of the concept of a state of all the people by Khrushchev made possible the systematization of Soviet governance. As the Soviet system matures the elements of order and constitutionalism are coming to predominate over arbitrariness and convention. The 1977 constitution further rehabilitated law in socialist society and tried to provide a framework for its stable operation. However, while the duties of Soviet citizens were specific, their political rights were general. According to Soviet theory law serves to protect the Soviet system itself rather than the rights of individuals. The regime has only hesitantly come to the position where it is prepared to obey its own laws and integrate prerogative law with due process. General slogans of revolutionary legality have gradually given way to a more settled system where in theory and mostly in practice the concept of 'Soviet legality' has come to dominate. The scope of arbitrary police action has been severely limited. To overcome Stalin's dominance of the judiciary and the security police, the party brought the judiciary within its own jurisdiction. The crucial further step is to free it from party tutelage and allow it a degree of independence within the Soviet constitution.

The Criminal Code in the Soviet Union is independent of the constitution and was last revised in 1961. The Soviet legal system is administered by the Procurator General, whose office oversees preliminary investigation, the prosecution of criminal cases on behalf of the state, and ensures that state bodies remain within the law. The judges of the Supreme Court of the USSR, and of the supreme courts of the union republics, together with the Procurator General, are elected by the respective supreme soviets for ten-year terms. The USSR Supreme Court acts as the final court of appeal for cases coming up from the people's courts. These lower courts are presided over by a professional judge and two lay assessors. Judges are elected for ten years by the local soviet and the lay assessors for a five-year term by open local elections. The procuracy acts as the state prosecution service. Official policy proclaims that sentencing is not only guided by a retributory impulse but is also designed to reform and re-educate the offender to deter further offences. The system to date has placed the emphasis not so much on the trial itself as on the pre-trial investigation, often without adequate representation by a defence lawyer, who until recently was not allowed to interview clients until after the police and counsel for the prosecution had done with them. The growing role of the market in the economy has raised the profile of the state arbitration service, which deals with the adjudication of enterprise and economic law.

Among his many initiatives Gorbachev is urging judicial reform. The motive is a shift from the 'utilitarian' basis of the rehabilitation of law to date to the theoretical 'humanitarianism' basic to Western law. The language of legal reform has changed from talk of restoring 'socialist legality', pursued by Khrushchev and Brezhnev, to the creation of a 'socialist legal state', announced by the nineteenth party conference in 1988. Debate over the reforms focuses on the following issues: greater powers for defence lawyers; a review of sentencing procedure, with an improved quality of judges and people's assessors, and possibly the reintroduction of twelve-person juries, abolished in 1917; less political interference, dispensing with 'hot lines' between local party bosses and the courts; greater protection for those accused of crimes, including the presumption of innocence; rewriting the Criminal Code to make it more humane, and possibly revision of the notorious Articles 70 and 190, dealing with political offences; decreasing the number of offences liable to the death penalty; and judicial review of legislation in the light of the constitution. To achieve this the nineteenth party conference resolved to create a powerful new Committee of Constitutional Review. In short, the aim is to develop greater independence for the judiciary. The population is to be inculcated with a legal consciousness based on the principle that 'everything is permitted that is not forbidden by law'. The problem is not the often asserted claim about the lack of a legal perspective in Russian political culture, but the demands of the Soviet political system, which for too long considered law a branch of the state. The protection of citizens from the state was regarded as anathema. The obstacles to achieving a strongly rooted legal system defended by an independent judiciary in a system where even overt political conduct has little relation to the provisions of the constitution remain formidable.

Notes

1 S. White, 'Communist Systems and the Iron Law of Political Pluralism', *British Journal of Political Science*, 8 (1978), p. 111.
2 Cited by Breslauer, *Khrushchev and Brezhnev as Leaders*, pp. 284-5.
3 Cited by W.E. Odom, 'The "Militarisation" of Soviet Society', *Problems of Communism*, 5 (September-October 1976), p. 34.
4 K. Gerner, *The Soviet Union and Central Europe in the Post-war Era* (Swedish Institute of International Affairs, Aldershot, 1985), p. 181.
5 T. Hasegawa, 'Soviets on Nuclear-war Fighting', *Problems of Communism*, 35, 4 (July-August 1986), pp. 68-79.
6 *Pravda*, 8 January 1987.
7 Cited by N. de Basily, *Russia under Soviet Rule: Twenty Years of Bolshevik Experiment* (Allen & Unwin, London, 1938), p. 171.

Key text

Hough, J., and M. Fainsod, *How the Soviet Union is Governed* (Harvard University Press, Cambridge, Mass., 1979)

Select bibliography

Constitutions, Supreme Soviet and government

Hill, R., 'Party-State Relations and Soviet Political Development', *British Journal of Political Science*, 10 (April 1980), pp. 149-95
Hough, J., 'Centralisation and Decentralisation in the Soviet System', in J. Hough, *The Soviet Union and Social Science Theory* (Harvard University Press, Cambridge, Mass., 1977), pp. 159-70.

Little, D. Richard, 'Legislative Authority in the Soviet Political System', *Slavic Review*, 30, 1 (March 1971), pp. 57–73.

Little, D. Richard, 'Soviet Parliamentary Committees after Khrushchev: Obstacles and Opportunities', *Soviet Studies*, 24 (July 1972), pp. 41–60.

Matthews, Mervyn, *Soviet Government: a Selection of Official Documents on Internal Policies* (part 2) (London, 1974)

Nelson, Daniel, and Stephen White (eds.), *Communist Legislatures in Comparative Perspective* (Macmillan, London, 1982)

Schneider, Eberhard, 'The Discussion of the new All-Union Constitution of the USSR', *Soviet Studies*, 31, 4 (October 1979), pp. 523–41

Sharlet, Robert, *The New Soviet Constitution of 1977: Analysis and Text* (Kings Cross, Brunswick, Oh., 1978)

Sharlet, Robert, 'Constitutional Implementation and the Juridicization of the Soviet System', in D.R. Kelley (ed.), *Soviet Politics in the Brezhnev Era* (Praeger, New York, 1980)

Unger, Aryeh L., *Constitutional Developments in the USSR: a Guide to the Soviet Constitutions* (Methuen, London, 1981)

Vanneman, Peter, *The Supreme Soviet: Politics and the Legislative Process in the Soviet Political System* (Duke University Press, Durham, N.C., 1977)

White, Stephen, 'The Supreme Soviet and Budgetary Politics in the USSR', in S. White and D. Nelson (eds.), *Communist Politics: a Reader* (Macmillan, London, 1986), pp. 55–72

The military

Agursky, M., and H. Adomeit, 'The Soviet Military-Industrial Complex', *Survey*, 24, 2 (1979), pp. 106–24

F. Barghoorn and R. Kolkowicz, chapters in H.G. Skilling and F. Griffiths (eds.), *Interest Groups in Soviet Politics* (Princeton, N.J., 1971)

Colton, Timothy, *Commissars, Commanders and Civilian Authority: the Structure of Soviet Military Politics* (Harvard University Press, Cambridge, Mass., 1979)

Colton, Timothy, 'The Impact of the Military on Soviet Society', in S. White and D. Nelson (eds.) *Communist Politics: a Reader* (Macmillan, London, 1986), pp. 243–59

Hasegawa, T., 'Soviets on Nuclear-War Fighting', *Problems of Communism*, 35, 4 (July-August 1986), pp. 68–79

Herspring, D.R., and I. Volgyes (eds.), *Civilian-Military Relations in Communist Systems* (Westview, Boulder, Colo., 1978)

Holloway, David, *The Soviet Union and the Arms Race* (Yale University Press, New Haven, Conn., 1983)

Holloway, David, and T.J. Sharp (eds.), *The Warsaw Pact: Alliance in Transition?* (Macmillan, London, 1984)

Jones, Ellen, *Red Army and Society: a Sociology of the Soviet Military* (Allen & Unwin, London, 1985)

Kolkowicz, Roman, 'The Military and Soviet Foreign Policy', in R. Kanet (ed.), *Soviet Foreign Policy in the 1980s* (Praeger, New York, 1982)

Kolkowicz, Roman, 'The Political Role of the Soviet Military', in J.L. Nogee (ed), *Soviet Politics: Russia after Brezhnev* (Praeger, New York, 1985)

Larabee, F. Stephen, 'Gorbachev and the Soviet Military', *Foreign Affairs*, 66, 5 (summer 1988), pp. 1002–26

Leebaert, Derek (ed.), *Soviet Military Thinking* (Allen & Unwin, London, 1981)

Odom, W.E., 'The "Militarisation" of Soviet Society', *Problems of Communism*, 25, 5 (September-October 1976), pp. 34–51

Sadykiewicz, M., 'Soviet Military Politics', *Survey*, 26, 1 (winter 1982), pp. 179–210

Scott, H.F. and W.F., *The Armed Forces of the USSR*, 2nd rev. edn (Westview, Boulder, Colo., 1984)

Simes, D.K., 'The Military and Militarism in Soviet Society', *International Security*, 6, 3 (1980–81)

Spielman, Karl F., 'Defence Industrialists in the USSR', *Problems of Communism*, 25, 5 (September-October 1976), pp. 52–69

Warner, Edward L., *The Military in Contemporary Soviet Politics* (Praeger, New York 1977)

The KGB

Barron, John, *KGB Today: the Hidden Hand* (Hodder and Stoughton, London, 1984)

Conquest, R., *The Soviet Police System* (Praeger, New York, 1968)

Corson, W.R., and R.T. Crowley, *The new KGB: Engine of Soviet Power* (Wheatsheaf, Brighton, 1985)

Dallin, A., and G.W. Breslauer, *Political Terror in Communist Systems* (Stanford University Press, Stanford, Cal., 1970)

Hingley, Ronald, *The Russian Secret Police* (Hutchinson, London, 1970)

Knight, Amy, *The KGB: Police and Politics in the Soviet Union* (Unwin Hyman, London, 1988)

Leggett, George H., *The Cheka: Lenin's Political Police* (Oxford University Press, Oxford, 1981)

Penkovsky, Oleg, *The Penkovsky Papers* (London, 1965)

Wolin, S., and R. Slusser, *The Soviet Secret Police* (London, 1957)

Justice

Barry, D., G. Ginsburgs, and P. Maggs (eds.), *Soviet Law after Stalin* (Sijthoff, Leiden, 1977–9)

Berman, Harold, *Justice in the USSR: an Interpretation of Soviet Law* rev. edn (Harvard University Press, Cambridge, Mass., 1966)

Butler, W.E., *Soviet Law* (Butterworth, London, 1983)

Feldbrugge, F., and W. Simon (eds.), *Perspectives on Soviet Law for the 1980s* (Nijhoff, The Hague, 1982)

Huskey, Eugene, *Russian Lawyers and the Soviet State: the Origins and Development of the Soviet Bar, 1917–1939* (Princeton University Press, Princeton, N.J., 1986)

Ioffe, Olimpiad S., and Peter B. Maggs, *Soviet Law in Theory and Practice* (Oceana, London, 1983)

Ioffe, Olimpiad S., *Soviet Law and Soviet Reality* (Nijhoff, Dordrecht, 1985)

Juviler, Peter, *Revolutionary Law and Order* (Free Press, New York, 1976)

Solomon, Peter, *Soviet Criminologists and Criminal Policy* (Columbia University Press, New York, 1978)

Solomon, Peter, 'Local Political Power and Soviet Criminal Justice, 1922–41', *Soviet Studies*, 37 (July 1985), pp. 305–29

Van den Berg, Ger P., *The Soviet System of Justice: Figures and Policy* (Nijhoff, Dordrecht, 1985)

Chapter seven

The communist party

The Communist Party of the Soviet Union is the linchpin of the political system. The major reason for an 'unwritten constitution' is the existence of a party with great although undefined powers. The party acts as a 'ministry of politics', but it does far more than that. The Bolshevik party was indeed, as Lenin claimed, a 'party of a new type', a unique combination of organizational and ideological innovations. Under Brezhnev the party's authority was eroded as its ideology stagnated, trust in cadres gave way to corruption, and policy stability to immobility. Gorbachev's ambitious intention is to restore the authority of the party through real moral leadership, effective policies, and identification with the aspirations of the population. There are some precedents for the attempt to redefine the party's relationship with society, stopping short of pluralism, and in this Gorbachev is in the tradition of Khrushchev, the Czechoslovak reformers of 1968, and the attempts at the internal renewal (*odnowa*) of the Polish party in the 1980s.

Recruitment

By 1988 the CPSU had achieved a membership of 19·5 million members and candidates, representing 9·7 per cent of the adult population. One in fifteen, or 6·8 per cent, of the entire population of 284 million is a party member. Recruitment policy is based on the idea that the party represents the cream of the population, the most dedicated and the most able, who wish to serve the country to the best of their ability. On this principle rests a large degree of the legitimacy of the party's dominance of Soviet political life. If the party were to be perceived as made up of time-servers and careerists its dominant role would be eroded and it would be forced to rely more openly on coercion.

Party members can be divided into three categories. The first group are the party *apparatchiki* who work full-time in the party's own bureaucracy. Their exact number is unknown but they make up a fairly small proportion, about 2 per cent of total party membership. Some of them are included in the second category, the party activists. In February 1986 there were 5·3 million elected officials, most of them part-time, representing 29 per cent of total CPSU membership.[1] The third group consists of the rank-and-file membership. Some of these are recruited not because of any particular dedication to the party but because they represent the elite in their professions. They fulfil the 'cadre' role in their chosen field, representing the party and its policies in their place of work. Their role is that of mass leadership, a channel for the transmission of information to and from their colleagues.

Lenin's idea of the communist as a dedicated revolutionary remains in force, and there are constant attempts to maintain a level of *aktivnost* (activity), contrasted to *passivnost* (passivity), in all spheres of a party member's life. Under Gorbachev the role of the individual party member has been much enhanced. The aim is to revitalize the political life of each communist and thereby revive the grass roots of the party for active participation in party and public affairs. While the CPSU was traditionally a cadre party, one made up of dedicated activists, it has now clearly also become a mass party. The distinction between the two has become blurred, though in a sense it is a mass party run by a cadre core. The fundamental dilemma is how to reconcile its mass functions with its vanguard, or leading, role. There appear to have been limits set on the party's size at about 10 per cent of the adult population in order to maintain the balance between the cadre and mass roles and to guard against its 'dissolution' into society.

In theory membership is open to any citizen of the USSR but there are various screening processes. Prospective members have to be invited to join, hence the decision is not so much the individual's as that of the party organization. Recruitment has become an extended system of co-option. The checks consist of references from communists of not less than five years' standing, approval by a party meeting, usually at the place of work, endorsement by party officials at the next highest administrative level, and a probationary period (candidature) of twelve months during which the candidate has to prove her or himself worthy of membership by attending party meetings, working well, and showing adequate political consciousness. During *perestroika* the conditions have become more exacting, with a preliminary discussion of the merits of candidates at their workplace to democratize recruitment. About 5 per cent of candidates fail to graduate to full membership. The system is a legacy of pre-revolutionary procedures designed to avoid infiltration by police spies.

The party stresses the duties associated with membership rather than the privileges. Yet there are advantages, such as access to certain posts and to what is called party information, a network of information not usually available to ordinary citizens. Communists can be more easily elected to responsible posts and have the right to criticize other communists. There is also the prestige of being one of the chosen few, but this factor was perhaps less marked under Brezhnev, giving way to a prevalent attitude of cynicism. In response the mystique of joining the party was inflated. The official view condemns the use of party membership to advance one's career, yet under Brezhnev the dangerous tendency emerged for party membership to be associated with particular jobs. Officials stress that people cannot join the party simply because they hold a certain post or as a family tradition. The personal qualities of the applicant are what is important, although certain social or national categories, such as workers, find it easier to join, since it suits the purposes of the central party leadership. On the other hand, certain top posts are almost always reserved for party members. This is particularly the case with senior military officers, where party membership is a prerequisite of promotion.

The pattern of recruitment since 1917 has alternated between periods of intensive and restricted growth. The first years saw a rapid expansion as the party acted as a massive 'conveyor belt' of workers into administration and military posts. The party's elect membership was diluted by the influx of 'Soviet bureaucrats' and illiterate workers and peasants, evoking fears about its degeneration. Lenin's death in 1924 and the industrialization drive from the late 1920s were followed by major enrolment drives. The late 1930s and the war years once again witnessed expansion, which slowed down after the war. Under Khrushchev there was sustained growth, especially in the years after 1957. The party grew by 65 per cent, with an annual growth rate of about 5 per cent, as Khrushchev attempted to catch up with population growth, increases in the number of workers, and educational progress. Excessive growth appeared to threaten the party's vanguard role and the growth rate was halved after 1965, and halved again in 1971–6. The decline also reflects demographic patterns, with a low birth rate during the war and again after the immediate post-war baby boom. Growth fell from an average of 762,000 per annum between 1962 and 1965 to 311,000 in 1981–6, an average of 1·7 per cent a year. The slowdown is a response to what John Miller calls the 'dilemma of party growth' whereby rapid increases undermine the party's vanguard position.[2]

While the party tries to ensure that its membership is representative of society at large, the principle of 'strict individual selection' remains the dominant entry criterion. The periods of slow-down in party growth usually coincide with a campaign to check the credentials of the existing membership. During war communism these campaigns were called re-registrations. They were systematized in 1921 when the party underwent the first full-scale purge. In 1971 the twenty-fourth party congress sanctioned a new purge, once again described as a re-registration, which saw 347,000 communists expelled by 1974. Even when no re-registration campaign is in progress there is a steady stream of expulsions from the party. Between 1981 and 1986 about 430,000 communists were reportedly expelled, reflecting the greater emphasis on discipline following the Solidarity crisis in Poland and Brezhnev's death. In 1988 a thorough report-and-election campaign was launched, to check on membership. It was designed to weed out 'careerists and time-servers', to leave a purified 'vanguard' to lead the process of *perestroika*.

The party's social composition has always been a matter of prime concern. Statistics describe the status of members on joining the party and do not reflect subsequent changes. In 1986 45 per cent were described as workers, 11·8 per cent as collective farmers, and 43·2 per cent as employees or in the army.[3] The party no longer claims to be only the vanguard of the working class but of the

Table 2 The CPSU in figures

	1971	1976	1981	1986
Total membership	14,455,321	15,694,187	17,480,768	19,037,946
Full members	13,810,089	15,058,017	16,763,009	18,309,693
Candidates	645,232	636,170	717,759	728,253
Population 20+	152,281,000	165,767,000	178,874,000	196,267,800
Communists as % of				
adults 20 and over	9·4	9·4	9·4	9·7
Social composition				
Workers	5,759,379	6,509,312	7,569,261	8,551,779
%	40·1	41·6	43·4	45·0
Peasants	2,169,437	2,169,813	2,223,674	2,248,166
%	15·1	13·9	12·8	11·8
Employees	6,443,747	6,959,766	7,637,478	8,204,433
%	44·8	44·5	43·8	43·2
Sexual composition				
Women	3,195,556	3,793,859	4,615,576	5,475,145
%	22·2	24·3	26·5	28·8
Recruitment (%)				
Workers		57·6	59·0	59·4
Peasants		11·3	10·3	9·9
Technical intelligentsia		24·5	25·4	26·1
Administrators		5·2	3·8	3·2
Students		1·4	1·5	1·4
Women		29·5	32·2	34·1
Education				
Higher	2,819,642	3,807,469	4,881,877	6,045,653
%	19·6	24·3	28·0	31·8
Incomplete higher	337,995	385,556	391,216	398,059
%	2·4	2·5	2·2	2·1
Secondary	4,932,958	6,022,397	7,297,089	8,451,480
%	34·3	38·5	41·9	44·5
Incomplete secondary	3,573,368	3,175,163	2,973,839	2,601,613
%	24·9	20·3	17·1	13·7
Primary	2,708,600	2,251,306	1,886,392	1,507,573
%	18·8	14·4	10·8	7·9

Note: The columns represent changes over the five-year period between congresses. The twenty-fourth party congress met in March 1971, the twenty-fifth in February 1976, the twenty-sixth in February 1981, and the twenty-seventh in February 1986.
Source: *Partiinaya zhizn*, 14 (July 1986), pp. 19–24.

whole society, in line with the concept of the state of all the people, and this has justified the recruitment of employees. The party still claims to have a special relationship with the working class, although since 1918 the working class have never comprised an absolute majority of membership. Khrushchev's policy of increasing the proportion of workers has been continued by his successors. By 1986 59·4 per cent of new members were workers, compared with 26·1 per cent employees, 3·2 per cent administrators and managers, 9·9 per cent collective farmers, and 1·4 per cent students[4] in a society made up of 61·7 per cent workers, 26·2 per cent employees, and 12·1 per cent collective farmers. Given rising educational levels, the increased proportion of new party members designated worker does not necessarily mean that they work manually or in a traditional industry. The emphasis has been on recruitment of workers employed in the forward-looking industries of electronics, communications, energy, and engineering.

In some professions party membership is vastly overrepresented, especially in ideologically sensitive posts in the soviets or the armed services. Three out of four journalists are party members, but only one artist in five, one in four engineers and teachers. In general there is a higher party 'saturation' of those with higher education. The typical party member is better educated than the average citizen and better qualified. Over 78 per cent of communists have completed secondary or higher education. About 12·5 per cent of the employed population have higher education, whereas in the party the figure is 32 per cent. Three-quarters of employees joining the party are skilled professionals, such as agronomists, engineers, teachers, doctors, and cultural figures. The obverse side of this is the danger that certain sectors of society, in particular the poor and undereducated, may find themselves unrepresented. The party has gradually become more solidly white-collar, better educated, and more urban than the population as a whole.

Party membership, especially at higher levels, can be broken down into generations. Recruitment has gone through successive phases, and these remain as geological layers in the party. The cohort schooled under Stalin is the one still in command but it is gradually giving way to a post-Stalinist and post-war generation. Andropov appealed both to the conservative authoritarianism of the old generation and to the younger technocrats. In the first years of Bolshevik power the average age of the party member was in the late 20s but by Khrushchev's period it was only slightly lower than the national average, and now the party has kept pace with the general ageing of the population as stable recruitment patterns have allowed the party to mature. There were some attempts to delay recruitment under Brezhnev to avoid the influx of too many 18-year-olds, the legal minimum age for joining. Nearly three-quarters of recruitment in the early 1980s was of Komsomol members, that is, those under 28 years old, and four-fifths were under 30. In 1986 17·6 per cent of membership was under 31, 23·7 per cent between 31 and 40, and 22·3 per cent between 41 and 50.[5] There is an increasing proportion of long-term members, with 68 per cent having been in the party for over ten years in 1986 compared to only about 50 per cent in 1967.

The national composition of the party is as much a matter of leadership concern as its social composition. Ethnic Russians make up about half the total population of the USSR, but in 1986 they comprised 59·1 per cent of the CPSU. This dominance has declined from 66 per cent in 1961 as the non-Russian republics have maintained a higher recruitment rate than the RSFSR (1·6 per cent). In 1986 the five main Central Asian peoples together made up only 5·7 per cent of the CPSU, while in 1979 they represented 9·9 per cent of the total population (see

Table 3 National composition of the party, 1986

Nationality	Number	%
Russians	11,241,958	59·1
Ukrainians	3,041,736	16·0
Belorussians	726,108	3·8
Uzbeks	465,443	2·4
Kazakhs	387,837	2·0
Azerbaidzhanis	337,904	1·8
Georgians	321,922	1·7
Armenians	291,081	1·5
Lithuanians	147,068	0·8
Moldavians	110,715	0·6
Tadzhiks	87,759	0·5
Latvians	78,193	0·4
Kirgiz	78,064	0·4
Turkmenians	76,786	0·4
Estonians	61,277	0·3
Others	1,550,527	8·2
Total	19,004,378	100·0

Source: *Partiinaya zhizn*, 14 (July 1986), p. 24.

Tables 3 and 8). The Uzbeks, for example, have been joining the party at an annual rate of 3 per cent, compared to the national average of 2 per cent. There are great variations between republics, with the rate of increase the highest in Moldavia, at 3·1 per cent a year, and the lowest in Georgia, possibly to offset earlier overrepresentation (see Table 4). There is a higher representation of Jews than of any other single nationality in the CPSU, at about 20 per cent of those over 20 years old. The Georgians are the next highest to be overrepresented, at 11·6 per cent of the total adult population, the Russians at 10·3 per cent, down to 3·5 per cent for Moldavians. A marked feature is the falling recruitment of ethnic groups without a national republic, such as the Tatars, Jews, and Chuvashis, while those with a union republic have consolidated their position. As time passes the CPSU is gradually losing its Russian face, but its features are still predominantly Slavic. The Slavic peoples (Russians, Belorussians, and Ukrainians) in 1986 made up 79 per cent of membership and 72·2 per cent of the total population. It seems clear that the leadership is unable to control ethnic recruitment quite so closely as it can socio-economic trends. The issue is an extremely sensitive one, and whatever strategy the party adopts one or another ethnic group is likely to be offended.

Women have always been greatly underrepresented. This was understandable when the party claimed to represent the industrial working class but is less so now. In 1920 women made up only 7·4 per cent of membership, and this rose to 22·2 per cent in 1971 and to 28·8 per cent in 1986. The official policy clearly aims to redress the imbalance. The immediate result has been that the proportion of women among those joining the party has risen from 29·5 per cent in the early 1970s to 34·1 per cent in the 1980s. Since there are more women than men in

Table 4 Party membership in the union republics, 1971–86

	1971	Growth %	1976	Growth %	1981	Growth %	1986
USSR	14,455,321	8·6	15,694,187	11·4	17,480,768	8·9	19,037,946
RSFSR[a]	9,253,243	6·7	9,875,562	10·2	10,885,704	7·7	11,730,254
Ukraine	2,378,789	10·1	2,625,808	11·7	2,933,564	8·7	3,188,854
Belorussia	434,527	16·5	506,229	17·6	595,311	12·2	667,980
Moldavia	115,164	17·5	135,303	21·1	163,902	15·6	189,403
Transcaucasia							
Azerbaidzhan	258,549	11·3	287,823	14·8	330,319	14·1	376,822
Georgia	296,375	7·4	318,371	10·1	350,435	9·4	383,472
Armenia	130,353	9·7	142,959	15·2	164,738	13·3	186,637
Central Asia							
Uzbekistan	428,507	13·8	487,507	16·6	568,243	13·0	642,025
Kazakhstan	575,439	14·2	657,141	11·0	729,498	11·1	810,776
Tadzhikistan	86,491	11·8	96,716	12·7	108,974	12·9	122,985
Kirgizstan	104,632	4·9	109,746	15·2	126,402	14·3	144,466
Turkmenistan	69,862	11·5	77,910	20·1	93,556	17·7	110,141
Baltic							
Lithuania	122,469	18·8	145,557	17·4	170,935	15·4	197,274
Latvia	127,753	12·2	143,305	12·5	161,264	9·9	177,258
Estonia	73,168	15·2	84,250	16·2	97,923	11·9	109,599

Note: [a]There is no republican party organization for the RSFSR: the figures given are the remainder after the subtraction of the fourteen other republics. Growth rates calculated from the table.
Source: *Partiinaya zhizn*, 14 (July 1986), p. 20.

the population (53 per cent), the underrepresentation has been even more severe than the above figures suggest (see Tables 2 and 5). This pattern is even more marked at higher echelons of the party.

Recruitment allows the party to act as a massive mechanism for the incorporation of society into the political system. Stable recruitment policies and patterns have been pursued since the fall of Khrushchev, and most sectors of society are adequately represented. Past imbalances are being ironed out, as in gender composition and decreasing the proportion of employees, but some new imbalances are creeping in, as in underrepresentation for nationalities without their own republic and the poorly educated. Recruitment has never been left to the market, and there is no doubt that it will remain a matter of concern to the party leadership.

Organization

The CPSU is organized as a pyramid, with the central bodies (the Central Committee, Politburo, and Secretariat) rising above successive stages of party committees from the primary party organizations. With the exception of the RSFSR, every union republic has its own communist party, and together they constitute the unitary CPSU (see Fig. 4).

The ideological perspectives of the party are contained in the party programme. It sums up the tasks and nature of a given period. The first programme was adopted at the second party congress in 1903, the second at the eighth congress in 1919 to

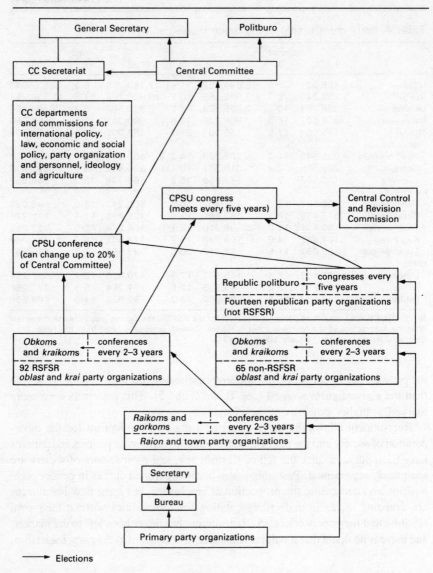

```
┌─────────────────────────┐        ┌──────────────┐
│   General Secretary     │        │  Politburo   │
└─────────────────────────┘        └──────────────┘
```

Elections

Figure 4 CPSU: organizational structure

reflect the coming to power of the Bolsheviks, and the third in 1961 to reflect Khrushchev's state of all the people. A new edition of the third programme was adopted by the twenty-seventh party congress in March 1986, though it is in effect a new programme. The very absence of explicit ideological innovations was remarkable and indicated that the Gorbachev period would be one of hard work rather than of grand theoretical reformulations. The new programme dropped some of the utopian aspirations of Khrushchev's text, such as the promise that 'this generation of Soviet people will live under communism', and some of the more grandiose ambitions — to overtake the USA by 1970 and to attain communism by 1980. The new version holds out few promises for the future.

The organization of the CPSU is governed by its statute, or rules, which are modified to reflect the concerns of the programme. The 1961 rules were amended in 1966 and 1971 to eliminate Khrushchev's 'excesses', like the obligatory turnover of personnel. The current rules were adopted in March 1986. Democratic centralism is the key principle governing the organization of the CPSU, and indeed of the whole polity. The concept was formulated by Lenin as one of the fundamental principles of party organization. It claims to combine effective central control with democratic practices from below. The rules speak of five key elements in democratic centralism (Rule 19):

(a) the election of all leading bodies, from the lowest to the highest;

(b) periodical reports of party bodies to their organizations and to higher bodies;

(c) strict party discipline and subordination of the minority to the majority;

(d) the obligatory nature of decisions by higher bodies for lower bodies; and

(e) collective spirit in the work of all organizations and the personal responsibility of every communist for the fulfilment of his [or her] party assignments.

The last point was a new addition. Traditionally, centralism has predominated over democracy, and the election process has been governed from the top down. Democratic centralism served to prevent the mass of the party membership controlling its own leadership. All party bodies are subordinated to the decisions of party congresses and conferences as interpreted on a day-to-day basis by the Politburo and lower-level party committees. Democratic centralism still provides the justification for keeping certain questions off the agenda and restricts groups within the party, so-called factions, from coming together. The current rules explicitly state that 'any manifestation of factionalism or group activity is incompatible with Marxist-Leninist principles and party membership'. Democratic centralism inhibits interest-group politics and justifies the 'monolithic unity' of the party. It guarantees that the lines of communication within the party are vertical, from top to bottom, rather than horizontal, between like-minded individuals, groups or committees.

The party rests on its base of 440,363 (January 1986) primary party organiztions (PPO, formerly called party cells). All party members must belong to a PPO and participate in its activities. Reflecting the Soviet conception of the individual primarily as a worker, PPOs are overwhelmingly organized in workplaces and only rarely on a territorial basis. In 1986 25·6 per cent were located in industry, 17·4 per cent in offices, 11·3 per cent on farms, and 16·7 per cent in colleges. They vary greatly in size, 39·8 per cent having from the minimum of three to fifteen, and 7·1 per cent ranging from 101 to several thousand. Average membership in industry is ninety-five, and about sixty on farms. All PPOs have a secretary, a bureau if the organization is large enough, and a committee in the 45,000 very large organizations. Party meetings are usually held once a month, at which new members are admitted and disciplinary measures passed. Executive officers are formally elected by members, but the initial candidatures before Gorbachev were usually proposed by a higher party committee and then only ratified by the membership. The PPO is responsible for recruiting, training, and disciplining its members. Individuals are assigned responsibilities, and the cell as a whole acts to mobilize the population. The PPO's committee or bureau in workplaces acts as a type of board of directors. It takes part in decision-making, although it is formally subordinate to the manager. The PPO's precise role depends on the circumstances of any given period, but there has always been great scope for conflict, owing to the ambiguous definition of the relationship between the party cell and management, described in terms of the 'right of supervision' (*pravo kontrolya*) and not 'control'.

The next stage consists of 3,550 *raion* (urban borough or rural county) committees. The *raikom* (*raion* committee) of eighty to a hundred members is elected by a conference of delegates from all the PPOs in the area. It meets in plenary session about six times a year, and leaves the running of current affairs to a bureau of about a dozen, most of whom are full-time officials. This bureau meets much more frequently than the plenum, usually about two or three times a month. The *raikom* oversees a number of party departments established to supervise the affairs of the district and the local soviet, reflecting the major industries of the area. In the countryside, for example, an agricultural department takes a keen interest in the affairs of the local farms to ensure that plans are fulfilled, and indeed this interest often spills over into a virtual replacement of local managers, the process known as *podmena*. All *raikomy* have an agitation and propaganda (agitprop) department to run the local ideological work of meetings, clubs, and lectures. The organization department is the focus of local personnel placement, and no significant appointment in a given locality can take place without its sanction.

Above the *raikomy* there are 889 city committees (*gorkomy*), ten area (*okrug*) committees, two city committees (*gorkomy*) with the rights of *obkomy* (Moscow and Kiev), 151 regional or *oblast* committees (*obkomy*), (ninety-two of whom cover the RSFSR), six *krai* committees (*kraikomy*) and fourteen republican party committees. There are no *oblasti* in the Baltic states. Separate revisional commissions without overlapping membership are elected at the same conferences as the party committees to oversee the latter's work and to ensure financial, moral, and organizational probity. The *obkomy* are larger versions of the *raikomy*, with the exception that they usually have a secretariat of full-time party workers (*apparatchiki*) distinct from the bureau. *Obkomy* have between 100 and 150 members and meet perhaps once a quarter, with day-to-day affairs run by a bureau. Most *obkomy* have separate departments for industry, agriculture, health, education, and so on. There is the ubiquitous duplication between party and state bodies, and the relationship between the two is ruled, as elsewhere, by convention. Of the 5·3 million elected party officials, 4·9 million are found in the PPOs, 407,000 in *gorkomy* and *raikomy*, and 31,900 in *obkomy*, *kraikomy*, and republican committees.

Party committees are responsible to party conferences, held every two to three years. The elections are indirect, with PPOs electing delegates to *raion* conferences, which elect the local committee, and so on up through a series of conferences to the national party congress. The voting at all party gatherings has traditionally been carefully controlled and takes place by a show of hands. The individual merits of particular candidates are not scrutinized particularly carefully. At the top the national party congress since 1961 has met every five years, usually gathering for about a week. It is timed to coincide with the adoption of the current five-year plan. The twenty-seventh congress in February–March 1986 had 5,000 delegates, 76·5 per cent of whom were elected for the first time, representing top party officials from the centre but also some rank-and-file delegates from the localities. The Central Committee Secretariat's organization department ensures that the proper mix of delegates is selected, with a certain proportion of women, minorities, soldiers, intellectuals, workers, officials, and so on. The party congress elects a Central Control and Revision Commission to ensure correct procedures in the party and the investigation of abuses.

The leadership's policies for the succeeding five years are legitimized as fulfilling the programmes outlined by the party congress. Under Brezhnev congresses became the scene of orchestrated unanimity, with all major speeches approved in advance by the Secretariat. This was not always the case, and some congresses before Stalin's dead hand stifled debate were the scene of bitter controversy. Against the backcloth of vigorous debate the tenth congress in March 1921 imposed the ban on factions which allowed Stalin to consolidate his administrative control over congresses. By the time of the seventeenth congress in 1934, celebrating collectivization and the completion of the first five-year plan, criticism of Stalin could at most be oblique. Few congresses met under Stalin, and none between 1939 and 1952. Congresses have met regularly in the post-Stalin period, though they have tended to become professional affairs, managed to ensure the smooth progress of motions earlier decided. Echoes of controversies have, however, slipped in, and careful analysis of speeches reveals subtle differences of emphasis. Under Gorbachev more open debate is permitted but it remains to be seen how far delegates will be able to modify leadership proposals.

National party conferences met frequently under Lenin, but died out completely under Stalin following the eighteenth in 1941. Conferences provide a forum for debate and the discussion of policy options, although their powers with respect to electing the Central Committee have been vague. By reviving the body in June 1988 Gorbachev hoped to achieve consensus for reform and to institutionalize his strategy of *perestroika* and democratization. In future, conferences will meet every two or three years and will have the right to replace up to 20 per cent of members of party committees, including the Central Committee.

Congresses leave one of their most important tasks until the end, namely the adoption of the list of Central Commmittee members put to it by the leadership. Under Lenin it was the equivalent of today's Politburo, a compact group of ten to twenty members. As the CC grew in size to become a condensed party congress its authority declined. The CC elected in March 1986 had 307 full members and 170 candidates (or non-voting members), a total of 477. Of the full members, 30·6 per cent were new, reflecting Gorbachev's unusually rapid personnel turnover and ability to consolidate his position. The CC represents the key sections of society and co-opts various notables like Valentina Tereshkova, the first woman in space. Members are usually selected because of the particular job that they hold, with CC membership only confirming the importance of the other job. The CC elected in 1986 contained no fewer than 104 regional party chiefs, half of whom were new to the CC; thirty-one came from the CC apparatus itself, fifty-six from the governmental ministries, twenty-four from the armed services, and five from the KGB.[6] The CC is the high gathering of the Soviet elite and has become a type of social parliament representing various institutions rather than individuals.

The Central Committee is the source of official legitimacy for policies between congresses, but it is not an autonomous policy-making body. Its political decline dates from the early 1920s, and between 1945 and Stalin's death it met only twice. After 1953 the CC plenum was restored as the supreme authority in the country between congresses. Khrushchev's appeal to the CC against the Politburo to reverse the anti-party group's vote to oust him in 1957 illustrated its importance. It was the CC, however, that in 1964 confirmed his dismissal. Under Brezhnev the CC tended to act as the platform for the announcement of policies and to ratify changes in personnel. The CC confirmed the successors to Brezhnev chosen by the Politburo in the early 1980s. Gorbachev has been adept at using CC meetings to launch major policy initiatives and debate, but not without a struggle. Freed from the stifling restrictions of his predecessors, the CC has become the forum of more open debate. New rules governing plenary sessions permit interventions from the floor during debates that are entered into the official minutes. The January 1987 plenum, which saw him launch his proposals for democratization, was three times postponed, and at that meeting thirty-four CC members spoke. The problem for a reformer like Gorbachev is the creation of too many 'dead souls', people who have lost the job that originally entitled them to join the CC but who still retain their membership. These people are liable to oppose the reforms that cost them their jobs. According to the party rules the CC must meet at least once every six months. Its agenda is typically limited to one or two questions, and it does not usually discuss military policy. The CC's Party Control Committee, which ensured the observance of party discipline and considered appeals against expulsion, was in 1988 merged into the new Central Control and Revision Committee. One of the key functions of the CC is to approve changes in the membership of the Politburo and the CC Secretariat.

The Politburo is elected by the Central Committee at the end of the party congress, and further changes between congresses are ratified by CC plenary meetings. Established in 1919 to reach quick decisions at a time of civil war, the Politburo (or Praesidium, as it was sometimes called) came to dominate party congresses and the CC until in its turn it was subordinated to Stalin himself. Under Khrushchev the Praesidium became the undisputed policy-making body, the focus of the Soviet system of government. No longer terrorized by a single individual, the Politburo collectively decides policies, allocates resources, and appoints key personnel. It is not impregnable, as evidenced by the role of the CC in 1957, but it certainly represents the super-elite. The Politburo consists of about a dozen voting members and half a dozen alternating or candidate members. The CC elects a General Secretary who theoretically is no more than 'first among equals' in the Politburo. Under Brezhnev the Politburo began to take on the features of a cabinet, that is, representing the major departments of state, the military or heavy industry, and some key geographical areas such as the Ukraine or Central Asia. It became, as Rigby put it, a 'self-stabilising oligarchy', balanced to avoid conflict. The Brezhnev Politburo was marked by the gradual ageing of its members as stability gave way to senescence, oligarchy to gerontocracy. However, the principle that an institution or geographical area has automatic membership of the Politburo has never been conceded and therefore it is far from being a genuine cabinet system of rule. Membership is formally at the discretion of the CC but in effect is controlled by the Politburo and the General Secretary.

The Politburo meets regularly once a week on Thursdays and since 1982 has published short reports of its deliberations. Its detailed operation is not known but it appears that in contrast to Khrushchev's adversarial style the modern General Secretary hopes to achieve unanimity rather than to impose decisions through voting. This is made easier by the detailed preparatory work carried out by the CC Secretariat, where a consensus view is hammered out. On most items there is no discussion, and Politburo members simply append their signatures to a prepared file. An average four-hour Politburo meeting can thus deal with a great number of issues without overloading the highly centralized system of decision-making.

The CC Secretariat itself is headed by the General Secretary and until 1988 consisted of about ten full members and half a dozen candidates elected by the CC, some of whom are also members of the Politburo. Leadership of the Secretariat buttresses the General Secretary's position in the Politburo. The Secretariat usually meets on Wednesdays to draft proposals for the next day's Politburo meeting. Each secretary was a powerful official, responsible for several key areas of policy covered by the Central Committee departments. A secretaryship is often a stepping stone to membership of the Politburo itself, and joint membership has conventionally been an essential condition of becoming General Secretary.

The Secretariat heads the *apparat*, the vast Central Committee apparatus of appointed officials divided into about twenty-five departments each of which is led by a departmental head, a first deputy, and a number of other deputies. Until 1988 groupings of departments were headed by a secretary. The key departments were administration, party organization, ideology, defence industries, and international (foreign affairs), with a special department for the KGB. In September 1988 the old departmental system was radically reorganized and six new policy commissions created (see Table 4). The Secretariat was a shadow ministerial system assisted by a staff of *apparatchiki*, the party's civil service (or indeed, a state within the state) which oversees the implementation of Politburo decisions. This is the party machine, the full-time salaried party functionaries controlled by the General Secretary and the Secretariat. In Moscow the *apparat* is based in the Central Committee building, not far from the Kremlin in Old Square. Each level in the giant pyramid, from the republican committees, *obkomi*, down to the *raikomy*, have their own staffs, which are estimated to number about a quarter of a million. The great majority (83 per cent) of party functionaries are employed by *gorkomy* and *raikomy*. From 1988 the Central Committee's full-time staff, and those of committees lower down, were cut back drastically. The apparatus plays a very important role not only in the party but also in the whole Soviet political system. The Secretariat departments had close links with the ministries and acted as a vast supervisory mechanism. In contrast, the role of the new commissions is to chart long-term policy rather than to manage day-to-day business. The Secretariat acts as host to various conferences at which party policy is hammered out.

The Central Committee Secretariat is the nerve centre of the vast system of centralized appointments, the *nomenklatura*. It appoints officials to key bodies such as the Komsomol, trade unions, and a myriad other state and public organizations as well as to the party itself. Local party secretariats also have their *nomenklatura* lists. At each level there is a list of posts to be filled (considered to be in a particular committee's *nomenklatura*); and a second list of people suitable to fill them. The *nomenklatura* of the Central Committee, for example, is managed by the Politburo and includes the top positions in the party, the soviets, the ministries, the armed forces, and the leading scientific, academic, and cultural institutions. The *nomenklatura* of a *raikom* would include the secretaries of the party cells, the chair of the village soviet, the chair of the *kolkhoz* and the director of the local factory. The *nomenklatura* system constitutes a vast system of patronage exercised by the party. Those on the *nomenklatura* lists constitute the top people in the Soviet system, but those on the list of the Central Committee are clearly very different from those at borough level. Those whose *nomenklatura* is held by a department of the CC are considered to have broken through into the inner circle. The very peak is made up of those whose *nomenklatura* is held by the Politburo or the Central Committee itself. The number of people on these lists is not known. Estimates vary from between 750,000 to 3 million, including posts in the party itself.[7] There is a certain amount of personnel movement between the party, state, and ministerial hierarchies, and the system is clearly conducive to confused lines of command.

Appointment to posts does not take place through open advertisement or competitive recruitment but through this sytem of extended co-option. Political as much as professional factors are taken into account in making appointments. This more than anything reveals the Soviet system as an imperfect bureaucracy, based not on clear performance criteria as in the Weberian model but on a variety of informal practices. Under Brezhnev the incompetent and corrupt were shielded from the consequences of their actions. The system of patronage and the extended development of patron-client relations began to challenge the *nomenklatura* system itself. Corruption allowed favouritism and bribery to determine appointments rather than political qualities. Even more alarming from the CC's point of view, it bypassed the Secretariat and the official system of appointments. One result of the anti-corruption campaign since Andropov has been to re-establish the party Secretariat's control over the party machinery. A marked feature of appointments from the mid-1980s has been the 'parachuting in' of newcomers untainted by local networks.

The system of party organization as developed in the first years of Soviet power and consolidated by Stalin allowed little scope for democracy in the party. The 'circular flow of power' from about 1921 allowed the inversion of democratic centralism so that in place of elections from the bottom up the party's electoral system was fused with the party apparatus, which proceeded to 'select' suitable candidates from the top down, who were then 'elected' by the body concerned. Instead of the Central Committee electing the Politburo, the Politburo chose the membership of the Central Committee, which was then confirmed by the party congress. Under Gorbachev these patterns have begun to change. Less emphasis has been placed on centralism and more on democracy. Gorbachev's intention of introducing elections in the appointment of posts challenges the *nomenklatura* system. All party officials, including the General Secretary, are to be limited to a maximum of two five-year terms. Democracy within the party is no longer considered a substitute for democracy in society. It has become clear that one cannot survive without the other.

Party, state and government

Article 6 of the 1977 constitution provides a general formula for the role of the communist party in the Soviet state:

> The leading and guiding force of Soviet society and the nucleus of its political system, of all state organizations and public organizations, is the Communist Party of the Soviet Union. The CPSU exists for the people and serves the people.
>
> The Communist Party, armed with Marxism-Leninism, determines the general perspectives of the development of society and the course of the home and foreign policy of the USSR, directs the great constructive work of the Soviet people, and imparts a planned, systematic, and theoretically substantiated character to their struggle for the victory of communism.
>
> All party organizations shall function within the framework of the Constitution of the USSR.

This provides only a general indication of the powers of the party in the system of soviets and ministries. The ambiguity of Soviet constitutionalism has meant that from the very beginning, much to the anger of the Democratic Centralists, the party-state relationship, as in other spheres of Soviet life, has been governed more by convention than by statute. The relationship between the party and the state is a complex one, since not only is the CPSU the kernel of the state, but it is potentially the state itself. The Soviet Union, in effect, has two operative governments, the party and the state system. The party, however, is not to be identified with the government or state, despite its close links with them. Since 1917 the communist party has ruled but not governed. The party is in effect the senior executive branch of the Soviet government, where all decisions are made or confirmed. The Supreme Soviet and the Council of Ministers act as the junior administrative branches, implementing decisions taken within the appropriate party committee. Such overlapping and lack of definition of functions is a natural consequence of the constitution's rejection of the separation of powers. The relationship between the party and the state is a crucial one, yet it changes over time, level in the hierarchy and area of the country. The power system is both fused and confused. As part of the concept of developed socialism, the 1977 constitution moved some way from the former notion of a state structure towards the idea of a 'political system', which implies a more subtle relationship between the constituent parts of the Soviet system of power.[8]

The party is not meant to act either as an organ of state or as an alternative to state structures, though in practice this injunction is not always upheld. Party control over the state and governmental system is achieved through six main mechanisms.

(i) The use of party fractions in the soviets, institutions, and mass organizations. The party group acts as a caucus which directs the work of the host body. In the smaller soviets the party fraction is often a minority (in over 43 per cent of soviets in 1980), but at higher levels communists are always in the majority, and the percentage rises the higher one goes. In 1984 71.7 per cent of the 1,500 Supreme Soviet deputies were communists. At the republican level in 1979 the percentage of communists was about 65 per cent, in *oblast* soviets 55 per cent in 1977, down to 41 per cent in village soviets. These proportions are bolstered by a solid group of Komsomol members who act as a junior version of the party. The fractions ensure the dominance of communists on soviet executive bodies. In 1979 12·1 per cent of the 2,229,785 deputies at *oblast* level and lower were members of executive committees., Of these 71·6 per cent were communists. At *oblast* level communists comprise 93 per cent of executive committees, and in villages 68 per cent. The caucus is subordinate to the local party committee. The party caucus in a given soviet usually meets prior to sessions to agree on co-ordinated policies. The caucus system is the heart of classical Leninism and ensures that party policy decided elsewhere is adopted by the host institution. The group of non-party deputies do not have the right to meet separately beforehand and therefore, if they so desired, could not put up coherent opposition.

(ii) The party's influence is channelled through the vast network of primary party organizations. The PPOs in factories, farms, and institutions perform a variety of functions. They supervise the local managements, disseminate the latest political directives and ensure the fulfilment of the plans. The party secretary in any enterprise is an important figure, and although limited to a one-year occupation of the post is usually re-elected year after year. The secretaries' precise rights with respect to management have never been clear. Essentially, they have a right of supervision (*pravo kontrolya*) over management. Since the manager is usually also a communist, he or she would in any case try to ensure that their decisions were in conformity with party directives. In undoing the Khrushchev reforms party dominance under Brezhnev was somewhat undermined by the devolution of authority to the ministries. Measures from 1971 to counter this trend proved ineffective.

(iii) All important posts are appointed through the *nomenklatura* system. In this way the party ensures the loyalty both of the people appointed and of the organization in which they work. The system permits the communist party to use its membership to the maximum effect by placing them in strategic positions.

(iv) The system of appointments is reinforced by extensive interlocking membership. Senior party figures in a locality are often the same people who lead the soviets or other public bodies. Following the defeat of the anti-party group in 1957, Bulganin was replaced as Premier by Khrushchev in addition to his post as head of the party. On Khrushchev's ousting in October 1964 it was decreed that in future no individual could occupy both posts simultaneously. However, no such stipulation regulated the other link in the triad, the party leadership and the presidency. Brezhnev's elevation to the presidency in 1977 while remaining General Secretary was the most spectacular instance of interlocking membership and established a precedent followed by Andropov, Chernenko, and Gorbachev. There is, however, no overlap between the Council of Ministers and the Praesidium of the Supreme Soviet. The nineteenth party conference formalized the link between the party and the soviets by proposing that the candidate for the chair of each soviet should be the corresponding first secretary. At the top this means that the party's General Secretary will become president of the new Congress of People's Deputies.

(v) The party is the ultimate decision-making body and retains final control over the formation of policy. Hill and Frank term the party programme the 'ideological constitution' of the country, in which the key theoretical principles of a given stage are outlined. The party acts as the brain of the country. The Central Committee apparatus maintains an extensive shadow ministerial network, reproduced on a smaller scale down through the system. The party is meant not to engage in the direct administration of industry or agriculture but to supervise the work of the relevant bodies. Its decisions are usually enacted through the relevant soviet or governmental machinery and thus gain the force of law.

(vi) Responsibility for making policy is closely associated with accountability for securing its implementation, a system of executive responsibility. The party has its parallel structure of committees and at all levels is the most important source of authority. Local soviet or ministerial officials have learnt to live with the interference of party officials in their work, and since most share a common allegiance to the party the relationship does not need to be unduly adversarial.

The local party organizations and their secretaries are the cornerstone of a powerful system of party control from the highest to the lowest level. The republican, *obkom* and city first secretaries are powerful officials in their districts. Hough has compared them to the French prefects, acting as the plenipotentiaries of central power to ensure the execution of economic and political programmes. They appoint personnel and supervise the performance of industry and agriculture.[9] Local party secretaries are responsible for effective economic performance and political stability. The 'prefects' are encouraged to take the larger view and ensure that the general conditions of workers, food supplies, and so on do not reach crisis point. Under Brezhnev the system on the whole worked effectively and there was no major confrontation with workers like the one in Novocherkassk in 1962.

The powers of a *gorkom*, for example, are large but not unlimited. Its purpose is to direct (*napravlyat*) the activities of the state, economic, and public organizations. It exercises executive leadership (*rukovodstvo*) over the life of the locality. Further, it maintains supervision (*kontrol*) over factories, but it tries not to replace one-person management by a form of collective leadership. The party has an auxiliary role. It is intended to settle questions of political principle but not day-to-day management policy. In the unreformed system everything was subordinated to plan fulfilment, and even the party sometimes had to accede to the demands of local managers. In places 'company towns' emerged, dominated by one factory or industry, where the responsible ministry wielded enormous power. To a degree the duplication between party, ministry, and soviet acts as a checking mechanism.

Since at all levels local party organizations maintain departments staffed with their own experts, one can assume that the level of detailed supervision is fairly high. Indeed, in 1971 party organizations in ministries and departments were mandated to ensure the implementation of policy in the light of party directives. Party and state structures are maintained in parallel to each other, and there is a certain duplication of knowledge and expertise. The theoretical demarcation of party and state spheres of competence has been increasingly blurred as the role of experts has increased. The party is meant to act as the supreme rational co-ordinator. However, the rationality is conditional upon a variety of considerations which can be at variance with the achievement of maximum economic efficiency. The party-state administrative structure under Brezhnev did not always generate a sufficient 'quantity of rational decisions'.[10] It is for this reason that Gorbachev reorganized the CC Secretariat in 1988.

The detailed involvement of party officials in administration through these six mechanisms suggests that in many ways the country is vastly overgoverned. The lack of precise definition of the party's leading role and its extensive powers tend to convert its guiding functions into substitution. *Podmena* has been a permanent feature of political life, but it is often apparent in the administrative sphere as well. The nature of the party's involvement with local soviets cannot but sometimes take the form of 'petty tutelage' or 'parallelism', condemned since the first days of Soviet power. As mentioned, the eighth party congress in March 1919 warned that the party should lead but not merge with the state administrative system.

For over seventy years it has been difficult to establish a workable balance, since the problem is a structural one and cannot be overcome by decrees alone. *Podmena* only marks occasions when the underlying power relationship surfaces. Given the political weakness of the soviets, such 'parallelism' is not surprising. Furthermore, local party secretaries are judged by their performance in ensuring social order and the fulfilment of economic plans, hence their careers depend on detailed involvement in affairs that properly lie in the domain of state or government officials. Attempts to delineate more clearly the functions of the party and the state during *perestroika* have been set back by making local party leaders simultaneously the chair of the local soviet. In effect *podmena* has become institutionalized.

The role of the local party organizations has changed with time, but their prefectorial role has remained the same. As Rigby puts it, they have become officers of a 'ministry of co-ordination'. Under Brezhnev this achieved a peak of stability. Although the system is in some senses an irrational duplication of resources, it appears to work effectively to achieve certain goals. The prefectorial system has overseen the industrialization of the country and the maintenance of social peace. The question increasingly arises, however, whether such a system, developed in different times and with different aims, remains suitable for a developed society and economy. The accustomed definition of the leading role of the party may have to change.

The leading role of the party

The party, state, and government are locked into a complicated relationship governed, as elsewhere in the Soviet polity, by informal relationships. The party's leading role is ensured by its dominance in definining policy and personnel appointments. The political levels of decision-making (legislation) and the administrative level of decision implementation (administration) have become thoroughly entwined. For this reason Kassof labelled the polity an 'administered society' where politics has given way to expanded administration. This is a fundamental legacy of the Leninist ideal of a self-administered commune-state with a high level of public participation guided into politically correct channels by the party. The model has no room for antagonistic conflicts but insists on social and political unity, which too often comes out as conformity. In a sense the party fulfils the role of Plato's guardians. The party acts as the gatekeeper in a fairly literal sense in establishing policy options and determining the access of various concerns to the polity. To paraphrase Marx, the communist party is nothing more than an executive committee for managing the collective affairs of the socialist state.

The nature of Soviet-type parties has long been a matter of debate. Can a party be a party at all in a one-party state? It lacks free recruitment, is controlled by its leadership and it dominates the body politic to the exclusion of any meaningful role for other political parties. Under high Stalinism the party lost some of the attributes of a political organization. At present it functions less ambiguously as a party in terms of organization and structure. The emergence of a series of *dirigiste* one-party states in the world has forced the concept of the party to be expanded beyond the definition applicable to liberal democracies. Its functions are unique to this 'party of a new type'. The party's crucial achievement has been to retain its separate organizational identity: it has neither taken over the functions of the state (though at times it has come perilously close to doing so) nor been captured by the state. Institutional fragmentation is constitutionally chaotic, yet it has allowed the party to retain its identity.

The CPSU is at one and the same time a mass party, attracting a large membership in society, a revolutionary party, a cadre (or leadership) party, and something on the Mexican model of the party of the institutionalized revolution. This is reflected in the three layers of membership performing different functions. The party sustains its revolutionary role in society and abroad, and at the same time performs a cadre role in society. The identification of the party with the new ruling class is clearly misleading, given the large spread of its membership. The party member working in the dairy of a *kolkhoz* or in the machine room of a factory is hardly a member of the social elite, though it would be fair to say that members perceive themselves as belonging to the political elite. The party is clearly an elite in that it has selective membership and proclaims its higher status through a greater devotion to duty. The division of the party into a small inner corps and a much larger mass membership is a useful one, with the inner party broadly corresponding to those holding *nomenklatura* posts. There is, however, a large spread in the importance of these posts also. The middle category of party activists plays a vital role in mediating between the party and society.

The party's functions include socialization through the vast agitprop network operating through the media, local party organizations, and special agitprop bodies. In 1986 there were over a million propagandists working with about 2·5 million agitators. The malaise and corruption of the later Brezhnev years indicate the ineffectiveness of much of this work. It has done little to eradicate the alleged ills of Soviet society such as passivity, consumerism, narrowmindedness, and philistinism, let alone averted the corruption of the political leaders themselves.

In a vast country stretching from the Pacific to Poland with dozens of languages and nationalities the CPSU acts as an integrating force. The party is as active in an economically backward region as in an advanced one. Its influence is exerted through the mechanisms described above, but it also acts as a symbolic unifying force with which all classes and nationalities can identify. The centrifugal tendencies of the federal state structure are countered by the centralized and unitary communist party. Information from communist party organizations all over the country arrives daily at party headquarters in Moscow and provides the leadership with its own source of information about conditions in the country. The party in the Soviet Union is effectively embedded in its society, whereas in Poland, and to a lesser extent in Czechoslovakia, a gulf remains which can be expressed as one between the *pays légal*, the official system, and the *pays réel*, the actual operation of society. This difference derives largely from the way that party rule was established in Eastern Europe after the war and from differing political cultures, but it also owes something to the fact that the Soviet party has been a much more astute political manager than, say, the Polish party. The sources of the CPSU's legitimacy are much firmer than those of its counterpart in Poland: it has been able to sustain itself as a hegemonic force and relies on coercion only in extreme instances. Melvin Croan argues that the party is not only 'well-rooted' in Soviet society, it is the basis of that society.[11] The mantle of power of the old regime was not simply transferred to the new one but thoroughly remoulded. The party generated a new political culture to replace the one it destroyed.

The history of the post-Stalin era has been the story of the party's defence of its 'leading role' in society, as the guiding force in Soviet-type political systems. Under Stalin the party as a functioning political institution waned in importance, although, as we have seen, it remained the source of legitimacy. Khrushchev's most enduring achievement was the reconstitution of the leading role of the party. Brezhnev's definition of developed socialism consolidated the theoretical basis of the party's dominance. While Marxism talked of the ultimate withering away of the state as class contradictions disappear, and elements of this were reflected in the idea of the state of all the people, proclaimed in 1961, there is no equivalent theory of the ultimate withering away of the party.

It is difficult to envisage the Soviet political system without the communist party. However, Khrushchev's restoration of the party could not go back to Lenin altogether, since conditions had drastically changed. The quickening pace of advances in science and technology increasingly raised the spectre that the party's leading role itself might obstruct the further development of society's productive forces. Already some of the attempts at economic reform, as in 1965, were aimed at replacing some of the administrative controls exercised by the interlocking administrative apparatus by economic mechanisms operating through elements of the market. The first steps were taken towards making the direct economic role of the party redundant by strengthening injunctions against the party involving itself in 'petty tutelage' over enterprise affairs. Opposition to the reform was in part resistance to the implicit downgrading of the role of the party in a more marketized economy. The threat was not only to the privileges of the bureaucratic elite; ultimately it challenged the political dominance of the party as well. Reform of the centralized command economy could threaten the whole machinery of the command society.

In 1968 the Czechoslovak communist party tried to broaden the definition of its leading role in order to establish an interactive relationship with diverse social forces. The party's Action Programme of April 1968 accepted that its authority did not derive from the once-and-for-ever act of taking power but was based on performance and had to be fought for and won daily. The party's leading role was to remain, not in the form of a monopolistic concentration of power in its hands but through hegemony. Communist absolutism was tempered as the party renounced its divine right to rule. This was not a new idea, since it had been raised by the Democratic Centralists in 1919–20 when they railed against the petty tutelage of the party, and it was taken up by the Workers' Opposition as regards the trade unions, but under Stalin the issue was taboo. Dubček's 'socialism with a human face' abolished censorship of the press, but the reform that really precipitated the Warsaw Pact invasion of August 1968 concerned inner-party organization. The party rules were democratized to allow internal elections to be held by secret ballot, and the regular turnover of party officials was envisaged. The Czechoslovak party attempted to repeal Lenin's 1921 ban on organized factions. Democratic centralism was in effect discarded as minority views were allowed within the party even after decisions had been taken.[12] The invasion took place not to restore the party's leading role, for that was never in doubt, but to ensure that it operated in the old way. The Soviet party resisted the ideas of the Action Programme and vigorously reaffirmed its right to rule in the old way. To a degree the absence of serious reform after 1968 reflected the Brezhnevite political *impasse* consolidated by the invasion. The economic reforms that did occur concentrated on the introduction of new technology, improving planning techniques, and extending the powers of central government.

The Leninist system is a highly effective mechanism for retaining power. The Soviet party has been almost too successful in resisting domestic and external challenges. The communist countries of Eastern Europe act as social laboratories, allowing the CPSU to learn by proxy how to avert the successive crises suffered by neighbouring ruling parties. However, although the Soviet party has successfully resisted the advance of political pluralism, it has found it necessary to reconcile itself to the onset of elements of social and institutional pluralism. Pyramidal lines of command cover the polity in a dense network of controls over functionally differentiated groups and institutions. The charismatic leader has given way to settled routines and the institutionalization of power. Richard Lowenthal describes the modification in the party's role in terms of a shift from a mobilization phase, when the industrial foundations of socialism are laid, to a post-mobilization phase when the era of major transformations comes to an end. The political monopoly of the party is more difficult to justify in the second phase and has to be placed on a different footing.[13] The stages, according to Samuel Huntington, are 'transformation', 'consolidation', and 'adaptation', the last stage being variously called the 'post-mobilization phase' or David Apter's 'reconciliation system', in which the regime gradually draws in the various strategic sectors of society, and ultimately incorporates dissent, to establish a politically stable system.[14] Kenneth Jowitt is more sanguine and argues that after the mobilization and adaptation phases the process of inclusion is neither inevitable nor irreversible, and in any case takes place on the regime's terms.[15] There remains a fundamental question over the success of the party in the 'inclusion' phase. Zygmunt Bauman talks of a long-term systemic crisis and not of long-term political stability.[16] Stagnation and not political development were indeed prevalent under Brezhnev. Mikhail Heller talks of the party as a parasite on society which is not necessary but justified on ideological grounds.

The polity centred on the party is challenged to adapt to the society that it has created. The challenge is not a new one, since in many respects the problem of greater inner-party democracy, though for long periods suppressed, has never entirely disappeared. The relationship between the ideology of the development of socialism and the Leninist theory of party organization has been a problematical one from the outset. Lenin's theory of 'consciousness', the preserve of an enlightened elite, imposed certain constraints on party organization and on the party's relationship with society. In Western Europe several communist parties, notably in Italy and Spain, have rejected Leninist vanguardism in favour of a Euro-communism which explores the possibilities of Czechoslovakia's reforms of 1968. In the Soviet Union itself the question has become ever more urgent. The 'temporary' ban on factions, imposed in 1921, appears ever more anachronistic. Why should party members not meet together to discuss matters of common interest. For how long can the party hold back the tide of social pluralism that is inextricably a part of modern industrial society?

The alternative to party control at present is either the emergence of a technocratic ethos of public administration or socialist democracy. The party has acted as an obstacle not only to democratization but to the emergence of an independent technical sphere dominated by the rule of the 'experts'. It should be noted, however, that the technocracy itself is increasingly dominated by party members, and there is no stark distinction between 'red' and 'expert' as there was in earlier days. Technocratic party and governmental officials are gradually merging with a managerial view of politics. The alternative to technocracy is proposed by some of the leading exponents of reform in the Soviet Union, such as Roy Medvedev, who have argued in favour of a clear definition of the leading role within the context of socialist democracy. This has now been taken up under the rubric of socialist pluralism. It allows a certain scope for independent social movements within the framework of the dominant party, whose powers are defined and therefore limited. The party makes more use of the state, soviets, mass organizations such as the Komsomol and the trade unions, and a variety of special-interest organizations, both as instruments of administration and opinion formation and as a means of sounding opinion and generating support, within the context of greater trust of non-party people and organizations. There should be legal guarantees against the arbitrariness of the authorities. Such a programme, moving from the restoration of socialist legality towards the creation of a socialist legal state, entails a re-evaluation of the role and nature of politics in the Soviet polity, but its viability remains questionable.

The party is closely involved in administration but it is more than a 'political broker' between various competing groups. Like the Bonapartist state, it does to some extent 'stand above' warring interests. Under Brezhnev the party lost some of its dynamism, and in practice some of its authority devolved to powerful specialist and interest groupings. Andropovism was in part a response to the social effects of this trend but did not tackle its political roots. The party under Gorbachev intends to remain the dominant political force but to shed some of its administrative functions. At a time of reform it is faced with a fundamental dilemma: on the one hand it needs to maintain its dominance over state and economic bodies in order to force reforms through; on the other, those reforms will ultimately succeed only if the party to a degree allows groups and forces in society to enter into a dynamic relationship with each other, and to do that the party's role has to be fundamentally redefined. The experience of NEP in the 1920s illustrates some of the issues involved. The relative autonomy granted to the market and social forces led to accumulating frustrations among sections of the leadership who felt that the party's role as the chief 'doer' was being undermined.

Dubček's 'socialism with a human face' has under Gorbachev become *perestroika* through the human factor, reviving some of the ideas of the Action Programme in linking economic reform to *glasnost*. Reform entails massive changes for the party. The most urgent is the retreat from detailed oversight of local economic management as greater autonomy is conceded to enterprises. The nineteenth party conference accepted that fundamental reform in the Soviet Union requires a reappraisal of the relationship between the party and the state, with much greater independence of the government from party supervision. The party should rule less by administrative means and more by political and legal persuasion. Chinese experience has shown that reform of the political structure requires the separation of the functions of the communist party from that of the government, transferring power to lower levels, and reforming administration and management. The Chinese party leader, Zhao Ziyang, in 1988 argued that the monolithic party-state would eventually be replaced by 'a mechanism of checks and balances' operating in the context of a strengthened legal system and a marketized economy.

Within the Soviet sphere of influence this has been taken the furthest in Hungary. There the parliament has witnessed genuine debate and the emergence of an embryonic opposition party in the shape of the Democratic Forum. Leading critics such as Rezso Nyers and Imre Pozsgay have been co-opted on to the Politburo and given ministerial responsibilities in a revitalised government headed by Miklos Nemeth. However, while party leader Karoly Grosz has openly entertained the prospect of a multi-party system within a decade, there is no evidence that the party's leading role would be dismantled. If Hungary cannot break out of the neo-Stalinist compromise, then the prospects of the USSR doing so are infinitesimal.

The reform process under Gorbachev stresses that the functions of the party and other bodies should not be mixed, and yet exhorts active party involvement to ensure the implementation of reforms. The party apparatus and the *nomenklatura* are forces which, for a time at least, have to remain outside the reform process in order to generate the desired changes, yet their presence inhibits the development of self-sustaining and irreversible reforms. For Gorbachev there is no contradiction. *Perestroika* was started on the initiative of the party and is being carried out under its guidance, yet he insists that the reform process requires a radical transformation in the way the party conducts its leading role. Command-and-administer methods have to give way to political methods of social management.

The Central Committee plenum of 29 July 1988 called for a slimmed-down party governed by democratic elections and ruling by example rather than by orders from above. The fundamental question is the extent to which the party has to modernize itself to generate rational decision-making in an increasingly complex and pluralistic society. The problem is the same one faced in the first years of Soviet power, namely the need not only to find the will to reform but also to generate the ideological justification for doing so.

Notes

1 *Partiinaya zhizn'*, 14 (July 1986), p. 28.
2 J.H. Miller, 'The Communist Party: Trends and Problems', in A. Brown and M. Kaser (eds.), *Soviet Policy for the 1980s* (Macmillan, London, 1982), p. 5.
3 *Partiinaya zhizn'*, 14 (July 1986), p. 22.
4 ibid., p. 21.
5 ibid., p. 22.
6 See Thane Gustafson and Dawn Mann, 'Gorbachev's next Gamble', *Problems of Communism*, 36, 4 (July–August 1987), pp. 1–20; J.F. Hough, 'Gorbachev Consolidates Power' in the same issue, pp. 21–43.
7 M. Voslensky, *Nomenklatura: Anatomy of the Soviet Ruling Class* (Bodley Head, London, 1984), pp. 92–6; R. Hill and P. Frank, *The Soviet Communist Party*, 3rd edn (Allen & Unwin, 1986), p. 89.
8 Hill and Frank, *Soviet Communist Party*, p. 108.
9 J.F. Hough, *The Soviet Prefects* (Harvard University Press, Cambridge, Mass., 1969).
10 J. Habermas, *Legitimation Crisis* (Heinemann, London, 1976), p. 49.
11 M. Croan, 'The Leading Role of the Party: Concepts and Contexts', in A. Janos (ed.), *Authoritarian Politics in Communist Europe* (University of California Press, Berkeley, 1976), pp. 159–61.
12 *The Action Programme of the Czechoslovak Communist Party*, Spokesman Pamphlet No. 8 (Nottingham, 1968); see also Galia Golan, *The Czechoslovak Reform Movement* (Cambridge University Press, Cambridge, 1971); H.G. Skilling, *Czechoslovakia's Interrupted Revolution* (Princeton, 1976).
13 R. Lowenthal, 'Development vs. Utopia in Communist Policy', in Chalmers Johnson (ed.), *Change in Communist Systems* (Stanford University Press, Stanford, Cal., 1970), pp. 33–116.
14 S.P. Huntington, 'Social and Institutional Dynamics of One-party Systems', in S.P. Huntington and C.H. Moore (eds.), *Authoritarian Politics in Modern Societies* (Basic Books, New York and London, 1970), pp. 3–47; D.E. Apter, *The Politics of Modernisation* (University of Chicago Press, Chicago, 1965), pp. 394–6.
15 K. Jowitt, 'Inclusion and mobilization in European Leninist Regimes', *World Politics*, 28, 1 (October 1975), pp. 69–96.
16 Z. Bauman, 'Systemic Crisis in Soviet-type Societies', *Problems of Communism* (November–December 1971), pp. 45–53.

Key Texts

Hill, Ron, and Peter Frank, *The Soviet Communist Party*, 3rd edn (Allen & Unwin, London, 1986)
Miller, John, B., 'The Soviet Communist Party: Trends and Problems', in S. White and D. Nelson (eds.), *Communist Politics: a Reader* (Macmillan, London, 1986), pp. 135–56

Schapiro, Leonard, *The Communist Party of the Soviet Union*, 2nd edn (Methuen, London, 1970)

Select bibliography

Blackwell, Robert E., 'Cadres Policy in the Brezhnev Era', *Problems of Communism*, 28, 2 (March–April 1979), pp. 29–42

CPSU Programme, 1986

Gill, G. (ed.), *The Rules of the CPSU* (Macmillan, London, 1988)
Hill, Ron J., 'Party-State Relations and Soviet Political Development', *British Journal of Political Science*, 10 (1980), pp. 149–65
Hough, J.F., *The Soviet Prefects: the Local Party Organs in Industrial Decision-making* (Harvard University Press, Cambridge, Mass., 1969)
Kassof, A., 'The Administered Society: Totalitarianism without Terror', *World Politics*, 16, 4 (July 1964), pp. 558–75
Laird, Roy D., *The Politburo: Demographic Trends, Gorbachev and the Future* (Westview, Boulder, Colo., 1986)
Löwenhardt, J., *The Soviet Politburo* (Canongate, Edinburgh, 1982)
Lowenthal, Richard, 'The Ruling Party in a Mature Society', in Mark G. Field (ed.), *Social Consequences of Modernization in Communist Societies* (Johns Hopkins University Press, Baltimore, Md, 1976), pp. 81–118
McAuley, Mary, 'Party Recruitment and the Nationalities in the USSR', *British Journal of Political Science*, 10 (1980), pp. 461–87
Matthews, Mervyn, 'Inside the CPSU Central Committee (Interview with A. Pravdin)', *Survey*, 20, 4 (autumn 1974), pp. 94–104
Rigby, T.H., *Communist Party Membership in the USSR, 1917–67* (Princeton University Press, Princeton, N.J., 1968)
Rigby, T.H., 'The Soviet Leadership: towards a Self-stabilising Oligarchy?', *Soviet Studies*, 22 (1970), pp. 167–91
Sartori, Giovanni, *Parties and Party-Systems: a Framework for Analysis* (Cambridge University Press, Cambridge, 1976)
Shakhnazarov, Georgy, *The Role of the Communist Party in Socialist Society* (Novosti, Moscow, 1974)
Shevtsov, V.S., *The CPSU and the Soviet State in Developed Socialist Society* (Progress, Moscow, 1978)
Waller, Michael, *Democratic Centralism: an Historical Commentary* (Manchester University Press, Manchester and St Martin's, New York, 1981)

Chapter eight

Local politics and participation

Local soviets and administration

The slogan 'All power to the soviets' was one of the most effective in the Bolsheviks' political armoury in 1917. Nevertheless, following the events of July that year, when Bolshevik dominance in the soviets seemed unattainable, the slogan was played down. It appeared that the soviets were not an essential part of the Bolshevik vision of the future. In October 1917 Trotsky led the Bolsheviks to military victory in Petrograd and only then presented the Second Congress of Soviets with a *fait accompli*. The soviets became the basis of the legitimacy of Bolshevik rule and were gradually purged of non-Bolshevik representatives. The soviets were transformed from revolutionary organizations into the kernel of the administrative system in the new republic. The party has continued to rule in their name ever since.

The 1918 constitution vested power in the soviets, headed by an All-Russian Congress of Soviets which elected a Central Executive Committee (CEC). However, effective power lay with the *Sovnarkom*, which had the right to issue decrees without previously consulting the CEC. From the first there emerged a gulf between the theory and the practice of Soviet government, complicated by the undefined though dominant role of the party. Under Stalin the representative role of the soviets declined as they became almost purely administrative bodies. Even this was severely limited by the burgeoning ministerial apparatus. The soviets were limited politically by the party and administratively by the ministries. Following Stalin's death the new leadership led by Khrushchev launched a campaign for the revival of 'Soviet democracy' and in particular of the soviets themselves. The attempt, significantly, began not with the soviets but with the party leadership. Khrushchev's policy was continued by his successors but with diminished vigour until the accession of Gorbachev.

The 1977 constitution (Article 2) states, 'All power in the USSR belongs to the people. The people exercise state power through soviets of people's deputies, which constitute the political foundation of the USSR'. Since 1977 soviets have been called 'soviets of people's deputies', in line with the concept of the all-people's state, no longer distinguishing between workers, peasants, and intelligentsia. As part of the rhetoric of returning to Leninist practices there has been a new emphasis on public or mass participation. The stress has been on the professionalism of soviet bodies, with more formal procedures and observance of rules within the context of the restoration of Soviet legality.

The soviet network in 1985 was made up of the USSR Supreme Soviet, fifteen supreme soviets of the union republics, twenty supreme soviets of autonomous republics, 129 *krai* and *oblast* soviets, eight soviets of autonomous *oblasti*, ten soviets of autonomous *okruga*, 3,113 *raion*, 2,137 city, 645 town-*raion*, 3,828 urban-type settlements and 42,176 village soviets, a total of 52,074 soviets of people's deputies.[1] The soviets have become a major link between the regime and the population, acting to implement the policies of the political leadership, and at the same time enabling it to keep in touch with grass-roots opinion. However, there is a tension between the maintenance of effective leadership and the attempt to upgrade the quality of mass involvement. Too often in the Soviet context participation without power remains simply mobilization, since, as Khrushchev discovered, the attempt to convert managerial participation into populist participation encounters severe resistance. Despite the limitations, a large proportion of the adult population is drawn (*privlechenie*) into local administration. The number of deputies at all levels from the Supreme Soviet to the smallest village increased from 1.5 million in 1957 to 2.3 million in 1985. Of these 44 per cent were classed as workers, 25 per cent were collective farm peasants and 31 per cent employees. Overall 43 per cent were party members or candidates, 34 per cent were under 30 years old, and 89 per cent had higher or secondary education.[2] In addition to these elected representatives there are some 30 million activists associated with the standing commissions of the local soviets, in electoral commissions, or involved in some other local public organization, such as the comrades' courts, the people's guards, street and house committees, and other largely voluntary bodies.

The structure of the soviets reflects their debt to the theory of commune democracy, the principle of participatory rather than representative democracy. The essential feature is direct democracy, reflected in the soviets as 'working bodies' rather than parliamentary 'talking shops'. Most soviet deputies have full-time jobs in addition to their electoral responsibilities. The June 1988 party conference proposed that deputies should be given greater opportunities to concentrate full-time on soviet affairs. Deputies are delegates rather than representatives. They are issued binding instructions (*nakazy izbiratelei*) by voters, and if they deviate from them they can in theory be recalled. In the early days of Soviet power this was frequently used as a strategem to remove Mensheviks and others. Deputies are obliged to give periodic reports (*otchety*) to their constituents on their work in the soviet and their fulfilment of the *nakaz*. A nationwide system of 'parliamentary' immunity designed to prevent a recurrence of Stalinist terror protects deputies from arrest, fines, or administrative actions while on the territory of their soviet without the agreement of the soviet.

The principles of commune democracy have been integrated into the practice of democratic centralism. Soviets combine both legislative (making policy) and executive (its implementation) functions in one body. This classic Marxist principle dispenses with the liberal notion of the separation of powers and instead focuses authority in a single unitary body. Roy Medvedev argues that the combination gives great scope for the concentration of power and the absence of popular accountability.[3] The executive bodies are strengthened at the expense of the legislative. In practice Soviet local government has been less about politics than about administration.[4] A further ramification of the theory of commune democracy is the effective abolition of politics in the sense that the unitary organs of power assume an identity of interest. In Lenin's commune ideal political conflict would be replaced by administration guided, it was implied, by the leading role of the party. Any conflicts that might emerge would be not so much political as technical or departmental.

Commune democracy facilitated the extension of democratic centralism from the party to the rest of society and thus Soviet governmental and administrative procedures reflect unitary organizational practice. Although formally federal in structure, local administration represents the single, indivisible authority of the state in a particular locality, and all Soviet institutions function as part of a single giant bureaucracy. The system operates within the framework of dual subordination in which departments of executive committees are accountable both to the local soviet and to higher executive committees and ministries. The higher bodies can set aside the decisions of lower bodies. Dual subordination operates within the framework of strict hierarchical divisions and yet in a system where there is overlapping control by state and party bodies (see Fig. 5).

Local soviets have departments coming to a head in an executive committee, and (with the exception of village soviets) a praesidium. From 1989 local soviets elect a chair by secret ballot who will normally be the first secretary of the local party organization. Each local soviet has a single chamber, ranging in membership from thirty-three deputies at the village level, seventy-eight in the *raiony*, 134 in the cities, to 218 in the *oblasti*. Until Gorbachev the attempt to revive soviet plenums *vis-à-vis* executive committees met with little success. Ordinary deputies were seldom involved in policy formulation, since the legislative plenum was relatively unimportant, meeting on average about six to seven times a year for sessions that usually lasted no more than a day each. The day-to-day running of affairs was left to the executive bodies. The communist party dominated the legislative proceedings, with the party caucus bound by the directives of the local party committee. There was usually unanimous approval of all legislation introduced, with voting taking place by a show of hands.

Soviet work is now based primarily on achieving a level of public consensus and the satisfaction of social needs. The change parallels the shift from Khrushchev's confrontational to Brezhnev's consensual leadership style. Central party direction of soviets does not always guarantee uniformity in their operation. Away from the gaze of international scrutiny local soviets can be more lively than central bodies. There is more scope for initiative in the choice of topics to

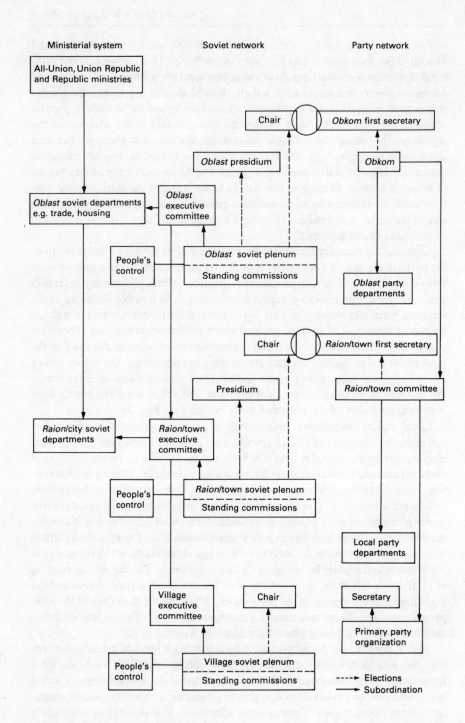

Ministerial system · Soviet network · Party network

All-Union, Union Republic and Republic ministries

Chair — Obkom first secretary

Oblast presidium

Obkom

Oblast soviet departments e.g. trade, housing

Oblast executive committee

People's control

Oblast soviet plenum

Standing commissions

Oblast party departments

Chair — Raion/town first secretary

Presidium

Raion/town committee

Raion/city soviet departments

Raion/town executive committee

People's control

Raion/town soviet plenum

Standing commissions

Local party departments

Village executive committee

Chair

Secretary

Primary party organization

People's control

Village soviet plenum

Standing commissions

- - - - → Elections
——→ Subordination

Figure 5 USSR: local government

be discussed, and the soviets are more representative of the local population. They contain a greater proportion of women and shop-floor workers.

The 337,000 standing commissions in local soviets and in the Supreme Soviet assist the executive bodies in their work. Locally they meet more frequently than their national counterparts and thus allow more consultation with deputies. The budget commissions, in particular, have gained influence over financial affairs. Committees like housing, industry, education, health, and agriculture, as in the Supreme Soviet, have an oversight and supervision function. About 80 per cent of local soviet deputies are members of standing commissions, and this high level of involvement to some extent offsets the infrequency with which soviets meet.

Local soviets are authorized to carry out a wider range of functions than their counterparts in the USA or Great Britain. However, in practice until the nineteenth party conference their real powers were much more circumscribed. This is partially due to the system of dual subordination, with all officials subordinate to the next rank in the chain as well as to the plenary session of their soviet. The powers of local soviets vary, depending on the field, since much is beyond the local soviet's purview, such as enterprises under all-union ministries and research institutions, and much heavy industry, defence establishments, and the railways. Until Gorbachev there was little fundamental change in the highly centralized system bequeathed by Stalin, in which the lowest state farm or factory was run by a ministry in Moscow.

Local soviets were severely weakened by tight central control over finance and their inability to raise taxes. Their main source of income is from sales taxes, which are collected locally but distributed nationally. The dominance of the all-union level in the allocation and distribution of resources deprives local politics of much of its excitement. The all-union centre limits the financial autonomy of the republics to ensure an equitable distribution of funds between richer and poorer areas. The pivotal role of local soviets in the local economy was to be much increased as part of *perestroika*. They are responsible for ensuring that local economic plans are fulfilled and that the decisions of higher authorities are implemented. Job placement programmes have been developing since the 1960s, and with the onset of *khozraschët* (cost accounting) in the 1980s, and the greater discretion for enterprises to shed workers, local soviets have gained primary responsibility for finding the displaced workers new jobs. Local soviets are responsible for running local transport, municipal shops, mains supplies, some industrial and construction enterprises, and cultural, welfare, and health services. The weakness of local soviets, however, is revealed by the generally poor level of infrastructural development. Under Gorbachev local soviets have been much criticized for their failure to use their existing powers to improve local services.

Housing provides the most dramatic example of the problems encountered by the soviets in their attempted revival. In 1936 the state devolved primary responsibility for housing to enterprises which could use this as an inducement to attract and keep scarce labour. Effective town planning was undermined, leading to unbalanced development. To compensate, local soviets since 1957 have become responsible for the co-ordination of local building, with all new land use having to be approved by them and with the ownership of all public housing concentrated in their hands. However, the attempt to encourage more rational local planning and the revival of the soviets is stymied by the government bureaucracy. Ministries and plants themselves still build housing for their workers and control their allocation, often with little or no consultation with the local soviet and its planning department. The problem is the larger one of controlling the vast centralized economy and the ministries. The vested interest groups fear the loss of their economic and political power. In a highly centralized system there is the paradoxical problem of power being diffused among a multitude of agencies. As Taubman points out, theoretically the Soviet system should be ideal for extended urban planning, but surprisingly enough it has the worst of both worlds in that it 'has managed the twin feats of reproducing the distortions of free enterprise under socialism and the pitfalls of pluralism in a centralised state'.[5] Despite strict controls urban expansion is unbalanced, with country towns denuded of services and facilities while Moscow, Leningrad, and the other big cities act as irresistible magnets. The population of Moscow by 1985 exceeded the planned target for the end of the century, while half Russia's villages are doomed to die if the trends of the era of stagnation continue.

The Brezhnev years saw attempts to balance enhanced central control over policy-making with greater initiative for local administration, yet the local soviets failed to achieve a breakthrough into a sustained sphere of independent action. Rather than the decentralization of power there was a degree of deconcentration unaccompanied by an expansion of local autonomy. The chief features of the revival have been the increased competence of local government bodies, strengthened budgetary rights, and an increased role for the soviet plenums as distinct from their executive committees. The role, status, and quality of the individual deputy above all have been enhanced. Despite their large cachet of responsibilities, local soviets lacked real powers in managing local affairs and have tended to act as agencies of the central authorities with little real independence. They were effectively bound by the principles of democratic centralism and dual subordination. The central government bureaucracy continued to dominate the local consumer and producer economy. Urban points out that even on a technical level the qualitative indicators of soviet performance were unimpressive. In the absence of ready access to technical information, elected delegates were unable effectively to partake in government. The stress on professionalism and the specialist under Brezhnev meant that standing commissions as much as individual deputies were unable to challenge their own administrative bodies owing to the lack of detailed information.[6] The obstacles to greater deputy involvement in policy formation and supervision proved formidable. As in other countries this was compounded, despite the rising educational accomplishments of deputies, by the lack of experience and expertise of most elected officials.

Since the actual powers of local soviets fall below their legal rights there remains much scope for the expansion of their activity. Gorbachev has returned to the vigorous espousal of Khrushchev's policy of revitalizing the soviets. There has been constant stress on improving their work to remove elements of 'formalism and show' (*paradnost*), to make soviets businesslike and more effective in *perestroika* and to eliminate 'paper' methods of management.[7] The link between the deputy and the electorate is to be strengthened by more feedback mechanisms, and legislative bodies are to be given more rights, to offset those of executives. Faced with powerful rivals in the localities, above all the party and the ministries, and with central policy tempered by powerful interest groups, the soviets will have to fight hard to achieve a significant improvement in their performance. There are powerful institutional and practical barriers to reform of local government in the Soviet Union.

One of the major factors affecting the revival of the soviets is the role of the party itself. The counterpart of dual subordination is the dual allegiance of state officials to their immediate superiors in the state hierarchy and to the parallel party organization. The *nomenklatura* system applies to local administration as to all other Soviet organizations. The local party committee oversees elections, establishes local priorities and ensures that centrally adopted policies are carried out. Taubman calls the party the 'super-mayor', represented above all by the party first secretary. The party is intended to work though the soviets and governmental agencies, but since local party officials take ultimate responsibility for plan fulfilment they have a tendency to take direct charge of economic affairs. The local party has the right of supervision (*pravo kontrolya*) over the local soviet, its departments and over the enterprises it manages. In the circumstances it is not surprising that the sixfold mechanism of supervision (see pp. 140–2) often leads to substitution (*podmena*).

The soviets are overshadowed by so many bodies that one can talk of their 'multisubordination'.[8] However, several Western analyses of local government in recent years have stressed that, when viewed in detail, there is a degree of liveliness in local politics. For example, Ron Hill challenges the view of the state apparatus as merely a facade for complete communist party control. He sees the overlapping membership of party and state organs at the local level as ensuring ultimate party control but providing the potential for more effective local political decision-making. One of the constant features of 'totalitarian administration' is its chaotic character. The two major interests in the locality, the party and the industrial managers, tend to cancel each other out, permitting a certain amount of local pluralism.[9] The 1970s saw much discussion of the extent of 'pluralism', 'participation', and 'feedback loops' as part of a unique Brezhnevite system of power. However, Gorbachev's revelations in the 1980s have convincingly demonstrated the inability of Brezhnevite mechanisms to overcome the distortions within Soviet administration caused by the overcentralization of planning and governmental processes.

Local deputies act as barometers of public opinion, but local administration as a whole is not constrained by an effective system of public accountability. The tenuous hold on some freedom of manoeuvre cannot be a permanent solution to the weakness of the soviets. The revival of the soviets as a party-directed process means that it is necessarily limited. The soviets are prevented from developing any autonomous and genuinely representative role. The basic issue is whether the creation of an effective participatory democracy is possible under conditions of party dominance. In 1968 the Czechoslovak Action Programme argued that to avoid an undue concentration of power a division of power was required whereby one agency could be checked and supervised by another agency of equal standing.[10] Both democratic centralism and commune principles were modified. In the USSR, however, the party still dominates every stage of local soviet affairs and determines the main lines of policies. Local conflicts are more often the politics of departmentalism than the reflection of a vigorous public life. Public officials are in constant struggle with each other for resources and favourable policy strategies but debate is confined to the administrative system as part of what has been called bureaucratic pluralism. Internal communications do play an important role at the local level, and indeed informal communication, in which the party usually plays a minimal role, does eliminate many of the frictions and irrationalities that persist in local administration, but bureaucratic crypto-politics[11] has not given way to what Jurgen Habermas calls communicative action, where an interactive relationship is established between the actors in political life.

Elections

Elections illustrate the nature of citizen participation in community decisions. Participation in the Soviet Union is mostly organized from above, but to a large extent it is voluntary. Elections to soviets have a special importance, since they involve citizens directly. Until 1989 deputies to local soviets were elected for two and a half years, as opposed to five years for republican and higher soviets. From 1989 all deputies serve a five-year-term to allow them more time to understand the working of local government. They are allowed only two successive terms. The widening role of local soviets in managing the local economy and services makes the choice of candidates increasingly important, and yet until Gorbachev the electoral system stagnated. Under Brezhnev the voting process through the single candidate system was refined to an art. In view of their limited impact the unofficial Polish term of 'voting' for elections was accurate.

In 1936 discrimination against 'anti-soviet' classes was dropped and since then elections have been open to all. Voting is direct in state elections, whereas in the communist party it is indirect. A secret ballot is used whereby the voter simply drops the printed ballot paper, on which there is usually only one name, into the box. Curtained booths are provided but their use has been suspect. Many voters under Brezhnev displayed ostentatious loyalty by simply folding the paper and dropping it into the urn in full public view. If the booth was used the person was suspected of crossing the name out, the way of registering a vote against the candidate. The premium is on unanimity, and as in the soviets, where a show of hands is used, there are social pressures to conform. Candidates are elected if they obtain more than 50 per cent of the registered votes in the constituencies (not just 50 per cent of those voting on the day). Between 1937 and 1981 about 30 million candidates had stood in elections to soviets at all levels, and until 1987 none faced an opponent. Remarkable turn-out figures are officially claimed. In the 1984 Supreme Soviet elections it peaked at 99·99 per cent! Direct elections show confidence in the authority's ability to 'manage' the results.

With such voting procedures the centre of attention focuses on the nomination process for the candidate. Not only is the CPSU the only political party, but until recently there was no choice within that party. The CPSU is involved at all stages, with the party's *raion* committee overseeing the local voting process. The 1977 constitution (Article 100) permits a range of social bodies to nominate a candidate, including the CPSU, trade unions, co-operatives, the Komsomol, and 'other social organizations'. The electoral law was tightened up in 1978 in order to prevent dissident groups constituting themselves as 'social organizations' and proposing their own candidates. The 1988 electoral law retained the principle that candidates can stand only if they are nominated by a recognized institution, but allowed more than one name to appear on the ballot paper. It is still hard for independent candidates to stand since nominations have to be proposed at meetings of not less than 500 people and accepted by at least half of those present. A second filtering takes place when the potential candidate has to be supported by more than half the people at a pre-election meeting. All candidates must be acceptable to the party, and, while they may be non-party, they cannot be anti-party.

The party established central guidelines in selecting candidates to obtain a desirable mix reflecting not so much the local population as national objectives. In the past the actual competence of the candidate was only a secondary consideration, with relatively strict central quotas applied for sex, Komsomol and party membership, age, occupation, education, and nationality. One aspect of this was the low but not disproportionate nomination rate of Jews. In national areas care is taken to ensure fair representation of ethnic groups. Local elections had a tendency not to produce individual candidates but groups of deputies (women, communists, workers, and so on). To balance this, as part of the revival of the soviets, there have been strong attempts to improve the quality of the candidates. The proportional principle loses force further up the hierarchy as individuals are chosen for their competence and loyalty.

In the absence of a free press, and with restrictions on printing and meeting, there is no adversarial election campaign. In the local elections of 1980 seventy-seven out of 2·27 million candidates failed to get elected because the number of scratched ballot papers exceeded those simply placed in the boxes. This is a very small, and declining, proportion and usually occurs in remote villages or if the official candidate is particularly obnoxious. A negative vote does not usually constitute a rejection of the Soviet system but reflects local grievances and local solidarity. However rare, the authorities try to avoid such incidents and aim to find acceptable candidates. It is no longer possible to nominate a defeated candidate a second time. If a person once elected proves to be particularly inept, or suffers from some personal problem, the nominating body of that deputy has the right to recall them. This is a fairly cumbersome procedure and the candidate is usually induced to resign.

The actual conduct of an electoral campaign reveals the organizing abilities of the system at its best, but the whole process under Brezhnev was imbued with formalism and cynicism. The heart of an election campaign is the agitation group, the *agitkollektiv*, which conducts the campaign at the grass roots. It is a permanent institution which is revived two or three months prior to an election. At the base of its hierarchical structure is the agitator, who is allocated about fifteen to twenty electors and instructed to ensure that they vote. About 7 per cent of the electorate actively participate in the campaign as members of the *agitkollektiv*. An equal number are involved in the district electoral commissions responsible for the formal registration of voters and for the counting. Hence a total of about 15 per cent are directly involved. Much of this activity is purely formal, as workers are delegated by enterprises or institutions as part of their social obligations, and participation is not marked by great enthusiasm.

The aim is to ensure that the voter registers at the offices of the district electoral commission. An individual can refuse on various grounds, including citing a specific grievance, or can say that he will be away on election day. Those claiming prior commitments obtain an absentee certificate. In some urban areas up to a quarter of voters get such a certificate. It is readily granted because it avoids forcing overt expressions of dissatisfaction. The much-quoted majorities of 99 per cent should therefore be seen in perspective. The figure excludes the 25 per cent or so of the population who have registered their absence and the unknown number who refuse to register or in any way have anything to do with elections. The 99 per cent represents those who register and turn out to vote, and hence the percentage of dissatisfied people is considerably higher than 1 per cent.

If elections do not perform the selective function typical of the West, why then are they held? They serve several practical functions. Elections permit the population to bargain with the authorities over matters of local significance, such as housing, broken pavements, or poor lighting. The local agitator's job is to listen to these complaints and report them to higher authorities. Workers sometimes even bargain for improved conditions and pay. Party loyalists and potential deviants can be identified during the voting process. Zaslavsky and Brym point out that this is particularly important in universities, where potential troublemakers can be identified early in their careers. The canvassers can conspicuously display their public-spiritedness and bring themselves to the notice of local officials. Elections serve as a channel of upward political mobility. Voting also serves general social control functions and helps to expose infringements of internal passport or registration regulations. Elections are also a useful pretext for periodically mobilizing the population behind the government and provide an opportunity for a ritual display of loyalty. They serve as a socializing device and enable the leadership to claim popular support. Electoral politics are colonized by the regime and inhibit the slogan of free elections becoming the rallying call of a potential opposition grouping. Soviet elections have traditionally served as a form of plebiscitary democracy. The inescapable conclusion is that the voting is less important than the campaign which precedes it. As Hough puts it, election day is merely the pretext for the election campaign.

It is usually argued that Soviet elections perform a legitimating function, and this was certainly the case under Stalin. But under Brezhnev it became clear that elections actually delegitimized the system by being so patently meaningless. There was much evidence of disillusionment with the system. In a sociological survey of the ZiL factory in Moscow in the early 1970s 18 per cent of respondents expressed outright dissatisfaction with the electoral system.[12] Despite widespread criticism of the single-candidate elections, Brezhnev set his face resolutely against electoral reform and indeed strengthened the system. Zaslavsky and Brym explain this in terms of the necessity of understanding the actual conduct of elections. Elections buttress the existing distribution of power in the USSR; they reinforce the recruitment of new people to the ruling elite; and they define the map of the political consciousness of the citizen by associating them with the pseudo-democratic process. By participating in hollow elections people display an act of consent or submission to the institutions and rituals of the political system and thus become accessories to its preservation. In certain respects the system resembles the eighteenth-century parliamentary elections in Britain before the formation of organized parties and where groupings were indeed known as 'factions'. Such 'elections without choice' are a parody of pluralist democracy and, according to Sakharov, 'an insult to common sense and human dignity'.

Perestroika forcibly raised the issue of electoral reform. The direction of possible changes has been seen in Eastern Europe. Elections in Hungary in 1985 for the first time gave voters the choice of two or more names rather than a single take-it-or-leave-it candidate, though none of the thirty-five independent candidates was elected.[13] In Poland, the GDR, and Cuba more than one candidate is sometimes nominated for office. Individual competition does not mean political opposition, but it helps achieve the regime's aim of improving the quality of the candidates. Obviously a multi-choice electoral system undermines the *nomenklatura* system of appointments. In his programme for the extension of 'socialist democracy', announced at the January 1987 CC plenum, Gorbachev accepted the logical consequence that multi-choice elections in the state raise the question of elections in factories for managerial and representative bodies and within the party. He called for greater use of the 'electoral principle' in soviets, the party, administration, and industry, with greater popular involvement in all stages of electoral campaigns.

The new electrocal law of December 1988 reformed the electoral system to the Congress of People's Deputies and other soviets and allowed contests between candidates in single-seat constituencies. Voters will have a choice of candidates from an approved list with one third of the deputies chosen by social organizations. There will be competitive electoral choice, though the campaigns will focus on personalities rather than policies. The option will be to cross out the name of an individual against whom there is an objection. The June 1987 local elections allowed a limited and experimental choice of candidates in about 5 per cent of seats. Gorbachev's plans for a choice of candidates and secret balloting in the party apply to all party committees from the shop floor up to the top. In 1987 experiments began with the election of enterprise managers by majority vote in secret ballots. The aim is to increase the authority of factory directors by making them more than simply the nominees of a distant ministry in Moscow. Gorbachev has extended the opportunities for loyal non-party people. Early experiments showed the limits to such developments. Officials used to organized elections placed restrictions on who could vote, on the choice of candidates, and on procedures (secret or open voting). The radical reform of elections is one of the main means of overcoming the legacy of *dirigisme* and commandism. The attempt to inculcate what Gorbachev calls the 'culture of democracy' into the Soviet political system challenges the practice of guided democracy.

Participation and socialization

The meaning of participation

Classical democracy is usually judged by the extent of participation, and there is no doubt that on a range of indicators the USSR is a highly participatory society. The nature of this participation, however, is ambiguous. It is more than what used to be called mobilization, the bureaucratic organization of consensus and enthusiasm, but less than voluntary effective public involvement in self-administration. Soviet participation has little to do with Western notions of participation as a form of control over political leaders, conducted by rational and informed citizens.[14] Pre-reform elections illustrate that the effective choice functions of participation have been overshadowed by the control functions of institutions and structures generated elsewhere in the political system. Participation has often been little more than an exercise in political socialization. To a degree the problem transcends political boundaries, and even before the foundation of the Soviet republic Max Weber had argued that in modern societies mass political participation will remain very limited.

The Soviet regime has always stressed the principle of direct participation, in the belief that the division of political labour between the rulers and the ruled could be transcended. In contrast to liberal democracy, the Soviet commune view of democracy insisted not only that everyone *could* but that everyone *should* take part in the management of the new society. The people (society) would take back the power hitherto delegated to 'special bodies' standing above them, such as ministries and armies. Mass involvement and the rotation of offices, Marx argued, would replace conventional parliamentary democracy.[15] State and society would become reintegrated, and the state, Engels added, would gradually wither away. In practice, exactly the opposite took place under the centralized system of the dictatorship of the proletariat. The state was massively strengthened and the individual in society was left defenceless. In addition to the class functions of the proletarian dictatorship the power of the state was bolstered by the economic programme of the Bolsheviks. While Lenin constantly urged maximum participation his period in power saw the emergence of a powerful state separate and distinct from society in which even the mass participatory bodies, such as the trade unions and Komsomol, became thoroughly bureaucratized. The institutions of participatory democracy could not operate effectively in the absence of open debate (*glasnost*) in society. The institutions designed to draw people into the building of communism and to extend party influence in society were dubbed by Lenin 'transmission belts', and they reached a peak of mechanical efficiency under Stalin. The totalitarian implications of theories of direct democracy have been denounced ever since Jean-Jacques Rousseau in *The Social Contract* first condemned the alienating and formal process of parliamentary democracy.[16]

Theories of totalitarianism have traditionally emphasized the conjunction of tight controls from above with the stimulation of mass participation from below. Stalin's mobilization of the Soviet population was not satisfied with passive acquiescence but demanded active enthusiasm. In the post-Stalin era enthusiastic mobilization has given way to routine participation as a half-hearted plebiscitary vote of confidence in regime policies and institutions. The transition in terminology from the dictatorship of the proletariat to the state of all the people reflects this shift. Khrushchev's populist attempt to transform managerial participation was designed to control the bureaucracy. Under Brezhnev popular participation remained important, but with a change of emphasis. Participation was no longer set against bureaucratic rule but was defined as its complement. The concept of developed socialism played down conflictual elements in Soviet society, and the stress on professionalism undermined the scope for popular checking of bureaucratic activity. Formal procedures and rule observance replaced Khrushchev's *ad hoc* frontal assaults against bureaucratic prerogatives. In the first flush of the computer revolution in the 1960s the language of cybernetics, the science of systems of control and communication, was applied to the management of socialist society. Soviet social scientists wrote in the technocratic language of the 'scientific management of society', which included provision for so-called 'feedback loops' whereby society could influence the leadership. The Brezhnev era saw the consolidation of formalized participation through greater public debate and discussions within administrative apparatuses, select academic institutions, specialist groupings, and party offices.

Rather than resurrecting populism, Andropov relied on one section of the administrative apparatus (the secret police) to combat the deficiencies in another (the corrupt officials in state and party posts). The post-interregnum leadership, however, has given a new impetus to the redefinition of participation from Brezhnevite formalism to a more active form of commune democracy. Gorbachev's reforms have the potential of transforming participation from the routine and managerial towards something closer to the liberal democratic model, eschewing populist exhortations of mass control over established procedures, and may go beyond liberal democracy and permit greater self-management of society. The development of the new people's control committees under the soviets might well offer expanded opportunities for popular supervision of bureaucratic agencies. Such participation is less than the grandiose ambitions of transcending the gulf between state and society of the early Bolsheviks, and more than hollow transmission-belt politics.

The 'democratic' participation in the West has been contrasted with the 'pseudo-participation' in Soviet-type systems. Studies from a comparative perspective, however, have blurred such a sharp distinction. Little, for instance, argues that most popular participation in the US and the USSR is unconnected with policy outcomes or leadership recruitment, and hence a similar qualitative approach can be adopted. In both systems participation is seen to have little impact on elite decision-making or on the satisfaction of popular demands.[17] Since economic self-management remains an aspiration, the soviets have become the focus of the debate over the democratic content of Soviet participation. The soviets combine a governing role and one of integrating citizens' demands. They are at one and the same time state organs and popular participatory bodies. The soviets are both the expression of the state and the seed for the withering away of the state as the community more and more manages its own affairs.

Contrary to the Leninist theory of public administration in the commune state, which spoke of the simplification of administrative tasks, Max Weber argued that modern industrial society leads to an increasing division and specialization of labour. This does not necessarily imply, however, that the extension of popular participation and democratic oversight over administrative procedures is a lost cause. Habermas distinguishes between practical-democratic decisions, such as whether to build a road, and technical-administrative issues, the question of what the road should be made of, a technical question which can be dealt with in the realm of administration. In the Soviet Union commune practices have removed both from the sphere of effective popular participation, with the party acting as a proxy for the public in the practical-democratic sphere, and the government monopolizing the technical-administrative side. The limited development of a public sphere, defined as 'a realm of social life where matters of general interest can be discussed, where differences of opinion can be settled by rational argumentation and not by recourse to established dogma or customs',[18] removes both from the purview of checking mechanisms and allows technocratic 'hyper-rationality' to run unhindered and permits those in power to advance their own status and power under the guise of an alleged technical rationality.[19] While popular participation everywhere may have little to do with the actual process of government and administration, the weakness of the public sphere undermines Soviet local government and effective participation. The encouragement of *glasnost* is an essential aspect of the revival of a public sphere and with it the regeneration of meaningful participation.

Institutional forms of participation

Participation can be divided into institutional and non-institutional forms. The institutional focuses on the formal mechanisms for socialization and for channelling public activity. In all political systems there is a balance between voluntary and coerced participation in the structures of social organization, a distinction which in the Soviet context is usually seen in terms of mobilized or autonomous participation. Soviet theory distinguishes between state bodies, such as the ministries, the military and the police, state committees and commissions, and so on, and the mass, voluntary organizations, of which the party is supreme, but joined by the trade unions, Komsomol, and other bodies. The soviets are unique in that they are designed to mediate between the two.

The majority of those who wish to participate can do so, but there is no doubt that of all the participatory mechanisms in the USSR party membership is the most effective. The degree of impact depends on the level within the party hierarchy. The contrast between the party official and the rank-and file membership has already been described: at higher levels the party official wields power, and at lower levels the party member exerts influence.

The designation of participatory mechanisms as solely downward transmission belts is now perhaps less true than previously, since they can also allow the upward transmission of information and complaints. The major body in this respect is the trade union organization, one of the most important mass institutions. Early hopes that the unions would ultimately take over the management of the economy gave way after the civil war to stressing their educative and defensive functions, especially under the mixed economy of the NEP. With the onset of rapid industrialization the tasks of the unions changed. In 1933 the separate labour ministry was abolished and the unions took over a wide range of functions which they retain to this day. They are responsible for the observance of safety regulations, administer social insurance, manage the complaints procedure, oversee the factory food distribution network (*zakazy*), run a massive network of social clubs, sports complexes, and housing, and own major resorts and rest homes. They are closely involved in efforts to raise labour productivity and maintain labour discipline.

There were about 125 million union members in 1988, covering virtually all those employed, with the exception of the military. Soviet unions are organized on production rather than on craft principles. Whole industries belong to a single union rather than being divided between electricians, welders, and so on. Nevertheless, the Soviet trade union movement has feet of clay in that the unions play only an advisory role in production issues and lack real powers in setting wages, although formally this is one of their main concerns. The status of the unions is comparable to that of a delegate at a conference with consultative rather than voting powers. The unions follow the line set by the government and have little input in policy formation, illustrated by the prolonged absence of trade union leaders from the Politburo. The post of trade union leader is used as a staging post for those going up (Grishin) or going down (Shelepin, 1968–75), and is firmly within the *nomenklatura* of the party. During *glasnost* it was admitted that, rather than protecting workers from the administration, unions tended to protect the administration from the workers. Unions do have an important, and often effective, role to play in defending the social rights of workers. This Gorbachev urged the February 1987 congress of Soviet trade unions to fulfil more vigorously.

Socialization of the child is the essential mechanism whereby a society reproduces its values and *mores*. In the USSR a variety of institutions have been established for this purpose, and participation is encouraged from an early age. Between the ages of 7 and 10 all children join the Young Octobrists, which had a membership of about 25 million in 1974. At age 10 children become Young Pioneers until the age of 14. The Pioneers have houses and 'palaces', and take part in activities geared towards nature and social participation. The organization is based in the classroom and involves almost all children of the relevant age group. Its socialization effort, like Soviet education itself, is highly politicized, with vows to love Lenin and to serve the communist party. The emphasis from the earliest age is on the group and support for the *kollektiv*. Individualism is frowned upon as a residue of bourgeois consciousness.

Both the above bodies are universal, but from the age of 14 the Komsomol (All-Union Leninist Communist League of Youth, or VLKSM) is more selective and membership is formally optional. Its entrance requirements are less stringent than for the party. Membership in 1987 was 38·4 million organized in the place of study or work. There are major advantages to active participation, and many a Soviet career began here by displays of political loyalty. The role of Komsomol activist is often the first step on a career in public life, as was the case with Andropov and Gorbachev. The Komsomol plays a major role in the socialization effort to inculcate party values among youth through such activities as lectures, meetings, and wall newspapers in factories, offices, and colleges. In addition the organization publishes dozens of newspapers, including one of the more lively national papers (*Komsomolskaya Pravda*), with a circulation of 10 million, and it runs three publishing houses, the major one being *Molodaya Gvardiya* (The Young Guard).

Komsomol acts as the junior branch of the CPSU for those between the ages of 14 and 28, with the party organizations at all levels taking a major supervisory role. A key function of Komsomol is as a preparation for party membership, and all those under 25 wishing to join the party require formal approval by the Komsomol. About 1·5 million Komsomol members also belong to the party, and the majority of party recruits come via the Komsomol. As with the unions, the leadership of Komsomol is firmly part of the *nomenklatura* system. The top position is usually occupied by an older party figure, such as Shelepin in 1952–8, when he was in his 40s. In many ways the Komsomol is an extension of the party apparatus. In foreign affairs it acts as the public representative among youth organizations of Soviet policies. International youth festivals provide an opportunity for the Soviet Union to proclaim its message. However, it is clear that really voluntary participation is rare, and too often the organization is used as a career path. Few members are genuine enthusiasts, and most do what is expected of them for fear that repeated absence from Komsomol meetings may lead to reprisals.[20] Reports from the Urals in the early 1980s suggested that over a third of young workers failed to join their factory Komsomol organization, claiming that it was a waste of time. The problem became a matter of acute leadership concern, and Chernenko sought to combat the alleged indiscipline of Soviet youth in the 1980s by the imaginative application of the methods of the 1930s. In the period of *glasnost* the First Secretary of Komsomol admitted at its twentieth congress in April 1987 that the organization failed to connect with a large proportion of youth. Gorbachev's view at the congress that there could be no socialism without genuine democracy was put into practice. For the first time since the ascendancy of Stalin voting was not unanimous, with a split vote over amendments to the Komsomol rules.

A further form of mass participation which can be briefly mentioned is military or police activity. Every year nearly 2 million Soviet men between the ages of 18 and 20 are conscripted to serve two years of military service. The army plays an important part in educating and socializing Soviet youth in collective values and Soviet patriotism. In addition, the highly developed civil defence programme, with reserve training and exercises, involves a large proportion of the under-30 population. There is enormous participation in policing through the *druzhiny*, the irregular militia groups organized by local soviets. The DOSAAF organization for voluntary assistance for the Soviet armed forces claimed a membership by 1988 of 80 million, or two-thirds of the entire adult population.

These major forms of institutional participation are designed by the regime to serve its own ends and do not necessarily reflect any fundamental underlying sense of unity. They are intended not to articulate social interests but to further the cohesion of the one-party state. At times of political breakdown the aggregation of social interests in Soviet-type regimes spontaneously takes on different forms. One of the commonest alternative 'genuine' participatory institutions is the workers' councils, institutionalized in Yugoslavia in the form of workers' self-management, which appeared in Hungary and Poland in 1956 and Czechoslovakia in 1968. In Czechoslovakia the youth organization was thoroughly reformed, and in Poland in 1980–1 the official trade union movement was abandoned as worthless.

Non-institutional forms of participation

Non-institutional forms of participation are highly formalized but are generated in a broad variety of anonymous and individual ways. Most important in this respect is the role of letters, which since the early 1960s have become an important link between the party and the population. Letters to the press, party, and Soviet institutions provide an important forum of public opinion. Regulations stipulate that every letter is to be answered, and they are all carefully indexed to give the government an indication of public concerns. In addition to the thousands of citizens received personally at the Central Committee offices in Moscow, there is a rising flood of letters, with over 3·5 million received between 1981 and 1986. Complaints predominate in the party's postbag, the major issue being housing. Most appeal for the redress of grievances. Letters are also sent to state bodies, especially to the Supreme Soviet and local soviets, and to the various ministries, particularly in a field such as health. Clearly, for every letter sent several more remain unposted, and the sheer scale of this activity can be taken to show the number of grievances that accumulate and the highly centralized nature of the system, where local complaints can only be resolved in Moscow.

By far the largest number of letters are sent to the press. The total is about 60 million to 70 million a year, and rising. Radio and television studios receive some 2 million letters annually, while a national newspaper receives an average of 75,000. The two major papers, *Pravda* and *Izvestiya*, each received nearly two-thirds of a million in 1987, the numbers rising with the onset of *glasnost*. Here again complaints predominate, with housing the major issue, but with poor organization in factories also important, and other concerns associated with *perestroika*. Even before *glasnost* the press acted as a significant para-political mechanism. The importance of these letters lies both in the symbolic value of the few that can be published, and in the fact that they are forwarded to the relevant agency to be dealt with. The press has increasingly emerged as a fourth estate, using the mirror of *glasnost* to amplify the themes of *perestroika*. The primary means to heal the many sores that festered under Brezhnev is a more active media which encourages the participation of the population in the struggle against corrupt and inefficient bureaucracies. The press, nevertheless, remains under strict party control and there are limits to how and what it can criticize.

The same applies to letter-writers if they wish to have their complaints dealt with. They must avoid directly implicating their immediate superiors, since it is not uncommon for writers to be victimized as a result of drawing attention to inadequacies. Anonymity is no cover, since unsigned letters under Gorbachev are automatically discounted. They must write in the spirit of a common dedication to improving the Soviet system. Letters allow the recipients to play an ombudsman role, and in the absence of other mechanisms letters indicate the mood of grass-roots opinion. They also provide a legitimating function, giving the appearance that citizen's requests are actually being considered. Letter-writers cover a wide spectrum of Soviet citizens, and the act of writing enhances a sense of community and the feeling that justice can be achieved.[21]

A range of voluntary or special-interest societies make up another kind of participation. By 1987 there were at least 135,000 of these, stimulated by a new law on 'Amateur Associations and Hobby Clubs' of May 1986. Formal groups have long been encouraged, but they have always been highly regulated and severely circumscribed by the regulation and control of local soviets. Already in 1920 Alexandra Kollontai had complained in her pamphlet *The Workers' Opposition* that the most minor of public activities was being stifled by a mass of bureaucratic regulation. Even today an approved sponsoring organization must be found, such as a trade union, a farm, or a cultural department of the local soviet. Those lacking formal approval, and even some with sponsorship, have gained the sobriquet of 'informals' (*neformaly*) because of their indeterminate status. Most activities are covered by an official organization, especially with sports activities and games clubs, and they often have workplace branches. Here, as elsewhere, party members in them form their own group. Ecology groups have proliferated, though the party now tries to take the lead on nature conservancy as a result of a steadily mounting wave of public concern. These societies act in turn as transmission belts, sending the party's message down and transmitting popular concerns upward. A range of groupings, such as the Soviet Sociological Association, are developing into genuine professional associations, advancing the cause of their members. Jim Riordan points out that Soviet sport is highly politicized and is used to implement and propagate official policy. It is encouraged as a patriotic endeavour. Literary policy is channelled through the Union of Soviet Writers, film policy through the Union of Film Makers, and so on. All these activities contribute to the attempt to create the 'new Soviet person'. As yet the Soviet state has not created a union of rock artists, and bands remain in a twilight zone of official intolerance.

Brezhnev particularly favoured the mass discussion before the adoption of legislation. This method reached its apogee before the adoption of the 1977 constitution. According to official figures a total of 140 million took part, 80 per cent of the adult population, and 400,000 amendments were received, 150 actually being accepted. It was a well publicized discussion of great noise and little content. The nationwide discussion was revived by Chernenko to air views on the educational reform of 1984. Although a reported 130 million people took part, it was formal, to say the least, though some changes were introduced in the final version of the legislation. Gorbachev reported that some 300000 comments had been received on the draft 1988 constitutional amendments, resulting in changes to about half the articles. To a lesser extent these discussions are encouraged on a range of practical issues, such as housing and alcoholism, which are of special concern to the regime. In June 1987 the Supreme Soviet adopted a law formalizing national discussions on major issues. Mass discussions are restricted to topics permitted by the authorities and cannot be taken to denote the existence of a public sphere. The failure of the Polish government to attain the minimum required votes in the referendum of November 1987 will inhibit the formalization of public debates into referendums.

In addition to the above, a system of complaints procedures allows citizens to participate in the correction of abuses. A law of 1987 strengthened complaints procedures by ordinary citizens against overbearing officialdom, though paradoxically weakened their rights against individual officials. Further, an extensive programme of meetings and lectures is organized to expound the party's views on current issues. Local party organizations and local soviet agitprop committees organize formal and informal meetings in the workplaces. A speaker then expounds on a current topic, such as 'recent events in China' or 'American imperialism in Central America'. It is not clear how useful these meetings are. A less political form of lecture programme is offered by the Znanie (Knowledge) Society, under whose auspices about 30 million lectures a year are organized. Another common form of participation is the officially organized mass demonstration to support

Soviet policies and condemn the United States. These really are 'demonstrations' — called to show the West that the Soviet Union also has demonstrations and to be reported in the press as examples of mass support for regime policies. With the onset of *perestroika* many demonstrations became genuinely spontaneous events. Several times a year, especially after the winter snows, a further form of participation is organized through the *subbotniki*, unpaid work on a Saturday, established to inculcate a sense of 'communist' labour for the common good and to generate a sense of civic consciousness.

The list is by no means complete, but it is enough to give an indication of the range and nature of participation in the Soviet Union. Clearly, the Soviet Union is a participatory society. It no longer needs to rule primarily by coercion but has achieved a high degree of acquiescence in its policies. However, there is only a small degree of bargaining between the rulers and the ruled. In an over-administered society even the participatory mechanisms are highly regulated, or, as current jargon puts it, 'over-organized'. Burks argues that 'The regime, while promoting a high degree of mass-participation at all levels, fears such participation equally. Participation may become effective "interference" in the prerogatives of the established authorities.'[22] Such was the danger of the participation encouraged by Khrushchev. The threat was removed by Brezhnev but the penalty was a widespread cynicism which came to replace fear as the cement of the polity. Participation in the Soviet Union is both voluntary and effective, but there are some missing ingredients: the ability not to participate; obstacles to the formation of groups; and the limits to lobbying. Dramatization of support for an issue through public protests, leaflets, or pickets is beyond the bounds of tolerated participation although increasingly witnesses as *perestroika* developed. The authorities set the agenda for participation. The ban on group activity reflects the politically atomized society. Since 1918 the Soviet regime has closely monitored lateral contacts between citizens (and indeed within the party) in order to suppress the sin of horizontalism. Democratic centralism ensures that participation is directed vertically between the individual citizen and the authorities. Political participation ensured not that authority was controlled by the populace but that the populace consented to being governed.

The official emphasis on mass participation is a legacy of the commune principles on which the Soviet state is built. Attempts to combine participation and administration, paradoxically, led to the radical separation of the two. Furthermore, in the USSR and elsewhere the technical administration of modern society does not intrinsically require participatory institutions. Extended bureaucracy inhibits the development of effective participation, although at the social level participatory networks are important. For most of Soviet history popular participation in decision-making was largely formalized and had little impact on the decisions themselves. Only with the onset of Gorbachev's reforms did the extension in the scope of mass participation since Stalin's death begin to alter the conduct of politics.

Notes

1 *Deputatu mestnogo soveta: sbornik normativnykh aktov*, chast' 1 (Moscow, 1985), p. 3.
2 ibid.
3 R. Medvedev, *On Socialist Democracy* (Spokesman Books, Nottingham, 1977), pp. 140–1.
4 W. Taubman, *Governing Soviet Cities: Bureaucratic Politics and Urban Development in the USSR* (Praeger, New York, 1973), p. 4.
5 ibid., p. 9.
6 M.E. Urban, 'Information and Participation in Soviet Local Government', *Journal of Politics*, 44 (1982), pp. 70, 85.
7 *Pravda*, 28 December 1986.
8 E.M. Jacobs, *Soviet Local Politics and Government* (Allen & Unwin, London, 1983), p. 8.
9 Taubman, *Governing Soviet Cities*, p. 113.
10 *The Action Programme of the Czechoslovak Communist Party*, p. 12.
11 The term is Rigby's, in T.H. Rigby *et al.* (eds.), *Authority, Power and Policy in the USSR* (Macmillan, London, 1982), p. 25.
12 V. Zaslavskii and R.J. Brym, 'The Function of Elections in the USSR', *Soviet Studies*, 30, 3 (July 1978), p. 36.
13 B. Racz, 'Political Participation and Developed Socialism: the Hungarian Elections of 1985', *Soviet Studies*, 39, 1 (January 1987), pp. 40–62.
14 D. Little, 'Mass Political Party Participation in the US and USSR: a Conceptual Analysis', *Comparative Political Studies*, 8, 4 (January 1976), p. 437.
15 K. Marx, *The Civil War in France*, with F. Engels, *Selected Works* (Lawrence & Wishart, London, 1968).
16 See J.L. Talmon, *The Origins of Totalitarian Democracy* (Secker & Warburg, London, 1952).
17 Little, 'Mass Political Party Participation', p. 453.
18 Introduction to J.B. Thompson and D. Held (eds.), *Habermas: Critical Debates* (MIT Press, Cambridge, Mass., 1982), p. 4.
19 Cf. Urban, 'Information and Participation', pp. 65–7.
20 A. Unger, 'Political Participation in the USSR: YCL and CPSU', *Soviet Studies*, 1 (January 1981), p. 111.
21 S. White, 'Political Communications in the USSR: Letters to Party, State and Press', *Political Studies*, 31 (1983), p. 48.
22 R.V. Burks, 'Popular Participation under Socialism', *Studies in Comparative Communism*, 15, 1–2 (spring/summer 1982), p. 149.

Key texts

Friedgut, Theodore H., *Political Participation in the USSR* (Princeton University Press, Princeton, N.J., 1979)
Jacobs, Everett M., *Soviet Local Politics and Government* (Allen & Unwin, London, 1983)
Zaslavsky, V., and R. Brym, 'The Function of Elections in the USSR', *Soviet Studies*, 30, 3 (July 1978), pp. 362–71

Select bibliography

Local soviets and administration

Andrusz, Greg, *Housing and Urban Development in the USSR* (Macmillan, London, 1984)

Cattell, David T., *Leningrad: a Case History of Soviet Urban Government* (Praeger, New York, 1968)

Frolic, B. Michael, 'Decision-making in Soviet Cities', *American Political Science Review*, 66, 1 (March 1972), pp. 38–52

Hill, Ron J., 'Patterns of Deputy Selection to Local Soviets', *Soviet Studies*, 25 (1973), pp. 196–212

Hill, Ron J., *Soviet Political Elites: the Case of Tiraspol* (Martin Robertson, London, 1977)

Hough, Jerry F., *The Soviet Prefects: Local Party Organs in Industrial Decision-Making* (Harvard University Press, Cambridge, Mass., 1969)

Lewis, Carol W., and S. Sternheimer, *Soviet Urban Management* (Praeger, New York, 1979)

Morton, H.W., and R.C. Stuart, *The Contemporary Soviet City* (Macmillan, London, 1984)

Nelson, Daniel N. (ed.), *Local Politics in Communist Countries* (University Press of Kentucky, Lexington, Ky, 1980)

Oliver, J.H. 'Turnover and family Circles in Soviet Administration', *Slavic Review*, 3 (September 1973), pp. 527–45

Ross, Cameron, *Local Government in the Soviet Union* (Croom Helm, London, 1987)

Smith, Gordon B. (ed.), *Public Policy and Administration in the Soviet Union* (Praeger, New York, 1980)

Stewart, Philip D., *Political Power in the Soviet Union: a Study of Decision-making in Stalingrad* (Bobbs-Merrill, Indianapolis and New York, 1968)

Taubman, William, *Governing Soviet Cities: Bureaucratic Politics and Urban Development in the USSR* (Praeger, New York, 1973)

Urban, Michael E., 'Information and Participation in Soviet Local Government', *Journal of Politics*, 44 (1982), pp. 64–85

Urban, Michael E., *The Ideology of Administration: American and Soviet Cases* (SUNY Press, Albany, N.Y., 1982)

Elections

Gilison, J.M., 'Soviet Elections as a Measure of Dissent: the Missing One per cent', *American Political Science Review*, 62 (1968), pp. 814–26

Hahn, Jeffrey, 'An Experiment in Competition: The 1987 Elections to the Local Soviets', *Slavic Review*, 47, 2 (Fall 1988), pp. 434–47

Hahn, Werner G., 'Electoral "Choice" in the Soviet Bloc', *Problems of Communism*, 36, 2 (March-April 1987), pp. 29–39

Hill, Ron J., 'The CPSU in a Soviet Election Campaign', *Soviet Studies*, 28, 4 (October 1976), pp. 590–8

Hill, Ron J., 'Soviet Literature on Electoral Reform', *Government and Opposition*, 11, 4 (October 1976), pp. 481–95

Jacobs, E.M., 'Soviet Local Elections: What they are and What they are not', *Soviet Studies*, 22 (1970), pp. 61–76

Pravda, Alex, 'Elections in Communist Party States', in S. White and D. Nelson (eds.), *Communist Politics: a Reader* (Macmillan, London, 1986), pp. 27–54

Participation

Adams, Jan S., 'Citizen Participation in Community Decisions in the USSR', in P.J. Potichnyj and J.S. Zacek, *Politics and Participation under Communist Rule* (Praeger, New York, 1983), pp. 178–95

Biddulph, Howard L., 'Local Interest Articulation at CPSU Congress', *World Politics* 36, 1 (October 1984), pp. 28–52

Bielasiak, Jack, 'Party Leadership and Mass Participation in Developed Socialism', in J. Seroka and M.D. Simon (eds), *Developed Socialism in the Soviet Bloc: Political Theory and Political Reality* (Westview, Boulder, Colo., 1982), p. 121–53

Burks, R.V., 'Popular Participation under Socialism', *Studies in Comparative Communism* 15, 1/2 (spring/summer 1982), pp. 141–50

Hahn, Jeffrey W., *Soviet Grassroots: Citizen Participation in Local Soviet Government* (Princeton University Press, Princeton, N.J., 1988)

Hough, Jerry F., 'Political Participation in the Soviet Union', *Soviet Studies*, 18, 1 (January 1976), pp. 3–20

Lampert, Nicholas, *Whistleblowing in the Soviet Union: Complaints and Abuses under State Socialism* (Macmillan, London, 1985)

LaPalombara, Joseph, 'Monoliths or Plural Systems: through Conceptual Lenses Darkly', *Studies in Comparative Communism*, 8, 3 (autumn 1975), pp. 305–32

Little, D., 'Mass Political Party Participation in the US and USSR: a Conceptual Analysis', *Comparative Political Studies*, 8, 4 (January 1976), pp. 437–60

Rigby, T.H., 'Hough on Political Participation in the Soviet Union', *Soviet Studies*, 18, 2 (April 1976), pp. 257–61

Riordan, Jim, *Sport in Soviet Society* (Cambridge University Press, Cambridge, 1977)

Ruble, Blair A., *Soviet Trade Unions* (Cambridge University Press, 1981)

Schulz, D., and Jan S. Adams (eds.), *Political Participation in Communist Systems* (Pergamon Press, Oxford, 1981)

Unger, A., 'Political Participation in the USSR: YCL and CPSU', *Soviet Studies*, 33, 1 (January 1981), pp. 107–24

White, Stephen, 'The Effectiveness of Political Propaganda in the USSR', *Soviet Studies*, 32 (1980), pp. 323–48

White, Stephen, 'Political Communications in the USSR: Letters to Party, State and Press', *Political Studies*, 31 (1983), pp. 43–60.

Chapter nine

Power and policy-making

In recent years there has been a move away from the view which saw policy in the Soviet Union emerging simply as calculated responses by a monolithic power structure to domestic or foreign challenges. This 'rational actor' model has given way to views which see policy as emerging out of the interaction of various individuals, institutions, and groups representing a variety of perspectives and interests. How these interests are integrated and articulated remains a matter of debate, since policy-making still takes place largely behind closed doors. We have looked at some of the formal institutions in the policy-making process — the ministries, the soviets, and above all the party. There are in addition a range of informal mechanisms. Policy does not simply emanate from above but there is an element of pressure from below, and ultimately 'society' itself imposes certain constraints on the exercise of power.

Politics, narrowly defined, is a contest over the distribution of political power. However, in the Soviet context such a definition is barely applicable, since policy arises out of the total political and cultural context of the polity, not only of the present but burdened by the past and coloured by a vision of the future. The policy process in the USSR is clouded by the divergence between constitutional provisions and informal practices. Policy-making can be analysed in various ways. The focus can be on the policy process at the local level, or on a specific field, such as foreign policy, which has received a generous share of attention. Policy-making changes over time, and over the type of issue involved. The focus can be on the institutions involved, on the process of policy initiation, policy resolution or on the way that policy is implemented, which often subtly changes the policy itself. In the absence of convincing methodological approaches the emphasis has tended to focus on specific case studies. To help understand policy-making in the Soviet Union our focus in this chapter and the next will be on the role of leadership, on various models of the Soviet polity, on the role of ideology, and on the general issues of legitimacy, political culture, and the nature of power.

The role of leadership

Marxism emphasizes the role of objective socio-economic processes in the development of human societies. Lenin's achievement was to assert the role of human will, or consciousness, in the revolutionary process, although he always placed his voluntarism within the framework of impersonal laws of development. Soviet history has convincingly demonstrated the decisive role that leadership and individuals play in the development of social systems. Lenin's own contribution is a major example, together with Stalin's personal dominance over policy for over two decades. The personality of the leader does make a significant difference, and the leadership principle appears to be an integral part of the Leninist power system. However, this impact is mediated through the party and other institutions and moderated by social processes.

The exaltation of the leader has been an inalienable part of the Soviet political process since Lenin's death in 1924 unleashed the leader cult. The leadership principle has played an important part in the functioning of the system itself, since the charisma of the leader consolidates the legitimacy of the whole system. However, while Bolshevik ideology stressed the role of human intervention in history it was never a theory of individual dominance. The cult of leadership is in conflict with the formally collectivist nature both of the Bolshevik political system and of the ideology of Marxism. Stalin's personality cult from 1929 offended against both principles and was forced to justify itself by appealing to new bases of legitimacy: Stalin's closeness to Lenin; his achievements in building socialism; and his skills as a theoretician laying the basis for Marxism–Leninism–Stalinism thought. Stalin's cult sought to establish its pedigree from Marxism–Leninism by claiming that 'Stalin is the Lenin of today'.[1] The history of the party itself had to be rewritten to eliminate any trace of an earlier ethos of debate and collective leadership. Those who had entered into controversy with Lenin were portrayed not as errant colleagues but as wicked counter-revolutionaries.

The leadership principle is an essential mechanism through which the original revolutionary ideology can be modified to take new circumstances into account. Leadership therefore acts as a means of ideological regeneration. Hence most communist leaders designate themselves as theoreticians and publish multi-volume editions of their works. Gill makes the important observation that the more grandiose the ambitions of the revolution the more a magnified leadership cult is liable to appear as a focus of orientation in a time of turbulent change. As revolutionary enthusiasm subsides the full-blown version of the leadership cult becomes a liability, and so when Khrushchev developed a minor personality cult of his own he was ousted. The leadership principle, though still powerful, has been redefined in the light of the bitter experience of Stalin and to suit a mature industrial society. In this context the inflation of Brezhnev's personality cult was a grotesque confirmation of Marx's dictum that in history tragedy repeats itself as farce. The cult of Brezhnev was largely a personal affair and was designed to buttress the existing system rather than to modify it. Gorbachev's rule to date has been marked by personal modesty and open impatience with the trappings of the leadership cult, like extended ovations and exaggerated obeisance, and yet he has been forced to regenerate the leadership principle to push his reforms through.

The personalities of Soviet leaders and the choice of policies are closely related. The major example is the decision to embark on accelerated industrialization and the full collectivization of agriculture in 1928–9. The policy was always an option in the 1920s, but the particular way it was implemented was very much of Stalin's choosing. Khrushchev's denunciation of Stalin was to be expected, but it none the less represented a major act of personal courage. Brezhnev's personal commitment to *détente* in the 1970s was a factor in its relative success, and Andropov's insistence on discipline was a reflection of his own preferences and background. Gorbachev's bold policies display a great deal of personal policy initiation and his individual style of conviction politics.

There is no constitutional basis to the fact that the General Secretary of the party will head the Politburo and the country. The Soviet General Secretary is not formally vested with executive power, as the President is in the USA, but is constrained by the principle of collective leadership. In theory he or she is only *primus inter pares*. Since the death of Stalin the personal rule of the individual General Secretary has been played down and the Politburo has been careful to restrict his powers. The 1986 party rules explicitly stress collective party leadership as a guarantee against a revival of the cult of personality. However, the Gorbachev succession was exceptional in that there was very little public emphasis on the principle of collective leadership, as there had been in the first years of both Khrushchev's and Brezhnev's rule. Overall the emphasis is on the collective rule of the CPSU, stressing that its policy choices are the only rational options in any particular circumstance. The stress is on unity and continuity, with the basic policy contours allegedly immutably established by ideology, the economic system, the geopolitical situation, and historical traditions. However, in the absence of constitutional limitations a Soviet leader has great scope for stamping his personality on a period.

Since 1953 all leaders have been constrained by the general framework of 'neo-Stalinism', not breaking out into liberalism or reverting to Stalinism. There has been a certain continuity in goals and methods, although the emphasis has changed between leaders. To a degree, Voslensky argues, the General Secretary is a 'prisoner' of the machine and cannot stray too far from representing the interests of the party apparatus, otherwise the apparatus will dismiss him, as it did Khrushchev in 1964. The elaborate rules against factionalism, such as the provisions passed in 1964 that no two members of the Politburo can meet alone (in order to prevent a plot), ensure that leadership links are focused through the party machinery itself.[2] This view perhaps has a tendency to reify the *nomenklatura* system, to give it a personality as if it had a life of its own. It plays down the degree to which a General Secretary might launch independent initiatives not wholly consonant with the interests of the *nomenklatura* office-holders.

There is no settled succession mechanism as such in the Soviet Union, for the simple reason that theoretically there is no succession. Nowhere is it decreed that the leader of the party will be the leader of the country. There are no general elections for the party leadership, and of course there is no choice between parties.

The creation of an executive presidency elected by the new Congress of People's Deputies regularized the position of the Soviet leader. It is most likely that the party's General Secretary will occupy the post and thus be given a popular mandate to act as leader of the country.

The three successions of 1924, 1953, and 1964 were accompanied by bitter contests, but overall the six successions since 1917 have seen a diminution in the intensity of the struggle. The procedure within the Politburo for nominating the General Secretary is shrouded in mystery, but the formal selection is the job of the Central Committee. The Brezhnev succession confirmed the pattern whereby the successful contender is conventionally simultaneously a member of the Politburo and the Secretariat. The nomination procedure worked very effectively in the 1980s, confounding some of the more alarmist predictions that chaos would follow Brezhnev's death. The lack of a constitutional mechanism however, reflects the absence of an open way of integrating conflicting interests. They are resolved, but behind closed doors, giving rise to much Kremlinological speculation. Pleas for more focus on long-term developmental processes such as changes in social mobility, education, and general sociological factors rather than the minute study of the entrails of power struggles within the Kremlin were undermined by the absence of *glasnost*. As growth falters and resources decline these informal mechanisms of conflict resolution may put an intolerable strain on the system. Only now is there beginning to be more actual legislation about what is, than fiction about what should be.

There was no established term for remaining in power until 1988. With the exception of Khrushchev all pre-Gorbachev party leaders have died in office. The lack of a tradition of honourable retirement has dire consequences for the country, since, as Brezhnev proved, the leader refuses to give up his job for fear of being discredited. At the same time, no Soviet leader is able to designate his successor, and the emergence of an individual as heir apparent usually signals his downfall as the other pretenders unite to destroy him. Lenin in his Last Testament set his putative successors at each other's throats by the inflammatory and derogatory terms in which he described them. By surrounding himself with men his own age Brezhnev tried to ensure that any heir apparent would be too old to displace him before his death as he himself had ousted Khrushchev in 1964.

The role of leadership in the Soviet political system is a variable which waxes and wanes and which is not derived from institutional sources of power alone but from a combination of personality factors, the tradition of the 'strong Tsar', and the presidential factor: the ability to inaugurate and promote policy initiatives in a system which has a tendency towards immobilism and inertia. The posts themselves can rise and fall, depending on the personalities of the incumbent. A distinction should be drawn between the 'power' of a leader and his or her 'powers'. Up to 1989 the formal powers did not derive from any constitutional provisions, but since then the Soviet presidency has begun to look rather like a classic presidential system, though without contested general elections. Actual power, which can be termed authority, depends on convention and the personality of the leader. Stalin had virtual complete mastery over policy-making, while Khrushchev's dual position as head of both party and government from early 1958 gave him great leverage. His formal powers were great, but his authority waned because of his inability to solve problems or to maintain a coalition of support. Brezhnev's leadership rested on a consensual approach, the building of policy coalitions and the gradual consolidation of his own personal position. There is constant faction-fighting at the top of the Soviet political system, but the power of the leader depends on shifting balances between individuals, factions, and institutions.[3]

The successions of the early 1980s proved that the Politburo hopes to choose someone who will not rise too far above them, but their collective preferences can be outbalanced by the Central Committee. Given time, luck, and energy, the General Secretary will be able to consolidate his position in two ways. The real substance of power comes from a combination of control over personnel and policy. Peter Frank points out that a new leader inherits a government rather than creates a new one,[4] and Bunce illustrates that 'Soviet leaders campaign after coming to office'.[5] Power comes from the ability to manipulate personnel; authority comes from success in policy.

The leader's first priority is to build a power base as part of the circular flow of power. The initial emphasis on collective leadership gradually gives way to the emergence of a powerful General Secretary as rivals are replaced. Stalin's bloodthirsty purges of the leadership were only the most extreme expression of the pattern whereby every major leader tries to remould the Politburo and the party apparatus to suit his needs. Before 1957 Khrushchev was able to replace a significant proportion of the Central Committee, and after 1957 of the Politburo and regional party leaderships. Brezhnev moved slowly and required six or seven years to consolidate his own personal position. In this period some observers considered that a stable system of oligarchical rule had developed, based on the collective leadership of Brezhnev, Podgorny, Kosygin, Suslov, and Kirilenko.[6] However, Brezhnev gradually emerged as the dominant figure and upset the balance. In policy terms also the rejection from 1976 of Kirilenko's high industrial investment strategy saw his demotion and the rise of Chernenko as the CC Secretary in charge of personnel.

Allied to the personalism of Brezhnev's political style a broad network of patron-client relations was allowed to develop which threatened the anonymous rule-governed aspects of the system. Patronage groups emerged at all levels, in which loyalty was rewarded by political and social benefits, bypassing the nomenklatura system and often degenerating into plain corruption. Brezhnev's group focused on the 'Dnepropetrovsk mafia' but also included many other institutional and regional interests, marking his progress through the political system. Such networks provide an important channel for the aspiring politician. Gorbachev's own rise from Stavropol to the Politburo as a client of Kulakov and ultimately of Suslov is a case in point. At its worst there 'was a trend to promote people often on the grounds of personal devotion', giving rise to a 'cult of mediocrity'.[7] For the patron these networks help consolidate his or her control over institutions and politicians. For a Soviet leader like Brezhnev they provided a way of integrating the formation of policy with its implementation and the general supervision of the governmental and party machinery. Of course, the existence of competing patronage networks acted as a check on his leadership and justified his consensual approach.[8] In the 1980s outsiders have been 'parachuted in', breaking up local patronage networks.

Brezhnev's policies for this reason represented the lowest common denominator of general agreement among the elite and reflected the conservative consensus. Much of the inertia of the Brezhnev years was due to decision-making procedures that sought to smooth over conflicts rather than resolve them. Gorbachev has committed himself to rectifying the situation where resolutions were passed and then left unfulfilled. It is for this reason that the attempt at reform in the 1980s has necessitated the exercise of political muscle by leaders. This may well in the long run lead to a change in the post-Stalinist situation where the General Secretary has dominated the Politburo but never totally controlled it.

However much power a General Secretary may wield, he must be able to establish his authority by posing as a successful problem-solver. This by 1979 Brezhnev had conspicuously failed to do, and, while his power appeared to be at a peak, his authority was waning and he began to lose his hold over the policy agenda. In the 1980s leaders have tried to consolidate their position very fast. Andropov launched several policy initiatives, such as the discipline campaign, and consolidated his power through substantial though not dramatic personnel changes. Andropov's many years away from the party apparatus in the relative backwater of the KGB meant that he lacked an extensive clientele network on whom he could rely and found himself in the strange position of a patron without clients. He quickly promoted his own supporters such as Aliev, Chebrikov, and Shevardnadze, but for the rest he had to turn to the former supporters of Kirilenko, those who had supported greater investment in industry in the 1970s, such as Ligachev, Vorotnikov, and Ryzhkov, with a technical or economic background. During his fifteen months in power thirty-five of the then 155 *obkom* first secretaries (22 per cent of the total), twenty-five ministers (20 per cent) and a quarter of the Politburo were replaced, dismissed, or retired. Andropov had to force these changes through against the Brezhnevites and their still active leader Chernenko. Andropov had much authority but relatively little power, despite taking on the presidency.

Following his death it was clear that there was considerable resistance to the appointment of the functionary Chernenko. Chernenko's appointment took several days, compared to the two days required to select Andropov and the few hours to confirm Gorbachev. Gorbachev came to power with much authority and substantial power, which he moved fast to consolidate. The sense of crisis provided an atmosphere conducive to the exercise of an activist leadership. In personnel terms Gorbachev was exceptionally fortunate, since a series of deaths left a number of vacancies on the Politburo which he could fill with like-minded people.

Ryzhkov was appointed premier, and Gorbachev took on greater personal responsibility for foreign policy by nominating the veteran foreign minister Andrei Gromyko president and replacing him by Shevardnadze. There was little emphasis on collective leadership but Gorbachev was forced to reckon with some of Andropov's appointments, above all Egor Ligachev, responsible for ideology, and Viktor Chebrikov at the head of the KGB. He launched a major challenge to the Council of Ministers, scathingly condemning the industrial ministries. The twenty-seventh party congress in March 1986 replaced 44 per cent of Central Committee members. He has capitalized on the need to rejuvenate the elite. The rapid consolidation of Gorbachev's power was achieved by the traditional means of creating a patronage network loyal to himself by the extensive transfer of personnel. His demand for loyalty, however, was tempered by an insistence on ability which takes primacy over the principle of 'stability of cadres'. However, part of the reason for the dismissal of the radical reformer, Boris Eltsin, from the post of Moscow city party leader in November 1987 was his obsession with moving personnel around, giving rise to a dangerous 'instability of cadres'. In personnel policy and in policy formation Gorbachev placed himself in a strong, but not unassailable, position. His authority can be sustained only by success in the fields in which he has chosen to invest his prestige.

It is clear that in the post-Stalinist Soviet political system the leader can no longer simply impose his will on his colleagues but has to operate within consensus politics. Policy emerges through the interaction of the leader, the leadership group, and certain vested interests. The General Secretary is first among equals and has to take into account the views of his Politburo colleagues over policy and appointments (or dismissals) from the Politburo. Archie Brown has summed up the general position: 'Each General Secretary has wielded less individual power over policy than his predecessor, but within his period in office has increased his power *vis-à-vis* his colleagues during his time in office.'[9] One could add that, following Brezhnev, the concentration of power accelerated, since any leader — irrespective of specific policy issues — could not resist the need to show a certain dynamism in policies. Within nine months Andropov was wielding more power and had accumulated as much authority as Brezhnev had done in nearly a decade. Chernenko was an anomaly and too sick to do more than hold back the tide of change for a year. The rapid consolidation of Gorbachev's power and authority, due as much to his dynamic personality and intrinsic abilities as to the undefined powers of his office, is capable of creating the novel situation of an 'imperial General Secretary', comparable to the 'imperial presidency' in the USA. Indeed, such a development was formalized by the creation of an executive presidency. Just as the liberals in the New Deal and the 1960s put their faith in a strong President to push through a reform programme, so it appears that solutions to the Soviet Union's problems will require the concentration of power to overcome vested interests. Already under Brezhnev the General Secretary had begun to maintain his personal staff, and Gorbachev has gathered round himself a select group of advisers making up a think-tank. They include the economist Abel Aganbegyan, the sociologist Tatyana Zaslavskaya, and the political scientist Georgy Shakhnazarov.

There is always the danger of a return to Stalin-style dictatorship or Khrushchevian wilfulness. However, the principle of collective leadership stands in the way of a full-blown imperial general-secretaryship, as do memories of the cult of personality. There has been unprecedented leadership turnover, and yet Gorbachev finds himself stubbornly opposed at all levels of the leadership and polity. Gorbachev's fight in his first years of power to implement a reform programme illustrates the limits to the power of the General Secretary. His struggle is rather like Lenin's attempt in the immediate post-1917 years to carry his policies. Such struggles may entail the revival of some of the features of civil war internal party life, such as open discussions, that were terminated so abruptly by the tenth party congress ban on factions in March 1921. Opposition can in part be seen as an attempt to prevent the General Secretary gaining too much power.

The issue of generational change is closely associated with the political changes of the 1980s. The succession of the early 1980s has been as much a generational as a political revolution. The old cohort came to power as a result of the massive upward social and political mobility of the early Stalin years, and they came to maturity managing his system in war and post-war reconstruction. This generation greyed under Khrushchev, and slowly slipped into senility under Brezhnev. The new generation, represented by Gorbachev, began to take up major posts in significant numbers under Andropov. What impact this will have on policy is not clear. The new generation were children during the war and came to maturity against the background of destalinization and the threat of nuclear war. They are better educated and have a larger view of the world than their predecessors. They are aware of the need for dynamism and international contacts to overcome economic and social stagnation, but the nature of their dynamism is unclear. There is little evidence that they will necessarily be more liberal than the old generation. The no-nonsense authoritarian style of the 1930s and the war may give way to the no less *dirigiste* style of the cold-blooded technocrat as the leather-jacketed Chekist gives way to Stalinists in white coats. The insertion of a new generation into the existing political structures may not mean much of a change at all. They were designed in the first place by the well educated and cosmopolitan leaders of Lenin's generation. The changing sociology of the leadership may make some differences in style and tone, but changes in content will take an act of political will rather than generational change.

There is a larger question of generations against which policy has to be seen. The Soviet people themselves have changed: the population is better educated and has achieved a basic Western standard of living. The prospect arises that, having achieved economic welfare, the people will increasingly resent their exclusion from meaningful political participation and the hollow formality of so much that passed for political life in the Soviet system. The neo-Stalinist compromise is breaking down, both because the regime is no longer able to offer steadily improving standards of living and because the people will no longer tolerate their political exclusion. A further aspect is the generational change of mood. After Stalin political society seemed to cry out for a leader who could invigorate the moribund political and social processes. In Khrushchev they found a dynamic personality, but after his ousting they looked for calm. Brezhnev's stability, however, was taken to excess, and once again the general mood is for change and dynamism. Even without Gorbachev the political system was ready for a period of change.

From the above account it is clear that new leaders do make a difference in the Soviet Union. Weber was clearly right in arguing that individual charisma is a historical force in its own right. The concentration of power in the Soviet system is such that despite elements of collective leadership and continuity the accession of a new leader broadens the scope for policy innovation. Individual leadership in the USSR reflects the fundamental *dirigisme* of the system as a whole. Policy change in some cases flows directly from struggles from within the elite. Bunce illustrates that in the 'honeymoon' period following accession to office a new leader makes his or her major policy innovations. These innovations then become routine until a new leader begins the process anew, dubbed by Bunce the 'policy cycle'.[10] However, in certain important respects a new Soviet leader does not make that much of a difference. The policy cycle inaugurated by the October revolution has become routinized and a change of leader allows some tilts to the rudder but not a fundamental change of course. Above all, despite six changes of leadership up to the mid-1980s, there was little fundamental change in the relationship between the state and society. No leader was prepared, or allowed, to concede an autonomous role for associations beyond the aegis of the state-party apparatus. Under Gorbachev there has been unprecedented debate over policy options. However, it remains to be seen whether this relative tolerance will extend to permitting criticism of reform policies once they have been implemented. All the leaders have shared the same fundamental views on the nature of the system, the role of the ideology and the way the system should operate. Post-Stalin leaders have been appointed to preserve the party's leading role, not to preside over its dismantling.

Models of Soviet power

An occupational hazard of Soviet studies is the proliferation of models of its politics. The various models on offer imply a different understanding of the dynamics of the Soviet state; each has its own contribution to make to understanding the policy process, and each has its drawbacks. The very selection of facts that one thinks relevant is dependent on the theory or model that one chooses. There are three main types of models: those that emphasize the concentration of power; those that stress its diffusion; and those that try to combine an understanding of the centralist elements of the Soviet system with the apparent devolution of influence.

Totalitarianism and concentration models

Totalitarianism can be taken as representative of concentration models. The term was first used by Benito Mussolini in the 1920s in Italy to signify his intention of consolidating power in a one-party state. In the late 1930s Western social scientists began to apply the term to the phenomenon of the massively expanded powers of the state in Germany and the USSR. It was developed into a political philosophy by Franz Borkenau, and Hannah Arendt argued that a new social form had emerged in Germany under Hitler and in the Soviet Union that was not synonymous with tyranny, dictatorship, or authoritarianism.

The classic definition of totalitarianism was provided by Carl Friedrich and Zbigniew Brzezinski.[11] They identified six key elements: (i) an official ideology to which adherence was demanded: the ideology was intended to achieve a 'perfect final stage of mankind'; (ii) a single mass party, hierarchically organized, closely interwoven with the state bureaucracy, and typically led by one man, the *Führerprinzip*; (iii) monopolistic control of the military by the party (as opposed to the state); (iv) a similar monopoly of the means of effective communication; (v) a system of terroristic police control; (vi) central direction and control of the entire economy. The original version very much stressed the role of the leader, known as the *vozhd* in Russian, and the mass party brooking no opposition and extending its tentacles into all other organizations. The role of terror, an aggressive ideology with a dynamic of external expansion, and a mass movement were also highlighted. Of the six points some are typical of many states that are not considered totalitarian.

Two novel features lie at the centre of totalitarianism. The first is the nature of the relationship at the heart of the system, between the totalitarian party and its supporters. Adherence is gained out of psychological 'impulses' as much as out of political belief, and even less out of personal greed. It is an impersonal appeal for loyalty to a higher goal in which loyalty is ideologically structured. When more base motivations become dominant, then one can talk of the decline of totalitarianism. Under Stalin the charismatic personality cult focused these ties on the leader, who was seen as fulfilling the historical needs of the movement. The unique feature of Stalin's rule was his control over the mass movement and the downgrading of the principles on which a party operates, namely routine, established procedures, and the dominance of organization over personal arbitrariness. The clash between charismatic and bureaucratic principles was resolved by the great purges, which firmly subordinated the bureaucracy to the cult of personality while allowing the latter to triumph over society.

The second feature is the relationship between the totalitarian apparatus and society. Totalitarianism focuses on the structure and application of power at the centre and stresses the destruction of alternative sources of power in society. In a totalitarian society all intermediate institutions between the party and the masses are eliminated. Among other things, law becomes subordinate to the power centre and in practice loses any semblance of independence from the state and party.

There are no legal, political, or moral restraints on power. This is usually described by the term atomization, the destruction of all social ties and groups not necessary for the maintenance of the totalitarian system. The regime obliterates the distinction between private and public spheres, and individuals are marked by loneliness, *anomie*, and alienation.

Parallels are often drawn between totalitarian theory and the organization of 'hydraulic societies'. In his *Oriental Despotism* Karl Wittfogel argued that Russia was never fundamentally a Western-type society but was instead characterized by the 'Asiatic Mode of Production'. This was marked by the dominance of the state over society, the absence of intermediary proprietors, the prominent role of the state in organizing or regulating production, and the concentration of economic surpluses in the hands of the state through taxation. This model remains profoundly subversive, for it suggests that Soviet statism has something in common with pre-industrial social formations.

The concept of totalitarianism was never wholeheartedly adopted by sovietologists, and has been under severe attack since the 1960s. As part of the movement to strip the social sciences of their normative connotations and to make them more value-free and objective, scholars tried to reduce the earlier stress on the USSR's exceptionalism and to study it within the terms of general social science methods applicable to any other society. The criticisms of totalitarianism can be summarized as follows. The theory tended to equate not Stalinism and fascism but communism and fascism, and therefore was not easily able to conceptualize the differences that may have existed between Lenin's regime and Stalin's, or between Khrushchev's and Brezhnev's. Even under Stalin the concept tried to bring together two very different systems, communism and fascism, whose internal dynamics were very different. Totalitarianism moreover was held to have described the state of affairs under Stalin and had therefore become anachronistic. With the era of mass terror giving way to the less arbitrary application of coercion against specific targets there was at the least a change from terroristic totalitarianism to 'totalitarianism without terror', or simple totalitarianism. The mass of the population are now allowed to get on with their own affairs as long as they do not make untoward political demands on the system. The era of mass mobilizations from above and the demand for belief have given way to a more relaxed approach. The concentration of power in the hands of a single leader has declined significantly since the death of Stalin. Khrushchev retained elements of one-person dominance, while Brezhnev was firmly constrained by the collective leadership. There is now a degree of interplay between the leader, the leadership, and some institutions.

The fundamental idea of totalitarianism that social relations become completely atomized and that rule becomes anomic and direct is questionable. Hannah Arendt's idea of totalitarianism was associated with the theory of mass society, which posits that atomization increases as group and class loyalties dissolve.[12] Atomisation is a vague concept and begs the question of whether such a condition, even if it existed, could be maintained for long. Natural solidarity remains, as in the family. The fundamental tenet of totalitarianism that a monolithic regime dominates a passive population has been belied by evidence of popular resistance and even political struggles throughout the Soviet period. Vera Dunham demonstrated that even under Stalin a Soviet middle class emerged with which the regime made a 'Big Deal'. The theory of totalitarianism exaggerated the success of official socialization, and tended to take the regime's self-evaluation at face value. There is some evidence which suggests that the party's ability to control popular beliefs and values is not as effective as its ability to control overt political behaviour. The resistance of society at all stages of Soviet power has continued in more or less subtle ways. At worst, resistance derived from atomization takes the form pointed out by Alexander Zinoviev, an active though cynical participation in political structures combined with the concentration on enhancing one's own life chances within smaller groups, or 'communes', in a Hobbesian war of all against all in a process of moral debasement, a victory for the regime.[13] At best, resistance has taken the form of the affirmation of certain inalienable human values.

Totalitarianism stressed the monolithic unity of the party and its partners in ruling the Soviet polity. As we have seen, there have been considerable shifts, and the tensions between institutions and their fragmented interaction can hardly be called monolithic. While the dominance of the institutions of the power elite over society is undoubted, this also can barely be called monolithic. In the Polish context, for example, intermediary forces remain between the state and society in the form of the Roman Catholic church and an independent peasantry, illustrating that a 'totalitarian' regime can accommodate itself to 'islands of separatism'. Of course, an independent trade union in Poland struck at the heart of the power system and could not be tolerated. To describe this reality B. Wolfe Jancar has rejected the term totalitarianism in favour of the term 'absolute monopoly', implying *exclusive* rather than *total* control.

The main charge against totalitarianism was that it was too static. It failed to take into account not only social and economic developments, but also the political changes since Stalin. The theory did not have a way of explaining political change other than through the leadership mechanism, and thus it ignored the many sources of change in Soviet-type systems. The understanding of the policy process was limited to the top leadership. An associated criticism is that the theory of totalitarianism overemphasized formal institutions at the expense of trying to locate Soviet-type power systems within their national and cultural contexts. Totalitarianism, it was argued, looks very different in Tallinn from in Baku, let alone in Warsaw or Tirana. Even if different societies approximate to the ideal type of totalitarianism, marked by omnipotent control and all-pervasive power, they have various distinctive features.[14]

The dynamics of industrial society themselves are considered to undermine the long-term viability of the more overt forms of totalitarianism. The classic totalitarianism of high Stalinism is allegedly undermined by a threefold process: institutional devolution encourages various forms of bureaucratic pluralism;

social factors bring to the fore the specialists, the cultural intelligentsia, and the huge class of the technical intelligentsia; and cultural interpenetration means that totalitarian regimes can no longer insulate themselves from the non-communist world. Given the changes in communist systems and the increasing national and cultural diversity, either the model had to keep being modified or one remains loyal to the original model, the 'ideal type', and measures the distance the Soviet Union deviates from it.

The theory of totalitarianism would appear to be crippled by insurmountable weaknesses. However, a solid case can be made in favour of retaining the concept. Virtually abandoned in the West after 1968, the concept of totalitarianism was taken up by independent political thinkers in Eastern Europe and the Soviet Union, shocked at the abrupt termination of hopes of communist reform in Czechoslovakia. While its defenders on the whole admit that the model has flaws they argue that in the absence of anything better it remains the best existing model of Soviet politics and should not be discarded lightly. Totalitarianism, they argue, emphasizes what is truly important in Soviet politics, above all the continuing pervasive level of political and ideological control. Totalitarianism in common usage is ultimately about the quality of political relationships. There remains a vast coercive apparatus which was unleashed against dissent after 1979. There are still no effective safeguards for the Soviet citizen against arbitrary police powers. While the authorities on occasion relax their control over intellectual life, overt rival intellectual currents are not tolerated. The 'institutionalized lie' (as independent thinkers put it) of Soviet ideology is still defended with all the authority of the state. The policy process remains highly centralized and usually operates in secrecy, and the state administrative apparatus pervades all of society. The division between public and personal is tolerated but not legitimized by a concept of privacy. The system remains a 'dictatorship over needs' in that the social project of equality, full employment, and so on retains priority over narrowly political concepts of individual freedom. Its advocates insist that totalitarianism is capable of acting as a comparative concept to analyse other communist systems. Totalitarianism, it is argued, should be defined more as the aspiration to obtain total control rather than its achievement. Above all, they argue, it would be difficult to study the early years of the Soviet system without using the concept. For the later stages the theory focuses attention on the factors that make the system less totalitarian.[15] This point allows totalitarianism to be used to analyse the changes, weakening the argument that the theory was too static. Of the original six points only the role of the leader has changed, and the decline in terror. It would be difficult to study Soviet-type systems without the concept of totalitarianism, or some version of it, in order to understand their authoritarian features. The decline in impersonal loyalty and the implicit appeal to self-interest under Brezhnev represented the social modification of totalitarianism while its political structures remained relatively intact.

Hence the concept of totalitarianism is back with a vengeance. In the 1960s it was often dropped for the wrong reasons.The concept had connotations not of academic study but of crude anti-communist politics. However, the division over the use of the term is no longer, if it ever was, simply a split between the left and the right. Those in favour of describing the Soviet Union as totalitarian include Soviet dissenters, East European critical intellectuals, democratic socialists, exiles from communist lands, and Western conservatives. It is now used by the more radical supporters of *perestroika* to describe the system before 1985. The term is sometimes used by Western socialists of the West, and by the Soviet Union to describe systems it finds odious. It was applied by Trotsky to describe the Soviet Union under Stalin. The concept is a broad one, but as Archie Brown points out the social sciences are full of key concepts that are not susceptible to simple definitions. Above all, the theory of totalitarianism has revived to some extent because the earlier optimism about modifications to such systems has been confounded. The theory of convergence from the 1950s predicted that social and economic developments would act to weaken the concentration of power. In fact, communist leaderships have tried to co-opt advances in technology (such as computers) to consolidate their power within the 'mono-organisational' system. Vaclav Havel in his *Power of the Powerless* referred to 'post-totalitarianism', but has since dropped the 'post' in the belief that the crude totalitarianism of Stalin only foreshadowed the more subtle totalitarianism now practised. The leading role of the party has been consolidated and communist political power has remained remarkably impervious to social and technological changes. The current phase of reforms has profound political implications and may mark a decisive break with totalitarianism, and thus put an end to the debate.

The group approach and diffusion models

One of the major theories to challenge totalitarianism is the group approach to Soviet politics. In the 1950s American political scientists, led by David Truman in his *The Governmental Process* (1951), inspired by Arthur F. Bentley's *The Process of Government* (1908), moved away from the study of legal structures and state institutions to informal processes and society. Analysis shifted to societal inputs to the policy process, above all the role of organized groups. In the 1960s the approach was applied to the Soviet Union in an explicit attempt to downgrade ideas of Soviet uniqueness and to integrate Soviet studies into mainstream social science. Totalitarianism tends to focus on the formal structures of Soviet politics, whereas the group approach focuses on how the system actually works in practice. The shift in interest was part of what is known as the behavioural revolution in political science, away from political institutions to informal processes and individuals, from government to politics. At its most developed the group approach is the basis of a pluralistic theory of politics, though the two are not synonymous. Pluralism implies conflict over political power and policies whereas the group approach specifies only that groups are an important factor in this competition.

Stalinist totalitarianism has allegedly been its own gravedigger as the society born of rapid industrialization has matured. The revolution has been consolidated and there is a growing institutionalization of Soviet political life. Although Soviet politics lacks an overtly competitive dynamic typical of liberal democracies, there are nevertheless contestatory processes involved in the allocation of resources and in the enjoyment of the fruits of power. Under Gorbachev the terminology of reformists and conservatives indicates the *de facto* emergence of two 'parties', though it has not been legitimized in any way. It is clear that any open debate about policies will entail a degree of lobbying, if not 'factionalism'. There is considerable conflict and diversity beneath the formalized surface of Soviet political life, and in particular there is much evidence of bureaucratic or group activity. An element of pluralist competition is pursued between individuals, groups, and the various offices and departments of the party and government. However, while the group approach highlights an important facet of Soviet political life there remain major limits to the diffusion of power. As Skilling warns, pluralism is not a group theory of politics, but a theory of groups in Soviet politics.[16]

Beneath the veneer of monolithic unity the USSR is as divided into national, class, professional, or religious groups as any other society. The actual classification of groups can take different forms. Skilling divides them into occupational and opinion groups. Occupational groups can be both bureaucratic and intellectual, while opinion formations cut across other groups and tend towards more unified views. Three categories can be derived from the occupational groups: leadership groups or factions which are involved in policy-making; official or bureaucratic groups, including the military, police, party apparatus, and industrial managers; and a broad group of brain workers such as scientists, writers, journalists, scholars, and other specialists and intellectuals. A fourth category includes a range of broadly based but not institutionalized social forces such as workers, peasants, nationalities, religious groups, regional, age, and gender groups and at the most general level social interests like consumers. The weakness of autonomous interests means that the focus in the Soviet context is very much on institutionalized interests and professional groupings such as economic managers and planners, teachers, and lawyers, rather than general groupings such as youth, women, race, or religion.[17]

Pluralism shifts the emphasis away from the concentration of power and the 'output' side of politics (the policies) and from supports (how the regime maintains itself in power) to the input side of politics, the demands that groups and individuals make on the system. Policies are initiated not only from above but also from below, and in their implementation are modified. Skilling insists that groups act on the leadership as much as they are acted upon. However, while it is easy to name groups, the immediate problem with the group approach is how to define a group and how to define an interest. An interest group, according to Skilling, is a collection of people who share a common position on an issue and act to fulfil their group ambitions. There is a question over how the imputed interests can be articulated. In the Soviet context groups are forced to behave in an informal way, with overt lobbying forbidden but discreet bargaining possible. The point however, is not whether the demands are made, but whether they will to some degree be satisfied, and indeed on the mechanism whereby they can be satisfied. While power is clearly concentrated in the USSR, the concept of 'more' and 'less' power suggests an element of diffusion. The role of leadership at all levels means that the aggregation of interest takes place in a fundamentally different way from in the West, and even there few claim that policy flows simply out of the clash of groups. Bentley exaggerated when he argued that once you have looked at the groups you have looked at everything: the suggestion that politics, including the government and parties, does not exist outside group processes.[18]

Groups have always played an important role in Soviet politics. From Lenin's time the notion of 'departmentalism' (or localism), where institutions or groups put their interests above those of society as a whole, has been condemned. There is evidence that groups influenced policy in the 1930s and 1940s even at the height of Stalinism. It is clear that policy conflicts are as endemic to the Soviet system as to any other. Skilling characterizes the Stalin period as quasi-totalitarianism, on the grounds that pure totalitarianism is a practical impossibility. Groups existed, but had little capacity for independent action and were manipulated by the leadership.[19] Douglas Weiner has shown that under Stalin a sustained covert struggle raged between the defenders of ecological *zapovedniki* (reserves) and a range of opponents led by the 'industry first' lobby.[20] The fundamental principle of the right of scientists to pursue their own research independent of state direction was never abandoned, despite the depredations of a charlatan like Lysenko. Dunmore and others have shown that under the ferocious though weakening gaze of the dictator in his declining years there were pluralist and bureaucratic elements in Soviet politics, with conflicts over consumer goods and agricultural policy, cultural and foreign policy. The Zhdanov 'party revivalist' faction were opposed by Malenkov, who put greater emphasis on state procedures as they had developed during the years of the war. Such factional activity is a reflection of personal conflicts, institutional jealousies, and genuine policy debate.

Under Khrushchev the professional and institutional groupings came into their own, despite continued support for Lysenko. The decline in political terror and mass mobilization permitted a degree of political competition between groups pursuing their own interests. The debate over the Virgin Lands Scheme showed the possibility of intra-elite conflict, and the 1958 educational reform demonstrated that a professional grouping could influence policy between its inception and implementation. Specific specialist interest groups and inchoate social resistance were able to modify the policies of the leader of an allegedly totalitarian state. The education reform revealed the limits to policy group activity as well, such as the need to build support within the apparatus, the need to avoid openly challenging party policy, that objections must be voiced in a non-political 'technocratic' language, and that success is possible only over relatively uncontroversial policy issues.[21] It perhaps showed less the importance of interest groups than the centrality of bureaucratic politics and indeed the strength of the social groups whose privileges were under attack. The announcement of the state of all the people limited the concept of 'one class — one party — one truth' and broadened the theoretical scope of group politics. The bureaucracy and the military, with the approval of social elites, played a key role in ousting Khrushchev in 1964.

Skilling characterized the Soviet Union under Brezhnev as post-totalitarianism, a form of 'consultative authoritarianism' or 'imperfect monism' in which the political leadership was secure but willing to consult experts. The expected next stage, which was long delayed, predicted more vigorous group activity which would be able occasionally to challenge official policies.[22] Under Brezhnev groups were able to establish themselves as a constraining rather than as an active promotional force. Stewart argued that Soviet interest groups lack the associational element found in the USA and instead institutional interest groups, lacking independent resources and yet consulted by the leadership in the making of policy, are the key actors.[23] Hough identified the development of 'institutional pluralism', which permitted a degree of administrative devolution to certain 'complexes' (termed 'policy whirlpools') as part of the larger corporatist style of politics, with a leadership effectively neutralized by Brezhnev's occupancy.[24] The currency of exchange with the leadership is specialized information, but the value of the currency depends on the group's strategic position within the system. The increasing complexity of administration made it more difficult for the checking mechanisms, primarily achieved through the party, to monitor the apparatus. This allowed officials to carve out areas of relative autonomy amidst the forest of rules and regulations, a form of bureaucratic pluralism. Andropov's accession showed the importance of the KGB both as an interest group and as a checking mechanism, while Gorbachev has admitted that certain groups are impeding his policy of *perestroika*. The military have been able to exert considerable influence on policy simply by the fact that they represent a cardinal concern of the whole body politic. Under Gorbachev this has given way to the primacy of civilian economic interests, the party apparatus, and the liberal intelligentsia. Groups such as lawyers and environmentalists have also achieved some success in influencing policy.

Despite the undoubted role of groups in Soviet politics there are strong arguments against the application of the idea of pluralism to the Soviet Union. Above all, there is a lack of formal legitimacy for group activity. The Soviet party and its allies do not accept political pluralism as either desirable or permissible. Pluralism runs directly counter to the foundations of Soviet ideology and organization, and there is no accepted philosophical basis for group activity. The concept of socialist pluralism became acceptable as part of Gorbachev's reform process, yet its scope remained restricted. Democratic centralism and the ban on factions apply as much to the rest of society as they do to internal party life. Groups are weak and non-inclusive and do not fully overcome the element of 'mass society' in Soviet politics. Some parties, as in Poland, have had to accommodate to the realities of pluralistic forces, such as the church, but threats to the leading role of the party have been suppressed. Under Dubček the Action Programme envisaged only a limited form of political pluralism, and even that was intolerable to the Brezhnev leadership. The 'normalization' process under Gustav Husak, following the invasion, was designed to root out all the shoots of pluralism that had emerged during the Prague Spring. Normalization has indeed been the normal state of Soviet-type systems to date. Even in Yugoslavia, where relatively independent social organizations are sanctioned, the political leadership has wide discretionary powers. While the theory of 'one class — one party' has given way to a state of all the people this has not signified a role for autonomous social forces or particularities in Soviet-type societies.

As far as policy formation is concerned, lack of formal legitimacy reduces the effectiveness of groups. Group interests must be articulated through the personal solicitation of support or indirect access to channels of influence. The group approach reacted against the study of formal institutional structures of political regimes in favour of the informal processes which determine decision-making. However, as Griffiths pointed out, groups are not central to the policy process in the USSR. The approach assumes that a polity is 'sub-system-dominant', where the whole can be explained by the sum of the parts or sub-systems, with interaction between autonomous interest groups, the government, and the party, whereas in the Soviet Union this is far from being the case. The Soviet polity is clearly system-dominant, and interaction with groups is not central to policy outcomes.[25] The group approach exaggerated the role of sub-system relationships and underestimated overarching factors such as leadership or ideology. Skilling and Griffiths conclude that groups influence only the form of policies, not the policies themselves, and then only on non-sensitive issues.

By definition pluralism is a system where political power is dispersed and yet the 'dictatorship' of the Politburo remains. In the context of weak legal traditions and a diffuse constitutionality there is a tendency for groups to form on the basis of 'patronage' and professional ties. However, one of the great strengths of the CPSU has been its ability to prevent itself degenerating into competing factions based on these groups, the sad fate of the Chinese communist party under Mao Zedong. There is a need for specialist advice, but the system has been able to incorporate various pressures and conflicting influences. The integrated power system has been preserved almost in its entirety, buttressed by democratic centralism and the continued ban on factions. The bonds of adherence at the heart of the regime, though tempered by corruption, have not yet given way to a non-ideological loyalty to the group, and hence the system retains, in this respect at least, the totalitarian emphasis on impersonal ties.

Group activity in the USSR operates within the context of universal nationalized property and is therefore based not on ownership but on a politically mediated differential access and role in the operation of the means of production. To a degree Soviet group activity simply reflects the division of labour within a single system. Intra-class differentiation is now a permitted field of sociological study but contradictions are regarded as non-antagonistic and therefore not the site of class struggle.

The cohesion of groups is open to question. Groups like the party *apparat*, military or state bureaucrats do not necessarily have a single view. In the Soviet Union, as in the West, there are concerns that cut across simple institutional divisions, such as ideological, national, generational, religious, gender, and social alignments which to some extent moderate the fundamental division between state and society. The boundaries between groups are blurred and members often act in several simultaneously. There is perhaps too much focus on groups and not enough on the individuals who compose them. There is no group organization to consolidate group identity and to advance their interests, and interaction between members is limited. Their views as a group are not sanctioned by any formal arrangements such as ballots or elections. There is always the danger of reifying groups, giving them personalities and characteristics, such as selfishness, and forgetting that they are no more than abstract categories.

There is little role for groups beyond the institutional system, although this is rapidly changing under Gorbachev. They operate within the framework of the administrative structure rather than appeal to society for support. The imperfect monism is reflected in the 'pluralism of elites' whereby competing forces and interests can be articulated by their leaders within the party and state mechanism. The emphasis on informal groups tends to neglect the centrality of the official groups. The analysis of groups has to be supplemented by analysis of the institutional context in which they operate, and by more nebulous concepts such as political culture. The highly formalized but non-constitutionalized nature of political relations endows Soviet politics with a fluidity which inhibits the consolidation of a patterned structure of group relations. Under Gorbachev the fluidity of organizational structure has been intensified, and while groups such as writers and journalists have been encouraged to play a more forthright role the major hint of the institutionalization of groups in the policy-making process is the development of 'popular fronts' to channel support for *perestroika*.

The group approach was developed to describe the realities of Western, and above all American, liberal democracy, and hence there is some doubt over its applicability to the Soviet Union. Pluralism *a priori* studies the diffusion of power, which in the Soviet Union is a questionable assumption. The use of the term is a case of what Giovanni Sartori calls 'conceptual stretching'. It forces an inappropriate conceptual framework on to a system in which conflicting group influence on policy is both theoretically and practically denigrated, and where power is monopolized to a great extent by a single institution, the party. Interest groups in the Soviet Union operate in a very different way from those in the United States. The proliferation of terms — institutional pluralism, bureaucratic pluralism, centralized pluralism, institutionalized pluralism — reflects the hesitancies and qualifications required to apply the concept to the Soviet Union. While the totalitarian approach entails the danger of reducing the United States and the Soviet Union to mirror images of each other, there is an equal danger in applying the group approach in that the enthusiasm for a value-free approach to the study of the changing Soviet polity can lead to the exaggeration of similarities between the two. There is a danger of ethnocentrism as familiar images are projected on to the 'other' in order to tame it. The ethnocentricity in the context of group politics comes down to the belief that groups by definition must be contestatory, the American pattern, whereas in other cultures and political systems groups may be compatible with overall integrative structures. The Farmers' Solidarity in 1980–1 in Poland, for example, refused to see itself simply as a 'lobby' working on behalf of its membership but wished to participate in the general social renewal process.

The theory of pluralism as applied to the Soviet Union does not focus on the autonomy of society but examines fragmentation within the power structure. Divisions can take various forms (individual, professional, or institutional) but their ability to influence policy is severely circumscribed. There has been some diffusion of influence to specialist and other groupings, but the overwhelming fact about the Soviet political system remains its centralization. The long-awaited revival of the soviets, for example, will come about not through the initiative of the soviets themselves but from the party leadership. The political system has historically been able to retain a degree of autonomy from the socio-economic 'base' on which it rests. Social pluralism does not necessarily entail political pluralism: economic and social developments have not been automatically reflected in political change in the Soviet system.

Corporatism and other approaches

The emergence of a number of non-dictatorial but authoritarian one-party systems in the wake of decolonization has stimulated the search for new approaches. A number of theories have sought to reconcile the insights of concentration and diffusion models. If totalitarianism was associated with the institutional approach to politics, and group theory with the 'behavioural revolution', then the intermediate models can schematically be identified with the methodology of functionalism, which argues that while political systems may vary widely in institutions certain functions are common to all. Inputs in the form of demands and supports pass through the gatekeeper (parties or interest groups) to the political system, which outputs in the form of authoritative decisions, which are connected with the inputs by a feedback loop.[26] Functions include political recruitment and socialization through to policy-making and implementation. Functionalism provides a ready-made arsenal of terms to analyse the Soviet system, though too often the wood gets lost in the trees of the verbiage of structural functionalism.

Corporatism is a way of combining 'output' models (totalitarianism) and 'input' models (pluralism). A distinction can be made between 'state corporatism' as practised in Latin America or the USSR, and 'societal corporatist systems' as in Great Britain in the 1970s. The difference is that in the latter the corporatist actors (such as trade unions or employers' organizations) retain the right to organize themselves and choose their own leaders, whereas in state corporatist systems the mass bodies act largely as state organizations, or transmission belts, with their leaders imposed on them by the state. But the similarity of corporatism with pluralism is clear,

193

since both stress the group input in policy formation. However, the theory obviates the necessity of developing a competitive theory of interest participation in the policy process and instead focuses on co-ordination.

Corporatism has come to take the place of pluralism as a key concept in studying the Soviet polity. In particular, it has been applied to explain the compromise between the leadership and various interests during the Brezhnev years. The lifting of Khrushchev's threats to the party and state bureaucrats in 1964 was consolidated by the lack of vigour in pursuing the aims of the 1965 economic reform against the vested interests of the economic bureaucrats. The compromise was broadened during the era of *détente* to satisfy most sectors of society. The major casualty was labour and factor productivity, as incentives were inadequate and industrial investment lagged. Brezhnev's conciliatory policy did little to change the structure of power. The major interests such as the KGB, trade unions, industrial ministries, republican party organizations, or research institutes of the USSR Academy of Sciences did not gain the ability either to select their own leaders or openly to articulate their own interests. Their heads are appointed by the *nomenklatura* system, and policy is formed elsewhere. Corporatism has developed the furthest in Yugoslavia and to a lesser extent in Hungary and provides a more accurate description of political reality than pluralism. The rest of the communist world may see a gradual transition to corporatism as groups are given more autonomy but not freed from the restraints of directed politics. The value of the corporatist model is that it contributes to an understanding of the central paradox of the power system in the Soviet Union: the multiplicity of institutions operating in an uninstitutionalized framework. It helps explain the diversity of groups in the Soviet Union and the limits of group activity. However, it seems anomalous to talk of corporatism, whether societal or state, in the Soviet context, given the ideological and organizational strictures against political corporations of any form beyond the direct control of the party. The same 'conceptual stretching' as with pluralism is involved here.

Monist models are similar to corporatism but focus more on the power centre. They incorporate some of the insights of diffusion theories by modifying the idea of the concentration of power while avoiding the pitfalls of totalitarianism. Monism is a society in which all power is public power resting in the hands of the state, which itself is controlled by a single political ruling group which manages the economy and society. This is rather similar to Rigby's mono-organizational model, which examines the means whereby the dominant party and leadership integrate the multiplicity of elites that emerge as society becomes more diverse under the impact of technological and social change. The pluralism of elites becomes reflected in the party leadership. The concentration of power is accommodated to take into account the post-totalitarianism of modern Soviet politics.

The move away from totalitarianism was accompanied by great interest in convergence models. In the 1960s the idea of convergence seemed to offer a theoretical framework for the common evaluation of industrial societies. Analysis took on a sociological flavour with the emergence of the 'development' model and of the 'mature industrial model'.[27] Classical versions of convergence theory place American-style pluralism and Soviet-style totalitarianism at opposite ends of an implicit continuum, and suggest that they are moving towards each other as the capitalist state takes on more of the functions of planning and social welfare, and the socialist state sheds some of its ideology and allows a certain play to market forces. One of the earliest theorists of this view, impressed by Khrushchev's relative liberalization and apparent move away from totalitarianism, was Talcott Parsons' functionalist approach to world history moving through three stages: primitive, intermediate, and modern. The modern stage affected communist countries as much as capitalist ones, with new patterns of industrial production and life characterized by state interventionism, bureaucratization, differentiation of functions, and competing interest groups.[28] Parsons argued that pluralist democracy was an 'evolutionary universal', essential to sustain a degree of consensus in a complex system composed of various groups. Such a consensus, he insisted, could not be achieved in an authoritarian system and thus the efficiency of the system was reduced by the lack of legitimacy.[29]

A gloomier version of convergence was put forward by Herbert Marcuse, who saw technological imperatives as integrating the mass of the population not only into the rhythms of factory production but also into the mental condition acceptable to industrial labour processes. The need for overt coercion in East and West decreases as individuals internalize the necessary discipline. People repress themselves and become one-dimensional individuals.[30] Elements of this view, though not from the perspective of convergence, are contained in the idea of a dictatorship over needs. The theory suggests a radical governmental manipulation not only over the physical needs of human beings but also over their mental lives.[31]

There are many different versions of convergence, yet they all suffer from an economic and political determinism. The argument is a crucial one, since Soviet studies have long been haunted by the determinism that asserts that the backwardness of Russian conditions forced the expansion of the state as a substitute for broader social movements such as entrepreneurs or revolutionary workers. The era of stagnation graphically illustrated that industrial development on its own does not weaken the power of a *dirigiste* power system. The same criticism of determinism can be made of those who hold that the Soviet Union is a transitional society whose development has been arrested midway between capitalism and socialism. From a Marxist perspective the sequence of change from feudalism through capitalism to socialism was historically determined, but the time sequence was not. The whole problem of a prolonged transitional society has been finessed by those who argue in favour of convergence: instead of socialist societies marking a radical divergence, they turn back on themselves to share certain features with capitalist states. The problem now is to understand what industrial societies have in common while remaining sensitive to their political differences.

One of the more interesting recent models of Soviet-type societies is the idea of communist neo-traditionalism. The approach accepts the total set of structures pertaining to communist systems as unique and evolving, while stressing the distinctive features employed to achieve the high level of social control typical of such systems. In contrast to the totalitarian emphasis on coercive means of control, it focuses on the positive incentives to compliance. The fusion of economic and political power allows neo-traditionalist systems to reward political loyalty with a patterned system of favours such as career advancement, privileges, and status. The theory explores the ambiguity between the demands at the heart of the system for impersonal loyalty and ideological standards of behaviour, and the dense network of patron-client relations through which that loyalty is rewarded. Hence a clientelist system is the unintended social effect of party policies. Moreover, this loyalty-reward relationship is posited to be at the heart of regime-society relations. Despite running counter to the party's ideological and organizational principles, the operation of the system encourages 'a rich subculture of instrumental-personal ties through which individuals circumvent formal regulations' to obtain goods, income and career opportunities.[32] These are to be found in political relations and at the workplace. Employment is not primarily a market relationship but the source both of work and of a variety of benefits, cultural life, and services. The workplace is also the centre of informal sub-cultural networks with other workers.

The neo-traditional argument accepts the group approach's view of competition and conflict for resources, but reasserts the centrality of communist political institutions not only in overt political processes but also in social consciousness itself. There is a creative tension between group loyalties and vertical allegiances. Perhaps the greatest insight offered by the neo-traditional image is the rejection of visions of convergence with the advanced capitalist state. It focuses on the uniqueness and complexity of communist patterns of rule. There is evolution and change in communist systems, but towards a historically distinctive social formation. The actual features of this formation can be disputed. For neo-traditionalists the novelty lies in the authority pattern of clientelism, characterized by a citizenry dependent on social institutions and leaders.[33] These are modernizing societies, but are becoming transformed from within by 'their pattern of economic organization and the ambiguities of their official ideology and political institutions'.[34] This evolutionary process was set in train from the very first days of the system and hence the model rejects any fundamental contrast between the 'mobilization' and 'post-mobilization' phases of Soviet history.

The theory of neo-traditionalism is not used to suggest a system that is not yet 'modern'. Instead it refers to the changes in Western Europe from the eighteenth century, analysed by Emile Durkheim, Talcott Parsons and others, in which 'the term *tradition* has come to be associated with dependence, deference, and particularism, and the term *modern* with independence, contract and universalism' marked by impersonality and anonymity.[35] The theory of the dictatorship over needs also makes the point that the Soviet system is stamped by a fundamentally pre-Enlightenment set of authority relationships and mind set locked on to a modern industrial context.

We have looked at some of the models which seek to explain the operation of the Soviet political system. All highlight aspects of the system, but each has major drawbacks. Between models which stress the concentration of power and those which highlight its diffusion, intermediary concepts which stress the uniqueness of the Soviet system and take note of the distinctive pattern of evolution seem to be the strongest. In particular, the theory of neo-traditionalism helps towards an understanding of the fundamental continuity in Soviet politics and the totality of the interaction between the party, ideology and economic organization, and developments in society. This review of models, however, would be incomplete without raising the issue of the nature of the Soviet state and referring back once again to the role of leadership. The pluralist view, which focuses on the societal input into policy formation, must clearly be tempered. The state-dominated structure of power is more than the arena of group conflict: it has interests of its own standing far above all other groups.

The great achievement of the many models is to highlight various aspects of the operation of the party-state and its relationship to groups and individuals in society. The fundamental paradox is that the diversification of economic, social, and political life has undermined the classical features of totalitarianism, and yet there has been no breakthrough into a liberalization of social life or the institutionalization of pluralism. The state (whose social nature will be examined in Chapter 11) remains absolutely dominant though in the process of decomposition from totalitarianism to authoritarianism tinged with elements of democratization. In this in-between land there is a healthy scope for the proliferation of models, but the essential point is that the Soviet Union can be understood only in its own terms as a unique and changing political formation. The power structure is a semi-autonomous actor with interests of its own. Soviet politics has largely been the history of state initiatives to control and restructure society, from collectivization to high-rise housing, and the story of the impact of state policies on society. It is a hitherto unique system where a section of society, the Bolshevik party, took control of the state and proceeded to use it to inaugurate a massive programme of social and political change. Soviet politics has also been the story of how, in fits and starts, socio-economic forces and society have gradually reduced the autonomy of the state and decreased the scope and effectiveness of state initiatives. There has been the gradual reconstitution of civil society, a sphere independent of the state though not yet guaranteed by law. It remains to be seen whether these forces will be translated into overtly political forms.

Notes

1 G. Gill, 'Personal Dominance and the Collective Principle', in T.H. Rigby and F. Feher (eds.), *Political Legitimation in Communist States* (Macmillan, London, 1982), pp. 95–6.
2 M. Voslensky, *Nomenklatura* (Bodley Head, London, 1984), chapter 6.
3 On power and authority see T.H. Rigby, 'A Conceptual Approach to Authority, Power and Policy in the Soviet Union', in T.H. Rigby *et al.* (eds.), *Authority, Power and Policy in the Soviet Union* (Macmillan, London, 1980); G.W. Breslauer, 'Power and Authority in Soviet Elite Politics', in J.L. Nogee (ed.), *Soviet Politics: Russia after Brezhnev* (Praeger, New York, 1985), pp. 15–33.

4 Peter Frank, 'Political Succession in the Soviet Union: Building a Power Base' (University of Essex, Russian and Soviet Studies Centre, Discussion Paper No. 2, Colchester, 1984), p. 1.

5 V. Bunce, 'The Political Economy of the Brezhnev Era', *British Journal of Political Science*, 13 (1983), p. 138.

6 T.H. Rigby, 'The Soviet Leadership: towards a self-stabilising Oligarchy?', *Soviet Studies*, 22 (October 1970), p. 2.

7 For a bitter critique of the Brezhnev years see *Kommunist*, 4 (March 1987), pp. 3–19.

8 See J.P. Willerton, 'Patronage Networks and Coalition-building in the Brezhnev Era', *Soviet Studies*, 39, 2 (April 1987), pp. 175–204.

9 A. Brown, in Rigby *et al.* (eds.), *Authority, Power and Policy in the USSR*, p. 136.

10 V. Bunce, *Do New Leaders make a Difference?* (Princeton University Press, Princeton, N.J., 1981).

11 C. Friedrich and Z. Brzezinski, *Totalitarian Dictatorship and Autocracy*, rev. edn (Praeger, New York, 1966), p. 22.

12 Hannah Arendt, *The Origins of Totalitarianism*; on mass society, see W. Kornhauser, *The Politics of Mass Society* (Routledge & Kegan Paul, London, 1960).

13 Alexander Zinoviev, *The Yawning Heights* (Penguin, Harmondsworth, 1979); *The Radiant Future* (Bodley Head, London, 1981); *The Reality of Communism* (Gollancz, London, 1984); see also Philip Hanson, 'Alexander Zinoviev: Totalitarianism from Below', *Survey*, 26, 1 (winter 1982), pp. 29–48.

14 See A. Brown, 'Political Power and the Soviet State: Western and Soviet Perspectives', in N. Harding (ed.), *The State in Socialist Society* (Macmillan, London, 1984), pp. 51–103.

15 W. Odom, 'A Dissenting View on the Group Approach to Soviet Politics', *World Politics*, 28 (July 1976), p. 567.

16 H.G. Skilling, 'Interest Groups and Communist Politics Revisited', *World Politics* 31, 1 (October 1983), p. 5.

17 See H.G. Skilling and F. Griffiths (eds.), *Interest Groups in Soviet Politics* (Princeton University Press, Princeton, N.J., 1971); S. Solomon (ed.), *Pluralism in the Soviet Union* (Macmillan, London, 1983).

18 A.F. Bentley, *The Process of Government* (Chicago, 1908), pp. 330–6.

19 Skilling, 'Interest Groups and Communist Politics: an Introduction', in *Interest Groups in Soviet Politics*, p. 17.

20 Douglas R. Weiner, *Models of Nature: Conservation and Community Ecology in the Soviet Union, 1917–1935* (Indiana University Press, Bloomington, 1988).

21 J.J. Schwartz and W.R. Keech, 'Public Influence and Educational Policy in the Soviet Union', in R.E. Kanet (ed.), *The Behavioural Revolution and Communist Studies* (Free Press, New York, 1971), pp. 151–86.

22 Skilling, 'Interest Groups and Communist Politics', p. 17.

23 P. Stewart, *Political Power in the Soviet Union* (Bobbs-Merrill, Indianapolis, 1968), pp. 4–5.

24 J.F. Hough, The Brezhnev Era: the Man and the System', *Problems of Communism* 25, 2 (March-April 1976), p. 14.

25 F. Griffiths, 'A Tendency Analysis of Soviet Policy-making', in Skilling and Griffiths (eds.), *Interest Groups in Soviet Politics*, p. 335.

26 D. Easton, *A Framework for Political Analysis* (Prentice-Hall, Englewood Cliffs, N.J., 1965); G. Almond and G. Powell, *Comparative Politics: System, Process and Policy* (Little Brown, Boston, Mass., 1978).

27 Alex Inkeles, 'Models and Issues in the Analysis of Soviet Society', *Survey*, 60 (July 1966), pp. 3–19.

28 Talcott Parsons, *Structures and Process in Modern Societies* (Free Press, Glencoe, Ill., 1960).

29 Talcott Parsons, 'Evolutionary Universals in Society', *American Sociological Review* (June 1964).
30 Herbert Marcuse, *One-dimensional Man* (Sphere, London, 1968).
31 F. Feher *et al.*, *Dictatorship over needs* (Blackwell, Oxford, 1983).
32 A.G. Walder, *Communist Neo-traditionalism: Work and Authority in Chinese Industry* (University of California Press, Berkeley, 1986), pp. 5–8.
33 ibid., p. 8.
34 K. Jowitt, 'Soviet Neotraditionalism: the Political Corruption of a Leninist Regime', *Soviet Studies*, 35, 3 (July 1983), pp. 275–97.
35 Walder, *Communist Neo-traditionalism*, p. 10.

Key texts

Brown, Archie, *Soviet Politics and Political Science* (Macmillan, London, 1974)
Brown, Archie, 'Political Power and the Soviet State', in Neil Harding (ed), *The State in Socialist Society* (Macmillan, London, 1984), pp. 51–103
Brown, Archie (ed.), *Political Leadership in the Soviet Union* (Macmillan, London, 1988)
Harasymiw, Bohdan, *Political Elite Recruitment in the Soviet Union* (Macmillan, London, 1984)
Janos, A. (ed.), *Authoritarian Politics in Communist Europe* (University of California Press, Berkeley, 1976)
Johnson, Chalmers (ed.), *Change in Communist Systems* (Stanford University Press, Stanford, Cal., 1970)
Hough, J. *The Soviet Union and Social Science Theory* (Harvard University Press, Cambridge, Mass., 1977)

Select bibliography

The role of leadership

Blondel, Jean, *Political Leadership* (Sage, London, 1987)
Breslauer, G.W., *Khrushchev and Brezhnev as Leaders* (Allen & Unwin, London, 1982)
Breslauer, G.W., 'Power and Authority in Soviet Politics', in J.L. Nogee (ed.), *Soviet Politics: Russia after Brezhnev* (Praeger, New York, 1985), pp. 15–33
Brown, Archie, 'The Power of the General Secretary of the CPSU', in T.H. Rigby, Archie Brown, and Peter Reddaway (eds.), *Authority, Power and Policy in the USSR* (Macmillan, London, 1980)
Brown, Archie, 'Leadership Succession and Policy Innovation', in A. Brown and M. Kaser (eds.), *Soviet Policy for the 1980s* (Macmillan, London, 1982), pp. 223–53
Bunce, V., *Do new Leaders make a Difference? Executive Succession and Public Policy under Capitalism and Socialism* (Princeton University Press, Princeton, N.J., 1981).
D'Agostino, Anthony, *Soviet Succession Struggles: Kremlinology and the Russian Question from Lenin to Gorbachev* (Unwin Hyman, London, 1988)
Gill, Graeme, 'The Soviet Leader Cult: Reflections on the Structure of Leadership in the Soviet Union', *British Journal of Political Science* 10 (April 1980), pp. 149–66.
Gill, Graeme, 'Political Myth and Stalin's Search for Authority in the Party', in T.H. Rigby, Archie Brown, and Peter Reddaway (eds.), *Authority, Power and Policy in the USSR* (Macmillan, London, 1980)
Gill, Graeme, 'Personal Dominance and the Collective Principle: Individual Legitimacy in Marxist-Leninist Systems', in T.H. Rigby and F. Feher (eds.), *Political Legitimation in Communist States* (Macmillan, London, 1982), pp. 87–118.

Gustafson, Thane, and Dawn Mann, 'Gorbachev's next Gamble', *Problems of Communism*, 36, 4 (July-August 1987), pp. 1–20

Hodnett, G., 'The Pattern of Leadership Politics', in S. Bialer (ed.), *The Domestic Context of Soviet Foreign Policy* (Westview, Boulder, Colo., 1981), pp. 87–118

Hoffman, E., 'Changing Soviet Perspectives on Leadership and Administration' in S.F. Cohen *et al.* (eds.), *The Soviet Union since Stalin* (1980)

Hough, J.F., 'The Soviet Elite: Groups and Individuals', *Problems of Communism*, 16, *1* (January-February 1967) pp. 28–35

Hough, J.F., *Soviet Leadership in Transition* (Brookings Institution, Washington, D.C., 1980)

Hough, J.F., 'Soviet Succession: Issues and Personalities', *Problems of Communism*, 31, 4 (July-August 1982), pp. 20–40

Hough, J.F., 'Gorbachev Consolidating Power', *Problems of Communism*, 36, 4 (July-August 1987), pp. 21–43

McCauley, Martin, and Stephen Carter, *Leadership and Succession in the Soviet Union, Eastern Europe and China* (Macmillan, London, 1986)

Mills, Richard M., 'The Soviet Leadership Problem', *World Politics*, 33, 4 (July 1981), pp. 590–613

Narkiewicz, Olga A., *Soviet Leaders: from the Cult of Personality to Collective Rule* (Wheatsheaf, Brighton, 1986)

Odom, W.E., 'Choice and Change in Soviet Politics', *Problems of Communism*, 32, 3 (May-June 1983), pp. 1–21

Ploss, S., 'Soviet Succession: Signs of Struggle', *Problems of Communism*, 31, 4 (July-August 1982), pp. 41–52

Rigby, T.H., 'The Soviet Leadership: towards a Self-stabilising Oligarchy?', *Soviet Studies*, 22, 2 (October 1970), pp. 167–91

Rigby, T.H., 'The Soviet Politburo: a Comparative Profile, 1951–1971', *Soviet Studies*, 24, 1 (1972-3), pp. 3–23

Rigby, T.H., 'Personal and Collective Leadership', in D. Simes *et al.*, *Soviet Succession* (Sage, Beverly Hills and London, 1978)

Rigby, T.H., 'A Conceptual Approach to Authority, Power and Policy in the Soviet Union', in T.H. Rigby *et al.* (eds.), *Authority, Power and Policy in the Soviet Union* (Macmillan, London, 1980)

Rigby, T.H., and Bohdan Harasymiw (eds.), *Leadership Selection and Patron-Client Relations in the USSR and Yugoslavia* (Allen & Unwin, London, 1983)

Tatu, Michel, *Power in the Kremlin* (Viking, New York, 1968)

Tucker, Robert C., 'The Rise of Stalin's Personality Cult', *American Historical Review*, 84 (1979), pp. 347–66

Tumarkin, Nina, *Lenin Lives! The Lenin Cult in Soviet Russia* (Harvard University Press, Cambridge, Mass., 1983)

Zaslavsky, Victor, 'The Rebirth of the Stalin Cult in the USSR', in *The Neo-Stalinist State* (Harvester, Brighton, 1982), pp. 3–21

The making of policy: general works

Aspaturian, Vernon V. (ed.), *Process and Power in Soviet Foreign Policy* (Little Brown, Boston, Mass., 1971)

Bell, Daniel, 'Ten Theories in Search of Reality', in *The End of Ideology*, rev. edn (Collier-Macmillan, London, 1960)

Bruce, James B., *The Politics of Soviet Policy Formation: Khrushchev's Innovative Policies in Education and Agriculture*, Monograph Series in World Affairs, vol. 13, book 4, (University of Denver, Denver, Colo.)

Brzezinski, Zbigniew, and Samuel P. Huntington, *Political Power: USA/USSR* (Viking, New York, 1965)

Conquest, Robert, *Power and Policy in the USSR* (Harper & Row, New York, 1967)

Etzioni, A., *Modern Organizations* (Prentice-Hall, Englewood Cliffs, N.J., 1964)

Fainsod, Merle, *How Russia is Ruled* (Harvard University Press, Cambridge, Mass., 1953)

Gallagher, Matthew P., and Karl F. Spielman, Jr., *Soviet Decision-making for Defense: a Critique of US Perspectives on the Arms Race* (Praeger, New York, 1972)

Gustafson, Thane, *Reform and Power in Soviet Politics: Lessons of Recent Policies on Land and Water* (Cambridge University Press, Cambridge, 1981)

Hammer, D.P., *USSR: the Politics of Oligarchy*, 2nd edn (Westview, Boulder, 1986)

Hough, J.F., and Fainsod, Merle, *How the Soviet Union is Governed* (Harvard University Press, London and Cambridge, Mass., 1979), chapter 14

Jowitt, Kenneth, 'Inclusion and Mobilisation in Leninist regimes', *World Politics*, 8, 1 (October 1975), pp. 69–96

Juviler, Peter H., and Henry W. Morton (eds.), *Soviet Policy-making: Studies of Communism in Transition* (Praeger, New York, 1967)

Lodge, Milton C., *Soviet Elite Attitudes since Stalin* (Merrill, Columbus, Oh., 1969)

Löwenhardt, John, *Decision-making in Soviet Politics* (Macmillan, London, 1981)

Moses, Joel C., *Regional Party Leadership and Policy-making in the USSR* (Praeger, New York, 1974)

Ploss, Sidney, *Conflict and Decision-making in Soviet Russia: a Case Study of Agricultural Policy, 1953–1963* (Princeton University Press, Princeton, N.J., 1965)

Ploss, Sidney I. (ed.), *The Soviet Political Process* (Ginn, Toronto and London, 1971)

Remnek, R.B. (ed.), *Social Scientists and Policy-making in the USSR* (Praeger, New York, 1977)

Stewart, Philip, *Political Power in the Soviet Union: a Study of Decision-making in Stalingrad* (Bobbs-Merrill, Indianapolis, Ind., 1968)

Valenta, Jiri, 'Soviet Decision-making and the Czechoslovak Crisis of 1968', *Studies in Comparative Communism*, 8, 1/2 (spring/summer 1975), pp. 147–73

Totalitarianism and concentration models

Arendt, Hannah, *The Origins of Totalitarianism* (Deutsch, London, 1986)

Armstrong, J.A., *The Politics of Totalitarianism: the CPSU from 1934 to the Present* (Random House, New York, 1961)

Barber, B., 'Conceptual Foundations of Totalitarianism', in C. Friedrich, M. Curtis and B. Barber *Totalitarianism in Perspective: Three Views* (Pall Mall Press, London, 1969)

Burrowes, Robert, 'Totalitarianism: the Revised Standard Version', *World Politics*, 21, 2 (January 1969), pp. 272–94

Curtis, M., *Totalitarianism* (Treemartin, USA, 1979)

Feher, Ferenc, and Agnes Heller, *Eastern Left, Western Left: Totalitarianism, Freedom and Democracy* (Polity, Cambridge, 1987)

Friedrich, Carl, and Z. Brzezinski, *Totalitarian Dictatorship and Autocracy* (Harvard University Press, Cambridge, Mass., 1956)

Friedrich, C.J., 'Totalitarianism: Recent Trends', *Problems of Communism*, 17, 3 (May-June 1968), pp. 32–43

Havel, Vaclav *et al.*, *The Power of the Powerless: Citizens against the State in Central-Eastern Europe* (Hutchinson, London, 1985)

Jancar, B. Wolfe, *Czechoslovakia and the Absolute Monopoly of Power* (Praeger, New York, 1971)

Kassof, A., 'The Administered Society? Totalitarianism without Terror', *World Politics*, 16, 4 (July 1964), pp. 558–75

Kassof, A. (ed.), *Prospects for Soviet Society* (Pall Mall Press, London, 1968)

Lane, David, *The Socialist Industrial State: towards a Political Sociology of State Socialism* (Allen & Unwin, London, 1972), chapter 2

Meissner, B., 'Totalitarian Rule and Social Change', *Problems of Communism*, 15, 6 (November-December 1966), pp. 56–61

Rigby, T.H., 'Traditional Market and Organisational Societies and the USSR', *World Politics*, 16, 4 (July 1964)

Rigby, T.H., ' "Totalitarianism" and Change in Communist Societies', *Comparative Politics*, 4, 3 (April 1972), pp. 433–53

Rigby, T.H., 'Politics in the Mono-organisational Society', in A.C. Janos (ed.), *Authoritarian Politics in Communist Europe* (University of California Press, Berkeley, 1976), pp. 31–80

Rigby, T.H., 'Stalinism and the Mono-organisational Society', in R.C. Tucker (ed.), *Stalinism: Essays in Historical Interpretation* (Norton, New York, 1977), pp. 53–76

Schapiro, Leonard, *Totalitarianism* (Macmillan, London, 1972)

Schapiro, L. (ed.), *Political Opposition in One-party States* (Macmillan, London, 1972), especially pp. 241–76

Tucker, R.C., *The Soviet Political Mind: Stalinism and Post-Stalin Change*, rev. edn (Allen & Unwin, London, 1972)

Wittfogel, K.A., *Oriental Despotism: a Comparative Study of Total Power* (Yale University Press, London and New Haven, Conn., 1957)

The group approach and diffusion models

Azrael, Jeremy, *Managerial Power and Soviet Politics* (Harvard University Press, Cambridge, Mass., 1966)

Bentley, Arthur F., *The Process of Government* (Chicago, 1908)

Biddulph, Howard L., 'Local Interest Articulation at CPSU Congresses', *World Politics*, 36, 1 (October 1983), pp. 28–52

Eckstein, Harry, 'Introduction: Group Theory and the Comparative Study of Pressure Groups', in H. Eckstein and D.E. Apter (eds.), *Comparative Politics: a Reader* (New York, Free Press of Glencoe, 1963)

Groth, Alexander J., 'USSR: Pluralist Monolith?', *British Journal of Political Science*, 9 (1979), pp. 445–64

Hough, Jerry F., 'The Soviet System: Petrification or Pluralism', *Problems of Communism*, 21, 2 (March-April 1972), pp. 25–45

Hough, J.F., ' "Interest Groups" and "Pluralism" in the Soviet Union', *Soviet Union/Union Soviétique*, 8, pt I (1981), pp. 103–9

Janos, Andrew C., 'Group Politics in Communist Society: a Second Look at the Pluralistic Model', in S.P. Huntington and C.H. Moore (eds.), *Authoritarian Politics in Modern Society* (Basic Books, New York, 1970), pp. 437–50

Kelley, Donald R., 'Interest Groups in the USSR: the Impact of Political Sensitivity on Group Influence', *Journal of Politics*, 34, 3 (August 1972), pp. 860–88

Langsam, David E., and David W. Paul, 'Soviet Politics and the Group Approach: a Conceptual Note', *Slavic Review*, 31, 1 (March 1972), pp. 136–41

Odom, W., 'A Dissenting View on the Group Approach to Soviet Politics' *World Politics*, 28 (July 1976), pp. 542–67

Schwartz, Joel J., and William R. Keech, 'Group Influence and the Policy Process in the Soviet Union', in Frederic J. Fleron (ed.), *Communist Studies and the Social Sciences* (Rand McNally, Chicago, 1969)

Skilling, H. Gordon, and Franklin Griffiths, *Interest Groups in Soviet Politics* (Princeton University Press, Princeton, N.J., 1971)

Skilling, H. Gordon, 'Group Conflict and Political Change', in Chalmers Johnson (ed.), *Change in Communist Systems* (Stanford University Press, Stanford, Cal., 1970), pp. 215–34

Skilling, H. Gordon, 'Interest Groups and Communist Politics', *World Politics*, 18, 3 (April 1966), pp. 435–51

Skilling, H. Gordon, 'Interest Groups and Communist Politics Revisited', *World Politics*, 36, 1 (October 1983), pp. 1–27; revised version in S. White and D. Nelson (eds.), *Communist Politics: a Reader* (Macmillan, London, 1986), pp. 221–42

Solomon, Peter, *Soviet Criminologists and Criminal Policy: Specialists in Policy-making* (Columbia University Press, New York, 1978)

Solomon, Susan (ed.), *Pluralism in the Soviet Union* (Macmillan, London, 1983)

Truman, David B., *The Governmental Process* (New York, 1951)

White, S., 'Communist Systems and the Iron Law of Political Pluralism', *British Journal of Political Science*, 8 (January 1978), pp. 101–17

Intermediate models

Bunce, Valerie, 'The Political Economy of the Brezhnev Era: the Rise and Fall of Corporatism', *British Journal of Political Science*, 13 (1983), pp. 129–58

Jowitt, Kenneth, 'Soviet Neotraditionalism: the Political Corruption of a Leninist Regime', *Soviet Studies*, 35, 3 (July 1983), pp. 275–97

McCain, Morrie A. Jr., 'Soviet Jurists Divided: a Case for Corporatism in the USSR?', *Comparative Politics*, 15 (1983), pp. 443–60

Meyer, Alfred G., 'Theories of Convergence', in Chalmers Johnson (ed.), *Change in Communist Systems* (Stanford University Press, Stanford, Cal., 1970), pp. 313–41

Schmitter, Philippe, 'Still the Century of Corporatism?', *Review of Politics*, 36, 1 (January 1974), pp. 85–131; and in Frederick B. Pike and Thomas Stritch (eds.), *The New Corporatism* (Notre Dame University Press, Notre Dame, Ind., 1974)

Walder, Andrew G., *Communist Neo-traditionalism: Work and Authority in Chinese Industry* (University of California Press, Berkeley, 1986)

Chapter ten

Ideology and authority

The meaning of ideology

Power and ideology are explicitly associated in the Soviet Union. As Lenin put it in *What is to be Done?*, 'Without theory there can be no revolutionary movement'. In the Russian and Soviet traditions not only do ideas matter, but intellectuals are listened to and respected, if not feared and imprisoned. Censorship can be seen as a back-handed compliment to the power of ideas, something the Old Bolsheviks very well understood, since many of them were intellectuals themselves. The Bolsheviks shared a view of the world made up of three cardinal features. The first, reminiscent of the Populists, was what Bauman calls 'the intellectual idiom', the belief in the need to change the world and that intellectuals know what is required.[1] The second aspect concerned the actual content of their beliefs, derived from Marxism. The third feature was the distinctively Leninist understanding of a mechanism to make the necessary changes, the revolutionary party. When these three factors came together in the Bolshevik party they were to have an explosive impact. The Bolsheviks came to power in the service of an idea, since they represented, in Bauman's chilling phrase, 'the despotism of the enlightened':[2] the belief that they, guided by reason, knew what was best for the people, and the people, once the dark clouds of ignorance were dispelled by education and agitprop, would gladly embrace this vision. Those who failed enthusiastically to respond to the glorious utopia opened up by the Bolshevik revolution were self-evidently not only deluded but criminal, and had to be swept away to allow the people to enter the communist paradise.

The party itself acted, in Gramsci's words, as the 'collective intellectual'. Hence any analysis of the party's novel organizational features must be supplemented by stressing its intellectual resources. The Bolsheviks were initially intellectuals in power, but even as Stalin destroyed the intellectuals the party clung ever more tenaciously to a dogmatized and shrivelled version of the original idea and to the belief that there should be a ruling idea. Ideology and organization are merged in the body of the party: it is not simply that the ideology buttresses the leading role of the party; or that the party supports the dominance of an ideology. They are organically linked, and the one could not survive without the other, though both are susceptible to change.

The problem remains, however, to define the meaning of ideology. Is it a system of beliefs or a mode of action? Marxists talk of *praxis*, the unity of theory and action. In this sense Bauman talks of the Soviet Union as the active utopia where certain goals are being achieved. In the United States there is a liberal tradition derived from Locke and based on individualism, but when one studies the actual operation of American politics it is clear that the ideology is modified by various class, social, race, and other factors. There are similar if not greater problems in the Soviet Union, with the major difference that the Soviet ideology specifies its own pre-eminence and explanatory role not only in the present but in the future as well. The Soviet Union has an official state ideology, believed by some and tolerated by many more, which refers to both what is and what will be, usually adding a rosier hue to both. Anthony Black distinguishes between ethos, the spontaneous convictions of everyday life that Gramsci called 'common sense'; ideology, the *ad hoc* (and according to Marx not necessarily conscious) presentation of a case; and philosophy, the systematic, rational examination of political norms.[3] Ideology in capitalist societies, according to Marxists, is a system of thought that reflects class interests while professing to express a universal world view. Ideology, in other words, masks the domination of the ruling class. Does ideology play a similar role in the Soviet Union? We will try to use philosophy to understand the relationship between ideology and authority in the USSR.

The basic elements of Soviet ideology can be summarized in nine bundles of related issues. (i) Soviet ideology is based on dialectical materialism, denoting a philosophical methodology critical of idealism (transcendant or God-based views of humanity) which stresses the notion of continual interaction, of movement and dynamism, in the development of nature, human society, and thought. In the dialectical method the thesis comes into contradiction with an antithesis and results in a synthesis. The practical application of this methodology is historical materialism, in which the changes in society are considered to be derived from the fundamental contradiction between classes, based on their different relationship to the means of production. Marx uses the base/superstructure metaphor to illustrate the dependence of the political on the economic. The final stage of the class struggle according to Marx was the overthrow of the bourgeoisie (thesis) by the proletariat (antithesis) to result in the transcendence of both (synthesis) in communism.

(ii) Lenin's major contribution to Marxism was the notion of consciousness, which underlay his theory of party organization. As we have seen, by 1902 Lenin was impatient with the slow development of the Russian working class and insisted on the need to imbue it with revolutionary class consciousness. This would have to come from outside, which in effect meant intellectuals. For Lenin ideology was not simply a reflection of the material base, the implication of Marx's base/superstructure metaphor; instead he drew attention to the conscious application of change in history. Lenin insisted that revolutions have to be organized, whereas Marx tended to think that history itself would bring the working class to power. Lenin's voluntarism, however, was located firmly in the historicist, or determinist, framework: the revolution was inevitable but needed active assistance. On coming to power Lenin's historicism revealed itself in the belief that since working-class power was inevitable the problems that arose *must* have a solution in history itself, and hence his rudimentary approach to the structure of working-class political power. Lenin was the original exponent of 'guided democracy' practised under the direction of a vanguard party. Under Stalin the idea of consciousness became an exaggerated theory of Bolshevik *dirigisme*, typified by the statement that there are 'no fortresses that a Bolshevik cannot storm'.

(iii) Soviet ideology has been marked by economism, the belief that the economic substructure of society determines the social relations within that society. Nationalization of the means of production, for instance, is taken to mean the establishment of socialism. Economism stresses the relationship between *things* and not the social relationships between *people*. It subordinates politics to economics, to so-called objective laws. Economism was triumphant during war communism and lies at the heart of Stalinism. Gorbachev's reform programme stressing the 'human factor' and the quality of social relationships is an explicit condemnation of economism and an implicit rejection of Stalinism. The human face is at last being put back on to socialism.

(iv) Marxism-Leninism is the cornerstone of Soviet ideology and provides the rationale for the existence of a dominant ruling party. It is said to embody scientific truths about society, and the CPSU claims that it, and it alone, clearly and correctly understands these truths. The role of the party is defined by the ideology, but the party constantly modifies the ideology to take into account changing circumstances. The important point is that however much it may change Marxism-Leninism is held to represent the truth at any particular time. The concept of a single 'truth' rejects the pluralist conception of partial and many truths. The party is the bearer of revolutionary tradition, hence it has a moral right to rule. The official elements of that tradition, and in particular the history of the CPSU, are incorporated into the Soviet version of Marxism-Leninism to establish a mutually reinforcing relationship between the ideology and party authority. The party becomes the only legitimate mouthpiece of the working class, even if the working class disagrees with it, because the party knows what is in its best interests. The party alone can decode the processes of history and interpret Marxist ideology. In the absence of war, overriding national tasks, free elections, or charismatic leadership Soviet ideology becomes ever more important to justify the party's leading role. Marxism-Leninism justifies the rule of a militant vanguard party which takes power in the name of the movement and nation.

(v) Marx's great achievement had been to put socialism on an allegedly scientific basis, dispensing with the idealistic dreams of a Robert Owen or a P.-J. Proudhon, and instead establishing the basis of 'scientific communism' from his study of material life. Marx never tried to provide detailed guidance on the organization of communist society, and dismissed such attempts as utopian. Scientific communism now denotes the short-range pronouncements on the detailed management of communist states. The revolution has undergone many metamorphoses as the domestic commitment to far-reaching change has gradually focused on maintaining stability. The 1961 party programme, for example, talked of the 'comprehensive building of communism by 1980', but his successors dropped Khrushchev's grandiose perspectives in favour of more modest ambitions. This was expressed above all in Brezhnev's concept of 'developed socialism', or 'developed socialist society'. After the storms of Stalinism and Khrushchev's flirtation with populism it signalled that the ethos of the new era was technology, professionalism, and controlled administrative change.

(vi) The technocratic element in Soviet ideology should be singled out more specifically. It is a crucial part of the concept of developed socialism and signals the adaptation of the 'intellectual idiom' to modern industrial society. The technocratic bias in Soviet ideology suggests that society is no longer to be transformed but to be managed. Brezhnev's concept of developed socialism embodied the 'scientism' implicit in the technocratic ideal, buttressed by two supplementary concepts. The first was the 'scientific-technological revolution' and the second the 'scientific management of society'. The scientific-technological revolution reiterated the Soviet belief in the leading role of technology in social change, but modified economism by stressing a scientific approach to enterprise management and labour relations. The notion of the scientific management of society only confirmed the role of scientific communism in providing the key to managing social processes. Political and economic management was restricted to a group of 'experts' with a privileged understanding of the allegedly real forces operating at any given time. However, the political restrictions on technocratic power meant that even under Brezhnev one could not talk of the triumph of the technocracy, the allegedly rational and depoliticized solution of existing problems. In the USSR problems are still dealt with as political issues rather than as technical matters subject to instrumental rationality alone. Gorbachev has condemned the technocratic elements in Brezhnev's rule and suggested that the concept of developed socialism was premature.

(vii) Stalin promoted the fusion of political ideology with social ethos, particularly during the war. The Brezhnev years witnessed the consolidation of what can be called patriotic-traditionalism. The already existing was raised to the level of the eternal, stifling critical responses to emerging problems. This was accompanied in his later years by the idea of 'the Soviet way of life', which closed the gap between doctrine and practice by lending the vision of communism a thoroughly Soviet face. The 'Soviet way of life' was a conservative mixture of patriotic xenophobia and self-praise which combined a contempt for 'Western' (liberal democratic) values with an aggressive nationalism and a submission to paternalistic authority.

(viii) Soviet ideology has always been marked by a strong teleological element, the belief that society is directed towards a historical goal and shaped by a purpose. The view of a rational world to come can lead to de-enlightenment, or irrationality, in the present. During war communism Soviet communists believed that the future could be attained in the present. After the low-key NEP Stalin used the teleological elements in Soviet ideology to whip the population into a frenzy of expectations which appeared to justify the sacrifices and cruelties. Post-Stalin expectations have declined, and Khrushchev's vision of communism in the 1961 programme was a fairly tame Sovietized version of consumer industrialism. Brezhnev's rule was marked by a sharp decline in ideological enthusiasm and represented a further turn in the downward spiral of expectations. The stress under Gorbachev is on the problems of real or 'developing socialism' rather than the socialism of the future. The replacement of enthusiasm by scepticism can be seen as a process of re-enlightenment as rational analysis takes the place of irrational expectations, philosophy the place of ideology.

(ix) This survey of Soviet ideology is enough to illustrate yet another of its major characteristics, its 'rigid flexibility', the counterpart of the 'organized chaos' in the administrative sphere. It is not clear whether the many shifts witnessed by the ideology since 1917 represent fundamental changes or simply adaptation to new circumstances. The very premise of dialectical materialism permits flexible, or dialectical, responses to actual processes. Hence, as Basily pointed out in 1938, the communist party 'differs from ordinary political bodies just as much by the rigidity of its doctrines as by the extreme instability of its immediate pro-gramme'.[4] Zaslavsky attributes the combination of stability and flexibility to the extraordinary explanatory strength and absorptive capacity of Marxism, its role as the sole official ideology in a single-party system (factions and feuds within the party are banned and hence intellectual debate is limited), and the role that Marxism plays as the dominant ideology of the international communist move-ment.[5] The operating ideology undergoes changes whereas the solid core provides stability.

Marxism-Leninism remains the hegemonic force in cultural and political life, but its hegemony is derived not from its innate dynamism but from its institu-tionalization as the 'state religion'. While weakened as a rational explicatory or predictive force, it remains at the centre of the Soviet power system. Marxism-Leninism contributes to a novel body of thought and belief that can be termed Soviet ideology. Soviet ideology is an amalgam of Marxism, traditional socialist precepts, the Bolshevik (or Leninist) interpretation of Marxism, and the tradi-tions and experience of seventy years of Soviet power. It operates within the context of a socialist economic basis, the political monopoly of the CPSU, a leader-ship cult focused on Lenin, the universal application of the principle of democratic centralism, and the memory of the revolutionary and Soviet past. The stability of Soviet ideology is derived in part from the fact that it is used primarily not as a means of intellectual exchange or debate but as part of a structure of authority. It is modified in response to the needs of the power system rather than to new currents of intellectual endeavour. The Soviet ideology as here defined is synonymous with the beliefs and actions of the Soviet power system. Over the years Soviet ideology has become transformed into the ethos of the system, and by the same token has lost some of the characteristics of philosophy.

The ideological apparatus

Historical materialism is determinist in its belief that people are conditioned by their social environment; or, as Marx put it, 'being determines consciousness'. The new communist society would produce a new person as the previous one had produced the old. However, instead of a new social consciousness arising spontaneously, the Soviet Union maintains a massive apparatus of ideological persuasion and control to make the 'new Soviet person'. Soviet practice concedes that consciousness can be changed irrespective of material conditions. The ideology which once inspired a small group of revolutionaries is now, with modification, imposed upon the rest of society as the only truth. The ideology is binding, otherwise it would become ineffective. In the administrative sphere Soviet democracy calls for the guidance of an elite political organization, so in the realm of ideas guidance is also required.

The ideological apparatus that emerged under Lenin was massively strengthened under Stalin. The party intervened directly, for example, in literary politics. In 1925 the party Central Committee declared that the class war had not ended on the literary front, and pronounced that neutral art was impossible. This resulted in draconian measures to impose unity on literature. During the cultural revolution from 1928 cultural and intellectual life began to be mobilized in a systematic way. Only after the cultural revolution had spent its energy by about 1931, however, did all spheres of academic and cultural life, in economics, philosophy, psychology, education, and history, become subordinated to the needs of the party apparatus and Stalin personally. In 1932 socialist realism was proclaimed as the only acceptable form of literature, and in 1934 it was given organizational form by the formation of the Union of Soviet Writers. In biology this period saw the triumph of Lysenko's spurious genetic theories. In history Pokrovskii's school of historiography, which concentrated on the role of the masses and revolutionary traditions in Russian history, were replaced by a greater stress on the role of monarchs, implying that Stalin the Great was carrying on the traditions of a Peter or Catherine. The consolidation of Stalinism was accompanied by the uneasy amalgamation of patriotic-traditionalism with Marxism-Leninism. The ideological apparatus is designed to propagate the ideology, popularize the current shifts and to ensure that the leadership can control the direction and degree of its flexibility.

Censorship lies at the heart of the system of ideological restriction. Censorship was strongly opposed by Marx, and Rosa Luxemburg argued that 'Freedom only for the supporters of the government, only for the members of one party — however numerous they may be — is no freedom at all. Freedom is always and exclusively for the one who thinks differently.'[6] From the first Lenin took a radically different view, and one of his first acts on coming to power in October 1917 was to close down the 'bourgeois' press to control the flow of ideas. Victory in the civil war saw the final suffocation of an independent press. Cultural and literary restrictions have to varying degrees stultified Soviet intellectual life ever since. Until recently Glavlit, the Main Administration for Safeguarding State

Secrets in the Press, was the organizer of censorship. Formed in 1922, by 1934 it had the power to control the press and journals, to remove books from libraries, decide which books would be published, and license imported publications. In libraries and museums there are 'special stores' in which sensitive materials are reserved for the use of trusted people. Glavlit's functions have been restricted by Gorbachev and are supplemented by a council of editors who monitor the 8,000 newspapers and 5,000 magazines now being published in the USSR. The methods of the censorship are not known precisely, but can be compared to the Black Book of Polish Censorship, a publication, smuggled to the West in the late 1970s, giving detailed instructions to the censors. Censorship is at its most effective when it is invisible, giving life an impression of immutable reality rather than being contingent on the whims of a bevy of censors. Once the censorship becomes visible, with blank spaces in papers, it begins to lose its credibility. A law on the mass media in Gorbachev's early years shifted the emphasis away from direct censorship towards more subtle forms of editorial control. Individual editors are now permitted a much greater choice of material to print, within certain guidelines established by the Central Committee.

One of the main functions of the ideological apparatus to date has been the insulation of the Soviet Union from foreign influences. The trial of Sinyavsky and Daniel in February 1966, which marked the end of Khrushchev's liberalism, was prompted by the publication of their works abroad. New laws passed that year included the fresh Article 190 of the RSFSR Criminal Code, making it an offence to disseminate in oral or written form 'conscious fabrications discrediting the Soviet state'. The definiton of 'fabrication' was left to the authorities. Mail from abroad is controlled, and the history of radio jamming illustrates Soviet relations with the west like a geological chart.

The attempt to mobilize the population to build communism is achieved through political education and the agitprop apparatus. As noted in Chapter 8, mass organizations such as the trade unions and Komsomol are vehicles not only of participation but also of socialization. Each major party committee has ideology and agitation and propaganda sections. At the local level the PPOs play a key role, supplemented by a widespread system of closed lectures delivered at workplaces and a network of circles (kruzhki) for political and party enlightenment. Socialization is reinforced through the Soviet festival and ritual system, notably the May Day and 7 November parades, which inculcate the ideology in a particularly vivid manner. The Soviet victory in World War II is used to imbue the population with patriotic values in a system of civic education.

The ideology is used as a social integrator and acts as a supra-national unifying force over and above national, religious, and ethnic divisions. The language and mission of socialist transformation still serve to establish the parameters of acceptable behaviour and beliefs. It was axiomatic in Soviet ideology that dissent would naturally wither away as the social basis for it disappeared. But in keeping with Bolshevik voluntarism, and the inevitable authoritarianism of the 'despotism of the enlightened', the stubborn persistence of dissent is ascribed to the pathological inadequacies of individuals rather than manifestations of social imbalance. A massive apparatus exists to ensure the withering away of alternative ways of thought both by coercion and by socialization. The ideological apparatus tries to inculcate in social consciousness not only the hope of a better tommorrow but also the conviction that the Soviet Union today is, despite its shortcomings, preferable to that of any other system. Under Gorbachev this increasingly hollow 'propaganda of success' has given way to a more sober examination of past and present inadequacies and has toned down the prospect of the future.

The socialization is imperfect, however, since it competes with a variety of other influences such as material life, careers, religion, and family interests. By the 1980s it had become increasingly clear that the years in which the agitprop apparatus had claimed increasing numbers of meetings, propaganda pamphlets published, meetings attended, had not given birth to the desired new person. The sheer statistical enumeration of agitprop activity said little about its effectiveness. Respect for ideology among the young appeared extremely low: classes in Marxist-Leninist ideology were to be endured rather than enjoyed. The generation numbed by Brezhnevite crassness are a particularly alienated group. Well aware of the problem, the Politburo in September 1987 called for 'drastic improvements' in the system of political education.

Cultural policy during *perestroika* revealed a tremulous uncertainty about the degree to which the party could allow the various cultural associations greater freedom. Brezhnevite functionaries were replaced, often by people who had seen their work shelved during the era of stagnation, and yet the attempt to overcome the administrative autonomy devolved to ministries under Brezhnev entailed the enhancement of party authority. The removal of the minister of culture, Peter Demichev, in 1986 was accompanied by criticism that the ministry had usurped some of the rights of the CC Secretariat in cultural affairs. Intervention by leading writers in public issues was encouraged as long as it was supportive of the broader goals of *perestroika*. The lessons of the Khrushchev years, which capitalized on the writers' ability to mobilize popular feelings in the destalinization campaign but unleashed forces that it could not control, have been learnt. The point at which discipline is reimposed will mark the boundary of *glasnost*.

Luxemburg's main argument against censorship was that the lack of criticism would lead to bureaucratism and corruption. In this she was amply proved correct, and Gorbachev's *glasnost* campaign is clearly an attempt to use greater openness to expose corruption and inadequacies. *Glasnost* does not signify the end of censorship or editorial control. It does mean, though, that there is a greater will-ingness to tolerate the public expression of ideas: Stalinist monophony has given way to polyphony. The nineteenth party conference resolved that the right to information by the public should be enshrined in the constitution as a sort of Freedom of Information Act. The category of 'offical secrets' was to be severely curtailed and statistics on economic and social affairs should be made available. The deliberations of party plenums, including those of the Central Committee, would be published. *Glasnost* represents the reconstitution of the rationality implied in Soviet Marxism, the belief that it is a scientific doctrine rather than a utopian project. *Glasnost* represents a weakening of the demand for belief in the infallibility of the party or the interpreters of ideology and thus broadens the scope of debate.

The role of ideology

The Marxist classics and Lenin offer no detailed guidelines about the policy choices of an urbanized, educated, and increasingly computer-literate society. While there is no doubt about the centrality of ideology to the Soviet system, its precise role is very much a matter of controversy. Is it a set of fundamental principles, a doctrine, remaining in the background, or is it an action programme determining policy? These contrasting views have been reflected in the debate between Solzhenitsyn and Sakharov. Solzhenitsyn argues that the Soviet state is guided by the overarching influence of Marxist ideology and that it has been responsible for all the disasters that have befallen the Soviet people. The only way forward lies in the country's liberation from the stifling ideology.[7] These views have been echoed by commentators such as Vladimir Bukovskii, Alexander Shtromas, Robert Conquest, and Richard Pipes, who insist that the West refuses to take Soviet ideology seriously at its own peril. They argue that it is an act of naivety to project Western values on to the 'power seekers' and 'hegemonists' of the Kremlin. On the other hand, Sakharov argues that the official state ideology is dead and that it is no longer taken seriously. It is therefore ridiculous to imagine that it could guide and shape practical policies. From this perspective R.V. Daniels argues that Marxism-Leninism is very much subordinate to such factors as Russian political culture in shaping policy.

Both views reflect different aspects of the truth, but any analysis which does not place ideology at the centre of the power system distorts the reality of Soviet politics. The Soviet state has ideology built into its foundations, to inspire and legitimize its actions and its very existence. The government itself justifies the political system in terms of its relationship to Marxism-Leninism. And yet too often even when the centrality of ideology is recognized it is applied as a very blunt explanatory instrument. The antinomies expressed by the Sakharov-Solzhenitsyn debate are fundamentally misleading. Ideology is not an external to be utilized or not as circumstances change but lies at the heart of the existing system of power. Furthermore, it is important to define which aspect of the ideology is being discussed.

The relationship of ideology to policy-making remains ambivalent. The question arises whether ideology is a guide to action or its justification. The ideology is absolutely indispensable to the operation of the Soviet system irrespective of how seriously it is taken or how crudely it is presented. This does not mean that in each and every decision ideological considerations are dominant. Decisions are taken within the context of an evolving Soviet ideology which continually modifies Marxism-Leninism in the light of current needs. Marxism-Leninism is part of the official ideology of the power structure of the Soviet Union but it does not serve as a blueprint for building communist society. The most that it can do is to identify the broad goals and assess the policies that are compatible with the building of communism. Just as the ideology retains a certain autonomy from the power structure, so the structure of decision-making is not wholly dependent on the ideology.

All policies are expressed in terms of their alleged contribution to the building of communism, but in detailed policy-making there is a balance between ideological and practical influences. Soviet policy has always been severely practical in foreign and domestic policies. The operating ideology restricts the types of demands that can be made by society, but it does not significantly reduce the freedom of manoeuvre of the power elite. Soviet history is the story of the flexible application of 'communist ideology', and indeed Stalinism can be defined as the subordination of the means to the end. There are few, if any, policy options excluded by the ideology as long as they can be made compatible with an evolving concept of socialism. These include the decollectivization of agriculture, and even the denationalization of industry. In foreign policy the ideology did not prevent a pact with Hitler's Germany or the invasion of fellow socialist states. The ideology does not specify the preponderance of heavy over light industry: that was a consequence of the preferences of a specific leadership group at a specific time. There is clearly a distinction between the ideology and the party line, the current political expedient based on immediate political considerations. A broad flexibility in tactics is permitted within the general strategic framework. However, rather than practice determining ideology, the ideology offers a way of identifying which interests and demands are compatible with the overall goal. The flexibility of the ideology is often manifest in current policies, but its rigidity still derives from the notion of an ideal society towards which the present society should be guided. Marxism-Leninism has become less of a prescription for action than a set of loose goals.

Alfred Meyer defined Soviet ideology as operating in two distinctive modes. In the first the ideology provides a language or a code for communication in the political sphere; and in the second it affirms certain values which serve to legitimate the role of leadership.[8] The philosopher Leszek Kolakowski argues that the ideology in Soviet-type systems is used primarily to legitimize the monopoly of power.[9] The irreducible element of contemporary Soviet ideology is the maintenance of the leading role of the party. The initial formulation of this has changed from the dictatorship of the proletariat to the state of all the people, but in the Soviet Union as elsewhere no communist system has challenged this fundamental idea, though in practice Stalin and other charismatic leaders have displaced the party as a functioning political institution. However, it would be an unwarrantedly narrow view to argue that the main role of Soviet ideology is to maintain the existing political system. The regime could probably well survive without an explicit ideology, and indeed in countries such as Poland its abandonment (as urged by Solzhenitsyn) would inestimably strengthen the system, although of course the operative ideology in Eastern Europe is *Soviet*, generated by an alien historical and political experience. The ideology in the Soviet Union is in any case buttressed by other legitimating factors such as victory in the war, great-power status, and until the late 1970s rising standards of living. The party's special relationship to ideology justifies its dominant role in the system: its task is to interpret and fulfil the laws of social development.

Since at least the 1950s there has been much talk about the end of ideology in the Soviet Union. Such statements can mean several things. First of all it depends on what aspect of ideology one has in mind, whether Marxism, or Leninism, or Soviet ideology. One could mean that no one believes in the ideology any more. For the Soviet Union this would probably be an exaggeration. However, in the sense that Marxism-Leninism in the Soviet Union is no longer regarded as infallible, and the communist utopia for an increasing number of Soviet citizens is no longer considered desirable, let alone achievable, then the statement that ideology is dead is correct. The process has been seen as the 'rationalization' or 'de-ideologization' of the communist movement as it loses its earlier chiliasm in favour of more limited and incremental objectives.[10] Communist rule changes from mobilizing to managing the society through rational organization. The Soviet Union shared, according to this view, certain aspects of modernity and could be studied in comparative political science terms. The process has if anything accelerated under Gorbachev's pragmatic and flexible approach, although the reforms remain located in the old ideological framework. While teleology is now a minor chord in the symphony of Soviet ideology, the *dirigiste* implications of the planned transformation of society remain.

Convergence theory and concepts of advanced industrial society hold that ideology will decline as power is devolved to specialist groupings and government becomes more instrumental. Daniel Bell in the late 1950s predicted that 'The STR . . . inevitably leads to the end of ideology . . . It always and everywhere produces commonality in technology and methods of industrial leadership, the development of similar ways of life among all peoples, and common social problems.'[11] This may well be correct, but it was at least thirty years premature. It presupposes a convergence of industrial societies, whereas two very different models of advanced industrial society exist, the Western and the Soviet type. In the West the emergence of a relatively affluent consumer-based economy eased class conflicts compared to the first stages of industrialization, but in the Soviet Union ideology is rooted not in the conflict of social classes but in the supremacy of the communist party, reinforced by the vitality of Soviet patriotic traditionalism. The ideology has become vested in a cohesive, bureaucratic, autonomous ruling elite, although the role of ideology cannot be reduced to the exercise of power. The component parts of Soviet ideology affect different groups in different ways. To date, this has acted as an integrating force, but as the coherence of the ideology declines each separate element may become magnified and act as the basis of intensified group or class conflict. John Dunlop sees the course of the decay of Marxist-Leninist ideology taking a path towards the development of nationalist and religious feelings. Hough argues that the ideology is declining and that its growing ambiguity allows the increased vitality of public policy debate.[12] Of course, greater debate may signify only greater confidence on the part of the power structure, rather than any change in the role of ideology. Either way, growing ideological flexibility will allow the reconstitution of a vigorous public sphere.

The death of Brezhnev has permitted a profound debate over the content and role of ideology in the Soviet Union. In his speech on the hundredth anniversary of the death of Marx in January 1983 Andropov revealed a pragmatic and flexible approach in arguing for a re-evaluation of the role of ideology. Battle was joined at the June 1983 'ideological plenum' of the Central Committee. Andropov spoke in favour of the 'creative use of ideology'. 'Marxism', he argued, 'does not give answers in ideology once and for all'. Chernenko countered, however, by asserting that 'there are eternal verities, some truths which cannot be changed'. His was the voice of an older generation unremittingly hostile to alien ideological influences. Andropov, in contrast, insisted that changes in the productive forces required changes in production relations, and he attacked 'formalism' and 'mechanical repetition'. Gorbachev has continued Andropov's arguments with renewed vigour. At the January 1987 CC plenum he argued that the party's theory was fixed in an outdated mould dating from the 1930s, implying that it was marked by Stalinist dogmatism and authoritarianism buttressing a conservative bureaucratic machinery. Gorbachev insisted that the Soviet system requires democracy like 'the air we breath'. However, Gorbachev explicitly stated at the plenum that he was not proposing a new theory for the period. Hence, as Zhores Medvedev notes, 'although Gorbachev did talk about theory, he did not actually talk theoretically'.[13] In domestic policy he worked within the framework of the theoretical innovations introduced by his predecessors. In the current period not only the diversity within Marxism-Leninism but the freedom with which some of the contentious issues are discussed is remarkable. In society debate has lost some of its allusive style, but within the party Aesopian mannerisms reflect the struggle between reformers and conservatives.

The fascinating feature of the Soviet system and the source of much of its dynamism is the cohabiting of incompatible elements, such as Marx's condemnation of censorship with one of the most severe censorship regimes in the world, or the belief in popular self-management combined with the radical negation of popular control and self-organization. The Andropov-Chernenko debate and Gorbachev's vigorous approach illustrate that Soviet ideology retains elements of critical reflection, possibly derived from its Marxist roots, of its own predicament. It is forced to adapt as an act of survival in order to avoid suffocating from its own complacency. Paradoxically, in the current debate over reform, ideology, considered the force most resistant to change, has proved to be the sphere where reformers have achieved their greatest successes in reinterpreting the current demands of the Soviet polity. A. Yakovlev, the onetime CC Secretary responsible for ideology, represented a sharp break with Suslov's dogmatic inflexibility.

215

Yet this is in a sense a compensation for having failed to obtain the support of the governmental machinery. All statements about beliefs and policies are still couched in the language of Marx and cast in terms of their loyalty to Lenin's bequest, but there is a greater sense of possibilities of interpretation of the sacred canon. The discussion is over means, not ends, and it is premature to speak of the end of ideology. Gorbachev's single greatest achievement to date has not been to bury the ideology, but to make it responsive to the requirements of modern Soviet society. Not only the economy but the ideology also required modernization.

Power, political culture and legitimacy

Soviet ideology has exercised a mobilizing function to justify the common ownership and management of large-scale property. It legitimated a fundamentally asocial political practice in which social forms of life were subordinated to goals generated beyond the real-life experience of the people. At its most violent peaks in the 1930s (comparable to the Chinese cultural revolution of 1966–76) the system lurched towards its own self-destruction and was forced to modify the extremism of its otherworldliness. From the first the enthusiasm of enlightenment couched in the language of development and historical progress provided the Soviet system with enormous reserves of popular support, even during its most sanguinary periods. Stalinism was not based purely on coercion but on a great degree of popular support for policies such as collectivization and industrialization. The image of a totalitarian regime dominating an atomized society through power techniques alone is exaggerated. The element of coercion in the Stalinist polity was projected as a necessary response to external crises and domestic emergency within the context of a culture of despotism buttressed by the *dirigisme* implicit in the ideology. Stalinist 'order' and paternalism still evoke a certain nostalgia.

Gramsci's insights on the role of hegemony in capitalist society are applicable to the Soviet system. Gramsci modified the traditional Marxist view of the state as an instrument of coercion and in its place developed an expanded view of the state as based upon both coercion and consent. Consent was achieved through hegemony, described by Gramsci as intellectual and moral leadership, as opposed to dictatorship or domination. His ideas have been taken up by Euro-communists in the notion of a 'democratic' road to socialism eschewing the need for insurrectionary politics, and were reflected in the Action Programme of the Czechoslovak communists in 1968. Domination gives way to leadership, and the idea of the dictatorship of the proletariat is replaced by the concept of the hegemony of the working people. Yet in the context of the reaffirmation of the leading role of the party, the formal nature of much participation, and sustained low-intensity coercion the achievement of consent operates in a radically different way from the West.[14] There is clearly a broad congruence between the immediate aspirations of the population and the welfare and paternalistic policies of the regime. Prices until 1988 remained reasonably stable, and the disciplinarian policies of the government gave the appearance of sustaining a high degree of 'law and order'. If democracy is defined as consent to rule, then the USSR is a highly democratic system. There are clearly many sources of political consensus in the Soviet Union, extending from the political to the sociological and psychological. To a degree, however, consent is manufactured by the ideological apparatus which is responsible for the bureaucratic organization of consensus, yet that is not the whole story. Consent to state policies does not take place in a vacuum but within the context of social, economic, and psychological relations. Models of the state based on consent or coercion, dictatorship or democracy, bureaucracy or participation are designed to further the analysis of how precisely the state really functions under socialism.

The concept of political culture is a broad one and is used in many senses. Political culture should be distinguished from Soviet ideology, the belief system of the authority structure. Political culture refers to both the operational pattern of decision-makers (the way they think and act) and the general psychological attitudes of the public. It is a concept that can be tested in specific cases of decision-making only with great difficulty. For example, the decision to invade Czechoslovakia in 1968 can be cited as an expression of Russian political culture in its attitude to neighbouring peoples. But such a statement is fairly meaningless. The term is usually restricted to analysis of the general context of decisions and processes. Tucker retreats from using the concept of political culture to explain specific processes, and refers to it as 'a complex of real and ideal culture patterns, including political roles and their interrelations, political structures, and so on'.[15] Archie Brown stresses that the best way to use the term is in terms of subjective orientation. Beliefs and values are to be kept distinct from behaviour.[16]

The study of Soviet politics has suffered grievously from the tendency to replace ideological determinism by a historical determinism based on political culture. The practices of the present are monolithically ascribed to the traditions of the past. The alleged congruence between elite values and popular aspirations is ascribed to the influence of a historically determined political culture whose major features were listed in Chapter 1. The historical experience of strong leadership from above and lack of formal restraints on the state within a centralized power structure, with few formal channels for popular involvement in politics, are the key features of the continuity theorists. Other factors include common attitudes towards authority and the state and the sense that there is a primordial legitimacy vested in a powerful Russian state as defender of the borders and provider in a paternalistic way of security and economic welfare. Another feature is the weakness of individualism in an economic and social sense. This is reflected in the underdevelopment of representative institutions and a traditional lack of focus on the role of law. In particular, hierarchy and bureaucratism are argued to have been transferred from Tsarism to the Soviet Union. The argument that the weakness of civil society actually pre-dated the creation of the Bolshevik regime has been much exaggerated.

It would be more accurate to focus on the distinctive Bolshevik combination of ideology and organization rather than on Russian political culture. The new system borrowed the elements of the old regime which were considered necessary for its own survival, rather than being burdened by a choiceless past. Even though Stalin has been seen as the 'Red Tsar', continuing a tradition of strong monarchs, he achieved a radical transformation of society that would have been incomprehensible to the Romanovs, with their religious and traditional values. The Tsars aimed to conserve and defend, whereas the Bolsheviks aimed to destroy and transform.

The Russian past was made up of many contradictory elements, and the concept of political culture cannot explain why some traditional patterns are incorporated into modern social and institutional structures while others are undermined and destroyed. Survival or destruction of earlier forms depends on their relationship to institutional or cultural patterns that serve to perpetuate the current system. It is the mechanics of this relationship that must be examined. The fundamental question is whether modern forms are grafted on to traditional structures or cultural norms and are thus subverted by them and forced to conform to older forms; or whether the older forms survive only because of their utility to the new social formation. The answer probably lies somewhere in between. Thoroughly modern functions are performed in the guise of traditional institutions. In any case, a very large proportion of the contemporary Soviet practices have no counterpart in pre-revolutionary traditions.

The debate over political culture contains an apologetic element: that Soviet socialism might well have worked better if only Russia had been different, if it had had more democratic institutions, and if it had not been tainted by oriental despotism and Byzantine mysticism, and if the working class had been stronger and the peasantry less numerous. This serves only to underline the point that Soviet socialism was not a stage following capitalism but, as Joan Robinson put it, an alternative to capitalist development. The fact that the debate over a long-term political culture still rages illustrates that, despite the vast social upheavals of the twentieth century, Soviet socialism has in a sense acted as a sarcophagus shielding the country from the enormous transformative power of modern capitalism.

An important facet of political culture is the relationship between popular attitudes and the structure of political power, a question that can be examined under the heading of legitimacy. It is clear that major changes have taken place since the era of high Stalinism and that the basis of the legitimacy of the Soviet regime has to some extent changed. Max Weber identified three main 'pure' types of legitimacy. The first is based on 'traditional domination', sanctioned by the preservation of ancient customs and based on patrimonial and patriarchal values. In a Soviet-type system traditional legitimacy 'is not seen as rooted in an "eternal past" but in the promise of a "better tomorrow"'. It is based on the 'belief in the inevitability and immutability of a given order, in the idea that no alternative to it can be conceived'.[17] The second is charismatic legitimation, where the individual leader, endowed with almost supernatural gifts, is venerated in the religious and political spheres. Examples are prophets, elected war lords, or political party leaders. The third type is based on 'legality', the acceptance of legal norms and a rational order in which each performs functions based on rules. The executives of the modern state and its bureaucracy fall within this category. The cult of personality under Stalin represented a form of charismatic rule. However, even under Lenin and to the present day elements of charismatic legitimation have been 'routinized' in the collective personality of the communist party. The charisma of the post-Stalin leader, in theory, is only the reflected brilliance of the party. In addition, as time passes there is an increasing development of legitimation based on the 'legal' processes of party governance in a developed and stable society. The bureaucratic nature of Soviet rule, one of its most distinctive features, finally becomes rule in a bureaucratic way, marked by clearly delineated rules, the demarcation of functions, and an end to arbitrariness in administrative and judicial procedures. At that stage the legitimacy of the Soviet regime would be solidly based on legality, and the charismatic or 'heroic' features would correspondingly decline.

The basis of the Soviet regime's legitimacy has changed over time. It shifts away from ideological and programmatic grounds to the regime's identification with the creation of the industrial basis of socialism. The growing complexity of the society generates a thick web of social relationships relatively independent of the power relations of the system, and the purely ideological forms of legitimation necessarily wane. The third type of Weberian legitimacy, the rational-legal, becomes increasingly important. Here social demands could be given a legal orientation, with rules and procedures for achieving consensus, the elements of a genuine social contract. But in the absence of the full emergence of a rational-legal order a series of socially generated forms of legitimation arise to fill the gap, such as defence of the national territory and patriotic traditionalism. They supplement Marxist-Leninist ideology in the ever-changing amalgam of Soviet ideology. The development of a socialist legal state will provide opportunities for philosophical challenges to be mounted against Soviet ideology on the grounds of rationality.

Among the latter-day bases of legitimacy is a characteristic identified by F. Feher, the role of paternalism as a mode of legitimation. The regime acts as a benevolent and protective entity which both removes the fear of disorder and constitutes a fear of freedom. The terror meant death for many, but for others the Stalinist system obviated the need for independent thought or initiative. The death of Stalin allowed the emergence of paternalism to replace charismatic legitimation. As part of the neo-Stalinist compromise, paternalistic dictatorship helped consolidate a fundamentally authoritarian system by making it responsive to the needs of the population. Arbitrary terror was removed but a degree of paternalistic coercion was ingrained in the system. The neo-Stalinist compromise permitted a slow improvement in living standards, but at the price of the continued depoliticization of society as the state retained a monopoly of political life. State paternalism is allied to the maintenance of a conservative family pattern which, according to Feher, sustains the 'authoritarian personality'.[18]

From 1936 the legal source of legitimacy was again proclaimed, though ignored in practice. Yet the battle for legality, socialist or otherwise, has gained the support of all post-Stalin leaders. It could be argued that from 1936 the rising modern strata of officialdom and technical specialists sought to consolidate their gains in legal form. For the polity, also, legality became an increasing political necessity as the period of revolutions from above came to an end. At present the consolidation of legality has become the concern of one of the most effective of the Soviet Union's 'interest groups', the jurists.[19] Whether consciously or not, the jurists provide the basis for the development of the Soviet system into a state governed by law, a socialist *Rechtsstaat*. Gorbachev's own legal training has helped make legal reform an essential part of *perestroika*.

In Brezhnev's last years certain indications of a fundamental 'legitimacy crisis' were beginning to become apparent. For Habermas a legitimation crisis (as applied to advanced capitalist states) is marked by the increasing inability of the political-administrative system to manage the economy.[20] In the Soviet Union there has not as yet been a moment of fundamental breakdown caused by legitimacy crisis comparable to Hungary in 1956 or Poland in 1980–1. Disappointed expectations have given rise to general dissatisfaction, but it would be an exaggeration to suggest that this constitutes a crisis in political legitimacy. Reform undoubtedly poses new challenges and hastens the transition to rational-legal forms of legitimation.

For Pye and Verba political culture represents the structure of popular attitudes which provide the context in which the authority system operates,[21] although the two may or may not be congruent. Almond and Verba went on to provide a threefold classification of political culture: parochial, subject, and participant. In the parochial culture the political system is regarded as something outside the individual's life experience. In the subject political culture individuals have a passive relationship to politics, and while they are aware of government they do not participate in it but simply react to political output. A participant culture entails interest and involvement in policy-making.[22] Soviet political culture in this scheme has changed from being overwhelmingly subject-parochial towards a more subject-participant form. The measurement of change in the USSR is hampered by the lack of broad social survey data, yet there is sufficient evidence to permit some broad generalizations.

Emigré studies of the 1950s showed that there was a basic level of support among the population for the Soviet system and a belief in the Soviet future. They showed a great deal of support for ideas of discipline, authority, and welfare, and civil liberties did not rank high among its preoccupations.[23] While economic concerns remain dominant, human rights have taken a much higher profile following the Helsinki process. The Soviet Interview Project of the 1980s showed that despite a generally high level of satisfaction in the USSR there were some worrying features, especially the sense of alienation provoked by the lack of incentives and poor work organization among the 'brightest and the best', those at the educational and professional peaks.[24] The old ideological input is increasingly ineffective and can no longer project an attractive vision of the future. The 1980s in particular have been marked by a decline in the old optimism. This is marked among intellectuals, disappointed by the reversal of destalinization, the crushing of the liberalization processes in Czechoslovakia and Poland, and the general tightening of political control up to the mid-1980s. The falling growth rate has depressed living standards, but the main criticisms are directed against the poor level of public services, in particular health, education, and social welfare. There is a shift of interest to the personal sphere. The problem will be to shed some of the regime's heavy-handed paternalism while retaining the popularly approved 'order'. Stephen White's broad review of Soviet and Western materials confirmed the conclusion of the earlier survey that the Soviet 'system' has achieved a broad degree of legitimacy, in that such policies as high welfare provision and public ownership of the means of production are widely popular, but the 'regime' or the institutions of the political system have failed to gain a similar legitimacy.[25]

There are elements of a rationality crisis in the debate over methods of resolving the conflicting demands of various sections of society. Is the myth of 'non-antagonistic' interests managed for the good of all by the communist party finally giving way to the realization that the effective crisis-management of the system was achieved by the overenthusiastic damping down of various demands rather than by integrating them in a rational manner? This may well be the case, but in contrast to most East European countries, whose peoples can draw on national traditions, the absence of a single vision of what the alternative order could be in the Soviet Union helps sustain the legitimacy of the existing system. Moreover, on the basis of the experience of the crushing of popular reform movements in Czechoslovakia in 1968 and Poland in 1981, a strong case could be argued that in the final analysis Soviet-type regimes are more concerned with staying in power than with their legitimacy. They have been forced to abandon mass terror as economically counterproductive, but in its place have had recourse to more subtle but no less sustained forms of oppression.[26] Such an approach helps explain the apparent paralysis and schematic nature of reforms in Soviet-type systems: reforms would endanger the political and social supremacy of the political and administrative elites even though they would considerably enlarge the legitimacy of the socialist system. Not only opponents of the existing systems are repressed but even, or indeed especially, overenthusiastic reformers. One has only to bear in mind the fate of Dubček and possibly Eltsin. It was enough for Gorbachev to talk of reforms to infuse the Soviet system with a legitimacy that had been waning under Brezhnev. Whether this will be enough to ensure his survival remains to be seen.

Notes

1 Z. Bauman, 'Intellectuals in East Central Europe: Continuity and Change', *Eastern European Politics and Societies*, 1, 2 (spring 1987), pp. 165–6.
2 ibid., p. 174.
3 A. Black, *Guilds and Civil Society in European Political Thought from the Twelfth*

Century to the Present (Macmillan, London, 1984), p. xiii.

4 N. de Basily, *Russia under Soviet Rule* (George Allen and Unwin, London, 1938), p. 105.

5 V. Zaslavsky, 'Socioeconomic Inequality and Changes in Soviet Ideology', *Theory and Society*, 2, 9 (March 1980), p. 395.

6 Rosa Luxemburg, *The Russian Revolution* (Ann Arbor Paperbacks, University of Michigan Press, 1961), p. 69.

7 A. Solzhenitsyn, *Warning to the West* (Farrar Straus & Giroux, New York, 1976), p. 114.

8 A. Meyer, 'The Functions of Ideology in the Soviet Political System', *Soviet Studies*, 17, 3 (July 1966), pp. 273–85.

9 Leszek Kolakowski, 'Ideology in Eastern Europe', in Milorach Drachkowitch (ed.), *East Central Europe: Yesterday — Today — Tomorrow* (Hoover Institution Press, Stanford, Cal., 1982), p. 45.

10 A. Janos, 'Systematic Models and the Theory of Change in the Comparative Study of Communist Politics', in A. Janos (ed.), *Authoritarian Politics in Communist Europe* (University of California Press, Berkeley, 1976), p. 19.

11 D. Bell, *The End of Ideology*, cited by J.F. Hough, *The Soviet Union and Social Science Theory* (Harvard University Press, Cambridge, Mass., 1977), p. 197.

12 Hough, *The Soviet Union and Social Science Theory*, p. 35.

13 Z. Medvedev, 'New Leaders, Old Problems New Solutions', *Labour Focus on Eastern Europe*, 8, 2 (May 1986), pp. 3–9.

14 J. Hoffman, 'The Coercion/Consent Analysis of the State under Socialism', in N. Harding (ed.), *The State in Socialist Society* (Macmillan, London, 1984), pp. 129–49.

15 R.C. Tucker, 'Culture, Political Culture and Communist Society', *Political Science Quarterly*, 88, 2 (June 1973), pp. 173–90.

16 A. Brown (ed.), *Political Culture and Communist Studies* (Macmillan, London, 1984), pp. 1–12.

17 A. Jasinska-Kania, 'Rationalization and Legitimation Crisis: the Relevance of Marxian and Weberian Works for an Explanation of the Political Order's Legitimacy Crisis in Poland', *Sociology*, 17, 2 (May 1983), p. 161.

18 F. Feher, 'Paternalism as a Mode of Legitimation in Soviet-type Societies', in T.H. Rigby and F. Feher (eds.), *Political Legitimation in Communist States* (Macmillan, London, 1982), p. 77.

19 D. Barry and H. Dernan, 'The Jurists', in Skilling and Griffiths (eds.), *Interest Groups in Soviet Politics*.

20 J. Habermas, *Legitimation Crisis* (Heinemann, London, 1976), pp. 46–9.

21 L.W. Pye and S. Verba, *Political Culture and Political Development* (Princeton University Press, Princeton, NJ, 1969).

22 G.A. Almond and S. Verba, *The Civic Culture* (Princeton University Press, Princeton, N.J., 1963).

23 A. Inkeless and R.A. Bauer, *The Soviet Citizen* (Harvard University Press, Cambridge, Mass., 1959).

24 James R. Millar and Peter Donhowe, 'Life, Work and Politics in Soviet Cities: First Findings of the Soviet Interview Project', *Problems of Communism*, 1, 36 (January–February 1987), pp. 46–55.

25 Stephen White, *Political Culture and Soviet Politics* (Macmillan, London, 1979), p. 189.

26 See Mark Wright, 'Ideology and Power in the Czechoslovak Political System', in Paul Lewis (ed.), *Eastern Europe: Political Crisis and Legitimation* (Croom Helm, London, 1984), pp. 111–53.

Key texts

Evans, Alfred B., 'The Decline of Developed Socialism? Some Trends in Recent Soviet Ideology', *Soviet Studies*, 38, 1 (January 1986), pp. 1–23

White, Stephen, and Alex Pravda (eds.), *Ideology and Soviet Politics* (Macmillan, London, 1988)

Select bibliography

Soviet ideology

Amalrik, A., 'Ideologies in Soviet Society' *Survey*, 22, 2 (spring 1976), pp. 1–11

Bell, Daniel, 'Ideology and Soviet Politics' and discussion, *Slavic Review*, 24, 4 (December 1965), pp. 591–621

Besancon, Alain, *The Rise of the Gulag: Intellectual Origins of Leninism* (Continuum, New York, 1981)

Brzezinski, Z., *Ideology and Power in Soviet Politics* (Praeger, New York, 1967)

Carew-Hunt, R.N., *The Theory and Practice of Communism* (Pelican, Harmondsworth, 1963)

Conquest, Robert, *The Politics of Ideas in the USSR* (Praeger, New York, 1967)

CPSU Programmes of 1961 (1986)

Evans, Alfred B., 'Developed Socialism in Soviet Ideology', *Soviet Studies*, 29, 3 (July 1977), pp. 409–28

Evans, Alfred B., 'The Polish Crisis in the 1980s and Adaptation in Soviet Ideology', *Journal of Communist Studies*, 2, 3 (September. 1986), pp. 263–85

Kanet, R.E., 'The Rise and Fall of the All-People's State', *Soviet Studies* (July 1978), pp. 81–93

Kelley, D.R., 'Developments in Ideology', in D.R. Kelley (ed.), *Soviet Politics in the Brezhnev Era* (Praeger, New York, 1980), pp. 182–99

Kolakowski, Leszek, *Main Currents of Marxism: its Origin, Growth, and Dissolution*, III, *The Breakdown* (Clarendon, Oxford, 1978)

Kuusinen, O. (ed.), *Fundamentals of Marxism-Leninism: Manual* (Lawrence & Wishart, London, 1961)

Leonhard, Wolfgang, *Three Faces of Marxism* (New York, 1974)

McLellan, David, *Ideology* (Open University Press, Milton Keynes, 1986)

Marcuse, Herbert, *Soviet Marxism: a Critical Analysis* (Pelican, Harmondsworth, 1971)

Meyer, Alfred G., *Leninism* (Harvard University Press, Cambridge, Mass., 1957)

Meyer, Alfred G., *Communism* (Random House, New York, 1960)

Meyer, Alfred G., 'The Function of Ideology in the Soviet Political System', *Soviet Studies*, 17, 3 (January 1966), pp. 273–85, and discussion in succeeding issues by Nove, Joravsky, Chambre, etc.

Meyers, Alfred G., 'Assessing the Ideological Commitment of a Regime', in J.L. Nogee (ed.), *Soviet Politics* (New York, 1985), pp. 107–21

Mills, C. Wright, *The Marxists* (Pelican, Harmondsworth, 1963)

Tiersky, Ronald, *Ordinary Stalinism: Democratic Centralism and the Question of Communist Political Development* (Allen & Unwin, London, 1985)

Tucker, R.C. (ed.), *The Marx-Engels Reader* (Norton, New York, 1972)

Tucker, R.C. (ed.), *The Lenin Anthology* (Norton, New York, 1975)

Zaslavsky, V., 'Socioeconomic Inequality and Changes in Soviet Ideology', *Theory and Society*, 2, 9 (March 1980), pp. 383–407

The ideological apparatus and political socialization

Benn, David Wedgwood, '*Glasnost*' in the Soviet Media: Liberalization or Public Relations', *Journal of Communist Studies*, 3, 3 (September 1987), pp. 267–76

Dewhirst, Martin, and Robert Farrell (eds.), *The Soviet Censorship* (Scarecrow, Metuchen N.J., 1973)

Dzirkals, L., T. Gustafson, and R. Johnson, *The Media and Intra-elite Communication* (Rand, Washington, D.C., 1982)

Hollander, Gayle, *Soviet Political Indoctrination: Developments in the Mass Media and Propaganda since Stalin* (Praeger, New York, 1972)

Hopkins, Mark, *Mass Media in the Soviet Union* (Pegasus, New York, 1970)

Kenez, Peter, *The Birth of the Propaganda State: Soviet Methods of Mass Mobilisation, 1917–1929* (Cambridge University Press, Cambridge, 1986)

Lane, Christel, *The Rites of Rulers: Ritual in Industrial Society: the Soviet Case* (Cambridge University Press, Cambridge, 1981)

Mickiewicz, Ellen P., *Media and the Russian Public* (Praeger, New York, 1981)

Mickiewicz, Ellen P., *Split Signals: Television and Politics in the Soviet Union* (Oxford University Press, New York, 1989)

O'Dell, Felicity Ann, *Socialisation through Children's Literature: the Soviet Example* (Cambridge University Press, Cambridge, 1978)

Roxburgh, Angus, *Pravda: Inside the Soviet News Machine* (Gollancz, London, 1987)

Wettig, G., *Broadcasting and Detente* (Hurst, London, 1977)

White, Stephen, 'The Effectiveness of Political Propaganda in the USSR', *Soviet Studies*, 32 (1980), pp. 323–48

White, Stephen, 'Propagating Communist Values in the USSR', *Problems of Communism*, 34, 6 (November–December 1985), pp. 1–17

Political culture and legitimacy

Brown, A., and J. Gray (eds.), *Political Culture and Change in Communist Systems* (Macmillan, London, 1977)

Brown, Archie (ed.), *Political Culture and Communist Studies* (Macmillan, London, 1984)

Brzezinski, Z., 'Soviet Politics: from the Future to the Past', in P. Cocks *et al.* (eds.), *The Dynamics of Soviet Politics* (Harvard University Press, Cambridge, Mass., 1976), pp. 337–51

Daniels, R.V., 'Russian Political Culture and the Post-revolutionary Impasse', *Russian Review*, 46, 2 (April 1987), pp. 165–76.

Golan, Galia, 'Elements of Russian Tradition in Soviet Socialism', in S.N. Eisenstadt (ed.), *Socialism and Tradition* (Humanities, Atlantic Highlands, N.J., 1975)

Habermas, Jurgen, *Legitimation Crisis* (Heinemann, London, 1976)

Inkeles, A., *Public Opinion in Soviet Russia* (Harvard University Press, Cambridge, Mass., 1950)

Jowitt, Kenneth, 'An Organisational Approach to the Study of Political Culture in Marxist-Leninist Systems', *American Political Science Review*, 68, 3 (September 1974), pp. 1171–91

Millar, James R., *Politics, Work and Daily Life in the USSR: a Survey of Former Soviet Citizens* (Cambridge University Press, Cambridge, 1988)

Paul, D.W., 'Political Culture and the Socialist Purpose', in J.P. Shapiro and P.J. Potichnyj (eds.), *Change and Adaptation in Soviet and East European Politics* (Praeger, New York, 1976)

Rigby, T.H., and Ferenc Feher (eds.), *Political Legitimation in Communist States* (Macmillan, London, 1982)

Samuel, R., and G. Stedman-Jones (eds.), *Culture, Ideology and Politics* (Routledge & Kegan Paul, London, 1982)

Szamuely, Tibor, *The Russian Tradition* (Secker & Warburg, London, 1974)

Tucker, R.C., 'Culture, Political Culture and Communist Society', *Political Science Quarterly*, 88, 2 (June 1973), pp. 173–90

Tucker, R.C., *The Political Culture of Soviet Russia: from Lenin to Gorbachev* (Wheatsheaf, Brighton, 1987)

White, Stephen, *Political Culture and Soviet Politics* (Macmillan, London, 1979)

White, Stephen, 'The USSR: Patterns of Autocracy and Industrialisation', in Brown, A., and J. Gray (eds.), *Political Culture and Change in Communist Systems* (Macmillan, London, 1979), pp. 25–65

Zaslavsky, V., 'The Problem of Legitimation in Soviet Society', in A. Vidich and R. Glassman (eds.), *Conflict and Control: Challenge to Legitimacy of Modern Governments* (Sage, Beverly Hills and London, 1979)

Chapter eleven

Class and gender

New class and *nomenklatura*

One of the paradoxes of the Soviet system has been that the abolition of private ownership of the means of production, considered by Marxists to be the main source of exploitation, did not eliminate inequality or hierarchy. New sources of economic, social, and political inequality rapidly emerged whose causes and operation, and indeed whose very existence, were long denied by Soviet commentators. The nationalization of economic life itself gave rise to new forms of stratification.

The defeat of Khrushchev's challenge to elite status during the educational reform of 1958 illustrated the strength of the new hierarchy. By the time Brezhnev died there were clear signs that the defence of elite privileges had given rise to widespread social corruption. On 13 February 1986 *Pravda* published a review of readers' letters which sharply condemned party privilege:

> When considering social justice, it is impossible to close one's eyes to the fact that party, soviet, trade union, economic, and even Komsomol leaders sometimes objectively intensify social inequality by their enjoyment of all kinds of special buffets, special shops, special hospitals, and so on.[1]

The call for a thorough purge of the *apparat* was supported by Boris Eltsin, and was partly responsible for his fall in November 1987. Even under *glasnost* direct attacks on official privileges are rare, although the general problem is frequently discussed and became a major issue at the nineteenth party conference. Gorbachev himself admitted that there had been an 'erosion of the ideological and moral values of our people'.[2]

A number of theories try to explain the nature and structure of the dominant 'new class', as it was termed by Milovan Djilas. The new class can be looked at in two ways. First, in terms of an elite in whose hands political power is concentrated. Second, in terms of the privileges enjoyed by that class, and the general inequalities in society. In other words, study of the characteristics of the elite can focus on political or social factors. The new class has privileged access to economic decisions and takes an inordinate share of the surplus generated. The

226

social ownership of property and the accompanying division of labour generate a class structure, irrespective of the greed or asceticism of the new class.

In capitalist countries social stratification arises from the working of the market and ownership of private property. Classes according to Marx derive from the ownership (and non-ownership) of property and the relationship of individuals and groups to the means of production. What this means in practice is not entirely clear. Even under capitalism the institutions of modern political society cannot be reduced to the class relations of the capitalist mode of production. In the Soviet Union the state owns almost all property and the market has been all but abolished. Differentials in wages and stratification are generated primarily by political rather than economic forces, making the application of Marxist class theory problematic. The pattern of inequality has little to do with the private ownership of the means of production. The political and administrative system is one of the major sources of stratification and power. The problem in the Soviet context is to distinguish between the occupational structure, based on the necessary division of labour, and a class structure, which can be defined broadly in either political or economic terms. Soviet theory insists that class differentiation is drawn horizontally as part of the socialist division of labour, rather than creating a social hierarchy when drawn vertically.

The unification of political and economic power was foreshadowed during war communism, when, as Karl Kautsky pointed out, the state's attempt to organize all social life forced it to substitute for social classes. The new state and party officialdom took over the functions of the former capitalist managers and owners.[3] The ruling party selects goals and implements them, legislates and enforces, all without particular reference to society. In communist societies the state is the owner of almost all the economy and so there is no institutional separation, as there is in capitalist societies, between the influence of property holders and control by the incumbents of political offices. Bauman distinguishes between officialdom and class. The officialdom is generated by the political structures and is sustained above all by the unquestioned authority over all appointments to office exercised through the party's *nomenklatura* system. The class structure is based on the inequalities that arise from the operation of the economic system and the black economy.[4] In practice, however, the officialdom and class are to a large extent one and the same, the new class. In the Soviet Union there is an integrated hierarchy of power and privilege which Nove calls a unihierarchical society. The likely outcome of Gorbachev's marketization of the economy will be the formal separation of officialdom and class to create a dual-type hierarchy.

The official Soviet view maintains that in the Soviet Union there are only two friendly classes, the peasantry and working class, and one stratum, the intelligentsia, in the process of evolution towards the classless society of communism. Officially, in 1987 61·8 per cent were classified as workers, 23·5 per cent as intelligentsia and 15·1 per cent as collective farmers.[5] The pattern is similar to that in other societies, with a shift from agriculture to industry, and from factory to service work. There is allegedly no class antagonism or class stratification.

The classes are based on different types of property: the working class is associated with state property (considered the highest form); the collective farm peasantry with co-operative property; and the intelligentsia, a broad category which includes employees, are designated as a stratum rather than a class, since they do not have property. The intelligentsia is a very broad catch-all category lacking much analytical precision. Under Stalin there was no pretence that this was an egalitarian society. Indeed, from 1932 there was a struggle against *uravnilovka* ('wage-levelling' or 'equality-mongering'). The aim was to use monetary incentives to increase production, and the resulting substantial inequalities were held to reflect not class privileges but different contributions to production.

Recent Soviet writing has introduced new ideas into the discussion but without repudiating the earlier image. Soviet society is seen as a hierarchical structure of social groups ranked according to 'higher' or 'lower' status, especially marked on the mental-manual labour continuum. The literature talks of various socio-occupational groups of different economic status, cultural level, and so on, including internal differentiation within classes. The general goal is equality, but the pace of equalizing work and rewards towards a fully homogeneous society is a controlled process. There is a sharp rejection of group struggles for betterment of conditions. The achievement of social equality is seen in terms of 'social management', the application by the party of 'scientific socialism' to the Soviet Union. The Soviet interpretation does not explain why substantial inequality continues to exist long after the elimination of private property and the bourgeoisie.[6] The image of society as a set of functional, non-antagonistic social groups remains dominant, though modified by a number of socio-occupational groups, such as unskilled labour, managers, and technical specialists. Just as the political equalization expected to result from commune democracy failed to materialize, so social inequality persists and, indeed, is partly derived from political stratification. Soviet Marxists have provided few analyses of the sources of economic and social differentiation in a socialist society. Too often it is ascribed to legacies of the past, economic backwardness, or the social division of labour. The traditional view asserted that inequality would disappear as a society of abundance was achieved. However, during *perestroika* there has been an increased willingness to concede that socialist society will not become more uniform as it advances towards communism, but that, on the contrary, it will become more complex and differentiated.

Various theories of bureaucracy are applied to the study of class and power in the Soviet Union. Most are inspired in one way or another by Max Weber or by Trotskyist analyses. The term 'bureaucracy' is used in three broad senses: it can describe a style of administrative management; a social group of functionaries; or more narrowly a political elite who rule rather than govern. The conditions for the consolidation of the bureaucracy were identified long ago by Luxemburg:

With the repression of political life in the land as a whole, life in the soviets must also become more and more crippled. Without general elections, without unrestricted freedom of the press and assembly, without a free struggle of opinion, life dies out in every public institution, becomes a mere semblance of life, in which only the bureaucracy remains as the active element'.[7]

Trotsky developed his theory of the Soviet Union as a degenerated workers' state after his exclusion from power in the mid-1920s. He identified the growth of a privileged bureaucracy, whose representative was Stalin, as the cause of the 'degeneration'. This was provoked, Trotsky argued, by Russia's isolation and economic backwardness, and resulted not in the emergence of a new capitalist ruling class but in a ruling bureaucratic caste living off the socialist foundations of nationalized property. It was a caste rather than a ruling class because its position and benefits derived from malfunctions in the distributive mechanism rather than from exploitation based on ownership of the system of production, as under capitalism. There is a certain lack of credibility in Trotsky's criticism of such features as the death of democracy within the party, since he contributed much to its extinction by his advocacy of militarization. There is the further problem of explaining the persistence of the bureaucratic caste, based on the state as the surrogate for capitalist industrialization, now that backwardness has been overcome and isolation reduced. The degeneration of the workers' state was based on the idea of impermanence, and yet the position of the working class in institutional terms has changed little over the years. According to Bahro the 'bureaucratic superstructure' continues to exist because the 'industrial underdevelopment' of socialist states remains, in comparison with more mature capitalist countries, and because of the pressures of competition with them.[8] Bureaucratic hierarchies in any case by definition have a self-perpetuating quality.

The bureaucratic interpretation expounded by Tony Cliff asserts that the Soviet Union is state-capitalist. According to him capitalism was restored in the Soviet Union about 1928 in a new, amalgamated form of state property. Under Stalin the national economy became a business run as one large enterprise headed by a collective capitalist, the Soviet elite or the bureaucracy, who forced through collectivization and industrialization. The state acted as substitute for market forces. The major problem with this approach (at least until the onset of *khozraschët*, or cost accounting) is how one can call the system capitalist when the major features of capitalism are lacking, such as profits and market competition between rival capitalist groupings. Production is controlled by and in the interests of a unified state, and most production is not for sale on competitive markets, hence it has traditionally been largely an economy of waste. Market regulation is replaced by attempts at the direct administration of economic life. Until 1988 there was no market competition between enterprises, so, strictly speaking, only export material was produced capitalistically in competition with other states. Cliff answers that the major spur to economic accumulation is the operation of a 'permanent arms economy' in competition with capitalist states, forcing the Soviet leaders to improve the efficiency of their giant factory. The concept of state capitalism tends to blur the distinctive pattern of Soviet development. Trotsky himself refused to label the Soviet Union as state-capitalist, since he insisted that state property remained socialist. In reducing socialism to property relations Trotsky was as guilty of economism as Stalin.

The Poles J. Kuron and K. Modzelewski provided a strong rebuttal of the view that there can be no contradictions between workers and 'their' state after the nationalization of the means of production. Their analysis of officialdom and class in a bureaucratic context led them to conclude that state ownership of the means of production is secondary to the exercise of the powers associated with ownership by the social groups in control of the state. Political power is consolidated by control over production and distribution. At the heart of the power system is the central political bureaucracy (CPB), which determines basic political and economic policy. They do not analyse the size or structure of the bureaucracy, but stress its role in society and in the social process of production. The bureaucratic elite identifies itself with the state and, in a perverse resuscitation of peasant commune principles, hold property collectively in the name of the state, a fact which determines their internal structure as a class. Its class nature derives from its relationship as a group to the means of production and its relationship to other social classes, principally the working class. The privileges of consumption and power are by-products of the ability to control production.

The bureaucratic interpretation of class has a managerial version. Bruno Rizzi in 1934 foresaw the fascist and communist states developing into a new type of 'bureaucratic collectivist' society in which the new class collectively owned the state and its economic apparatus. This perspective was developed by James Burnham in 1941. From his studies of European countries he came to believe, contrary to his original intention, that modern managers have a positive role to play in the technocratic systems of modern 'managerial societies'. The number of managers increases to keep pace with the changing nature of production, and they secure their position by taking over the state. Recent versions shift the emphasis from the concept of totalitarianism towards an organizational approach focusing on 'rationality' and 'efficiency' stripped of the need for terror. Managerial theories now talk in terms of 'administered societies' (Kassof). The major problem with managerial/bureaucratic theories is that they tend to exaggerate the similarities between industrial societies, irrespective of whether they are capitalist or socialist. Such reductionism leads to the absurd assertion that from the class point of view there is no difference between American and Soviet workers. This is neither analytically nor politically helpful, since it is clear that life expectations and possibilities, the nature of class conflict and the conduct of politics are radically different in the two systems. The theory moreover exaggerates the elements of unity in the managerial class.

The term 'bureaucracy' fulfils a multitude of purposes but on its own tells us little about the nature of Soviet society. The Soviets usually use the term primarily to denote 'inadequacies of the mechanism', petty bureaucratic failings in an otherwise splendidly functioning system. In the West the term is usually understood in the Weberian sense of an apparatus of professional officials operating according to hierarchical principles and constrained by rules and regulations. It is difficult to characterize the Soviet bureaucracy as bureaucratic in a Weberian sense. Most elements of rationality — professionalism, established procedures, and steadiness of expectations — are missing. Hough points out that the bureaucracy in the Soviet Union is plagued by particularism and irrationality. The involvement of party officials in administration indeed prevents clear lines of authority from becoming established, a process Hough considers positive.[9] Rules and regulations are plentiful but act not so much as standards codifying procedures than to consolidate the control of superior bodies over inferior ones.[10] To understand the phenomenon, sociological investigation or studies in social administration have to be supplemented by more narrowly political analyses.

The division between a political level, represented by the leadership, and the social level, focused on the bureaucracy, is a crucial one for evaluating the political independence of the bureaucracy in the USSR. Trotsky's major point was that in the Soviet Union a 'sovereign bureaucracy' had emerged which does not compete with other bureaucracies. The declining role of charismatic leadership and the consolidation of an institutionalized style of governance, accompanied by the decay of the teleological ideology, have allowed the bureaucracy to consolidate itself. Soviet ideology has gradually lost its anti-bureaucratic and egalitarian elements and has emerged in a symbiotic and mutually supportive relationship with the bureaucracy. As Bauman points out, the bureaucracy is no longer simply the 'civil service' that implements the policies of a force beyond the bureaucracy such as the charismatic leader, but has become an intrinsic part of the structure of power itself.[11] Its subordination to the political elite is questionable, and in a sense the political elite emanates from the bureaucracy.[12] The argument is questionable, since it is the party that gives coherence to the existing administrative system. The bureaucratic or managerial class has been in existence since 1918; under Stalin it grew in social power but it depended, and ultimately continues to depend, on the political elite's favour for its continued privileges. It has much power and many privileges, but its power is derivative. The Cultural Revolution in China serves as a warning to theories of bureaucratic power in communist systems. The political officialdom during *perestroika* has been forced to squeeze the privileges of the bureaucratic and managerial class to achieve economic and political reform. The managerial class receives stipends and privileges for its work, but they are meant for conspicuous consumption, as with the aristocrats of old. It has not been able to usurp the party and translate its privileges into political power. Political functionaries remain dominant over the social bureaucracy.

Another major theory of class in the Soviet Union focuses on the role of the intellectuals. At the turn of the century the Russian-born Pole Waclaw Makhaisky systematized Bakunin's earlier nostrums against the intelligentsia and warned of the dangers of the intellectual domination of the working class by the social democratic intelligentsia. He claimed that Marxism was used first to mobilize the masses to achieve power, and then to legitimate the rule of the intelligentsia over them. Such a development was implicit, as Luxemburg had warned, in Lenin's theory of consciousness. The ideological expropriation of the working class later led on to their political expropriation. Awareness of the issue was evident in the criticisms of the Workers' Opposition during war communism, though their response in calling for the increased workerization of administrative structures only exacerbated the problem. Bureaucrats of worker origin behaved no differently from those of intelligentsia provenance. Theorists like Trotsky, Djilas, and Kuron consider the state and party bureaucracy the main force opposing the working class. However, Konrad and Szelenyi argue that this contrast is secondary to the overriding contradiction between the working class and the intellectuals, of which the bureaucracy is only a part. They argue that the ideal of the planned society is a project of the intellectual imagination imposed on the actual producers, giving rise to what was called earlier the 'despotism of the enlightened'. Gouldner claims that intellectuals are not as selfless and free-floating as they like to portray themselves but a class with specific interests. There is a form of critical discourse in the currency of scientific and cultural communication within the Soviet elite that distinguishes it from the consumers of their product. This intelligentsia, from superficial observation, do have a relatively high degree of social group consciousness. Their internal communication acts as a functional substitute for a public sphere.

The major problem with theories that put the intellectual at the heart of class analysis is they they still work within the 'economistic' critical categories of Marxist class analysis, though they shift the subject from the working class to the intellectuals. By insisting that the main forms of stratification are class-based they remain lodged in a methodology that is questionable in the Soviet context of the dominance of 'political' and non-class-based forms of hierarchy. All class theories are assailed by the boundary problem: at what point does one class end and another begin in the endless series of gradations which typify a modern functionally differentiated society? Are the millions of low-paid workers by brain, such as the 2·2 million teachers, to be included as part of the ruling class? In the jigsaw of society class boundaries do not always coincide with professional demarcations, and politically an individual may simultaneously be a member of the CPSU, a member of a trade union, and a teacher. The intelligentsia, or specialists, have been produced in greater numbers than the unreformed Soviet socio-political system could absorb, rising from 10 per cent of the population to 20 per cent during Brezhnev's rule. This has given greater weight to the Soviet middle class, but has strained any sense of class cohesion as the leadership struggles to cut back on bloated offices and research establishments. The disappointed expectations of graduates who must resign themselves to jobs below their educational attainments is a major problem for the government during *perestroika*.

Elite theory is an alternative to trying to apply the concept of class. Vilfredo Pareto denied the viability of social democracy in modern societies by arguing that they will inevitably generate elites of two sorts: a governing elite dominating politics and a non-governing elite dominant in society. Gaetano Mosca insisted that human history is characterized by the emergence of 'a class that rules and a class that is ruled'. All societies, he argued, were dominated by a minority, with the rulers being a cohesive and self-conscious category. The theory was far too static and impermeable to permit an understanding of the process of change. It confused the ruling class and the political elite, who actually do the ruling. Pareto took a more complex systems approach, identifying a fixed hierarchy, an aristocracy, which is an inalienable part of human society. Both views have been criticized on the grounds that modern industrial societies are fragmented into a multiplicity of elites. The plurality of competing elites takes a distinctive form in the USSR, since it is expressed in institutional forms and is mitigated by the unified system of political control. The hierarchies of wealth, power, and status are to a degree one and the same. There is functional differentiation within the system, but ultimately political power is concentrated in a single hierarchy.

Mosca's follower Robert Michels directly confronted the notion of commune or participatory democracy, arguing that the 'iron law of oligarchy' operated in political parties no less than in other human organizations. Classical elite theorists pointed out that the Bolshevik revolution in Russia only 'bureaucratized' the revolution. The fusion of economic and political power engendered a unified elite with expanded powers. Pareto's notion of the circulation of elites saw lions alternating with foxes: lions rule by force, foxes by cunning. To a degree we are witnessing a shift from the Soviet lions like Stalin to the foxes, ruling by subtlety and persuasion, like Gorbachev.

It should be fairly easy to identify the political elite in the Soviet Union, since the existence of the *nomenklatura* clearly indicates who the system considers important. However, the task is not so easy, since the list covers an enormous spectrum of posts. Is the elite the Politburo alone, the party apparatus, or the whole *nomenklatura*? Even if we restrict ourselves to the top section we learn nothing about the cohesion of the bureaucrats staffing various parts of the machinery. Mosca stressed the importance of sub-elites mediating between the government and the masses. In the Soviet context, given the traditional importance of the intelligentsia in Russian society, this would clearly include leading cultural figures and possibly the cultural intelligentsia as a whole.

The word caste is inadequate to describe the elite because it suggests fixed hereditary status. There is a significant level of inherited privilege, but the elite is still not self-perpetuating. For proponents of state-capitalist theories the absence of significant private property inheritance does not nullify the fact that the dominant class collectively controls property through the state and hence has only to reproduce itself to maintain its position. In this respect the 'new class' is embodied 'human capital' characterized, according to Gouldner, by its intellectual traits.[12] The educational system increasingly fixes people in their class position. The traditional picture of the Soviet Union as a country of high social mobility stimulated by rapid industrialization, the expansion of the working class, and the creation of a new intelligentsia has given way to an increasing rigidity of the class structure. Mobility is supplemented by the party, the military, and other apparatuses, yet the educational system remains the fundamental channel of advancement, all the more so in the context of declining economic growth rates. The party under Khrushchev consciously tried to boost social fluidity, while under Brezhnev the jump between secondary and higher education was increasingly monopolized by the elite, especially at a time of a slowdown in the growth of higher education. The over-supply of educated people in comparison with the number of suitable jobs has led the authorities since the 1960s to try to lower the expectations of school pupils. This was partially the aim of the 1984 educational reform. Between 1966 and 1986 the gainfully employed population increased by 55 per cent while the number of specialists with higher education increased fourfold. Brezhnev tried to ease blockages on upward mobility by launching programmes to encourage working-class participation in higher education, by combating bribery in access to higher education, and by increasing the attractiveness of technical-vocational schools and blue-collar professions by raising wages. In a direct sense, education is now associated with state or party office as a new technocratic class emerges whose ability counts as much as ideological acceptability. The Soviet Union, as other advanced industrial countries, has witnessed an ever-growing expansion of the educated elite: the old workers and peasant classes are being inexorably squeezed as the society 'post-industrializes'. The functional elite or technocracy is a new social class in formation.

The above discussion clearly shows the problem of defining class in the Soviet context and the need to distinguish between political and social relationships. For Marxists there is a clear logic of class formation in the differentiated access of various groups to control over the means of production. This does not fully explain the relationship between 'the masses' and the 'elite'. Is it a subjective 'we-they' relationship or simply a gradation of more or less power? Should this entire elite be restricted to a political category, or a social one as well (a class)? The decline of the totalitarian model has increased awareness about elements of pluralism, but is the alleged dispersion of power accompanied by a dispersion of privilege? Hough urges the abandonment of the 'all or nothing' concept of political power and instead stresses the importance of the nature and quality of political relationships.[14] Effective social and political power is concentrated in the hands of an elite, but its rule is very difficult to define in class terms.

There is a division in the Soviet Union between officialdom and class. Andropov's anti-corruption campaign sought to reverse the dangerous trend for the party's leading role to be confused with the social dominance of the *nomenklatura*. Under Gorbachev the bureaucracy is less secure than it was during the Brezhnev years. The various theories posit the rise of a new stratum whose very existence depends on the political regime. Its actual name is not important: new class, stratum, caste, elite, bureaucracy, *nomenklatura*, partocracy, or central political bureacracy. Ultimately we are talking about a ruling group whose power derives from a combination of ideological factors, the belief that society is moving towards a final end, and the institutional relationship to the means of production. Non-economic forms of stratification and domination have allowed the Soviet Union to evolve into a hierarchical society where status and power depend on rank. Rule is enjoyed by a political elite, but its privileges are incidental to the fundamental juridical relationship to the mass of workers. The dominance of the political elite simply reflects the dominance of the state over society.

The politics of gender

Analysis of the politics of gender in any society helps identify the fundamental political and social processes within that society. However, one must be sensitive to cultural differences. While the symptoms of gender exploitation in the West and in the USSR might be similar, the processes whereby inequalities are integrated into the operation of each society are very different. There are major difficulties in applying Western concepts of feminism to the Soviet Union, a country which has undergone seventy years of socialist transformation. Feminism itself must be defined and can be categorized into three broad tendencies: liberal, radical, and Marxist. A distinction can further be made between movements for 'women's rights', in the sense of civil and political equality, and 'women's emancipation', in the sense of a broader striving for freedom from patriarchy and oppressive restrictions imposed by sex and for self-determination and autonomy. The first tendency, the liberal view, does not necessarily imply an equality of roles between men and women. It can be seen as an equality in terms of moral and rational worth. The second definition, closer to the radical view, implies a sustained difference, since self-determination and autonomy might well emphasize the separation between the sexes. Self-determination is possible but autonomy is illusory in the Soviet context.

The Soviet view, derived from the writings of Marx, Engels, and August Bebel, is balanced between the two concepts. Western feminist notions are often rejected in the Soviet Union, as in much of the Third World, as part of imperialism and derided as 'bourgeois feminism'. Bebel condemned women's struggles for equality as essentially bourgeois, and involvement in the struggle for sexual liberation was regarded as a distraction from the main task — the class struggle. Soviet theory is a variation of the general socialist programme which argues that gender exploitation can be overcome only as part of the socialist transformation of society. The abolition of class exploitation will entail the ending of gender divisions. This may not take place immediately, but as the state promotes development the changes in the economic sphere will wreak changes in the social sphere. But, in a dialectical manner, changes in the social sphere are seen as a way of accelerating the transformation in the economic sphere. Hence the USSR takes women's emancipation as far as it is useful for economic development, namely to release the economic potential of women in the labour force.

The first act of most socialist countries is to remove restrictions on female employment and legal status. The economic and political modernization of the

USSR required the mobilization of a number of previously disadvantaged groups as part of the broader process of social transformation. Equality for women, as much as egalitarianism, is a basic socialist goal; but it is also seen as part of the developmental goal. To a degree these two principles are in conflict. In contrast to theories that rely on naturalistic and biological causation, but in keeping with the economism of much of Soviet theory, women's historical subordination is seen as deriving from economic causes. But even in Soviet practice there is much emphasis on 'women's qualities' in the nurturing and caring professions. The induction of women into the labour force is considered an an act of economic, and hence social, liberation, but at the same time women remain primarily responsible for the domestic sphere. This is the theoretical and practical origin of the notorious 'double shift' for women: a full-time job combined with primary responsibility in the domestic sphere. Women's emancipation in Soviet theory does not take the crucial step of analysing the ideological factors that give rise to the subordination of women in work and in the home.

The history of the women's movement in the Soviet Union has gone through several phases. During the civil war the various tides of 'bourgeois feminism' in Russia were exhausted. From 1919 special women's departments (*zhenotdely*) began to be formed under Bolshevik party committees, though they were starved of resources in an atmosphere of male communist scorn. The outstanding figure of this period was Alexandra Kollontai, who played an active part in the Workers' Opposition of 1920–1. The organized women's movement in Soviet Russia gained very limited autonomy. As Lenin put it, 'We derive our organisational ideas from our ideological conceptions. We want no separate organisations of communist women. She who is a communist belongs as a member of the party, just as he who is a communist.'[15] Bolshevik and feminist policy in this first phase was to break up the patterns of life inherited from the old regime, such as the family, and to create a 'new Soviet woman'. Under the impetus of war communist ideological enthusiasm all sorts of experimental ideas were tried out. In Vladimir in 1918 a decree was issued proclaiming all women state property on reaching the age of 18.[16] This was the time of the great boom in companionate marriage.

The *zhenotdel* activists sought to stimulate a growing women's movement to support the Bolsheviks, but were wary of any autonomous developments that might challenge party hegemony. The women's organization was subordinated to the party since, quite apart from any political threat that it might have represented, an independent women's movement would have challenged male complacency. Working women, and especially peasant women, of this period were often considered 'backward' and unreceptive to Bolshevik ideas. As the years passed the image of the 'new woman' was gradually modified to fit in with changes in Soviet reality, above all with a greater stress on the nurturing role, to be all things — worker, wife, and mother. As Clements points out, whatever the changing content, the image of the 'new Soviet woman' was always at the service of the new regime.[17] In *Literature and Revolution*, published in 1924, Trotsky took a typically male Bolshevik condescending view of the poets Anna Akhmatova and

Marina Tsvetaeva. In the 1920s Kollontai's own subordination to Stalin was typical of the submissive attitude of the *zhenotdely* to the consolidation of the authoritarian regime. The *zhenotdely* tried to change the *byt* (daily life) of women through the organization of canteens and emphasizing the social functions of the place of work. They believed that under socialism it was the duty of the state to take over the major functions of the family. Communal facilities staffed by paid labourers would free women of the burden of domestic labour and endow them with economic and social independence.

This was the time of major campaigns in Soviet Central Asia against the most obscurantist of Moslem practices in regard to women, such as seclusion and the wearing of the *chaydor*. They provoked religious anti-Bolshevik crusades. Bolshevik policy had two purposes: to weaken the Islamic male dominance over women and to establish legal equality and access to education; and to weaken the structures of traditional authority in order to facilitate the consolidation of the Bolshevik regime in those areas. Women's emancipation was part of the process of advancing the revolution.

The consolidation of Stalinism was accompanied by the stabilization of the Soviet family. The 1926 Code of Common Law placed a multitude of obligations on the husband and wife, but above all guaranteed child support and alimony to spouses in common-law marriages, whereas the 1918 marriage law stated that alimony was available only for state marriages. The care of children was now the responsibility of the family. The 1926 alimony law was designed to strengthen the family and placed the burden of child-rearing on women. From that point the official representation of women has stressed their child-bearing and nurturing role. The dialectic of production and reproduction saw a narrowing of the scope of specifically feminist ideas. The abolition of even the semi-autonomous *Zhenotdel* in 1930 set the tone for the massive uptake of women in employment during Stalin's five-year plans. A booklet published in 1934 stated that the women's question was solved. A decree of 8 July 1944 recognized civil marriage alone as legal and, reversing the 1926 law, no longer accepted common-law marriages. The consolidation of the state and of the family were parallel processes, though no automatic relationship can be drawn between the authoritarian state and the patriarchal family. Both, however, can be seen as part of the attempt of the post-revolutionary regime to find an optimum means of sustaining its power. Following Stalin's death more flexible methods have been sought to achieve the regime's aims in family and gender policy.

Soviet practice today can be examined under the four major headings of education, work, politics, and the family. Education is the basic means of building the new society, and the curriculum of schools is moulded to meet the needs of socialist development. Socialization in schools stresses the advantages of female employment both as a means of self-development and as a patriotic duty. Strong gender typing begins at an early age, reinforced by the fact that the majority of teachers are women. There is equal access for men and women to education, and indeed the educational accomplishments of women are the same as men's, but the type of course chosen reveals a diverging pattern. Women dominate in the caring professions such as education, health, and welfare. As in most industrialized countries engineering remains a male preserve, even though women make up an unusually high 40 per cent of the profession.

Women once represented a 'reserve army', to be drafted into the economy to sustain rapid economic growth and to overcome the huge demographic losses of collectivization, war, and purges (see Table 5). An exceptionally high proportion of women work outside the family, the number rising from 19 million in 1950 to 51 million in 1974. Between 1959 and 1970 the number of female homemakers fell from 18 million to 6 million. Women make up 53 per cent of the total population and 51 per cent of the labour force, compared to 42 per cent in Britain, constituting the highest proportion of any country in the world. The process has now reached its natural limits. Furthermore, given the low average wages, there has been enormous pressure for women to go to work to make up a living family wage, especially if there are dependent children. At present 86 per cent of women of working age have an occupation outside the home (7·5 per cent of them students); and 44 per cent of the total female population are employed, of whom 80 per cent are between 20 and 39 years old, the period of highest fertility.

Table 5 Gender composition of the population

Year	Total population (millions)	Of whom		As % of total population	
		Men	Women	Men	Women
1913	159.2	79.1	80.1	49.7	50.3
1940	194.1	93.0	101.1	47.9	52.1
1959	208.8	94.0	114.8	45.0	55.0
1970	241.7	111.4	130.3	46.1	53.9
1979	262.4	122.3	140.1	46.6	53.4
1981	266.6	124.5	142.1	46.7	53.3
1987	281.7	132.5	149.2	47.0	53.0

Source: *SSSR v tsifrakh v 1986 godu* (Moscow, 1987), p. 27.

Entry of women to paid employment is seen as the key to the success of the emancipation of women. It is also convenient in stimulating socialist accumulation. There is usually equal pay for equal work, but the occupational status of employed women is generally inferior to that of men. The pursuit of economic growth has led to the down-playing of the idea of equality. For example, two-thirds of female manual workers are classified as unskilled, but only one-fifth of men. Many manual, unskilled occupations are reserved for women, especially in the countryside. Most dairy operatives are women, whereas most tractor drivers are men: men are lathe operators; women are auxiliaries. On average women do 50 per cent more manual work than men. In the non-manual sector gender divisions are as persistent but less obvious. Women tend to fall behind in terms of career advancement. For example, women make up 77 per cent of the medical profession but comprise only 52 per cent of consultants. Women are considered an unstable element in the labour force. Their productivity tends to be lower and there is a higher absenteeism rate as the burden of the 'double shift' forces them to stay at home to look after sick children. As the proportion of women rises in an occupation, like education or medicine, the occupation tends to become 'deskilled'. Status devaluation takes place as men move out and pay levels fall. Women's earnings are an average 30–35 per cent below men's. This is true not only between sectors of the economy but also within particular professions. Where women are concentrated wages and prestige are lower, such as in the service sectors of the economy, where average wages are one-third lower than in male-dominated professions. Women's representation at the higher levels of economic decision-making is minimal. Only 9 per cent of enterprise directors in 1975 were women, but this was a great improvement over 1 per cent in 1956. It is clear that in both form and effect the sexual division of labour in socialist countries is similar to that in capitalist countries, although Gorbachev has led a concerted drive to improve the status of such professions as teaching and medicine. However, with the prospect of a mass shake-out of the work force as *perestroika* starts to bite, once again the official image has praised the 'womanly mission' to prepare women for unemployment.

In politics the traditional Western pattern of women playing a secondary role in terms of political participation, especially in the higher echelons of administration and political leadership, has been replicated. The low percentage of women in the party is compounded by the fact that only 5 per cent of women between 31 and 60 are members, compared to 22 per cent of men. There are great variations in female participation, depending on geographical factors and field. As one rises through executive bodies the proportion of women decreases and there is a relatively low female impact in policy-making bodies. In 1986 only 3·5 per cent of the Central Committee were women, and only two women have ever been on the Politburo, Ekaterina Furtsova (1956–61) and Alexandra Biryukova (1988–), and then only as candidate members. The appointment of Biryukova to the CC Secretariat in 1986 broke a long tradition but was redolent of tokenism, as she was assigned responsibility for the 'nurturing' field of social welfare. The only two female ministers since the 1920s have been Furtsova (minister of culture 1960–74) and Maria D. Kovrigina (minister of health in the mid-1950s). There are very few top women in the republican and *oblast* leaderships, and none of the regional party secretaries has been a woman. To balance the picture, there is high participation in policy bodies with high formal authority but little actual power. Women make up one-third of the Supreme Soviet, and the proportion rises to half in local soviets. There is high participation in the trade unions and the Komsomol, but neither body has ever been led by a woman. In general, the impact of women is marked in such policy areas as health, education, and welfare, and they have achieved influence at the very summit of these bodies, especially in the localities. Women are well represented in certain professions which influence policy, such as college teaching, science, journalism and writing, economics and planning.

There are many reasons for the low achievement of women in politics. Rejection of the idea of 'mechanical equalization' has inhibited the development of positive equal opportunities programmes. The burden of combining full-time work with running the home keeps the participation of women in public life low and hampers them from acquiring the necessary education and experience. In Moslem areas this reticence is reinforced by tradition. Weighed down by a multitude of responsibilities, women are reluctant to take on extra commitments which would take up precious time and constitute a third burden. The overall level of female participation declines precipitously with marriage, and especially with the birth of a child. At the same time, political structures and male prejudices themselves screen women out. Party recruitment policies stress the activist and leadership image, which, given their socialization and lack of time, discourages women. There may simply not be enough women with the necessary experience and education.

The official definition of femininity is a farrago of sex-role stereotypes which are used to reconcile women to their domestic and employment roles. Following the abolition of *Zhenotdel* in 1930 there was no organized women's movement as such in the USSR, and the Soviet women's committee plays a largely propagandistic role. Khrushchev revived the special commissions for women under the trade unions (*zhensovety*), but there was no separate mass women's movement under the party. The reason for this derives from the party's conviction that the women's question has been settled and that sexual inequalities no longer exist. However, under Gorbachev the women's question has clearly been put back on the agenda of Soviet politics. The *zhensovety* have become a nationwide system of women's councils in workplaces and neighbourhoods, intended to become actively involved in 'managing the affairs of state and society'. Their ability — indeed, their desire — to encourage a sense of solidarity among women is questionable.

There is no tolerance of unofficial women's organizations. In 1979 a group of Leningrad women, including Tatyana Mamonova, published an almanac entitled *Women and Russia* which disagreed with the official view that the women's question had been solved. The magazine was banned and the authors were persecuted, though it still appears clandestinely. The journal deals with some of the main problems women face, such as the lack of sex education, male brutality in the home and intimate relations, a repressive official puritanism, and a pervasive hypocrisy about stymied career opportunities. The authority's response revealed once again that feminism was regarded as subversive. With the onset of *glasnost* informal women's groups have emerged to take up the themes of the Leningrad group.

In the fourth area, traditional Marxism predicted that the family would ultimately disappear, although it would remain in the transition to socialism. Engels dismissed the bourgeois family as a microcosm of capitalist class relations and as organized prostitution. The father represented the bourgeoisie while the wife and children were the proletariat. Under socialism the family was to be stripped of its economic functions. The Bolsheviks expected that all the problems would be solved by instituting legal equality between the sexes and economic emancipation for women. This economistic thinking led the Bolsheviks to perpetuate traditional values on the division of power and labour within the family. Soviet family legislation reinforces heterosexual monogamy and tries to ensure its stability. In 1970 90 per cent of the Soviet population lived in a family.

Government policy towards the family reflects demographic concerns. The Soviet Union has pursued strongly pro-natalist policies to compensate for the demographic disasters by providing incentives for marriage and have tried to mould social values in favour of large families. The reproductive functions of the family are often painted in glowing patriotic terms, and Stalin inaugurated the order of Mother Heroine for mothers of ten children or more. The politics of population are a sensitive issue, since the attempts to increase fertility by improving living standards and other such measures are clearly oriented towards the European part of the Soviet Union. A population explosion of sorts is taking place in Soviet Central Asia, whereas one-child families are the norm in European USSR. A variety of incentives are offered for large families. One of the major taxes is the 'childlessness tax' levied on married women and men. There is little individual choice in the question of contraception. Abortion was legalized in 1920, banned in 1936, and once again legalized in 1955. It is now free, and indeed is the major form of contraception. It has been estimated that 67 per cent of women who have been pregnant have had an abortion, the average Soviet woman having had six to eight abortions in her lifetime, giving rise to a host of complications, not least of which is sterility. Concern over the spread of AIDS has encouraged the greater provision of condoms. Women are encouraged to enter paid labour, and so the state takes on the provision of certain child-care facilities, although their quality and availability are very uneven.

The birth rate in European USSR is depressed by a variety of social and economic factors. The burden of domestic labour weighs heavily on women in the absence of the broad availability of labour-saving devices of adequate quality. Men play a small part in domestic tasks, though official policy now tries to redistribute the burden to the other members of the family, especially between the sexes. This has been most successful among the intelligentsia. At present little encouragement is given to alternative forms of household management, and Khrushchev's communal apartments, not surprisingly, are in disfavour. The majority of families (34 million out of 59 million) live in towns, often in apartments where several generations live together. Marriages are put under severe strain, adding to the high divorce rate. Between a third and half of marriages end in divorce, the rate being especially high in the early years of marriage. When no children are involved the procedure involves no more than a simple three-month wait.

The dual image of women as paid workers and primary home-makers is reflected in the dual burden that falls to their lot. They have entered employment in great numbers and the routes of political advancement have been opened. However, women suffer from material disadvantages by comparison with men in terms of lower average wages and depressed career opportunities. Inequalities persist beneath formal equality, and the official view of the female question and the family is conservative. There is a persistence in the sexual division of labour, and the major burden of domestic work falls on women. Legal and professional equality, economic independence, the socialization of the means of production, and the abolition of the directly economic functions of the family have not of their own created equality for women. The developmental functions of female emancipation have taken priority over examination of the psychological and social aspects of inequality.

Is there a women's problem in the USSR, or is the official view that it has been solved correct? Gorbachev's speech to the twenty-seventh party congress conceded the need to improve the context of women's lives by supporting the family and improving social and work conditions. There is widespread dissatisfaction among women over unfair treatment at work, poor promotion prospects, income differentials, and the burden of housework. Much has been published in the Soviet Union on the hardness of the woman's lot. Especially noteworthy is Natalia Baranskaya's 'A Week Like any Other,' published in the journal *Novy Mir*. However, perhaps surprisingly, this dissatisfaction does not usually take the form of the sense of grievance found among Western feminists. Not much more can be achieved through legislation in the Soviet Union on a formal level of equality. There is a broad acceptance that advances can be achieved only through cultural changes rather than political acts. Soviet women, even intellectuals, know little of the substantive arguments of Western feminists and are often prepared to accept differences of treatment on 'commonsense' grounds. For instance, teachers' wages in a profession dominated by women can be low since they usually represent a second wage. There is much greater acceptance of the conventional image of the 'biological essence' of women and their motherly mission as teachers and trainers. There is a complex cultural difference between Soviet women and their Western counterparts. Whether it represents a success for government socialization, political culture, or something more profound is not clear. For better or worse the Soviet Union missed out on the 1960s sexual revolution and increased female militancy of the West. Despite the massive social changes, beneath the carapace of Soviet power society has to some extent been shielded from the constant changes engendered by capitalism. This is above all true in the area of gender relations. There is little real pressure from within the socialist state, or indeed society, for radical change. The impression is that liberal reforms limited to bringing the man into the family rather than taking the woman out would be the limit of most Soviet women's ambitions.

The main reason for the general lack of resonance of radical feminism in the Soviet Union is that it does not mesh with Soviet socio-political realities. The

Soviet family is no longer an economically productive unit (though this is being reversed by the emergence of family-based businesses) but provides a variety of functions. From a demographic point of view it reproduces workers and soldiers, and it acts as the major unit of consumption. The family has been to some extent co-opted into the Soviet state, typified by the Stalinist glorification of the boy Pavlik Morozov, who informed on his parents during collectivization. And yet the family, ultimately, is a bastion of social autonomy against the pervasive state, and hence any theories that threaten this last redoubt of independence will not resonate in society.[18] Whatever the external circumstances, it manages to preserve a relative autonomy: its formation, growth, or dissolution all depend in the last analysis on personal decisions. The socialization that a child receives in the family is often at variance with that received from the state. The family is often a crucial psychological haven. A radical feminism which seeks to dissolve the family may well be socially progressive, but in the Soviet context it is profoundly politically reactionary.

Notes

1 See Peter Frank, 'Gorbachev's Dilemma: Social Justice or Political Instability?', *The World Today*, 42, 6, (June 1986), p. 94.
2 M.S. Gorbachev, *Perestroika*, p. 21.
3 Karl Kautsky, *Terrorism and Communism* (London, 1920).
4 Z. Bauman, 'Officialdom and Class', in F. Parkin (ed.), *The Social Analysis of Class Structure* (Tavistock, London, 1974).
5 *The USSR in Figures, 1917–1987* (Moscow, 1987).
6 See M.S. Yanowitch *Social and Economic Inequality in the USSR* (Martin Robertson, London, 1977), pp. 5–20; D. Lane and F. O'Dell, *The Soviet Industrial Worker: Social Class, Education and Control* (Martin Robertson, London, 1978).
7 Rosa Luxemburg, *The Russian Revolution* (Ann Arbor, Michigan, 1961), p. 71.
8 Rudolf Bahro, *The Alternative in Eastern Europe* (NLB/Verso, London, 1978).
9 J.F. Hough, *The Soviet Prefects* (Harvard University Press, Cambridge, Mass., 1969) p. 3.
10 M. Hirszowicz, *The Bureaucratic Leviathan* (Martin Robertson, Oxford, 1980), p. 26.
11 Z. Bauman, 'The Party in the System — Management Phase: Change and Continuity', in Janos (ed.), *Authoritarian Politics in Communist Europe*, pp. 83–4.
12 M. Hirszowicz, *The Bureaucratic Leviathan*, pp. 16–17.
13 Alvin Gouldner, *The Future of Intellectuals and the Rise of the New Class* (Macmillan, London, 1979).
14 J.F. Hough, *The Soviet Union and Social Science Theory* (Harvard University Press, Cambridge, Mass., 1977), pp. 203, 215, 217.
15 Cited by G.W. Lapidus, 'Political Mobilization, Participation and Leadership', *Comparative Politics* (October 1975), p. 94.
16 B. Kerblay, *Modern Soviet Society* (Methuen, London, 1983), p. 113.
17 B.A. Clements, 'Birth of the New Soviet Woman', in A. Gleason *et al.* (eds.), *Bolshevik Culture* (Indiana University Press,, Bloomington, Ind., 1985), pp. 230, 233.
18 For Western feminist views of the family see Michèle Barrett and Mary McIntosh *The Anti-social Family* (Verso/NLB, London, 1982).

Key texts

Atkinson, Dorothy, Alexander Dallin, and Gail Warhofsky Lapidus (eds.), *Women in Russia* (Harvester, Sussex, 1978)
Buckley, Mary, *Women and Ideology in the Soviet Union* (Wheatsheaf, Brighton, 1988)
Holland, B. (ed.), *Soviet Sisterhood: British Feminists on Women in the USSR* (Fourth Estate, London, 1985)
Lapidus, G.W. (ed), *Women, Work and Family in the Soviet Union: Equality, Development and Social Change* (Sharpe, New York, 1982)
Nove, A., 'Is there a Ruling Class in the USSR?', *Soviet Studies*, 27, 4 (October 1975), pp. 615–38
Nove, A., 'The Class Nature of the Soviet Union Revisited', *Soviet Studies*, 35, 3 (July 1983), pp. 298–312
Yanowitch, M., *The Social Structure of the USSR* (Westview, Boulder, Colo., 1987)

Select bibliography

New class and nomenklatura

Burnham, James, *The Managerial Revolutions* (Putnam, London, 1942)
Churchward, L.G., *The Soviet Intelligentsia* (Routledge & Kegan Paul, London, 1973)
Cliff, Tony, *Russia: a Marxist Analysis* (Socialist Review, London, 1964)
Cliff, Tony, *State Capitalism in Russia* (Pluto, London, 1974)
Crozier, M., *The Bureaucratic Phenomenon*, IV (Chicago University Press, Chicago, Ill., 1964)
Dahrendorf, Ralph, *Class and Class Conflict in Industrial Society* (Routledge & Kegan Paul, London, 1959)
Djilas, Milovan, *The New Class: an Analysis of the Communist System* (Praeger, New York, 1957)
Gouldner, Alvin, *The Future of Intellectuals and the Rise of the New Class* (Macmillan, London, 1979)
Harasymiw, Bohdan, *Political Elite Recruitment in the Soviet Union* (Macmillan, London, 1984)
Herlemann, H. (ed.), *Quality of Life in the Soviet Union* (Westview, Boulder, Colo., 1987)
Hirszowicz, Maria, *The Bureaucratic Leviathan: a Study in the Sociology of Communism* (Martin Robertson, Oxford, 1980)
Hough, J.F., 'The Soviet Elite: Groups and Individuals', *Problems of Communism*, (January-February 1967), pp. 28–35
Inkeles, Alex, *Social Change in Soviet Russia* (Harvard University Press, Cambridge, Mass., 1968)
Konrad, G., and I. Szelenyi, *The Intellectuals on the Road to Class Power* (Harvester, Brighton, 1979)
Kuron, Jacek, and K. Modzelewski, *An Open Letter to the Party* (Pluto, London, n.d.)
Lane, David, *The End of Social Inequality? Class, Status and Power under State Socialism* (Allen & Unwin, London, 1982)
Littlejohn, Gary, *A Sociology of the Soviet Union* (Macmillan, London, 1984)
Makhaisky, Waclaw, *The Intellectual Worker* (Geneva, 1905)
Matthews, Mervyn, *Class and Society in Soviet Russia* (Penguin, Harmondsworth, 1972)
Matthews, Mervyn, *Privilege in the Soviet Union: a Study of Elite Lifestyles Under Communism* (Allen & Unwin, London, 1978)
Matthews, M., *Poverty in the Soviet Union: the Lifestyles of the Underprivileged in Recent*

Years (Cambridge University Press, Cambridge, 1986)
Meissner, B., 'The Power Elite and the Intelligentsia', in K. London (ed.), *The Soviet Union* (Johns Hopkins University Press, Baltimore, Md, 1968)
Michels, Robert, *Political Parties* (Free Press, Glencoe, Ill., 1958)
Mosca, Gaetano, *The Ruling Class* (McGraw-Hill, New York, 1939)
Pareto, Vilfredo, *The Mind and Society* (Harcourt Brace, New York, 1935)
Parkin, Frank, *Class, Inequality and Political Order: Social Stratification in Capitalist and Communist Countries* (McGibbon & Kee, London, 1971)
Rizzi, Bruno, *The Bureaucratization of the World. The USSR: Bureaucratic Collectivism* (Tavistock, London and New York, 1939/1985)
Sik, Ota, *The Communist Power System* (Praeger, New York, 1981)
Simis, Konstantin, *USSR: Secrets of a Corrupt Society* (Dent, London, 1982)
Yanowitch, M., *Social and Economic Inequality in the USSR* (Martin Robertson, London, 1977)
Zemtsov, Ilya, *Private Life of the Soviet Elite* (Crane Russak, New York, 1985)

The politics of gender

Bebel, August, *Woman under Socialism* (Schocken, New York, 1975)
Browning, Genia, *Women and Politics in the USSR: Consciousness Raising and Soviet Women's Groups* (Wheatsheaf, Brighton, 1987)
Buckley, Mary, 'Women in the Soviet Union', *Feminist Review*, 8 (summer 1981), pp. 79–106
Clements, Barbara Evans, *Bolshevik Feminist: the Life of Aleksandra Kollontai* (Indiana University Press, Bloomington and London, 1979)
Clements, Barbara Evans, 'The Birth of the New Soviet Woman', in Abbott Gleason *et al.* (eds.), *Bolshevik Culture* (Indiana University Press, Bloomington, 1985), pp. 220–37
Danilova, Y.Z. *et al.* (eds.), *Soviet Women: Some Aspects of the Status of Women in the USSR* (Progress, Moscow, 1975)
Edmondson, Linda, *Feminism in Russia, 1900–1917* (Stanford University Press, Stanford, Cal., 1984)
Engels, Barbara Alpern, *Mothers and Daughters: Women of the Intelligentsia in Nineteenth Century Russia* (Cambridge University Press, Cambridge, 1983)
Engels, F., *The Origin of the Family, Private Property and the State* (Lawrence & Wishart, London, 1972)
Farnsworth, Beatrice, *Aleksandra Kollontai: Socialism, Feminism and the Bolshevik Revolution* (Stanford University Press, Stanford, Cal., 1980)
Glickman, Rose L., *Russian Factory Women: Workplace and Society, 1880–1914* (University of California Press, Berkeley, Ca., 1984)
Hannson, C., and Liden, K., *Moscow Women: Thirteen Interviews* (Alison & Busby, London, 1984)
Hayden, Carol Eubanks, 'The Zhenotdel and the Bolshevik Party', *Russian History*, 3, 2 (1976), pp. 150–73
Heitlinger, Alena, *Women and State Socialism: Women in the Soviet Union and Czechoslovakia* (Macmillan, London, 1979)
Heitlinger, Alena, *Reproduction, Medicine and the Socialist State* (Macmillan, London, 1987)
Holt, Alix (ed.), *Selected Writings of Aleksandra Kollontai* (Lawrence Hill, Westport, Conn., 1977)
Jancar, B.W., 'Women and Soviet Politics', in H. Morton and R. Tokes (eds.), *Soviet Politics and Society in the 1970s* (Free Press, New York, 1974)

Jancar, B.W., *Women under Communism* (Johns Hopkins University Press, Baltimore, Md, 1978)

Kerblay, Basile, *Modern Soviet Society*, (Methuen, London, 1983)

Lapidus, Gail Warhofsky, 'Political Mobilisation, Participation and Leadership: Women in Soviet Politics', *Comparative Politics*, 8, 1 (October 1975), pp. 90–118

Lapidus, Gail Warhofsky, *Women in Soviet Society: Equality, Development and Social Change* (University of California Press, Berkeley, 1978)

Lenin, V.I., *On the Emancipation of Women* (New York, 1934)

Lubin, N., 'Women in Soviet Central Asia: Progress and Contradiction, *Soviet Studies*, 33, 2 (April 1981), pp. 182–203

McAuley, Alistair, *Women's Work and Wages in the Soviet Union* (Allen & Unwin, London, 1981)

Mamonova, Tatyana (ed.), *Women and Russia: Feminist Writings from the Soviet Union* (Blackwell, Oxford, 1984)

Molyneux, M., 'Socialist Societies Old and New: Progress towards Women's Emancipation?', *Feminist Review*, 8 (summer 1981), pp. 1–34

Nikolayeva, Anna, 'Women in Soviet Society', *New World Review*, 53, 2 (March-April 1985)

Rzhanitsina, L., *Female Labour under Socialism: the Socio-Economic Aspects* (Progress, Moscow, 1983)

Sacks, Michael, *Women's Work in Soviet Russia* (Praeger, New York, 1976)

Sidorova, T.N. (ed), *Soviet Women* (Progress, Moscow, 1975)

Stites, R., *The Women's Liberation Movement in Russia: Feminism, Nihilism and Bolshevism, 1860–1930* (Princeton University Press, Princeton, N.J., 1978)

Chapter twelve

The command economy and reform

Political economy and the Soviet Union

Political economy is related to historical materialism and seeks to explain the relationship between economics and politics. Marx believed that after the revolution political economy as a subject would become redundant, since in the absence of capitalist exploitation socialist economic relations would become transparent. Reluctantly, however, Soviet scholars were forced to concede the need to study their own political economy. This was made all the more acute since, instead of inheriting a mature economic system ripe for socialism, the Bolsheviks took over from capitalism an unevenly developed country dislocated by years of war. The Soviet Union became what Alexander Eckstein called a mobilization regime devoted to rapid economic progress. Economic performance and governmental practice became linked.

Economic affairs lay at the heart of Soviet political concerns as industrialization became the *raison d'être* of the state. This has not been a simple process of 'modernization', since the process was as contradictory as the term itself. The Soviet economy has been able to achieve most of the goals it set itself despite limited foreign assistance. The Soviet Union has joined the front rank of industrial powers through its ability to mobilize resources on such prestige projects as Magnitogorsk, the Kama River truck plant, or the Baikal-Amur Main-line railway (BAM). This campaign approach to economic development led Oskar Lange to liken the Soviet economy to a war economy where all resources are concentrated on certain narrow ends.

Soviet economic achievements have been gained through a centralized planning mechanism (see p. 44). About 80 per cent of all the ministries represented in the USSR Council of Ministers have a primarily economic function. The specific branch ministries, such as those for steel or power, are joined by sectoral ones covering statistics or finances. Above all, there is the Gosplan (state plan) committee, responsible for co-ordinating the whole economic life of the country. The five-year plan establishes general priorities, such as the balance between heavy and consumer goods, and sets more detailed directives to individual plants. By 1987 Gosplan had the unenviable task of reconciling the interests of over 37,000

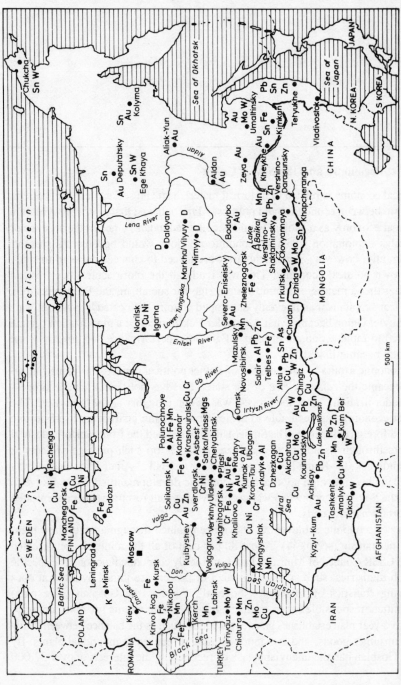

Figure 6 USSR: natural resources. Key to minerals: *Al* aluminium, *As* asbestos, *Cr* chrome, *Cu* copper, *D* diamonds, *Au* gold, *Fe* iron, *Mgs* magnesite, *Mn* manganese, *Mo* molybdenum, *Ni* nickel, *K* potash, *Sn* tin, *W* tungsten, *Zn* zinc

enterprises and production associations, and 26,300 collective and 23,000 state farms, with a total work force of 128 million dealing with over 300,000 items. It tries to integrate the various demands from the ministries with the general priorities of the government and with resources.

Planning has increasingly become directive planning rather than direct administration as elements of the market have crept in. The USSR is not so much a planned economy as a command one, or perhaps increasingly an administered economy, since the plans are in a constant state of revision and the behaviour of an enterprise in seeking to fulfil its own plans lies outside the plan. One could talk of the anti-plan process whereby, to fulfil the official plan, lower bodies engage in a variety of unorthodox stratagems. To make up lost time due to supply bottlenecks, for example, enterprises engage in 'storming', the chaotic attempt to fulfil orders, at the end of plan periods. The problems of detailed centralized planning became more acute as the economy grew in size and complexity. There is endless talk about 'improving the planning mechanism' but the problems require more radical changes. Most reform ideas challenge the efficacy of the direct link, established by Stalin, between production and consumption without the mediation of the market.

The party acts as the general co-ordinator and implementer of economic plans. Economic management is not divorced from public administration in the Soviet Union, and both are equally prone to political interference. Party control over the economy is ensured through the *nomenklatura* system and the other methods outlined in Chapter 7. Until 1988 about half the Central Committee's twenty-four departments were concerned with economic matters. They acted as shadow ministries, responsible for the detailed supervision of economic affairs. The governmental economic bureaucracy is buttressed by a specifically party hierarchy which reviews the state plans and budgets. The vast network of party committees down to the primary party organizations oversee the implementation of the plan, and the very survival of a party secretary often depends on successful plan fulfilment. A debate rages over whether party involvement actually promoted economic performance (Hough's view in *The Soviet Prefects*) or engendered chronic instability and disorganization. In 1988 the CC departments were replaced by an economic and social commission restricted to the general oversight of the economy.

In the mid-1950s the achievements of the Stalinist industrial system were the admiration of socialists and non-socialists alike. The launching of the first sputnik in 1957 seemed to support Khrushchev's contention that production *per capita* could exceed that of Western countries by the 1970s. Stalin's aim of 'catching up and overtaking' the West seemed to be within a hair's breadth of fulfilment. Khrushchev's ousting in 1964 led to a more modest assessment, and by the late 1970s the talk was more frankly of crisis. Food shortages, the lack of consumer goods, the massive waste of materials and labour power, the over-reliance on technologically obsolete coal-based industries, poor utilization of managerial skills, and so on became the currency of discussions about the economy. But can we really talk of a fundamental crisis of the Soviet economic system by the 1980s?

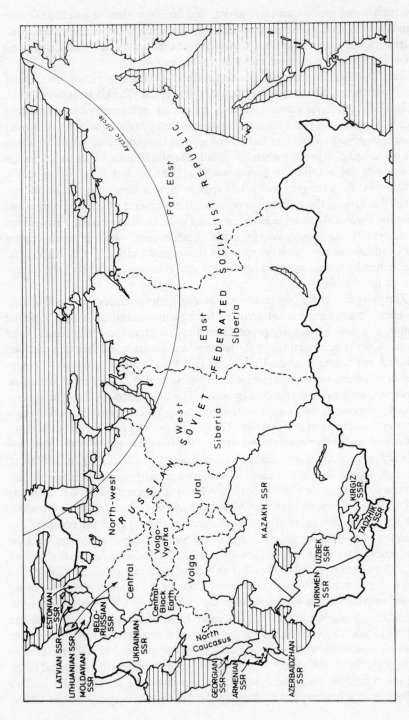

Figure 7 Republics and economic planning regions

Under Soviet power industrial output has increased sevenfold, agricultural output has grown 5·4 times, GNP has quadrupled, and *per capita* consumption tripled.[1] Critics such as Alain Besançon, however, point out that despite the enormous sacrifices the average Soviet wage in terms of purchasing power is half that of Brazil. The great number of workers on the land, double that of Western Europe and North America combined, cannot feed the country.[2] Peasant personal plots cover 4 per cent of the cultivated land and yet produce an estimated 60 per cent of potatoes, 30 per cent of vegetables, and a large proportion of meat, milk, and eggs. Moreover, the figures of Soviet economic growth are probably highly exaggerated, as some Soviet economists themselves have now admitted.[3]

The problem has become ever more acute of how the Soviet Union can sustain its global aspirations at a time when the gap between the world economy and the level of Soviet development is widening. There has been a secular decline in the growth rate of the Soviet economy, especially marked since the early 1960s. Annual growth rates during the first five-year plan reached 21 per cent, falling to an average 6·7 per cent per annum in the 1950s, to 4·2 per cent in the early 1970s, and down to 2–3 per cent in the 1980s. In 1982 the growth rate appeared to have fallen to zero. Soviet GNP is still, despite Khrushchev's hopes of overtaking the USA by the late 1960s, only 54 per cent that of the USA (falling from 58 per cent in 1975), and the USSR's position as the world's second largest economy has been challenged by Japan, with less than half its population. The *per capita* GNP of the Soviet people is 48 per cent of the US level and fell from fifty-sixth place in the world in 1976 to seventieth in 1982 (see Table 6). For most of the 1980s living standards stagnated. The productivity of Soviet industrial labour is 55 per cent that of the USA, and in agriculture a quarter. The technological gap has put the Soviet Union about ten to fifteen years behind the West.

Table 6 Comparison of the Soviet economy and the world

	Population (millions)	GNP US $ (billions)	GNP USA = 100	Per capita GNP US$	Per capita GNP USA = 100	GNP per employee US$	GNP per employee USA = 100
USA	234·5	3,310·5	100·0	14,120	100·0	29,400	100·0
USSR	272·5	1,843·4	55·7	6·760	47·9	13,600	46·3
Japan	119·3	1,157·0	34·9	9,700	68·7	20,000	68·0
West Germany	61·5	657·7	19·9	10,690	75·7	23,000	78·2
France	54·7	514·9	15·6	9,410	66·6	21,900	74·5
Great Britain	56·0	448·2	13·6	8,020	56·8	16,900	57·5
China	1,020·9	341·7	10·3	335	2·4	—	—
Canada	24·9	326·9	9·9	13,130	93·9	27,500	93·5
Brazil	131·3	296·8	9·0	2,260	16·0	—	—

Note: US dollars at 1983 values.
Sources: *Handbook of Economic Statistics* (National Foreign Assessment Centre, Washington, D.C., 1984), pp. 22 ff.; calculated in *Soviet Union, 1984–85: Events, Problems, Perspectives*, edited by the Federal Institute for East European and International Studies (Westview, Boulder, Colo., and London, 1986), p. 326; and using same data to compare the Soviet and American economies, see Paul R. Gregory and R.C. Stuart, *Soviet Economic Structure and Performance*, 3rd edn (Harper & Row, New York, 1986), p. 18.

The pattern of Soviet economic development has been unbalanced. Stalin set the country the task of 'catching up and overtaking' the West during the first five-year plans. The Soviet Union has caught up and overtaken — but in terms of already outmoded indices. The emphasis has been on heavy industry, and the annual production of steel, oil, cement, pig iron, and fertilizers has surpassed the United States, and massive achievements have been registered in the space and military fields. However, consumer goods and services have been neglected, and the Soviet information revolution has barely begun. The USSR is strong in precisely those areas that characterize an emerging economy, and weak in areas that mark out a mature economy. Just at the moment when all the sacrifices of the Soviet people should have come to fruition, the definition of modernization has changed and condemned the Soviet Union to yet more exertions. Instead of decreasing, as predicted by Khrushchev, the gap between the developed capitalist countries and the USSR is widening. Gorbachev has constantly stressed the depth of the economic crisis bequeathed by the era of stagnation. The Soviet Union has become industrialized when the advanced countries are moving into the post-industrial era when services and information are more important than smoke stack industries. Alvin and Heidi Toffler describe this as the 'third wave', following on from the agricultural and industrial revolutions, and marking a general crisis of industrialism, socialist as well as capitalist. The Soviets were well aware of the changes at least from the mid-1970s, but Brezhnev lacked the will to tackle the problem. The major question is whether the Soviet Union has to change fundamentally, allowing the freer flow of information and initiative, in order to compete. Can the Soviet Union somehow finesse the problems associated with decentralizing the economy while retaining the centralized political system?

The problems are not confined to the economy but amount to a crisis in Soviet society. Leading Soviet and Western commentators have identified a weakening in the political and social coherence and integrity of the Soviet polity. One of the key concepts in Gorbachev's twenty-seventh congress speech was the idea of 'social justice', which focuses on receiving income only for work performed but also includes a range of values such as the abolition of privileges and rights to labour, education, medical assistance, and social security. It also suggests such concepts as equality before the law, strengthened discipline and morality, and respect for the dignity of the person irrespective of social position or nationality. In other words, the vaunted Soviet political stability is seen as dependent upon social justice. It is in this context that the campaigns against corruption, against carbuncular architecture and the destruction of historic monuments, and against the excessive privileges of the elite have to be considered. Boris Eltsin displayed a barely concealed fear that the equilibrium was being upset: duty has given way to privilege, and the rhetoric of service that sustains rulers in power has weakened. Hence the reform process in the Soviet Union is more than a narrow attempt to improve economic performance but tries to assert certain basic social values to enhance the viability of society itself and thus strengthen political stability.

The existing organization of the Soviet economy is under challenge. There is a questioning of the economic suitability of a system designed to achieve the first stages of industrialization in the more complex circumstances of the late twentieth century. The historical conjuncture is the transition from an extensive economy to an intensive one: from one concerned with building steel plants, railways and suchlike to an economy which focuses on what goes on inside the factory, the productivity of labour, the effectiveness of the machine tools, and the quality of the goods produced — not more shoes, but better ones. The problem is now to move from a labour-intensive economy to a technologically advanced capital-intensive labour-productive economy.

The economic sociologist Tatyana Zaslavskaya in her important discussion paper of April 1983, dubbed the Novosibirsk Report, argued that the system of management created for the old-style command economy of fifty years ago remains in operation today in very different circumstances. It is now holding back the further development of the country's economy. Her analysis is a rare example of the application of a critical Marxism to the operation of the Soviet system itself. Her argument refers to Marx's famous passage: 'At a certain stage of their development, the material production forces of society come into conflict with the existing relations of production . . . From forms of development of productive forces these relations turn into their fetters.'[4] The underlying premise is a Soviet version of convergence, where the imperatives of industrial society force changes in the political system. She castigates the over-concentration of decision-making in the hands of central institutions, thus diminishing opportunities for participation from below. Popular initiative is no longer considered a luxury but essential for the further development of the economy and polity. On the grounds of rationality she argues that a more complex economy requires a more responsive managing centre. Furthermore, the very legitimacy of the government is jeopardized by its lack of adaptability to the new circumstances, giving rise to morbid symptoms such as a crisis in social justice. The existing economic arrangements, she argues, have appalling social consequences, a theme echoed by Gorbachev. She calls for a shift to the market to complement the administrative allocation of resources. In political terms the requirements of the moment can be seen as the transformation of nationalized property into more socialized forms.

The balance established in the post-Stalin years between economic development and political stability appears to be changing. The neo-Stalinist compromise from 1953 was based on an implicit deal whereby political opposition was subdued by the state's commitment to improving the standard of living. Now the post-Stalin era is coming to an end as the enormous economic and social costs of sustaining the bargain are becoming apparent. The compromise indeed has to be broken to reinvigorate the economy and to tackle the roots of the Brezhnev malaise. As yet it would be premature to argue that the population demands political autonomy, but society is beginning to emerge from the tutelage of the state. As the experience of Poland has shown, any economic dislocation has political consequences. The state's direct responsibility for the economy at a time of declining economic performance and stagnation in living standards means that economic resentments are directed against the political leadership. Moreover, there is a fundamental social, or class, dimension to the problem identified by Zaslavskaya. Since in the Soviet Union political control over the means of production is an unusually direct one, it follows that economic reform entails a fundamental adjustment in political relations. According to Marx a revolution takes place when the political superstructure is out of alignment with the economic base. Gorbachev's 'revolution without shots' reflects such a fundamental readjustment.

History of economic reform

There are two types of problem facing the Soviet economy. The first is general conjunctural issues, which include such factors as demographic changes, labour shortages, technological advances posing new challenges, and the condition of the world market. The second type is systemic problems that stem from factors internal to the socialist economy, and which can be remedied by actions taken by the leadership itself. Most of the latter arise from the pattern of Stalinist industrialization, which created a vast, top-heavy bureaucracy managing the country's economic life. At a certain stage the enormous costs and wastage involved in maintaining the managing mechanism, the heart of the command economy, condemn Soviet-type economies to relative stagnation. In the absence of the 'invisible hand' of capitalist market forces, and the increasingly palsied condition of the visible hand of command planning, such economies have no self-sustaining mechanism to fire them with dynamism. They do not operate, at root, by cumulative gains and benefits, but by constant wasteful exertion. Instead of performing as a stimulus to the growth of the rest of the economy, the expansion of the consumer sector, for example, acts as a depressant and is considered a diversion of resources from the heavy industrial or agricultural sectors. Instead of all sectors mutually sustaining one another, they struggle for scarce resources.

These problems are not new and have long been discussed in the USSR. The issue of economic reform has been on or near the top of the agenda at least since the death of Stalin. In 1957 Khrushchev focused on decentralization by breaking up the ministries and creating over 100 local economic councils (*sovnarkhozy*) (see p. 74). The highly centralized economic ministries, and some of their bureaucrats, were abolished. However, no effective way was found of integrating the councils, and by 1962–3 there was a recentralization. Khrushchev's attempt to improve efficiency by deconcentration proved a failure and was dismissed as one of his 'harebrained schemes'.

The debate continued, however, and the 1960s saw a boom in socialist reform economics. There was agreement that the old ministerial network had been guilty of excessive centralization, but there was also a consensus that Khrushchev's decentralization had not been an effective solution. At one pole reformers called for market socialism; others urged cybernetic planning through the increased application of computers; while the conservatives insisted on the return of the old centralized system. Under Khrushchev a series of reforms had been proposed by Evsei Liberman to break down the old Stalinist economic model whose main thrust was to free the enterprises from centralized administrative control and give them greater freedom and responsibility. Planning was to retreat and concern itself with the major decisions. Industry was to be decentralized and influenced by the internal, and even the external, market. Liberman proposed replacing 'gross output' by 'profit on total assets' as the main indicator of enterprise performance. Output as a measure of performance led to the hoarding of labour as managers produced more labour-intensive goods, and in general tried to avoid increases in their production norms. Similar ideas were put forward by Ota Šik in Czechoslovakia and have been taken furthest in Yugoslavia, and to a lesser extent in Hungary.

In September 1965 Premier Aleksei Kosygin introduced an economic reform which incorporated some of Liberman's ideas: the regional economic councils were abolished; a system of managerial incentives was introduced; efficiency and technical rationality were to replace 'voluntarism'; and plans were to be 'directive' rather than specific. The main aim of the 1965 economic reform was to give greater responsibility to individual enterprises by decreasing central direction from the recentralized ministries in order to improve efficiency and raise output. Managerial success was to be judged primarily by criteria of sales and profitability rather than the old method based on gross output. Managers were given some powers to allocate local resources and promote technological innovation. The reform itself was fairly limited in scope and restricted itself to altering institutional relationships. The reforms soon ran out of steam and were quickly forgotten. Bureaucratic reforms are always easy prey to 'sabotage' by bureaucrats. The leadership, and Kosygin personally, mindful of Khrushchev's recent fate, did not press the reforms for fear of endangering their political control. Economic reform once again lost out to political considerations.

A follow-up to the 1965 economic reform was a more narrow attempt to deal administratively with low labour productivity and underemployment. The Shchekino experiment of 1967 was conducted in a chemical plant near Tula in which wage and bonus funds were integrated and managers given the right to make workers redundant without having to find them alternative employment. They were permitted to use half the resulting wage savings to increase incentive payments to the remaining workers. The local soviets expanded their job centres to find alternative employment for those made redundant. The results were impressive as a reduced work force increased output, productivity, and wage levels. By 1980 Shchekino methods had been introduced in over 2,000 production associations, and another 7,250 were using aspects of the method, but still this covered only 10 per cent of the Soviet economy. It was only reluctantly introduced by the central ministries, well aware of the broad social and political implications of the reform. Large-scale redundancies could turn into high unemployment. Such reforms are constrained by the 1977 constitution's guarantee of a job for every citizen, a commitment at the heart of Soviet labour policy since

1929. The attempt to achieve greater efficiency by giving more autonomy to the enterprises met with great resistance from the central economic and political bureaucracy.

Brezhnev launched a small reform in 1973 in the form of production associations. These were created by the amalgamation of several allied enterprises and giving them more autonomy than the individual enterprises. The reform represented an attempt to eliminate some bureaucratic duplication and to improve managerial efficiency. It presented an implicit challenge to the ministries, who correspondingly dragged their feet in implementing the measure. By 1980 the associations produced only about half of Soviet industrial output with half the industrial workers. The same fate befell N. Zlobin's contract brigade method in the construction industry whereby payment depended on the performance of the financially autonomous brigade. There is some evidence that a group around Kirilenko in the 1970s were working towards an economic reform which would have introduced higher productive investment and wider differentials among workers, but the regime settled for social stability at the cost of economic stagnation. A new faith in long-range planning and computerization of planning and economic management promised great rewards while leaving social relationships undisturbed. Continuing weak Soviet economic performance, however, forced Brezhnev to launch a mini-reform in 1979. The aim was to improve planning indicators, but in some ways simple quantitative indicators were restored by a stress on quantity and the amount of goods sold. Over the last twenty years there has been a slow drift to cost-accounting or self-financing (*khozraschët*) principles. The clear pattern of the last thirty years of economic reforms is that they and the associated avalanche of edicts not only failed to tackle the problems but have in many cases only exacerbated them.

There is the genuine problem of deciding what is appropriate for the Soviet Union. Something has to be done, but what? The hesitancy in launching economic reforms after Khrushchev stemmed in part not only from the lack of political will but from the real inability to decide the appropriate course of action. Marx and Lenin have little to offer in the current situation. The Hungarian New Economic Mechanism (NEM), launched in 1968, cannot simply be copied, since Hungary has only some 800 enterprises and a relatively homogeneous population of 11 million, whereas the Soviet Union has a population of 284 million and is made up of over 100 nationalities. In any case, the NEM suffers from major drawbacks of its own. East Germany's reforms of industry and the planning system have made its economy one of the most successful in Eastern Europe, though the problem of low productivity has not been overcome. A comparison with the Chinese reforms is instructive. With ever greater conviction since 1978 the Chinese leadership under Deng Xiaoping have condemned the harm caused by tight planning and called for economic decentralization and the introduction of market mechanisms of managing the economy. Only about 30 per cent of the economy is still run by the state. The extension of reforms to political and social life is openly discussed. However, Gorbachev has declared that the Chinese approach to solving the problems of mature socialist economies is not applicable to the Soviet Union. There are no easy options, and any reform carries its own risks, especially in the transition period. A huge economy places its own limitations on reform.

Berliner identified four models of reform. The conservative model followed by Brezhnev retained the *status quo* while making some piecemeal reforms. It focused on administrative reforms such as creating or dismantling the production associations, changing the success indicators for managers, increasing the emphasis on profit and improvements to the planning mechanism. It condemns the Soviet Union to permanent technological backwardness and consigns the Soviet population to a low standard of living. The second approach is the reactionary model, which retains the basic Stalinist economic system but reverses some of the changes in social relations introduced since Stalin's death. Increased police power and coercion would ensure discipline and order. A frequent reaction when facing mounting problems in a Soviet-type system is to reassert central control rather than to decrease it. High investment and a low standard of living would accompany the emphasis on large, centralized enterprises. The third model is that of radical reform, somewhat along the lines of Yugoslavia and Hungary. It entails the decentralization of planning and management, with the emphasis on profit, and the greater dominance of market forces. But it would be limited by considerations of job security and limitations on income differentiation. Gorbachev has not hidden his respect for the achievements of Hungary's economic reform. The fourth model is the liberal one. It is a compromise solution, since it retains the traditional planning methods for most of the economy while liberalizing the present restrictions on private initiative. It is reminiscent of the NEP and its mixed economy, with planning restricted to the commanding heights of the economy. There would be private initiative in certain sectors of the economy, such as services, handicrafts, retailing, and construction.[5] The first two models enhance the powers of the bureaucracy, the second two undermine them.

Gorbachev's reforms to date combine the radical and liberal models. The Brezhnevite pattern of piecemeal adjustments to the 'economic mechanism' has been replaced by broad-ranging initiatives, focusing in particular on *khozraschët*. Gorbachev stresses the 'intensification' of the economy, the 'acceleration' and 'invigoration' of social and economic changes, in a programme called *perestroika*. Of course, the attempt to raise the tempo of economic growth through acceleration may actually hinder restructuring, though the latter in the long run is a condition of the former. The focus has been on the creation of super-ministries to co-ordinate long-term development, the shedding of some of the vast bureaucracy, accompanied by greater powers for individual enterprises and their increased participation in drafting plans. Gorbachev's economic policies contain the potential of a revival of some of the practices of the NEP, including elements of the market and the equivalent of a tax in kind to replace the delivery quotas. For Gorbachev *perestroika* means above all the rationalization of the Soviet administered economy to take advantage of the scientific-technological revolution. It will be an extended process involving restructuring the managerial system, increasing the participation of workers in management, and dealing with the social problems of Soviet society to create social justice, though not equality. The aim is to realize the potential of socialism through the use of the 'human factor'. Gorbachev calls all this 'revolutionary' and has admitted that there would be a struggle to achieve it, just as Lenin had to fight for the introduction of the NEP.

From 1985 a working party headed by the then director of Gosplan, Nikolai V. Talyzin, and including Leonid I. Abalkin, Oleg T. Bogomolov, and Abel G. Aganbegyan sought to develop a programme of economic reform suitable for Soviet conditions. Their main suggestions were adopted by the June 1987 Central Committee plenum in the document 'Main Provisions for Fundamentally Reorganizing Economic Management'. The meeting finally tackled the inertia caused by fifty years of Stalinist centralization. Gorbachev was by then sufficiently radicalized to realize that his earlier reforms would fail unless carried further. This conviction was supported by his reform economists, his travels round the country, and by the flood of letters complaining about the slow pace of improvements. The reforms adopted in June 1987 focused on four key features: reshaping the central planning system into a long-range mechanism giving guidance rather than specific orders; giving managers and enterprises more independence and allowing competition, with the uncompetitive ones going to the wall; eliminating the government-controlled pricing system and subsidies; and greater labour mobility, including redundancies. One of the leading reformers, Aganbegyan, sees the future economy as being characterized by intensive rather than extensive growth, more receptive to technological developments, oriented towards the consumer and marked by democratic public self-management. The long-term strategy is for the development of the 'socialist market', which Soviet commentators insist is not to be confused with market socialism: the stress is on socialism rather than the market.

The rights of Soviet enterprises and farms will be drastically expanded and partially released from plans handed down from Moscow. The state plan will become a general guideline while factories will deal with each other on the basis of signing contracts based on negotiated prices rather than by prices set by state agencies. On 1 January 1988 about 60 per cent of Soviet industry began to go over to the *khozraschët* or self-financing system. An estimated 13 per cent of enterprises operate at a loss, and thousands are in danger of going bankrupt if *khozraschët* is seriously introduced. The details of bankruptcy proceedings remain vague. The reform was accompanied by the radical reorganization of foreign trade. Direct links were encouraged between enterprises and Western trading partners, together with hopes of joint ventures between them. By May 1988 about thirty-five had been set up, and later even the 49 per cent limit on foreign ownership was dropped. Factory managers were forced to change the habits of a lifetime in a matter of months and sought continued guidance from the centre. The economic ministries only reluctantly relinquished their control. *Perestroika* has set a premium on the improved training of managers and officials in order to generate a 'managerial culture'.

The problems of agriculture typify those of the economy as a whole. Ninety-five million (34 per cent) of the Soviet population live in rural areas, and 24 million (19 per cent) of the work force of 128 million actually work on the land, much higher than the 2–5 per cent in advanced capitalist countries. And yet, far from being a net exporter of grain, as before the revolution, the Soviet Union is forced to spend valuable hard currency on the purchase of foreign foodstuffs. Agriculture is no longer exploited for industry; instead, under Brezhnev, it became a burden on the rest of the economy, devouring 27 per cent of total investment between 1976 and 1980. Between 1970 and 1988 agriculture absorbed £680 billion but output rose by a mere 25 per cent. The poor harvests from 1979 revealed that its problems are structural and social rather than due to any single factor such as lack of capital or infrastructure. The formation of about 9,000 agro-industrial complexes since the early 1970s as part of the attempt to industrialize farming caused even more bureaucracy and restricted the rights of farm management. Administrative reforms have often been used as a way of avoiding political reforms. This was clearly illustrated by the response to the Akchi experiment in Central Asia in the 1960s, which combined administrative and labour reorganization. It was an attempt to change the political relationships on the farm by establishing new patterns of authority, with rotation of offices and elections to fixed terms. The results were impressive, but the experiment was aborted and its organizer, Ivan Khudenko, imprisoned.

Gorbachev has raised the status and power of the agriculture ministry by creating the new 'super-ministry' Gosagroprom, cutting 22,000 bureaucrats at the same time. However, the reforms are going beyond purely administrative changes and are permitting a devolution of authority to the farms to allow more local decision-making over what to produce, in order to overcome excessive centralized direction and misplanning. Whether this will go so far as full decollectivization remains to be seen. The Chinese experiment in decommunalizing agriculture has been rewarded by massive increases in output and a significant rise in rural incomes. The reforms initially focused on labour reorganization, especially the development of the autonomous work tier, or link (*beznaryadnoe zveno*). In earlier versions a small group of about five or six people worked a piece of land collectively and were paid by results. The system is now called *kollektivnyi podryad*, or group contract work, and is actively encouraged by Gorbachev. The June 1987 CC plenum envisaged the expansion of small-scale family farming, with only loose affiliation with the collective or state farms. The main problems are whether the groups will receive the necessary support from farm managers, whose powers and prestige are threatened by the reforms, whether there will be sufficient incentive to work harder in the absence of goods on which to spend extra income, and the fundamental contradiction of personal initiative in the context of socialist collectivism and party interference. The Gorbachevites, disappointed by continued shortages of food and lengthening queues, went even further at the CC plenum on 9 July 1988 and planned to introduce universal long-term leasing of land to farmers for periods of up to fifty years. The declared aim was to restore sovereignty to the peasant, making him or her 'master of the land'. Gorbachev was careful to defend the impeccably socialist nature of his proposals.

Agricultural reforms were accompanied by the planned phasing out of subsidized prices, one of the linchpins of Soviet socialism, by the early 1990s. Food price subsidies by 1987 cost the Soviet government an annual R57 billion, 13·2 per cent of the state budget of R430 billion. In 1986 the prices of 200,000 commodities were still set centrally. While salaries would be raised, subsidies would be decreased and then removed from many items from bread to housing, remaining only for medicine, education, care for the elderly, and book publishing. Each family would be entitled to a minimal apartment with subsidized rents, but prices will soar for extra space and amenities. The savings on consumer subsidies would release funds for investment elsewhere. The outlook for the Soviet consumer in the short-term is not promising.

The example of Poland in the 1970s illustrates that investment strategy is at the root of political and social stability. Spending on consumer welfare in communist states can no longer be considered a luxury, a residual, but an integral part of improving general economic performance. In any economic system there are basically three demands on national resources: capital investment, consumption, and defence. During *perestroika* the government pursued a policy of dizzy investment in industry, planning between 1986 and 1990 to lay out R175 billion in capital investments, almost 50 per cent more than in the preceding five years. Gorbachev has set very ambitious tasks for the economy, and it is not clear how he plans to achieve them. The necessary dramatic improvements in labour and capital productivity could be achieved only by giving enterprises and ministries a much greater stake in achieving profitability. Otherwise the lack of correspondence between increased capital investment and steady defence spending will mean a squeeze on social consumption on 'non-productive' sectors such as health, education, housing, and culture.

Soviet technology has proved its abilities in the armed forces and space exploration, yet most of the civilian economy suffers from backwardness. The introduction of new technology is inhibited by institutional conservatism, restrictive price organization and lack of incentives. As elsewhere, the problem is the transition from extensive to intensive economic growth but exacerbated in the sphere of semiconductor technology by the rapid pace of change in the rest of the world. The old cumbersome central planning machinery has become a brake on development. The USSR is challenged by the need of modern economies for the free and rapid flow of information. The major experiment of the mid-1970s in developing a post-industrial service sector was the Fakel' (Torch) combine, established to provide enterprises with tailor-made software programs and various forms of consultancy work. The group was suppressed and its leader gaoled. The failure of the Soviet Union to sustain an effective alternative form of social and technological organization threatens to condemn it to sterility as an economic formation. In this field the Soviet Union has been condemned in most areas to the role of perpetual runner-up, always catching up on a world that moved on fifteen years ago. Gorbachev is aware that information is the key to any advanced economy, but technological advance does not operate in a social vacuum: it is tied ever more closely to culture and to social structure. *Glasnost* reflects the need for the free movement of information, if not ideas. The challenge of what Daniel Bell calls post-industrialism, where the emphasis is on services and information, entails a psychological shift of perceptions away from the USSR's romance with smokestack industrial development.

Perestroika aimed to give the Soviet employment structure less of a blue-collar look and make it conform more to a 'post-industrial' pattern. At present 96 million (including 24 million farm workers) of the USSR's 128 million workers are in what Soviet economists call material production. While the Soviet social structure broadly approximates that of the West, there has been a much slower shift from the primary to the secondary and tertiary sectors of employment (see Table 7). Gorbachev's reforms, however, will if anything in the short term tend to increase the already disproportionate share of labour in the capital-goods and metalworking sectors of industry. Furthermore, about 18 million people, or 14 per cent of those employed, are occupied in administrative posts, of whom 2·5 million are in various administrative bodies such as ministries, while the rest are in the management of production associations, enterprises, and offices. Gorbachev's aim is to drain the bloated administrative apparatus — and the number fell for the first time in many years in 1986 — to compensate for the perceived shortage of labour.

Table 7 Distribution of the work force according to sectors (%)

	1940	1965	1970	1979	1984
Agriculture and forestry	54	31	25	21	20
Secondary industry (including construction, transport and communication)	28	44	46	48	47
Tertiary (including trade, finance, health, education, science, administration, etc.)	18	25	29	31	33
Total	100	100	100	100	100

Source: L.G. Churchward, *Soviet Socialism: Social and Political Essays* (Routledge, London, 1987), p. 30.

There has been a transition from abundant labour to labour scarcity, and in future, as Gorbachev has noted, nearly all economic growth will have to come from increases in labour productivity. He insists that there is no shortage but just a misuse of existing resources and underemployment. The key problem is that while the Stalinist command economy ended open unemployment, it failed to create a self-sustaining mechanism for achieving gains in labour productivity or for rewarding the productive workers while penalizing slackers. Despite a system of labour allocation for graduates, with the exception of the war years there has been a relatively free labour market in the USSR. Workers not only have the right to work, they are obliged to do so, but for most purposes they can choose where, for how long and how hard to work. The trend until 1987 was towards greater equalization in earned incomes, leading to the weakening of material incentives. Zaslavskaya has constantly stressed the social repercussions of an economy which encourages corruption and makes people dishonest. The majority of economic reformers advocate pay differentials in order to provide incentives for more productive workers and managers alike. It is in response to this perhaps more than anything else that the ideological premise of Marxist socialism, the promise of guaranteed employment, comes into conflict with the strategy of economic reform and raising industrial productivity. Fear of dismissal and unemployment would weaken the legitimating ideology: and yet alternative strategies avoiding market-competitive individualism as a means of raising labour productivity remain at best vague.

The Soviet system has devoted itself to suppressing individual initiative for most of its existence. A case in point is the long campaign waged on ideological grounds by the government to restrict the *shabashniki*, the itinerant freelance construction teams active in the countryside. Gorbachev admits that people have lost the habit of thinking and acting responsibly on their own initiative. His strategy is based on the attempt to apply the 'human factor' in the economy by freeing people's capacity to work and to stimulate economic and social initiative. These attempts come into sharp conflict with fears of the social and political consequences of growing inequality and personal enrichment. This was revealed at its starkest when measures to stimulate official economic initiative were preceded by harsh measures against unofficial private initiative. The Supreme Soviet in July 1986 passed a law against unearned income aimed at a whole section of the population who survived on the margins of society, especially a generation of semi-dissidents who lived by giving private lessons. From May 1987 the 'Law on Individual Enterprise' sanctioned certain kinds of businesses. Groups of family members living under the same roof working in their spare time from a state job are permitted to open small businesses, from restaurants to toy factories, and to provide a range of services, from repairs to tuition and translation. Such activities are to be brought out of the twilight second economy so that they can be monitored and taxed by the government. There has been a much-expanded role for co-operatives, primarily in service industries.

Andropov expanded the contract brigade experiment of a decade earlier. A law on worker collectives gave workers' groups certain rights to participate in the organization of their work and to discipline their members (see p. 94). The 'brigade method' of shop-floor organization was endorsed by the twenty-seventh congress, but its results to date are ambiguous. The intention has been to overcome the chronic problems of low pay and poor working conditions by stimulating greater worker autonomy in the workplace. It shares many common problems with participation as a whole in the USSR. The degree to which the workplace can be transformed into a democratic and egalitarian venue is as much a political as an economic question. These measures have been accompanied by the extension of voting rights. Furthermore, under *glasnost* the unions are to take a more active role in defending the social rights of workers, ending the situation condemned by Gorbachev at the eighteenth Soviet trade union conference in February 1985 of 'trade union officials dancing cheek to cheek with economic managers'. They are to counteract the technocratic tendencies in the economy. In the struggle, as Gorbachev puts it, between democracy and social inertia and conservatism the unions should take the lead in reinvigorating work collectives and self-management.

The Soviet economy suffers both from certain problems specific to itself and from others which reflect social or international factors and the quickening pace of change in all industrial societies. Above all, the problem is overcentralization and lack of responsiveness to new demands, new technologies, and new ideas. Within its own terms the Soviet economy has registered massive achievements, albeit at equally massive costs. Steady, though declining, growth rates have been maintained. The problem is not one of economic collapse but of reducing the economic and social costs of an antiquated command system.

Problems of reform

The era of stagnation saw the development of what is now called a 'pre-crisis' which would have led on to full-blown crisis if remedial action had not been taken. The question arises whether the Soviet Union has reached one of those turning points in history, like 1861 or 1905, when the need for reform is apparent to all. But, as on earlier occasions, will the opportunity be missed or taken up too half-heartedly, and will events inexorably lead on to the Soviet Union's own 1917? Economic and allied reforms have now come to the fore in the third phase of the 'great debate', taking up the themes of the previous two of the nineteenth century and the 1920s. The modern debate focuses on the correct balance between 'plan' and 'market'. The fundamental problem is the growing irrationality of the attempt to maintain the command economy and the administrative allocation of resources in a society and economy making increasingly complex claims on the system. Demands for high-quality goods and services are supplemented by calls for greater individual autonomy. There is the ironic problem of a lack of meaningful information, an information crisis, in a system overburdened with information. But if the economic issues, if not solutions, are clear, the political issue, as under Khrushchev, comes down to a contest between the forces of reform and political conservatism.

While the restructuring to date is linked indissolubly with Gorbachev personally, the rationale of the reforms is self-evident. Gorbachev pointed out to the Italian Communist Party newspaper *L'Unita* in June 1987 that '*perestroika* was not an enlightenment that came all of a sudden, within a single night'. The growing links between the Soviet and the world economy push the country towards more reforms, otherwise the leadership will preside over its decline to the status of a third-rate power. The concept of interdependence within a single world economy implies that the sustained vigour of capitalism is as much in the Soviet interest as it is in the West's. However, while the necessity for change has become self-evident, it does not mean that the reforms cannot fail. The need for reform has been evident for at least thirty years, yet they were resisted and a policy of 'muddling through' was adopted. While necessity may be the mother of invention, she often goes barren.

The course of economic reform will be anything but smooth. There is opposition at the very heart of the process. The prevention of breaches in ideological probity by cautious reformers such as Ligachev can undermine the purpose of reforms, as revealed by the law on unearned income of July 1986 and the restrictions hedging the law on individual enterprise of May 1987. Clearly party and state bureaucrats have not taken kindly to the torrent of abuse launched at them. Gorbachev has condemned lethargy, incompetence, and corruption among party, public, and economic officials. In his Krasnodar speech of September 1986 he noted the opposition to restructuring on the part of workers, peasants, and even 'leading people in the apparatus. They can even be found among our intelligentsia.' In a speech of late October 1986 he argued that the bureaucracy was threatening the whole plan for the future.[6]

There are five major problems associated with the reform process. The first concerns the social consequences of reform. The major question is how to combine economic dynamism with a commitment to social justice. While the attractions of the market mechanism are often proposed as a universal panacea, reform might lead to social instability. A reduction in job security through the wholesale application of Shchekino methods would give rise to the fear of unemployment. At the June 1987 plenum Gorbachev pledged that new jobs would be found for the 15 million industrial workers who would be made redundant over the next twelve years, and yet women might be pushed back into the home. Marketization would affect equality in incomes and services and bring out into the open existing privileges and inequalities. The measurement of inequality in candidly monetary terms, rather than access to the old closed shops, special housing, and so on, would to some extent establish a new hierarchy of status. Economic reform condemns wage levelling and would benefit the most skilled and best educated, both in terms of wages and with the better consumer goods available. A weakening of the centralized economic controls could be seen as corrosive of workers' economic rights and as exposing them to the arbitrariness of the local economic or state authorities. Low prices have been at the heart of the social contract between the regime and the people, yet marketization of the economy raises the spectre of inflation as managers fight to remain solvent. Price increases carry a political danger, as the authorities in Poland have discovered several times, especially if lower-income groups are not adequately compensated from the very beginning. Further, some people would perhaps do too well out of a reform, with the emergence of prosperous latter-day NEP-persons and Soviet yuppies attracting the envy of the less successful.

The second problem focuses on the political consequences of reform. There is the fear that the decentralization of authority could lead to political fragmentation, especially in the non-Russian republics. Already Estonia has gone a long way towards claiming regional autonomy for its economy. A sustained economic reform would give rise to unpredictable political consequences, however beneficial to the regime in the long run. Ultimately, meaningful economic reform would raise the question of the party's dominance over all aspects of political and economic life, and it would certainly change the context of the party's leading role. Economic reforms leading to the market could give rise to a form of political pluralism. The democratization that Gorbachev sees as essential for effective economic restructuring is an open-ended process. Chinese experience shows that effective reforms entail the loosening of political controls over economic organizations. These economic organizations, producers and consumers, would then have to find a way of relating to each other, functioning as economic interest groups. The extent to which such groups could interact in a pluralist manner, defending not only economic but also political interests, would be a matter of concern to the political leadership. Their aim would be to ensure a continued depoliticization of the economy. It would be a political tightrope act to gain the benefits of an economic reform while restraining its political implications. The Chinese reform process to date suggests that with adroit leadership it can be done.

A third factor in the reform process is the influence of strategic and defence issues on domestic change. The Soviet reform process has traditionally been hostage to the international environment. The argument that the 'international situation' does not permit reform has always been a sure winner for conservatives, and it has been Gorbachev's achievement to change the rules in this respect. Nevertheless, however pressing the need for reform, success is contingent upon stability in world affairs: a stability to which the USSR itself can contribute much. A renewed arms race might foreclose the option of economic reform as the conservatives rally.

The fourth factor which shapes the pattern of economic reform is the role of ideology. How can the market be used in the Soviet system, which has devoted seventy years to its elimination? The ideology has stressed production for use rather than exchange as a commodity on the market. Party conservatives are worried about the ideological implications of an economic reform which increases the role of the market and raises the spectre of creeping capitalism. Socialism has long had an intrinsic bias against 'consumerism' in which individually defined needs have been regarded as frivolous by comparison with the allegedly rationally defined needs of the producers. In China the conservative reformer Chen Yun put forward his famous 'birdcage theory', which asserted that economic reform is like a bird which must be contained within the cage of socialist planning. The market deprives the central political elite of control over individual needs. There is furthermore an element of ideological conviction to policies which would give rise to large income differentials. The remnants of 'leftism' in China have hindered the programme of reform and defended the rights of the party in economic management. Such 'leftism' is much more deeply entrenched in the Soviet Union and will be more difficult to overcome than in China, where it was discredited by the excesses of the Cultural Revolution.

The basic argument focuses on what is and what is not socialism. Would a partial restoration of market relations undermine the fundamental ideological premise of Marxism that there is a rational alternative to capitalism? The conservatives argue that liberal or radical economic reforms of Soviet-type systems undermine Marx's belief that communism is an alternative in which a community of producers could in a conscious way shape social relations and organize production. The reformers argue that economic reform is precisely the prerequisite for the fulfilment of this ideal, and in addition it would help alleviate the all too palpable alienation in Soviet society. Marxism-Leninism has in any case proved to be relatively flexible, permitting the personal plot and the free peasant market, the use of the incentive system since the 1930s, and great inequality. The black economy of market relations already exists, caused by the disparity between supply and demand. There is furthermore a strong ideological current which can be used to justify reform focusing on the concept of 'advanced modernization', the economic equivalent of developed socialism, and the scientific-technological revolution. But the ideology does place limits on economic reform. Gorbachev is careful to guard himself against accusations of 'revisionism', the worst charge in the communist lexicon of abuse. He insists that the changes should not be seen as a repudiation of principles but that, on the contrary, they are designed to develop, in his words, the potential and superiority of the socialist system.

The fifth factor on which the success of restructuring depends is its ability to overcome opposition. Strategies for overcoming the crisis can be considered in terms of the social forces that are served by one or another reform programme and, perhaps more important, whose interests are threatened. Opposition to reform is both social and political: the social elite defends its privileges, and political resistance takes the form of defending ideological traditions. Resistance focuses on four key groups: the economic bureaucrats; the political elite; the military; and the workers, which in effect means the population at large. The opposition of the economic and political bureaucrats to the reforms in Hungary and China has been well documented. Their powers and privileges are eroded by the marketization of the economy. Zaslavskaya argues that there is a social basis to opposition to economic reform, in effect admitting that there are contradictory social relations in the Soviet Union. Among bureaucrats she locates the main source of opposition as the middle level of economic management in the ministries. Gorbachev is ruthlessly purging and criticizing the ministries, to whom there was a major devolution of power under Brezhnev. The major contradiction of the first phase of *perestroika* has been between the rights granted to enterprises by the Law on State Enterprises which came into effect in January 1988 and the existing powers of the ministries. The huge Gosplan agency, employing thousands of employees, in particular has become used to directing the operations of the economy, and its conversion to a long-range planning agency will be a major task, not least because of the lack of long-range planners. The views of plant managers are split, and those who do not adjust in time to the new climate will not survive. Gorbachev has been able to weaken the institutional obstacles to economic reform by a combination of reorganization and *glasnost*, mobilizing public and specialist opinion against bureaucratic resistance and inertia.

Certain sections of the political elite are clearly against liberal or radical reform. The very unpredictability and loss of control over social processes runs against the grain of the Soviet system. The party apparatus might find the *nomenklatura* system of appointments weakened. An increased role for the market, furthermore, presupposes the stable rule of impartial law. This in turn suggests a partial autonomy of the departments of state from the political system, encouraging a growing divergence between the party and the government. Further, a self-regulating economic mechanism would be viable only in the context of a relatively free flow of information and access to accurate government statistics, implying a relaxation of the government's monopoly of information.

There is no homogeneity in views of any of the groups, including the party bureaucracy, who are split by age, experience, and background. The division between the centre and the localities is probably the most significant one, rather than between central Moscow institutions. It is doubtful whether the whole party apparatus is in favour of maintaining discipline, centralized controls, and the absolute priority of heavy industry. Indeed, Gorbachev's main institutional support in the struggle for reform appears to be the Central Committee Secretariat, where he has been able to consolidate his allies. However, groups worried about exposure in a sustained anti-corruption drive or loss of power with the introduction of mandatory retirement are strong on the Central Committee.

The attitude of the defence, heavy industry, and security establishment to economic reform is ambiguous. The usual assumption is that reform would have to be financed by a decrease in military expenditure. But the armed services are well aware that military power in the final analysis depends on the level of economic growth and efficiency relative to the main adversary. It is not clear whether the defence establishment is more interested in its privileges or in maintaining genuine military parity with the United States. If the latter, it would appear that their long-term interests would predispose them to encourage improved Soviet economic performance, whether they would be willing to entertain short-term cuts in their budget is another matter. The degree to which the KGB stands outside the reform process is a measure of its reversibility.

Resistance to Gorbachev comes from ordinary citizens who so far have felt only the negative effects of his reforms on their everyday lives, his anti-alcoholism and anti-corruption campaigns. There was widespread resistance among the working class to the first phase of Gorbachev's reform programme as the imposition of severe quality standards cut bonuses and wages. The introduction of disruptive double or treble-shift systems dislocated traditional work patterns. Reformers have constantly stressed the need for improved social provision, such as shopping, transport, and health facilities, but real improvements have been slow in coming. Gorbachev admitted to the eighteenth trade union congress in February 1987 that there would be short-term losers in the reforms, and many of them by 1988 had already participated in a wave of strikes. In the long run *perestroika* promises higher living standards and greater opportunities for personal initiative, yet in the short run it means higher prices, intensified work patterns, and loss of unearned bonuses.

These five sources of opposition to reform are fragmented and cannot unite on an alternative policy. It is generally accepted that there can be no return to the Brezhnev approach, and yet an alternative policy is available in Andropov's authoritarian reform programme. For radical or liberal reforms to succeed, a 'reform coalition' must be created, sustained by a convincing rationale and marked by effective leadership. The distinctive feature of the reform process under Gorbachev, in sharp contrast to the abortive reforms under Brezhnev, is his personal commitment and political courage. His forceful style of leadership is willing to challenge the entrenched interests of institutional and social interest groups. Reform appeals to different sections of the population in different ways, and the reform coalition is made up of perhaps unexpected elements. Support comes from people in technology and defence industries, specialists at research institutes, sections of the party apparatus, women, who applaud the anti-alcohol campaign, young engineers, scientists, economists, and part of the technocratic elite. A pro-reform public in the Soviet Union could be garnered if the positive results of the reforms came through quickly enough. However, one of the fundamental dilemmas of reform is that after over seventy years of promises about the glorious future the threshold of tolerance for yet more short-term sacrifices is probably not high. Whatever the dangers, Gorbachev has understood that there comes a time when it is politically more dangerous to do nothing than to reform. As the conservative motto puts it, one must change a little in order to avoid changing a lot.

Notes

1 M.I. Goldman, *USSR in Crisis: the Failure of an Economic System* (Norton, New York, 1983), p. 174.
2 Alain Besançon, 'Andropov and his Soviet Union', *Policy Review* (summer 1983).
3 The figures have possibly been exaggerated by a factor of ten. For a radical downward revision of official figures on economic growth between 1928 and 1985, see V. Selyunin and G. Khanin, *'Lukavaya tsifra'*, *Novyi mir*, 2 (February 1987), p. 191–201.
4 K. Marx, *Contribution to the Critique of Political Economy, Selected Works* (Moscow, 1968), p. 182.
5 J.S. Berliner, 'Managing the USSR Economy: Alternative Models', *Problems of Communism*, 1 (January–February 1983), pp. 40–56.
6 *Pravda*, 30 October 1986.

Key texts

Aganbegyan, Abel, *The Challenge: Economics of Perestroika* (Hutchinson, London, 1988)

Colton, T.J., *The Dilemma of Reform in the Soviet Union*, rev. edn (Council on Foreign Relations, New York, 1986)

Lane, David, *Soviet Economy and Society* (Blackwell, Oxford, 1985)

Nove, Alex, *An Economic History of the USSR* (Penguin, Harmondsworth, 1972)

Nove, Alec, *The Soviet Economic System*, 3rd edn (Unwin Hyman, London, 1981)

Zaslavskaya, Tatyana, 'The Novosibirsk Report', introduced by Phil Hanson, *Survey*, 28, 1 (spring 1984), pp. 83–108

Select bibliography

Amann, Ronald, and Julian Cooper (eds.), *Technical Progress and Soviet Economic Development* (Blackwell, Oxford, 1986)

Arnot, Bob, *Controlling Soviet Labour: Experimental Change from Brezhnev to Gorbachev* (Macmillan, London, 1988)

Bergson, A., and H.S. Levine (eds.), *The Soviet Economy: Towards the Year 2000* (Allen & Unwin, London, 1983)

Berliner, J., 'Managing the Soviet Economy: Alternative Models', *Problems of Communism*, 1 (January-February 1983), pp. 40–56.

Bornstein, Morris (ed.), *The Soviet Economy: Continuity and Change* (Westview, Boulder, Colo., 1981)

Brus, W., *The Economics and Politics of Socialism* (Routledge & Kegan Paul, London, 1973)

Cole, John, and Trevor Buck, *Modern Soviet Economic Performance* (Blackwell, Oxford, 1986)

Dobb, M., *Soviet Economic Development since 1917* (International, New York, 1948)

Dyker, David A., *The Soviet Economy* (Crosby Lockwood Staples, London, 1976)

Dyker, David A., *The Future of the Soviet Economic Planning System* (Sharpe, Armonk, N.Y., 1985)

Gey, Peter, Jiri Kosta, and Wolfgang Quaisser (eds.), *Crisis and Reform in Socialist Economies* (Westview, Boulder, Colo., 1987)

Goldman, Marshall I., *USSR in Crisis: the Failure of an Economic System* (Norton, New York, 1983)

Goldman, Marshall I., 'Gorbachev and Economic Reform', *Foreign Affairs*, 64, 1 (fall 1985), pp. 56–73

Grossman, Gregory, 'The "Second Economy" of the USSR', *Problems of Communism*, 26, 5 (September-October 1977), pp. 25–40

Grossman, Gregory (ed.), *Studies in the Second Economy of Communist Countries* (forthcoming)

Hirszowicz, Maria, *Coercion and Control in Communist Society: the Visible Hand in a Command Economy* (Wheatsheaf, Brighton, 1986)

Hoffmann, E.P., and R.F. Laird, *The Politics of Economic Modernisation in the Soviet Union* (Cornell University Press, Ithaca, N.Y., 1982)

Hoffmann, E.P., and R.F. Laird, *Technocratic Socialism: the Soviet Union in the Advanced Industrial Era* (Duke University Press, Durham, N.C., 1985)

Hohmann, Hans-Hermann, Alex Nove, and Heinrich Vogel (eds.) *Economics and Politics in the USSR: Problems of Interdependence* (Westview, Boulder, Colo., 1986)

Ioffe, Olimpiad S., and Peter B. Maggs, *The Soviet Economic System: a Legal Analysis* (Westview, Boulder, Colo., 1987)

Kahan, A., and B. Ruble, *Industrial Labour in the USSR* (Pergamon, New York, 1979)

Kushnirsky, F., 'The Limits of Soviet Economic Reform', *Problems of Communism*, 33, 4 (July-August 1984), pp. 33–43

Lane, David (ed.), *Labour and Employment in the USSR* (Wheatsheaf, Brighton, 1986)

Lane, David, and F. O'Dell, *The Soviet Industrial Worker* (Martin Robertson, Oxford, 1978)

Lavigne, Marie, *The Socialist Economies of the Soviet Union and Eastern Europe*, trans. T.G. Waywell (Martin Robertson, Oxford, 1974)

Leites, Nathan, *Soviet Style in Management* (Crane Russak, New York, 1985)

Lewin, Moshe, *Political Undercurrents in Soviet Economic Debates: from Bukharin to the Modern Reformers* (Pluto, London, 1975)

Nove, Alex, *Political Economy and Soviet Socialism* (Allen & Unwin, London, 1979)

Nove, Alex, *The Economics of Feasible Socialism* (Allen & Unwin, London, 1983)

Prybyla, Jan S., *Market and Plan Under Socialism: the Bird in the Cage* (Hoover Institution Press, Stanford, Cal., 1987)

Rutland, Peter *The Myth of the Plan: Lessons of Soviet Planning Experience* (Hutchinson, London, 1985)

Schapiro, L., and J. Godson (eds.), *The Soviet Worker: from Lenin to Andropov* (Macmillan, London, 1984)

Smith, Keith (ed.), *Soviet Industrialisation and Soviet Modernity* (Routledge & Kegan Paul, London, 1986)

Wiles, Peter, *The Political Economy of Communism* (Harvard University Press, Cambridge, Mass., 1964)

Zaslavsky, V., 'The Regime and the Working Class in the USSR', *Telos*, 42 (winter 1979–80), pp. 5–20; also in his *The Neo-Stalinist State* (Harvester, Brighton, 1982), pp. 44–65

Ziegler, Charles E., 'Worker Participation and Worker Discontent in the Soviet Union', *Political Science Quarterly*, 98, 2 (summer 1983), pp. 235–53.

Chapter thirteen

Foreign and defence policy

The course of Soviet foreign policy

Soviet foreign policy has traditionally emerged from the interplay between national interest and the idea of communism as a world system. Marx believed that the proletariat had no national home and that as classes disappeared so would the state. There is therefore a tension between the internationalism of communism and the form in which it is contained, the nation state. Soviet foreign policy has been marked by a dualism, torn between defensive concerns and the thoroughly expansive theory of communism whose spread was considered only a matter of time. In practice, however, apart from the debate over the Treaty of Brest-Litovsk, no destructive conflict between the two principles has arisen. Soviet foreign policy can be interpreted through the realist school of international relations theory.

In keeping with Lenin's theory of imperialism the new leaders after the October revolution expected the revolution to spread rapidly once the 'weakest link' in the imperialist chain had been broken. Trotsky, the first Commissar of Foreign Affairs, indeed took a dim view of his new post, reflecting as it did the contempt-ible secret diplomacy and shady deals made by the great powers which had characterized the First World War. He entered his new offices only after a con-siderable delay and instead a few days after the revolution announced, 'I will issue a few revolutionary proclamations to the peoples of the world and then shut up shop.' Just as Lenin and the Bolsheviks considered that traditional politics would disappear after the revolution as the whole revolutionary nation set about managing its own affairs, so in the international sphere it was expected that diplomacy would give way to fraternal relations between the free countries of a socialist commonwealth. The concept of the 'permanent revolution' was not Trotsky's alone. The whole Bolshevik party believed that the revolution in Russia was but the harbinger of the world revolution. However, the revolution did not spread to industrially developed countries and the Soviet republic remained isolated, apart from Mongolia, between 1917 and 1939. The emphasis on defence industries in the industrialization drive of the first five-year plans was justified by this isolation.

The tension between world revolution and socialism in one country was particularly marked while Lenin lived. The controversy in the Bolshevik party in 1918 over whether to accept the German peace terms at Brest-Litovsk was bitterly divisive (see p. 26). Bukharin and the Left Communists insisted that a revolutionary war should be launched, accompanied by appeals to the German soldiers and working class. Lenin's approach was a pragmatic and realistic one, given Russia's military weakness. He no doubt remembered that the war had contributed to the fall of Tsarism and the Provisional Government in 1917. Lenin accepted the need to make concessions and for a time at least, much to the anger of the left, he was willing to put the survival of the Soviet state above utopian hopes of international revolution. The conflict between Soviet nationalism and world communism thus appeared in the first days of Soviet power. It is a moot point whether the calls for revolutionary war would have been effective against the might of the German war machine, but a Bolshevik call in March 1918 to rally to the defence of the nation against Germany might well have gained the Bolsheviks a wide spectrum of support.

With the collapse of Germany in November 1918 Lenin's tactic proved partially justified, and the territories of the old Russian empire, with the exception of Poland, Finland, and the Baltic republics, were recovered by the end of the civil war. The creation of a spate of short-lived 'soviet republics' in 1919 in Hungary, Slovakia, and Bavaria seemed to confirm the belief that the Russian revolution was only the first break in the imperialist chain. The establishment of the Third Communist International (Comintern) in March 1919 was designed to assist the spread of the world revolution. At a time of civil war and foreign intervention the Comintern was an attempt to utilize all the means at the disposal of the Bolsheviks to take the war to the enemy. The Comintern, however, was soon subordinated to state interests and became an instrument of Soviet foreign policy. The coexistence of the Comintern with a Commissariat of Foreign Affairs symbolized the tension between ideology and expediency. In 1920 certain elements of the revolutionary war strategy were revived with the war against Poland, which was seen as a bridge to the resources and support of the German economy. The Polish war of 1920 saw the emergence of a 'revolutionary jingoism' as socialist internationalism merged with Soviet nationalism.

Lenin's foreign policy in general was marked by a pragmatism that was to become characteristic of Soviet foreign policy. Already in 1918 the Soviet state had begun to practise the art of diplomacy, albeit rather crudely at first with Trotsky's tirades against the German generals at Brest-Litovsk. At the peace conference at Versailles in 1919–20 the French Premier Georges Clemenceau hoped to establish a *cordon sanitaire* around the Soviet republic. The Russo-German treaty signed at Rapallo in 1922 between the two outcast nations of inter-war Europe signalled the end of Soviet Russia's diplomatic isolation. Nevertheless, the Bolsheviks still expected revolution in the West, and their diplomatic initiatives were regarded as little more than holding actions. With the final defeat of the German revolution in October 1923 the isolation of Soviet communism was confirmed, although the Soviet state was recognized by a number of countries in the early 1920s. A new balance was required between Soviet diplomacy and world revolution.

The two aims, however, were in many ways incompatible. Lenin was cautious in his foreign policy but he remained a committed internationalist in that he saw international relations through the prism of the class struggle. Although Stalin remained contemptuous of the long-term prospects of peace with the capitalist states, under his leadership the USSR less equivocally defined its policies towards other states in terms of Soviet national interests, which he claimed represented the highest interests of the international working class at the given stage of development. Stalin's policy of socialism in one country from 1924 led to the subordination of the workers' revolution to the needs of Soviet diplomacy. The Comintern was launched in the belief that a revolutionary wave would destroy capitalism, but in the 1920s it was forced to accommodate itself to a period of revolutionary stagnation. Under Stalin almost every internal change of policy was reflected by shifts in foreign policy. The NEP was marked by revolutionary compromises. During the ten-day General Strike of May 1926 in Britain the Soviet Union supported the more moderate TUC through the Anglo-Russian Trade Union Council. In China Stalin insisted on the continuation of the alliance of the Chinese communists with the Nationalist Guomingdang under Jiang Jieshi. Comintern moderation was discredited by the Nationalist massacres of communists in Shanghai in April 1927.

Only three Comintern conferences met under Stalin, whereas under Lenin four were held in a much shorter period. The fifth congress in 1924 ordered the denunciation of Trotsky throughout the communist parties of the world. In December 1927, following the Chinese *débâcle* and his turn to the left against the NEP, Stalin declared that the 'stabilization of capitalism' had come to an end. The sixth congress in 1928 eliminated the influence of Bukharin and the 'Right Deviation' and inaugurated the notorious Third Phase in Soviet foreign relations of 1929–34. The policy was marked internally by collectivization and externally by the denunciation of social democracy. The bizarre reflection of internal policies in the extreme leftist foreign policy proved a disaster. In Germany the condemnation of the Social Democratic Party as social fascists, the most dangerous enemies of communism, smoothed the path of the Nazis to power under Hitler in January 1933. Out of fear of the traditional opponents of the USSR, Britain and France, Stalin clung stubbornly to the policy of Rapallo and ties with Germany.

With the consolidation of the virulently anti-communist Nazis in Germany Soviet policy dropped the extremism of the Third Phase and began a search for security. The seventh Comintern congress in 1934 inaugurated the era of the popular fronts whose aim was to forge defensive alliances and internal blocs against fascism. The USSR joined the League of Nations at this time and the Soviet foreign minister, Maxim Litvinov, used the forum to try and establish 'collective security' against aggressors. A Russo-French agreement was reached at Locarno, but Soviet hopes of an 'Eastern Locarno' of defensive pacts with its bordering states of East Europe was hampered by news of the great purges at home. Internal purges and external security agreements proved incompatible, and indeed at this time the purges took on an international dimension. In the Spanish civil war of 1936–9 Stalin fought a second war, organized by his secret services, against Republican forces who did not owe primary allegiance to the Soviet Union. The destruction of the Trotskyist POUM in Barcelona, described by George Orwell in *Homage to Catalonia*, was only the most publicized case.

Stalin's search for security was not an unambiguous policy. The destruction of the anti-German Tukhachevskii and the Soviet High Command in the purges of 1937 was perhaps an attempt to keep his options open to Germany (see p. 53). Following the Munich agreement of September 1938, in which Britain and France capitulated to German demands over Czechoslovakia, there was a gradual realignment of Soviet foreign policy. Stalin considered Munich an inducement by the West for Germany to look eastwards. Soviet assertions of readiness to go to war over Czechoslovakia appear rather unrealistic, given the condition and disposition of Soviet forces. There was now little talk of collective security, as Stalin understood Chamberlain's policy as an attempt to keep Russia out of Europe. Stalin increasingly saw advantages in reviving the spirit of Rapallo. At the eighteenth party congress in March 1939 he attacked the forthcoming 'imperialist war' while simultaneously denouncing appeasement and urging France and Britain to prepare for war with Germany. The months prior to open hostilities offered the undignified spectacle of all major powers hoping to divert the attention of the Nazi Moloch to their opponents. In mid-1939 Hitler talked of attacking Poland but not Russia, and in May Stalin replaced his Jewish foreign minister, Litvinov, who favoured alliance with the West, by Molotov. On 23 August 1939 the Soviet Union and Germany signed the Molotov-Ribbentrop non-aggression pact at the expense of Poland and Western Europe. A secret protocol provided for the reversion of the Baltic republics, eastern Poland, Bessarabia, and Finland to the USSR. Like Alexander I at Tilsit, Stalin hoped thereby to gain time. Nine days later Germany invaded Poland and World War II began.

Soviet expansionism in the period following the Nazi-Soviet pact can, at a pinch, be understood as fuelled by the search for security. Less understandable, however, is the thoroughness with which Stalin pacified the regions brought under his control. The Nazi *Blitzkrieg* from 1 September swiftly brought Poland to its knees. On 17 September Soviet forces entered Poland, and while the Nazis committed genocide in the western area, Soviet forces conducted 'classicide' in the east. About 1·5 million Poles, in particular the intelligentsia, were deported to Soviet labour camps, and 5,000 officers were murdered at Katyn, near Smolensk, in 1940; the whereabouts of another 10,000 is still not known. The damage inflicted on the Soviet army by the purges was reflected in its poor performance against the Finns in the Winter War of 1939–40. Early in 1940 Soviet forces occupied Latvia, Lithuania, and Estonia, and shortly afterwards incorporated them into the Soviet republic. Socialism was exported at the point of a bayonet but socialism remained in one country, albeit an enlarged one. The breathing space bought by the Nazi-Soviet pact was not used effectively to prepare for war. Defences along the

Figure 8 Territorial changes in the West, 1939–41

old border were dismantled but, for fear of offending Hitler, the new border was left almost defenceless. Stalin was dismayed by the 'phony war' in the West, and suspected that Britain and France (cowering behind the 'impregnable' Maginot Line) were waiting for Germany to attack the Soviet Union. He therefore compensated by redoubled assurances of good faith in holding to the Nazi-Soviet pact. His dismay was completed by the rapid collapse of France under the impact of *Blitzkrieg* in May 1940.

Stalin's attempts to appease Hitler proved of no avail, and on 22 June 1941 German forces launched a massive assault. Stalin appears to have had a nervous collapse at this betrayal and disappeared for ten days. He had ignored Allied warnings and those of his own secret service (especially those from the Soviet agent Richard Sorge in Tokyo) of the impending German attack. In his desperate attempts to maintain the agreement he continued to supply Germany with fuel and food. Stalin's role as a war leader has been much debated. His conduct was marked by the wasteful use of human resources and petty interference in operational questions. He refused to allow a retreat in the first days of the war, even though the German forces were better armed and more numerous. He refused to sign the Geneva Convention on Prisoners of War, allowing 3 out of 5 million Soviet soldiers to die in German camps. Soviet labour camps were kept full of people who could have fought. Soviet forces waited at the gates of Warsaw from the summer of 1944 to early 1945 while the uprising was destroyed. Victory was marked by the deportation of whole nations accused of collaboration with the occupying forces, even though the German army had not reached some of them.

Nevertheless, as a symbolic rallying force and overall strategist Stalin played a powerful role in the Allied defeat of the Nazis. The industrial base in the eastern areas developed during his five-year plans, reinforced by the evacuation of factories from the west at the beginning of the war, became the vital manufactory of war *matériel*. Stalin became a symbol of Soviet resolve, epitomized by the battle of Stalingrad from September 1942, which halted the German advance. He did not wage the war as a revolutionary war or under the banner of socialism, but was able to exploit the emotional power of Russian nationalism. In May 1943 the Comintern was abolished and a concordat was reached with the Russian Orthodox church. The battle was to be fought as a national war, with great prestige accruing to the army. Ranks and insignia were restored to stress the continuity with Russian traditions. Some of the restrictions on the peasant personal plots were relaxed for the duration. At this time Soviet nationalism became solidly based on Russian themes. Stalin promoted new commanders like Zhukov and Konev and dropped the incompetent ones such as his long-time supporters Voroshilov and Budenny. From 1942 he downgraded the political commissars and introduced a unified command under regular officers.

The German attack was so powerful that it appeared in the first weeks of the war that the regime would collapse. However, any sympathy that the Germans might have been able to exploit in favour of the overthrow of Soviet power swiftly turned to hostility as the bestial nature of Nazi policies and practices became clear. The sheer size of the country, the harsh winter of 1941-2 which blunted the German advance at the gates of Moscow, and the policies pursued by Stalin were able to defeat the aggressor. The alliance forged with the Western powers provided the USSR with vital supplies. However, Stalin was haunted by fears of a separate peace between Germany and the Allies, or that the West would remain on the sidelines as the Soviet Union and Germany exhausted each other. He sought guarantees by insisting on the speedy creation of a second front, and fought for Allied recognition of the 1941 frontiers (that is, the inclusion of parts of Poland and Finland, Bessarabia, and the Baltic states). The suspicions among the allies during the war were the seeds that grew into the Cold War.

Stalin's bargaining position grew ever stronger as the eastern front advanced from Stalingrad in early 1943 through Kursk and to Germany's borders by late 1944. In May 1945 the Soviet flag was raised over Berlin, and during the few days in July 1945 that the Soviet Union was at war with Japan it was able to gain the Southern Kurile Islands. The victory raised Stalin to unprecedented heights, and the Soviet Union emerged as a major power on the world stage. The communist regime had finally found a national legitimacy as the organizer of the defence of the motherland against the German attack. However, the losses were devastating, with about 7·5 million military losses and another 6-8 million civilian deaths. Soviet forces occupied most of Eastern Europe and promoted the spread of communist power. Once again, as in 1917, the revolution had not developed as predicted by Marx. Victory meant the end of socialism in one country, but the transplantation of Soviet communism to Eastern Europe was a long and complex affair. The dialectic between socialism and Soviet armed force was to give rise to an on-going instability in Eastern Europe as nationalism and communism contended.

Three conferences between the Allies had tried to establish a pattern for the post-war settlement. At Teheran in late 1943 agreement was reached over Poland and for an offensive either in the Balkans (Churchill) or France (Stalin and Roosevelt). In October 1944 at a meeting between Churchill and Stalin in Moscow the idea of zones of influence was accepted, with the infamous 'percentages agreement' giving, for example, the USSR an 80 per cent influence in Hungary to the West's 20 per cent. The Warsaw uprising from August 1944 strained relations between the Allies. The fate of post-war Eastern Europe was settled at the meeting of Stalin, Churchill, and Roosevelt at Yalta in February 1945. Soviet foreign policy interests in Eastern Europe were legitimated and the basic design of the division of Europe into spheres of influence was accepted. The plan was imposed at Potsdam in July-August 1945, in the shadow of the first nuclear explosion on 16 July 1945. The war ended with the major elements of the post-war world in place: the advent of nuclear weapons (used against Hiroshima on 3 August and Nagasaki on 6 August 1945); Soviet-American rivalry to gain world ascendance to replace a debilitated Europe; disputes over the institutionalization of Soviet influence in Eastern Europe; and a divided Germany symbolized by the partition of Berlin.

With the demise of the common enemy who had provided the bond for coalition, the Cold War developed with an inexorable logic based on irreconcilable conflicts of interest between the former allies and a profound ideological incompatibility. The Cold War, however, did not spring full-blown from the defeat of Nazi Germany but emerged only over a period of years. Controversy over

Figure 9 USSR and Eastern Europe since 1945

the fate of Germany was compounded by conflicts over Eastern Europe. The course of East-West and Soviet-East European relations mirrored each other. The first period of Soviet occupation of Eastern Europe saw the establishment of coalition governments designated people's democracies: the avoidance of the term 'dictatorship of the proletariat' signalled that these regimes were to be coalitions of workers, peasants, and intelligentsia. The establishment of a Soviet-type regime in Poland, however, particularly exacerbated relations between the former allies. The elections promised at Yalta were delayed until January 1947, by which time the communists were able to manipulate the result to defeat the popular Peasants' Party led by the deputy Prime Minister, Stanislaw Mikolajczyk.

Following the victory over fascism each country hoped to find its own path to socialism, and hence there was an implicit contradiction with the Soviet Union as a great power — all the more so since the Second World War was a battle of nationalities against the supra-national policy of the Germans. National paths had been legitimated by the dissolution of the Comintern and seemed to augur greater autonomy for individual communist parties. Between 1945 and 1948 various 'national roads to communism' were tried out. Wladislaw Gomulka in Poland, for instance, hoped to achieve a distinctively national form of communism in the shadow of a Soviet Union aspiring to regional hegemony.

Alarmed by the ruthlessness with which Soviet power had been consolidated in Poland and elsewhere, in a speech at Fulton, Missouri, on 5 March 1946 Churchill warned that 'From Stettin in the Baltic to Trieste in the Adriatic, an iron curtain has descended across the continent'. He called for an Anglo-American alliance to contain the Soviet threat. The announcement of the Truman Doctrine in March 1947 for the 'containment' of the USSR, followed by the Marshall Plan for the economic reconstruction of Europe, was pursued under the nuclear umbrella. The doctrine was based on the idea that the Soviet Union had a messianic urge to conquer the world, a view which argued that traditional Russian expansionism was bolstered by aggressive Marxist-Leninist ideology. George Kennan provided the most coherent rationale for this belief in his famous 'Mr X' article 'The sources of Soviet conduct' in July 1947 although he insisted later that he meant a political rather than a military response.[1] The Cold War represented the sharpening of pre-war conflicts by the struggle for mastery over Europe and ultimately the world.

As long as Stalin hoped to maintain elements of the wartime coalition he tolerated some national autonomy in Eastern Europe. With the deterioration in East-West relations he perceived a growing divergence between national roads and Soviet security interests. From 1948 the Stalinist model was imposed irrespective of local conditions. In Yugoslavia in mid-1948 the attempt to establish Stalinist hegemony met with resistance from Josif Broz-Tito and the Yugoslav communists. They had come to power largely by their own efforts and were not dependent on the Red Army. Stalin had no model of how to conduct relations between communist countries other than by the methods he had used to consolidate his power within the Soviet Union. But such methods raised powerful emotions when applied to relations between sovereign nation states and with peoples who had never been part of the Russian empire. The break between Yugoslavia and the Soviet Union in 1948 owed nothing to ideology, and everything to the dialectics of nationalism. It was the first major example of an East European state seeking to pursue its national interests within a communist framework. Similar problems were to appear following the coming to power of Mao Zedong and the Chinese communists in 1949. The spread of communism was not an unmitigated blessing for Stalin, as Moscow's position as the centre of communism was eroded by the development of other models of socialism in Belgrade and Beijing. The spread of communism came into contradiction with the Soviet Union's great-power status. The wheel had come full circle as socialism in one country gave way to a multinational communist movement in power.

The spread of communism, however, did not alter the manner in which Stalin ruled, and he chose Soviet state interests over the formation of a socialist commonwealth. Shocked by the temerity of the Yugoslav communists, he proceeded to impose draconian regimes in the countries within the Soviet sphere of influence. Already the Communist Information Bureau (Cominform) had been established as a successor to the Comintern at a conference of European communist leaders in the Polish Silesian town of Szklarska Poreba in September 1947. The creation of the Cominform reflected frustration at the failure of communist parties to come to power in France and Italy, but above all it was designed to contain Western influence in the East rather than to advance communism in Western Europe. National paths to socialism were discredited, and its exponents, such as Gomulka in Poland, were lucky if they escaped with their lives. 'Little Stalins' emerged in most East European countries between 1948 and 1953 — Mátyás Rákosi in Hungary, Boleslaw Beirut in Poland, Klement Gottwald in Czechoslovakia — who proceeded to stage their own show trials. The Soviet model of development was imposed on these countries irrespective of local conditions or their previous level of development. Collectivization of agriculture was accompanied by the same irrational concentration on heavy industry that had marked the Soviet pattern of development. In the Soviet Union this was merely wasteful, but in more developed countries such as Czechoslovakia it proved disastrous and entailed regression to a more primitive pattern of economic development. In addition, the imposition of the Soviet political system in such relatively advanced countries as Poland and Czechoslovakia, with Western-oriented political cultures dating back a millenium, imposed massive political strains. The Soviet Bloc was formed as a defensive barrier for the USSR, and hence these countries' own internal revolutionary development was subordinated to the state interests of the USSR. The extension of Stalinism was validated by the international power structure, confirmed at Yalta, and was reinforced by the Soviet Union's emergence as the supreme military power in the East.

The death of Stalin in March 1953 marked the onset of a new period in international relations. The deployment of nuclear weapons forced a re-evaluation of the 'inevitability of war' between the superpowers. Stalin himself in his last work, *Economic Problems of Socialism in the USSR*, had modified his position on the grounds that 'powerful popular forces had come forward in defence of peace'. Gradually the doctrine of peaceful coexistence emerged. It did not mean that conflict between East and West had ended, only that its forms had changed. The emphasis was now on ideological rather than military struggle. The basic premise was that there had been a shift in the 'correlation of forces' in favour of the USSR: socialism had been extended to Eastern Europe, creating a socialist bloc of 'peace-loving' states; the colonial powers had declined and their empires were challenged by socialist or nationalist movements opposed to imperialism; the military and economic power of the USSR had increased and the Soviet Union possessed thermo-nuclear weapons to counter 'imperialist aggression'. The view of peaceful coexistence as the active pursuit of Soviet interests as socialism allegedly became the ascendant historical force was to lie at the root of the failure of *détente* in the 1970s.

The change from the defensive coexistence of 1917–53 was marked by a much more forward Soviet posture in the Third World, symbolized by the extension of Soviet influence in Egypt and Ghana. Khrushchev's rule saw a temporary breakdown of the synthesis of communism and Soviet nationalism as scarce funds were expended in support of the world revolution. The legacy of this period was the massive drain on Soviet resources to Cuba. Stalin's death allowed relations to be improved with Yugoslavia. Tito was rehabilitated and the Belgrade Declaration of 1955 acknowledged the diversity of national paths to socialism. The creation of the Warsaw Treaty Organization in 1955, together with the revival of the Council for Mutual Economic Assistance (formed in 1949), was, among other things, an attempt to depersonalize Soviet-East European relations. Khrushchev hoped to provide a more reciprocal, multinational institutional framework to replace Stalin's pattern of exploitative bilateral relations. At the twentieth party congress in February 1956 Khrushchev's denunciation of Stalin's cult of personality was accompanied by an attack on his heavy-handed dominance over Eastern Europe. Destalinization in Eastern Europe released pent-up resentments (see p. 69–70). The attempt to reconcile nationalism with socialism in a specifically Hungarian way was crushed by Soviet tanks. A paradoxical effect of the liberalization under Khrushchev was that some national leaders, notably in Albania and China, joined later by Romania, became anti-Soviet Stalinists.

In foreign policy, as in domestic policy, Khrushchev followed a zigzag path. In 1958 Yugoslavia was once again condemned. In 1960 came the momentous break with China precipitated by Khrushchev's sudden withdrawal of Soviet experts and assistance. Here again, as with Yugoslavia, national suspicions played a much greater part in provoking the split than ideology. The on-going Berlin confrontation was exacerbated between 1958 and 1961 by Khrushchev's aggressive posturing. Khrushchev's erratic behaviour climaxed with the confrontation over the placing of Soviet strategic missiles in Cuba in October 1962. The world came to the brink of nuclear war but Khrushchev's retreat with the face-saving formula of an American commitment not to invade the island in return for the removal of the missiles averted the catastrophe. Amidst widespread alarm at the near-disaster, a 'hot line' was installed between Moscow and Washington, and in 1963 the Partial Test Ban Treaty prohibited atmospheric testing of atomic weapons.

The reformism associated with Khrushchev served to throw the communist parties of Eastern Europe back on to their own national communist traditions and to weaken their dependence on the Soviet Union. This was a period of slow dissolution of the blocs as Western Europe grew stronger in relation to the USA and the Cold War thawed slightly. The relatively slow economic progress of the USSR, its setback in Cuba in 1962, the failure over Berlin, the split with China, all accelerated moves towards greater independence and polycentrism. Khrushchev's foreign policy saw the extension of Soviet influence around the globe, but the failures, as over Cuba and China, were cited as part of the reason for his overthrow in 1964. His major achievement was to establish a new framework for East-West relations and to modify relations with Eastern Europe.

The Brezhnev era saw the transformation of the Soviet Union from a regional to a world power. Soviet military potential increased steadily from the early 1960s as Soviet military planners sought to remedy the perceived weakness revealed by the Cuban missile crisis. By the end of Brezhnev's rule the Soviet Union had fulfilled its post-war ambition to achieve strategic parity with the United States and to become a truly global power. The decision to invade Czechoslovakia in 1968 and thus to abort the reform process under Dubček reflected Soviet domestic conservatism as much as its desire to maintain hegemony over Eastern Europe. The 'Brezhnev doctrine' of limited sovereignty underwrote bloc cohesion in Eastern Europe. Soviet gains were legitimized internationally by the Helsinki Conference on Security and Co-operation in Europe in 1975. The conference ratified the post-war borders, but the Soviet Union was forced to concede certain human rights commitments.

Under Stalin foreign policy played a primarily defensive role, even when the Soviet Union was expanding. Peaceful coexistence saw the shifting of the struggle between East and West on to the ideological plane, but it did not eliminate the conflicts on other levels. Starting under Khrushchev, and even more under Brezhnev, Soviet foreign policy changed its bearings and became more active and more visible, and in some ways independent of domestic concerns. The slogan of peaceful coexistence of the Khrushchev era was continued under Brezhnev under the name of *détente*. The Basic Principles Agreement and SALT I (Strategic Arms Limitation Talks, placing limits on the *growth* of nuclear arms) of 1972 laid the basis of *détente*. *Détente* ultimately failed because the US and the USSR had different perceptions of what it meant. For the US it meant Soviet restraint in the Third World, a slow-down of military growth, and some liberalization of human rights. From the Soviet point of view *détente* meant that recognition of strategic parity with the US would also lead to political equality and co-responsibility for managing world affairs. *Détente* failed to provide the expected economic rewards. The USA did not grant the USSR most-favoured-nation trading status or low-cost trade credits. *Détente* had not prevented the United States from pursuing a resolute policy of excluding the Soviet Union from the Middle East peace process or from playing the China 'card' in a remorselessly hostile manner. As far as the Soviet Union was concerned, *détente* did not mean stepping aside from the world revolutionary process, and when the revolutionary forces in Angola, Ethiopia, or elsewhere demanded Soviet assistance, it was provided. In late 1979 it became increasingly clear that Congress would not ratify SALT II. In addition, as the Soviet leaders saw it, *détente* gave the United States the illusion that under the guise of concern for dissidents it could interfere in the Soviet Union's domestic affairs. With hindsight it can be seen that *détente* permitted technological and economic exchange with the West to delay domestic economic reform.

Despite many successes in the international arena, the Brezhnev era ended in discord and failure as a new Cold War took the place of *détente*. From 1979 East–West relations deteriorated markedly. The Soviet invasion of Afghanistan in December 1979 was not the cause of the end of *détente* but a symptom. Opposition in the West to *détente* was marked by the coming to power of Margaret Thatcher in Britain in 1979 and Ronald Reagan in America in 1980. The imposition of martial law in Poland on 13 December 1981 further worsened relations. Soviet perceptions were marked by the fear of a 'new encirclement' by the USA, China, Japan, and Western Europe. The American use of economic warfare against the Soviet Union further exacerbated relations. Reagan's announcement of the Strategic Defence Initiative (Star Wars) in 1982, and talk of the winnability of nuclear war, all increased tension, as did the gross mishandling by the Soviets of the shooting down of a Korean airliner in September 1983. The dissolution of *détente*, economic problems, indebtedness, world recession, arguments over the placing of American intermediate nuclear forces (INF), Cruise and Pershing II, in response to the Soviet deployment of SS20 missiles all marked a thirty-year low in East–West relations. The succession struggles in the Soviet Union furthermore led to a paralysis of Soviet decision-making. By 1985 the USSR had achieved the remarkable feat of alienating almost every country in the world, communist and non-communist alike.

Of necessity Gorbachev was forced to retrieve the situation. His accession radically changed the international atmosphere and established a new context for East–West dialogue. The succession was over and the scene was set for a period of new realism in Soviet foreign policy. His rule was immediately marked by a new vigour. The attempts to re-establish some sort of arms control agreement were matched by a series of concrete proposals which were no longer directed mainly at Western public opinion but to policy-makers. In the United States Reagan's fading presidency was prepared to enter into a series of arms reduction agreements. The meeting between Reagan and Gorbachev in Geneva in late 1985 was the first summit for nearly a decade. The encounter between them in Reykjavik in October 1986 saw astonishing proposals and counter-proposals for the complete elimination of nuclear weapons. An INF treaty actually eliminating categories of nuclear weapons was signed at the Washington summit in December 1987.

The arms control process continued towards a START (Strategic Arms Reduction Talks) treaty at the Moscow summit of May 1988. Gorbachev's spirit of revived *détente* differs significantly from that pursued by Brezhnev. While for Brezhnev the inflow of Western technology was of crucial importance, for Gorbachev it is designed as a complement rather than a substitute for domestic reform. Gorbachev's strategy is to reform Soviet society to achieve political comparability with the West in international affairs.

The making of foreign policy

With the assumption of a global role Soviet policy-makers have had to pay far more attention to foreign issues. Except in wartime, policy-making is not usually dominated by a single overriding ambition but arises out of the interplay of various motives and factors, not all of which are compatible. Western analysis of Soviet foreign policy veers between, on the one hand, the Riga axioms (named after a hostile group of inter-war specialists in Latvia), which emphasize the Soviet desire for world hegemony; and, on the other, the Yalta axioms, which stress the Soviet search for accommodation and the desire to be recognized as an equal and legitimate great power. Factors contributing to Soviet foreign policy include the following.

There are certain geopolitical constraints which can be seen to be in the tradition of Tsarist foreign policy. The argument that 'communism is Tsarism in overalls' assigns an important role to permanent features which would influence policy-makers based in Moscow of whatever hue. These strategic factors include insecure borders and the territorial imperative for a power based on the Eurasian land mass. An associated feature is the role of political culture, a view which often suggests that Russia has an irresistible urge to expand, owing to the nature of the country itself. Arrogant leaders combined with a boorish, xenophobic people, Kennan argued in 1947, provide the conditions for expansionism. R.V. Daniels stresses the continuity in centralized, autocratic rule buttressed by an official belief system, police control, and the absence of effective law restraining the state as lending Soviet foreign policy its Tsarist colours.[2] The problems associated with a concept of political culture which confuses Tsarist authoritarianism with Bolshevik *dirigisme* have been noted, and the idea does little to illuminate the contemporary concerns of Soviet policy.

The analysis of Soviet foreign policy is complicated to a greater extent than in most other countries by the ambiguous role of ideology. Does adherence to Marxism-Leninism reinforce traditional Russian concerns and drive the Soviet Union to establish a Pax Sovietica across the globe? The Soviet Union has become a world power in military terms, but it also has a world, or universalistic, ideology whose precise role in Soviet foreign policy is ambivalent. Every great power develops an imperial creed to justify its actions as a world historical mission. However, whether Soviet ideology is used in an instrumental way, to justify an expansionism based on its traditional great-power interests, or whether it is itself the major motor in a logic of expansionism, is not clear. Soviet ideology is an amalgam of Marxism-Leninism and pragmatic considerations which temper the chiliastic ambitions to a world united under the banner of socialism.

The original Leninist ideology was internationalist, committed to the goal of world socialism, though the means of achieving it were the subject of controversy. It shows great antagonism to other social systems but the socialist state was forced to deal with other systems. The ideology has therefore taken on a nationalist colour expressed in terms of loyalty to the Soviet state. From the political culture point of view, Marxism is redundant in explaining Soviet foreign policy. However, the Soviet view of the world is still tempered by the contribution of its ideological foundations. International affairs are not viewed simply as the interplay of nation states, the nineteenth-century view, but as a continuing struggle among various domestic and international interests. For most of Soviet history international relations were seen as the class struggle waged in the international arena in the form of the contest for global dominance between imperialism and socialism. Under Stalin the theory of the 'two camps' saw the world polarized around two hostile axes, neither of which could destroy the other, and so war was inevitable. The associated theory of capitalist encirclement helped explain the ideological inconsistency between hopes of the withering away of the state and its monstrous strengthening under Stalin. Neither theory altogether precluded a notion of peaceful coexistence, since Soviet foreign policy has always aimed at securing the best possible conditions for the building of socialism at home and abroad. As in domestic ideology, Marxist-Leninist doctrine is combined with great-power nationalism to sustain the hybrid Soviet ideology as the legitimating and motivating force of policy-making and popular support. Ideology is not the determining but a conditioning factor in Soviet foreign policy.

Another view would see Soviet foreign policy as the straightforward defence of national interest in which ideology plays a subordinate role. As Churchill put it in a radio broadcast of 1 October 1939, 'I cannot forecast to you the action of Russia. It is a riddle wrapped in a mystery inside an enigma; but perhaps there is a key. That key is Russian national interest.' It was at this period that the USSR was maintaining a pact with its sworn ideological enemy, Nazi Germany. The concept of national interest is a contentious one, since policy-making is rational calculation of interest at any particular time. There is no final court of appeal which can establish what in the long term comprises national interest.

A common view of Soviet foreign policy sees it as driven by a relentless opportunism which exploits and exacerbates regional conflicts for its own ends. Such a view is not incompatible with the opinion which regards Soviet policy as simply crisis management, a reactive approach to developing challenges. This minimalist view of policy processes gives little scope for leadership initiative or long-term strategic goals. Soviet foreign policy can be seen as the search for recognition and equality in the world order of sovereign nation states. This it has largely achieved, and its aim now is to gain a commensurate status in the management of the evolving international system.

Another view sees the Soviet Union as an authoritarian system in which the external threats, real or imagined, are required by the power system to justify its own dominance over the polity. An ambitious foreign policy serves to redirect the force of popular frustrations from domestic shortcomings to an external foe. The constant threat of the 'enemy without', imperialism, justifies repression against the 'enemy within' and the maintenance of the security state.

These views of the factors contributing to Soviet foreign policy are reflected in three major models of how the Soviet Union deals with foreign-policy decisions. The first is the counterpart of totalitarianism applied in international relations, the rational actor model (RAM) located in the realist school of foreign policy analysis. It thinks in terms of a single centralized monolithic policy-making process which plans foreign policy moves and responses. This centre is considered unbuffeted by departmental, institutional, or interest-group pressures and devoid of personality. The model plays down disagreements within the Soviet foreign policy establishment. The RAM model suffers from conflating centralization of policy-making with the suggestion that policy outcomes will therefore be rational. Under Stalin the Soviet foreign policy process was highly centralized, but Stalin's policies were not thereby any more coherent.

The pluralist model takes the opposite view and considers foreign policy the outcome of the interplay of interest groups. In this organizational processes model decisions emerge out of political bargaining between various bureaucratic and specialist groups. Brezhnev's consensual style of policy management certainly encouraged this tendency. The implication is that decisions are not always rational but the result of a particular balance of forces at any one time. A group's ability to forward its own interests can count for more than the long-term interests of the Soviet Union. The military clearly occupied this role under Brezhnev. But as with interest-group theory in general there is a tendency to exaggerate the cohesion of groups, although the theory when applied to the West does include bargaining within organizations. The military itself is probably divided over policy choices. Furthermore, the autonomy of the decision-making centres from social or institutional interests tends to be underrated. Even under Brezhnev the decision-making process was not disjointed or fragmented among individuals and groups but remained firmly in the hands of the Politburo.

The style of policy-making does not necessarily have any automatic effect on the type of policies that emerge. Consensual pluralism, for example, does not mean that Soviet foreign policy becomes more conservative or marked by greater restraint. The decision to invade Czechoslovakia in August 1968 is a classic case of policy resulting from the vigorous interplay of bureaucratic institutions and personalities. With his own position apparently in jeopardy, Brezhnev was forced to side with the emerging consensus view of the military, KGB, and party leaders in the western USSR afraid of being contaminated by 'socialism with a human face'. One can assume, however, that interests such as agriculture or consumer industries are in favour of a less ambitious foreign policy.

The third model takes a mid-path and suggests an emerging controlled pluralism in which interest groups do express certain views but within strict limits. In the political bargaining model policy outcomes are dependent on the interplay of the participants and what is acceptable as a politically viable solution. This sort of pluralism can be termed structural bureaucratic and is confined to certain institutions and elites involved in foreign policy formation. This model most closely approximates to Soviet reality.[3]

The new realism in foreign policy since 1985 has been reflected in the modernization of the Soviet foreign policy establishment. The bodies involved in foreign policy-making include the Defence Council and the Ministry of Defence itself, which, with the KGB, provides a major channel for information, monitoring, and formulating policy options. The purge of Soviet military officers in the western military district during the Polish crisis of 1980–1 suggests a taming of military ambitions and influence. The role of the military has been discussed earlier (pp. 113–17) but it is worth stressing that under *perestroika* the emphasis on shifting resources from defence to the modernization of the civilian economy means that military influence on policy formation has declined. The dominance of the military over the arms control process, for example, was broken by the creation of a civilian arms control section within the International Department of the Central Committee Secretariat.

Up to 1988 the CPSU Central Committee Secretariat had departments covering the main foreign policy fields. Together they constituted the nerve centre of decision-making. Gorbachev placed diplomats acquainted with the West in key positions at home. Anatolii Dobrynin, the long-serving Soviet ambassador to Washington, was recalled to Moscow and played a key role at the head of a revitalized International Department, advising on East–West relations. Aleksander Yakovlev, who spent ten years as ambassador to Canada and then headed IMEMO (the Institute of World Economy and International Relations), is now a full member of the Politburo and headed the Secretariat's ideology and propaganda department, and took a keen interest in relations with the Third World. Relations with the socialist world were handled by the Department for Relations with Communist and Workers' Parties of Socialist Countries, headed by Vadim Medvedev. From September 1988 the departments were merged into a new International Policy Commission headed by Yakovlev with the brief to formulate the long-term perspectives of Soviet foreign policy.

To reflect the greater sophistication of Soviet foreign policy since 1985 the Ministry of Foreign Affairs (MFA) under Shevardnadze has been revitalized, including the appointment of the smooth, professional spokesperson Gennadi Gerasimov, to put over the Soviet view. Some of the old absurdities like placing the Australian and New Zealand desks under Britain, the legacy of empire, have been done away with and they are now under a remodelled South Pacific section.

Specialist bodies such as IMEMO and the USA and Canada Institute, long headed by Georgy Arbatov, are increasingly important sources of specialized information and advice to the leadership. The move away from the old obsession with US-Soviet relations has been reflected in the creation of a new Institute of

European Affairs under the USSR Academy of Sciences. The new institute, significantly, will study not only Western but also Eastern Europe. Relations with the East are moving away from the old party-to-party basis towards a broader state-to-state footing. These institutes have played a critical role in the modernization of Soviet diplomacy under Gorbachev.

The politics of security

After 1945 Soviet socialism was no longer restricted to one country but became first a regional and later a global force. The Soviet Union's own role has changed dramatically as it has become one of the superpowers, with a voice and influence matching in many respects that of the United States. The Gorbachev period has seen a spate of unprecedented foreign policy initiatives, particularly in the sphere of arms control. Gorbachev clearly demonstrated that he was neither a prisoner of his foreign policy establishment nor of interest-group pressures. There was a clear desire to exploit new opportunities, to develop trade and technology, to establish a peaceful international environment to allow domestic modernization, and to raise Soviet prestige on the world stage. This can be achieved, the Soviets now believe, by establishing formal limits to East–West competition that go beyond the old formula of peaceful coexistence as a form of the class struggle. Soviet foreign policy is not only being refined but fundamentally reshaped.

Under Gorbachev Soviet foreign policy has come to be dominated by what is called 'the new political thinking' (NPT), which modifies the old approach to international relations. It is motivated by a new sense of the unwinnable nature of nuclear war and by a re-evaluation of *détente*. The strengthening of the military power of the Soviet Union did not on its own automatically strengthen peace, and indeed threatened it. Too much attention and excessive resources were devoted to the military aspects of countering 'imperialism', Gorbachev argued at the June 1988 party conference, leading to the failure to take advantage of new political opportunities in the world. The nuclear threat has been rethought and the idea of 'reasonable sufficiency' advanced, allowing a certain amount of 'disarmament for development'. Deterrence has been played down and to a degree nuclear weapons have been delegitimized.

The new political thinking has prompted a new analysis of the military, economic, and political interdependence between East and West. Above all, the emphasis is on the interdependence of the human race for survival, accompanied by the stress on international economic security. At the same time the 'correlation of forces' is no longer seen as ineluctably tilting in the USSR's favour. Peaceful coexistence and *détente* were underpinned by the Soviet belief that the long-term struggle between the two systems would inevitably be won by the progressive forces led by the USSR. The evaporation of the old optimism has encouraged the new realism of the NPT. This has been accompanied by modifications to the notion of 'imperialism', which is no longer seen in quite the same stark terms as previously. Against the background of the idea of interdependence there are hints that inter-system rivalries have moderated, allowing the development of more positive relations.

The new political thinking has modified the Soviet view of international relations. It no longer sees them as the playing out of the class struggle in the international arena, and, instead of emphasizing what divides the world, focuses on the world's common problems. The role of the USSR in the world has begun to be rethought. However, the new thinking is not universally accepted. Ligachev, for example, has constantly stressed that Soviet diplomacy should continue to base itself on the 'class character of international relations'. Despite this, there is no doubt that the post-war pattern of Soviet foreign policy has begun to change.

Just as there is no single motive to Soviet foreign policy, there is no single focus either. Soviet decision-makers are faced by a multiplicity of issues and problems. At the top of the list in the 1980s was the debate between economic reform and military commitments. The achievement of the Soviet Union's global status has been at huge domestic cost in financial and political terms. Shevardnadze has talked in terms of what can be called *khozraschët* in the international sphere: making foreign policy more cost-effective by avoiding wasteful expenditure on defence and excessive foreign commitments. The defence sector, the nineteenth party conference resolved, must concentrate on improving quality through science and technology, not on quantity alone. The central question remains whether the economic reform programme is compatible with the existing levels of spending on armaments. The Soviets maintain that their armed forces can be modernized within the existing defence budget.

Closely related is the crucial issue of arms control. Gorbachev's overriding aim is to free economic and foreign policy alike from the burdens imposed by the arms race. The nuclear threat has meant, in Gorbachev's words, that 'the human race has lost its immortality'. This understanding, together with the decline of the old optimism that history was working in the Soviet Union's favour, has led to a shift away from the view that peace could be assured only by the advance of socialism and that, on the contrary, peace was a condition of socialist development. The new emphasis is on 'necessary military sufficiency' for defence rather than an open-ended commitment to military expenditure. The Strategic Defence Initiative, however, struck directly at this doctrine by extending the arms race to space and converting it into a race of technologies. The START negotiations face formidable obstacles because of the complexity of the issues involved and the balance to be drawn between nuclear and conventional forces. The NPT has opened the door to fruitful talks, since the Soviets now accept the need for deep, and not necessarily symmetrical, cuts in weaponry and the need for extensive verification.

Another major concern of Soviet foreign policy is more narrowly the relationship with the United States. Both are guarantors of world security, and have the capacity to destroy not only themselves but the rest of the world with them. Both play a dominant role in their respective halves of Europe. The US has dominated the globe economically and politically, but is now being challenged militarily. The two superpowers have long seen the mirror image of themselves in the other, but there is much evidence that the bipolar structure of international relations that was established at Yalta in February 1945 is declining. The consolidation of the European Community (EC) and the emergence of regional powers such as China and Japan, Brazil and India, create a more complex world. Soviet foreign policy after the Second World War was based on the premise that international relations were determined by two contending camps. The Soviet Union was content to dominate its own camp and tolerated US domination of the industrialized non-communist world since it provided a mechanism for controlling German revanchism and Japanese militarism. Under Andropov there was a shift to a more multipolar view, and under Gorbachev relations improved with Germany, Japan, the EC, and Latin America. The veteran foreign minister Gromyko, the main proponent of the bipolar view, was relieved of his foreign affairs portfolio. The German question is no longer such a divisive issue, and Japan has turned its energies to economic development. There is, however, little to indicate the imminent dissolution of the blocs. However much the Soviet Union diversifies its foreign policy — and it has much ground to make up in that respect — superpower rivalry will remain the dominant theme. A degree of bipolarity will remain a constant in world affairs, though perhaps with less of an ideological edge as it becomes coloured by nineteenth-century balance-of-power diplomacy, no longer confined to the concert of Europe but enacted on a world stage.

Under Shevardnadze Soviet foreign policy has become much more sophisticated. It is no longer as obsessed with its relations with Washington as it was for so many years under Gromyko. A range of regional policies have been developed for most parts of the globe. There is absolutely nothing to suggest that Soviet foreign policy will retreat into some form of 'socialist isolationism'. Closer ties are being established with Western Europe, but the USSR is well aware that overt attempts to drive a wedge between the two wings of the Atlantic alliance would be counterproductive. The Soviet Union is looking to acquire a voice in a Middle East settlement, and to develop multilateral security systems for everywhere from Latin America to South Asia. There has been no scaling down of Soviet ambitions, although they are no longer couched in the messianic terms of world revolution. Gorbachev has increased the range and scope of the global adversarial stance towards the United States. The long neglect of the Pacific basin, for example, was remedied by Gorbachev's sharp reminder in a speech in Vladivostok in July 1986 that the Soviet Union regards itself as 'an Asian and Pacific country'. It is important to remember that Soviet specialist opinion is often divided and hence the Soviet approach to the Third World and elsewhere is less likely to be a single monolithic policy than a more variegated approach.

Soviet relations with the Third World moved into a new phase with the accession of Gorbachev. In the first post-war years the USSR was more concerned with its relations with the West and with consolidating its power in Eastern Europe. Under Khrushchev a new period of activism was launched, and from the late 1960s the Soviet Union was willing to use its growing military power in Africa and Asia. During the interventionist phase Soviet policy appears not to have been the outcome of an expansionist design but the opportunistic exploitation of favourable local and international circumstances, the American disarray following defeat in Vietnam, and the crises in Angola, Ethiopia, and Afghanistan. One of the major factors precipitating America's disillusionment with *détente* in the 1970s was direct Soviet involvement in a number of Third World conflicts. Whether intervention was justified or not is a matter of debate, but in *Realpolitik* terms all that had changed was that Soviet capabilities could now match those of the USA. The Soviet Union had taken advantage of opportunities rather than actively seeking avenues of advancement. However, it became clear to the Gorbachev leadership that Soviet activism in the Third World had hindered other foreign policy efforts, above all relations with the US in the form of *détente*.

Soviet arms sales help to cement political ties but are designed primarily to earn foreign currency. Even where Soviet military or economic assistance has been crucial it would be a mistake to characterize the recipients as 'client states', however limited their room for maneouvre might be. The Soviet Union has to deal with formidable nationalisms from Cuba to Ethiopia and Vietnam. In Afghanistan, however, the revolutionary forces were almost entirely dependent on the Soviet Union. Bitter disputes among warring factions in the ruling party, combined with the nature of the terrain and the dedication of the resistance, led to defeat in what has been called the Soviet Union's Vietnam. By the beginning of the withdrawal of the 'limited contingent' of some 115,000 men in May 1988 Soviet forces had lost 13,310 men killed and 35,478 wounded.

The heavy burden of client states led to a significant shift in Soviet relations with the Third World. Interventionism has given way to a greater concentration on economic relations and domestic reform. The grudging support given to the Sandinista regime in Nicaragua reveals the wish to avoid an onerous open-ended commitment to 'another Cuba'. There is a clear awareness that revolutions require a sufficiently developed economic base to be viable, otherwise they will require Soviet assistance. According to the Rand Corporation the USSR spends up to $40 billion annually in supporting dependent states, rising from $14 billion in the early 1970s. Soviet attention has shifted to the industrializing and newly industrialized countries. In November 1986 *Pravda* warned Third World Marxist movements that violence may no longer be justified in overthrowing capitalism because of the dangers posed by nuclear weapons. The world revolutionary process, in other words, was to be subordinated to Soviet developmental and security needs. Under Gorbachev there is a clear intention to reduce Soviet global military expenditure and to avoid superpower confrontation in the Third World. The weakening of bipolarity is reflected in much greater Soviet tolerance of the Non-aligned Movement.

The relationship of the Soviet Union to the world communist movement has undergone significant changes. The USSR has renounced its claims to be the directing centre, and there is now a degree of acceptance of polycentrism and the idea that each country must find its own road to socialism. Sino-Soviet relations improved steadily in the 1980s as both countries launched ambitious reform programmes. Ideological denunciations gave way to the practical development of economic contacts. Soviet policy has traditionally had two main aims in Eastern Europe: to maintain the cohesion of what used to be called the Soviet Bloc; and to ensure the stability of the individual regimes. These goals are not always compatible, since the enforcement of bloc unity can be destabilizing in terms of popular support. The association of socialism with the state interests of the Soviet Union has undermined the legitimacy of the local governments.

The whole region is suffering from declining economic dynamism. The Eastern European countries hold important lessons for the USSR itself in illustrating that the attempt to 'muddle through' is becoming less of an option and that more comprehensive reform efforts are unavoidable if the aim of regime stability is to be attained. *Perestroika* has led to changes in Comecon — focusing on the development of economic co-operation between member countries, improving its own organization, and working out strategic perspectives for long-term co-operation. The aim of economic integration, espoused by Khrushchev, has been shelved. Joint enterprises between Soviet and East European companies have been launched to share technological expertise, marketing, and resources. Expensive rescue efforts for inefficient alliance partners put an intolerable strain on the Soviet economy's own attempts to reform.

The Soviet link prior to Gorbachev acted as a brake on the political renewal of these countries. Soviet–East European relations were long governed by the principle of proletarian internationalism, which severely limited the policy options and allowed a high level of Soviet interventionism in day-to-day affairs. Contemporary relations are described by the term socialist internationalism, implying a looser form of unity and greater consultation. Alliance dynamics have never been simply the imposition of Soviet views, although the USSR as the senior partner and major supplier of arms has clearly dominated relations. In the Warsaw Pact, as in other areas, the national factor has increasingly cut across broader ties of ideology, institutional structures, and military necessity. The nineteenth party conference propounded the doctrine of 'freedom of choice' for states to choose their own social systems, though the degree to which this will apply to Eastern Europe remains unclear. What is clear is that the old pattern of power politics in the region has given way to attempts to develop a 'socialist commonwealth'.

A shift towards less centralized management of the Soviet economy implies that Soviet–East European relations should be placed on a new footing. The Stalinist concept of direct power may be transformed to one where the Soviet Union is happy to maintain its influence through more informal mechanisms rather than military occupation and party control. The principles governing such a relationship of independence of parties and socialist countries were adopted in the Soviet-Yugoslav declaration of March 1988 at the end of Gorbachev's visit. The declaration represented a formal repudiation of the Brezhnev doctrine of limited sovereignty. The Soviet leadership under Gorbachev has not repeated the mistakes of the post-Stalin leadership in forcing allied countries to follow each twist and of Soviet domestic struggles. *Glasnost* had not yet had the same impact on Eastern Europe as destalinization, although the communist world cannot ignore the reform process. Gorbachev's policy has been to allow indigenous leaderships to maintain their own stability, though hinting that the stability can be better achieved by timely economic and political reforms. Even Vietnam, long suffering from a particularly virulent and typically disastrous form of war communism, has begun to talk about reform. Changes are complicated by the fact that, while the succession in the Soviet Union may have been settled, the rest of the communist world is undergoing a prolonged replacement of the neo-Stalinist generation of leaders.

Prior to *perestroika* the completeness of the USSR as a superpower was questioned. Its military power was not matched by economic creativity or cultural dynamism. While the US has a myriad non-military ways of extending its power and influence, from Coca-Cola culture to computers, Moscow's global status was forced to rely more unequivocally on military power in the absence of the proven success of its economic system or ideology. It was a one-dimensional world power.[4] The Soviet Union learnt that foreign technology can easily lose its effectiveness when deprived of the social relations that gave it birth. Gorbachev's aim is to create the social conditions for the maximum viability of international economic relations. He insists that Soviet foreign policy stems directly from domestic policy.

Soviet foreign policy continues to be dominated by the tension between Soviet nationalism and communism as an international phenomenon. Even at a time of profound reform the question remains of which vision of the Soviet role in the world is most applicable: the 'hawks' of the Riga school who stress 'communist expansionism', or the 'doves' of Yalta who emphasize the legitimate interests of a major state continuing the traditions of Russia. Both views suffer from a narrowness of vision, since it is clear that Soviet foreign policy derives from the complex interaction of ideology and opportunities, elite perceptions and economic realities. Both Gorbachev and Shevardnadze have played down the role of ideology in international relations. Moreover, the freedom of manoeuvre of superpowers in the age of nuclear weapons is limited. Gorbachev has stressed the problems the USSR has in developing its own territories, let alone expanding to control more. Nevertheless, while Soviet policy is undoubtedly defensive in character, the definition of 'defence' is problematical. The USSR has traditionally seen the world as a hostile and alien place and has therefore maintained an aggressive and absolute concept of defence which the rest of the world has seen as threatening. It has been Gorbachev's achievement to tame the world in the perceptions of the Soviet leadership and thus open the door to fruitful diplomacy. The Soviet view of international relations as the class war in the world arena has not been altogether abandoned, yet Gorbachev is the first Soviet leader to have broken out of the narrow definition of Soviet interests to accept the implications of the increasing interdependence and integrity of the world as a global system. Despite this, Soviet perceptions of the world remain within a strong ideological framework which, while not determining foreign policy, creates the framework in which foreign policy is determined.

Notes

1 George Kennan, 'The Sources of Soviet Conduct', *Foreign Affairs*, 25, 4 (July 1947). This article developed the themes of Kennan's 'long telegram' of 22 February 1946.
2 Robert V. Daniels, *Russia: the Roots of Confrontation* (Harvard University Press, Cambridge, Mass, 1985).
3 The three basic models are discussed in D. Simes 'The Politics of Defence in the Soviet Union', in J. Valenta and W. Potter (eds.), *Soviet Decision-making for National Security* (Allen & Unwin, London, 1984), pp. 74–84.
4 See S. Bialer, *The Soviet Paradox: External Expansion, Internal Decline* (Tauris, London, 1986), and P. Dibb, *The Soviet Union: the Incomplete Superpower* (Macmillan, London, 1986).

Key texts

Light, Margot, *The Soviet Theory of International Politics* (Wheatsheaf, Brighton, 1987)
Nogee, J.L., and R.H. Donaldson, *Soviet Foreign Policy since World War II*, 3rd edn (Pergamon, New York, 1987)
Rubinstein, Alvin Z., *Soviet Foreign Policy since World War II: Imperial and Global*, 2nd edn (Little Brown, Boston and Toronto, 1985)
Ulam, Adam, *Expansion and Coexistence: Soviet Foreign Policy, 1917–1973* (Holt Rinehart & Winston, New York, 1974)
Valenta, J., and W. Potter (eds.), *Soviet Decision-making for National Security* (Allen & Unwin, London, 1984)

Select bibliography

Bialer, S., *The Soviet Paradox: External Expansion, Internal Decline* (Tauris, London, 1986)
Bialer, S. (ed.), *The Domestic Context of Soviet Foreign Policy*, 2nd edn (Westview, Boulder, Colo., 1988)
Carr, E.H., *The Twilight of Comintern, 1930–1935* (Macmillan, London, 1982)
Daniels, Robert V., *Russia: the Roots of Confrontation* (Harvard University Press, Cambridge, Mass., 1985)
Dawisha, Karen, and Phil Hanson (eds.), *Soviet-East European Dilemmas* (Heinemann, London, 1981)
Dawisha, Karen, *Eastern Europe, Gorbachev and Reform: the Great Challenge* (Cambridge University Press, Cambridge, 1988)
Dibb, Paul, *The Soviet Union: the Incomplete Superpower* (Macmillan, London, 1986)
Donald, Robert H., *The Soviet Union in the Third World: Success and Failures* (Croom Helm, London, 1981)
Duncan, W.R., *The Soviet Union and Cuba: Interests and Influence* (Praeger, New York, 1985)
Edmonds, R., *Soviet Foreign Policy: the Brezhnev Years* (Oxford University Press, Oxford, 1983)
Garthoff, Raymond, *Détente and Confrontation: American-Soviet Relations, Nixon to Reagan* (Brookings Institution, Washington, D.C., 1985)
Gelman, Harry, *The Brezhnev Politburo and the Decline of Détente* (Cornell University Press, Ithaca, N.Y., 1984)
George, Alexander L. (ed.), *Managing US-Soviet Rivalry* (Westview, Boulder, Colo., 1983)
Girardet, E.R., *Afghanistan: the Soviet War* (Croom Helm, London, 1985)
Gupta, B.S. *Afghanistan: Politics, Economy and Society* (Pinter, London, 1985)

Haigh, R.H., *et al.* (eds.), *Soviet Foreign Policy, the League of Nations and Europe, 1917–39* (Gower, Aldershot, 1986)

Halliday, Fred, *The Making of the Second Cold War*, 2nd edn (Verso/NLB, London, 1986)

Haslam, Jonathan, *The Soviet Union and the Struggle for Collective Security in Europe, 1933–1939* (Macmillan, London, 1984)

Hoffman, E.P., and F.J. Fleron (eds.), *The Conduct of Soviet Foreign Policy* (Aldine, Chicago, 1980)

Holloway, David, *The Soviet Union and the Arms Race*, 2nd edn (Yale University Press, London and New Haven, Conn., 1984)

Hough, J.F., *The Struggle for the Third World: Soviet Debates and American Options* (Brookings Institution, Washington, D.C., 1986)

Kanet, R. (ed.), *Soviet Foreign Policy and East–West Relations in the 1980s* (Praeger, New York, 1982)

Kanet, Roger E. (ed.), *Soviet Foreign Policy in the 1980s* (Praeger, New York, 1982)

Kanet, Roger E. (ed.), *The Soviet Union, Eastern Europe and the Third World* (Cambridge University Press, Cambridge, 1988)

Laird, Robbin F. (ed.) *Soviet Foreign Policy* (Proceedings of the Academy of Political Science, New York, 1987)

Laird, Robbin F. and Erik P. Hoffmann (eds.) *Soviet Foreign Policy in a Changing World* (Walter de Gruyter, Berlin and New York, 1986)

Lynch, Allen, *The Soviet Study of International Relations* (Cambridge University Press, Cambridge, 1987)

McCauley, Martin, *The Origins of the Cold War* (Longman, London, 1983)

Medvedev, Roy, *China and the Superpowers* (Blackwell, Oxford, 1986)

Papp, Daniel S., *Soviet Perceptions of the Developing World in the 1980s: the Ideological Basis* (Lexington Books, Lexington, Mass., 1985)

Pick, Otto, *Soviet Foreign Policy: an Analysis of Power and Ideology* (Wheatsheaf, Brighton, 1987)

Pike, D., *Vietnam and the Soviet Union: Anatomy of an Alliance* (Westview, Boulder, Colo., 1987)

Pravda, Alex, *Soviet Foreign Policy Priorities Under Gorbachev* (Routledge, London, 1988)

Saivetz, Carol R., and Sylvia Woodby, *Soviet–Third World Relations* (Westview, Boulder, Colo., 1985)

Shearman, P., *The Soviet Union and Cuba* (Routledge, London, 1987)

Shearman, Peter, 'Gorbachev and the Third World: an Era of Reform?', *Third World Quarterly*, 9, 4 (October 1987), pp. 1083–117

Shearman, P., and Phil. Williams (eds.), *The Superpowers, Central America and the Middle East* (Brassey's, London, 1988)

Simes, Dimitri K., 'Gorbachev: a New Foreign Policy?', *Foreign Affairs*, 65, 3 (1987), pp. 477–500

Steele, Jonathan, *The Limits of Soviet Power* (Penguin, Harmondsworth, 1985)

Stevenson, R.W., *The Rise and Fall of Détente* (Macmillan, London, 1985)

Terry, S.M. (ed.), *Soviet Policy in Eastern Europe* (Yale University Press, New Haven and London, 1984)

Valkenier, Elizabeth, *The Soviet Union and the Third World: the Economic Bind* (Praeger, New York, 1983)

White, Stephen, *The Origins of Détente* (Cambridge University Press, Cambridge, 1986)

Williams, P., and M. Bowker, *Superpower Détente* (Routledge, London, 1988)

Yanov, A., *Détente after Brezhnev: the Domestic Roots of Soviet Foreign Policy* (University of California Press, Berkeley, Cal., 1977)

Yergin, D., *The Shattered Peace: the Origins of the Cold War and the National Security State* (Houghton Mifflin, Boston, Mass., 1977)

Chapter fourteen

Nationality politics

The Tsarist empire was dubbed by Marx 'the prison house of peoples', and yet the Soviet Union has recreated a multinational state made up of some 126 nationalities and over 200 languages. Only a few of the peoples, however, make a significant impact on the Soviet polity. According to the 1979 census there were twenty-three ethnic groups with over a million members (see Table 8), fifteen of whom have their own union republics. The political repercussions of the existence of such a state in an era of nationalism and the dismemberment of empires has been

Table 8 Ethnic composition of the population

		No ('000)			as % of total population	
		1959		1979	1959	1979
	Total population	208,827		262,085	100	100
1	Russians	114,114	(1)	137,397	54.6	52.5
2	Ukrainians	37,253	(2)	42,347	17.8	16.2
3	Uzbeks	6,015	(4)	12,456	2.9	4.8
4	Belorussians	7,913	(3)	9,463	3.8	3.6
5	Kazakhs	3,622	(6)	6,556	1.7	2.5
6	Tatars	4,968	(5)	6,317	2.4	2.4
7	Azerbaidzhanis	2,940	(7)	5,447	1.4	2.1
8	Armenians	2,787	(8)	4,151	1.3	1.6
9	Georgians	2,692	(9)	3,571	1.3	1.4
10	Moldavians	2,214	(12)	2,968	1.1	1.1
11	Tadzhiks	1,397	(16)	2,898	0.7	1.1
12	Lithuanians	2,326	(10)	2,851	1.1	1.1
13	Turkmenians	1,002	(19)	2,028	0.5	0.8
14	Germans	1,620	(13)	1,936	0.7	0.7
15	Kirgiz	969	(22)	1,906	0.5	0.7
16	Jews	2,268	(11)	1,811	1.1	0.7
17	Chuvash	1,470	(14)	1,751	0.7	0.7
18	Latvians	1,400	(15)	1,439	0.7	0.5
19	Bashkirs	989	(20)	1,371	0.5	0.5
20	Mordvinians	1,285	(18)	1,192	0.6	0.5
21	Poles	1,380	(17)	1,151	0.7	0.4
22	Estonians	989	(21)	1,020	0.5	0.4

Notes: Figures in brackets refer to ranking order in 1959. Figures for 1979 refer to the permanently resident population as distinct from the population resident on the day of the census, 17 January 1979. The table excludes the 1.66 million ethnically heterogeneous Dagestanis.
Sources: *Narodnoe khozyaistvo SSSR v 1959 godu* (Moscow, 1960), p. 14; *SSSR v tsifrakh v 1986 godu* (Moscow, 1987), p. 32. *Chislennost' i sostav naseleniya SSR* (Moscow, 1985), p. 71.

much debated and posed in terms of whether there is a nationality problem in the Soviet Union. The Soviet view is clear. The revised party programme adopted in 1986 proclaimed that 'The national question, a legacy of the past, has been success- fully solved in the USSR.' This somewhat dismissive view was modified by the Soviet leadership in the light of the many contentious issues in nationality politics revealed by *glasnost*.

National sensitivities were exposed by the ousting of the long-time head of the party organization in the Kazakh republic, D. Kunaev, in December 1986 and the 'parachuting in' of a Russian replacement, G. Kolbin, leading to riots in which several people died. At the January 1987 CC plenum Gorbachev spoke with obvious concern about the threat to the integrity of the USSR posed by nationalist groups. Demonstrations in the Baltic republics from 1987 illustrated the strength of national feeling in areas with recent memories of independent statehood. The vote of the Supreme Soviet of the Nagorno-Karabakh autonomous region in 1988 to leave Azerbaidzhan to unite with Armenia revealed the implications of political democratization on nationality issues. Such incidents, however, may only represent the attempt to resolve long-suppressed grievances and do not necessarily signify catastrophic crisis tendencies in the multinational state. They do nevertheless indicate that nationality issues require a constant high level of attention by Soviet leaders.

Soviet constitutions and federalism

In his pamphlet of 1916, *The Socialist Revolution and the Right of Nations to Self-determination*, Lenin argued in favour of self-determination for peoples, in part to encourage the break-up of the old empires. His view that class should take precedence over national interest gave rise to the principle of proletarian internationalism. Lenin remained loyal to this internationalist vision of socialism during the First World War, in contrast to the compromises with nationalism reach- ed by many other socialist leaders. After the Russian revolution the long-run aim was not merely to draw the Soviet peoples together but to bring about their merger. This distinction Lenin drew between the 'drawing together' (*sblizhenie*) of nations and their 'merger' (*sliyanie*) is crucial for later developments.

Soviet constitutions

The first years of Soviet power were marked by debates over the form that the new republic should take. The July 1918 constitution created a federal state, though within a centralized administrative framework, known as the Russian Soviet Federated Socialist Republic (RSFSR), covering the Russian heartlands. By the end of the civil war most of the historical lands of the old Russian empire were under Soviet control (with the exception of Poland, the Baltic republics, Finland, and the Far Eastern republic of Tuva), and hence the problem arose of how to administer the territory now under Soviet rule. Stalin, the long-time Bolshevik specialist on national affairs and Commissar of Nationalities, envisaged a unitary state with some autonomy for the regions and nationalities (the autonomization plan). This would have made the regions units of a centralized Soviet state. Stalin insisted that the minority peoples should not be allowed to regress to a more backward system once they had become socialist. Hence, he argued, there was no need for the self-determination as earlier propounded by Lenin. The communist party itself was organized on unitary principles, with its centre in Moscow and branches in the republics. Attempts by the Ukrainian Bolshevik party in 1920 to achieve some autonomy were vigorously suppressed by the Moscow leadership. Lenin rejected Stalin's autonomization plan, bitterly distressed as he was at the time by the Great Russian chauvinism displayed by Stalin towards the Georgian communists, and insisted on the association of formally equal nations in a federal system.

Table 9 Nationality regions of the USSR

Union republics	Autonomous republics ASSR	Autonomous oblasti (regions)	Autonomous okruga (districts)
USSR			
RSFSR	Bashkir	Adyegai	Agin-Buryat
	Buryat	Gorno-Altai	Komi-
	Chechen-Ingush	Jewish	Permyatskii
	Chuvash	(Birobidzhan)	Koryak
	Dagestan	Karachai-	Henet
	Kabardino-	Circassian	Taimyr
	Balkir	Khakas	Ust-Ordyn-
	Kalmyk		Buryat
	Karelian		Kanty-
	Komi		Mansiiskii
	Mari		Chukotskii
	Mordvin		Evenk
	North Ossetian		Yamalo-
	Tatar		Nenet
	Tuva		
	Udmurt		
	Yakut		
Ukraine			
Belorussia			
Moldavia			
Transcaucasia			
Azerbaidzhan	Nakhichevan	Nagorno-	
		Karabakh	
Georgia	Abkhazian	South	
	Adzharian	Ossetian	
Armenia			
Central Asia			
Uzbekistan	Karakalpak		
Kazakhstan			
Tadzhikistan		Gorno-	
		Badakhshan	
Kirgizstan			
Turkmenistan			
Baltic			
Lithuania			
Latvia			
Estonia			

The Union of Soviet Socialist Republics (USSR) came into being in December 1922, and its creation was marked by the implementation of a new constitution in January 1924 which outlined the system which remains at the base of Soviet federalism today. It was not as loose a federation as the USA, Canada, or Australia, and the central authorities in Moscow reserved certain powers, such as the right to declare war, enter into treaties, and develop a general economic plan for the country as a whole. The guiding principle of Soviet federalism, as Stalin put it, was to be 'national in form but socialist in content'. The right to secede was only nominal. The structure of the USSR is replicated at lower levels, since some of the constituent republics are themselves federated (see Table 9). The fifteen 'union republics' in principle have the right to manage their own affairs, and even the right of seceding from the union. The twenty autonomous Soviet socialist republics (ASSR) belong to one or another union republic and are populated by national minorities. Their rights include a degree of local self-management and they are represented in the affairs of the local republic and on the Soviet of Nationalities of the USSR Supreme Soviet. The eight autonomous regions (*oblasti*) and ten autonomous districts (*okruga*) represent enclaves of national minorities and have few powers to manage their own affairs.

In the 1920s nationality politics was conducted in a relatively tolerant climate. A Latinized alphabet was devised for the Turkic languages of the Central Asian peoples to replace the Arabic script, on the pattern adopted by Turkey itself. However, with the consolidation of Stalin's dominance, even though he was a Georgian, nationality policy took on a more chauvinistic and Russian face. The Turkic peoples were compelled to change their alphabet yet again and adopt the Cyrillic script. A peculiarly Stalinist cult of Russian glory was inflated, and the historical and cultural traditions of minority peoples were undermined. Marxism-Leninism was combined with Soviet communism on the basis of a distinctively Russian version of the substance of Soviet nationalism. As in Stalinist Eastern Europe after the war, national cultures were reduced to folklore, and intellectual traditions that proved intractable were repressed. The accord with Russian nationalism and the church during the Second World War proved temporary, but it ensured the identification of Soviet power with Russian national interests. Stalin's Russification policy was pursued not out of respect for Russian traditions but for perceived state interests.

Under Khrushchev policy emphasized the imminent merger (*sliyanie*) of nationalities. The concept of the new Soviet person was promoted as a supranational entity whose loyalty to the socialist commonwealth would take precedence over ethnic affiliation. The concept of *rassvet*, of cultural unification on a higher level, joined the lexicon of Soviet nationality policy. Economic concerns also encouraged closer national integration, since the existing republican boundaries were not logical from the point of view of economic planning.

The tension between ethno-federalism and a unitary state planning for the whole country was reflected in the discussions from 1959 leading to the adoption of the 1977 constitution. Certain officials sought to change the system on the grounds of institutional parallelism, unclear jurisdictional boundaries, and the fact that demographic changes had made several titular nationalities minorities in their own republics, as in Kirgizia and Kazakhstan. Brezhnev admitted that proposals had been made to abolish federal divisions in favour of a unitary state, but fears of an ethnic backlash and charges of Russification prevented their implementation. The sensitivity of national feelings was starkly revealed over the language issue in the Caucasian republics (Georgia, Armenia, and Azerbaidzhan). Earlier local constitutions had stipulated that the national language was the 'state language of the republic', whereas the new draft republican constitutions implied that official status should be shared with Russian. The proposals evoked a sharp response, including demonstrations in Tbilisi in April 1978 in which a reported 20,000 demonstrators took to the streets, demanding the restoration of Georgia to its former status. In an unprecedented concession to popular forces, the demonstrators achieved their demands in the three republics. The Brezhnev period as a whole saw the strengthening of ethno-federalism as the dominant mode of managing the national question. A centralizing ethos, however, ensured that republican powers were left vague while those of the union were consolidated, especially in economic affairs. The institutional groundwork was laid for the 'drawing together of nations' (*sblizhenie*). The federal structure was retained as a concession to national feelings and did not contradict the goal of integration.

Soviet federalism

The Soviet constitution recognizes a large degree of local autonomy, and yet because of the superimposition of various overlapping administrative structures, between whom there is no clear demarcation, local autonomy is often weakened. The ministerial system, for example, is highly centralized and allows little scope for the republican or union-republican ministries. The rights of the republics are always subordinate to the larger interests of the Soviet state. As in other areas, the ethos of Soviet federalism is democratic centralism.

The definition of a nation or nationality group put forward by Stalin in 1913 remains the Soviet view today: 'A nation is a historically constituted and stable community of people formed on the basis of a common language, territory, economic life, and psychological make-up, revealed in a common culture'. However, the criteria for inclusion as a republic established by Stalin in 1936, when some autonomous republics were elevated to union republic status excluded some nationalities which fitted this description. He listed three necessary factors for becoming a republic: (i) sufficient population, considered to be over one million; (ii) compactness of population, which excluded the Jews, who were scattered throughout the USSR; and (iii) location on the borders of the USSR in case of secession. This provision excluded the Tatars and Bashkirs, who in terms of size and compactness of population deserved to become republics. It has also been suggested that these criteria were supplemented by whether peoples had resisted Soviet power, as in Central Asia, or had accepted the change relatively peacefully

(Tatars and Bashkirs) and thus posed no threat. The fragility of Soviet constitutional guarantees of the rights of republics and peoples was demonstrated by the wholesale deportations during the Second World War and the summary dissolution of the Finno-Karelian republic by Khrushchev in 1956 once hopes were abandoned of the incorporation of Finland into the Soviet Union.

The right to secede remains a legacy of early Bolshevik ideas on the national question. It is a symbolic right and underlines the claim of the 1977 constitution that union republics are sovereign. Nevertheless, the constitution's emphasis on the unity of the Soviet state makes the right virtually meaningless in practice. Since 1957 union republics have had the legal right to enact their own codes of law (a power lost in 1936). The powers in this respect are very limited and are designed to allow some regional variations to take into account local customs and traditions. Compared to American states the budgetary rights of Soviet republics are very weak. They are not permitted to raise taxes other than sales taxes or to dispose of their own revenues. The central government adopts a budget for the whole nation and allocates a share to each republic.

In 1944 union republics were authorized to conduct their own foreign relations and allowed diplomatic representation. The aim was to gain extra seats in the United Nations, being formed at the time. In the event only two republics achieved this right, the Ukraine and Belorussia, which they exercise to this day. The same provisions in 1944 permitted union republics to maintain military forces, albeit with the centre retaining ultimate control. The 1977 constitution dropped all reference to this right, even though all the other symbols of republican sovereignty were retained. The army, like the party, was confirmed as being centralized and unitary.

Soviet federalism today is marked by the notion of a 'new historical community of people' in the process of creation, the Soviet people, in which ethnic feelings should take second place. While the Soviet Union has never accepted the 'melting pot' theory of national assimilation the idea of *sblizhenie* suggests that the family of Soviet nations should be expected to mould themselves to the norms of their Russian 'elder brother'. Notions of Soviet patriotism and socialist internationalism downgrade pride in ethnicity. Nevertheless, at the present stage the government is careful not to force the pace of *sliyanie* and instead talks of 'complete unity' (*polnoe edinstvo*), which excludes biological homogenization. The fear of a 'yellowing' of the Slavic peoples is an element in Soviet policy.

Tensions in the Soviet practice of federalism are apparent. There is a potentially dangerous dualism in a federalism which in practice denies any but the slimmest margins of autonomy to the constituent nationalities and yet provides them with the symbolic institutions and administrative framework of autonomy. Every union republic has the trappings of its own nationhood, which, given the right circumstances, could form the core of a revived independent national identity.[1] This indeed began to occur from 1988 in the Baltic republics and elsewhere. The 'dialectic of nationality' in the Soviet Union therefore entails a considerable emphasis on maintaining the unity and peace of the nation and combating centrifugal tendencies. The heterogeneity of the USSR has acted as a powerful buttress to maintaining a centralized system of government. The fear of centrifugal forces in the polity provides the rationale for maintaining both a unitary party and its dominance over society. Nationalist tendencies also affect the nature and scope of economic reform and political democratization. A formula must be found by the reformers which does nothing to weaken the unity of the state while reflecting the size and diversity of the nation.

Nationalism in the USSR

While the national problem may claim to have been solved in the USSR, the question of what Olzhas Suleimenov calls 'inter-nation relations' remains sharp. Nationalism in the Soviet context is particularly difficult to define. The two entries in the Soviet passport for citizenship and nationality reflect and perpetuate the dual nature of nationality in the USSR. Loyalty to the smaller nationality is encompassed within a broader loyalty to citizenship of the USSR. The smaller nationality is based on ties of language, culture, and tradition, whereas the broader loyalty makes an overtly political appeal to the unity of the Soviet peoples. There is clearly plenty of scope for tension between these two principles and no lack of evidence that they can sometimes erupt into conflict. Manifestations of nationalism can operate in a vertical or horizontal manner: vertically when they are counterposed to the central authorities; and horizontally when they take the form of inter-ethnic rivalry or conflict. The USSR cannot be compared to the Austro-Hungarian, or even the British, empires, which were based on very different dynamics. Rutland goes so far as to argue that it is quite possible that 'national identity can be channelled in ways that are integrative and system-supporting, rather than constituting a purely negative political force'.[2] Just as ethnic pride in the USA does not always pose a political challenge, so a rise in both Russian and minority nationalism does not necessarily threaten the stability of the USSR — and indeed, if managed correctly, might enhance it. Nationalism is an evolving concept, responsive to political and economic developments, and in the Soviet context manifestations of nationalism do not necessarily indicate a major nationality problem.

Rakowska-Harmstone divides nationalism into two categories: orthodox, or within the system; and unorthodox, which in some way challenges the system. The distinction between the two is flexible, with much of the ambiguity deriving from the dynamics of the relationship between Russians and non-Russians. Orthodox nationalism can take many forms, and in contemporary parlance the issue of 'national justice' has become the counterpart of social justice as various peoples seek political justice to redress long-standing grievances. The national elites are permitted within certain bounds to defend the interests of their locality. This can take the form of encouraging acceptable expressions of cultural nationalism, local arts, and traditions. But above all orthodox nationalism takes the form of defending regional economic interests. In a centralized system such as the USSR this is expressed by attempts to achieve some local autonomy to manage the economy, to gain a greater share of investment from the centre, to obtain preferential access to scarce consumer goods, and in general to modify national economic policy to the advantage of the republic.

The national implications of military deployment were illustrated in the case of the war in Afghanistan. The initial assignment of Central Asian forces in Afghanistan proved unsuccessful and they were replaced by non-Moslem forces. Hopes of creating local militia forces founder on the danger that they would be unreliable in case of disturbances in their own areas. During the 1956 riots in Tbilisi following the denunciation of Stalin the predominantly Georgian units in the locality were not used. The worker unrest in Novocherkassk in 1962 could be suppressed only after the local forces had been replaced by loyal troops brought in from outside. Requests by Estonia for its recruits to be deployed in the republic were refused, though a similar request in Kazakhstan was regarded more favourably. Furthermore, demographic changes mean that an increasing proportion of conscripts come from the predominantly rural populations of Central Asia, often with little knowledge of the Russian language or Russian customs.

Investment policy in particular is bound up with national sentiments. If resources are assigned to the Slavic parts of the country the anger of the non-Slavs is aroused, and if to other republics, the Slavs feel aggrieved. Such elite nationalism often merges into unorthodoxy. For example, under Khrushchev Latvian officials

Table 10 Titular nationalities in the USSR

	Population of republic			% urban, 1979	Ethnic composition 1979 (%)	
	1980 (millions)	1987	% increase		Titular nationality	Russian
USSR	264·5	281·7	6·5	63	–	52·3
RSFSR	138·4	145·3	5·0	70	82·5	82·5
Ukraine	50·0	51·2	2·4	62	73·6	21·0
Belorussia	9·6	10·1	5·2	56	79·4	11·9
Moldavia	4·0	4·2	5·0	40	63·9	12·8
Transcaucasia	14·2	16·0	12·7	57		
Azerbaidzhan	6·1	6·8	11·8	53	78·1	7·8
Georgia	5·0	5·8	16·0	52	68·8	7·4
Armenia	3·1	3·4	9·7	66	89·7	2·3
Central Asia	41·0	47·5	15·8	43		
Uzbekistan	15·8	19·0	20·2	41	68·7	10·8
Kazakhstan	14·9	16·2	8·7	54	36·0	40·8
Tadzhikistan	3·9	4·8	23·1	35	58·8	10·3
Kirgizstan	3·6	4·1	13·9	39	47·9	25·8
Turkmenistan	2·8	3·4	21·4	48	68·4	12·6
Baltic	7·4	7·9	6·8	67		
Lithuania	3·4	3·6	5·9	62	80·0	8·9
Latvia	2·5	2·7	8·0	69	53·7	32·8
Estonia	1·5	1·6	6·7	70	64·7	27.9

Sources: Calculations from *SSSR v tsifrakh v 1986 godu* (Moscow, 1987), pp. 28, 32–3; Paul R. Gregory and R.C. Stuart, *Soviet Economic Structure and Performance*, 3rd edn (Harper & Row, New York, 1986), p. 7; M. Ryan and R. Prentice, *Social Trends in the Soviet Union from 1950* (Macmillan, London, 1987), pp. 7, 61.

opposed the expansion of the republic's heavy industry on the grounds that it would lead to the further dilution of the proportion of Latvians in the republic. This led to a purge of top officials. The forecast of local officials opposed to the Virgin Lands Scheme in Kazakhstan that it would mean a vast influx of Russians proved correct and Kazakhs became an even smaller minority in their own republic (see Table 10). In the case of Armenia, however, such considerations were respected and the Erevan underground railway system was built by Russian *Gastarbeiters* (guest workers), housed in tents so that they would not stay after the job was completed. The Ukrainian First Secretary, Peter Shelest, opposed large-scale investment in Siberia and the north on the grounds that it would divert resources from the industrial heartlands of the Ukraine. He also sought to defend Ukrainian intellectuals from persecution by the central authorities, until he was purged himself. Such nationalism is not only manifested by minorities but applies equally to Russians. Politburo members D. Polyanskii and A. Shelepin allegedly headed a 'Russia first' faction, a position which G. Romanov was reputed to share and which may have contributed to his fall on Gorbachev's accession in 1985.

Unorthodox nationalism takes many forms and is reflected in a mass of *samizdat* (self-published) literature, much of which came out into the open with the onset of *glasnost*. As yet most is based on religious, cultural, or historical concerns, and to a lesser extent poses a directly political challenge to existing policies. There has been an upsurge of national self-consciousness focusing on language and ecological issues. It is not restricted to students and intellectuals but penetrates the mass of the population. Much goes beyond the tolerated limits. At the extreme there is the rise of a militant nationalism which challenges the very principles of Soviet federalism. In certain areas there are demands for the independence of certain republics or support for long-standing irredentist demands.

The largest single national group is the Russians, with a population in 1987 of 145·3 million representing 52·4 per cent of the Soviet population. By the end of the century the proportion will have fallen to about 46 per cent, though in reality the ethnic Russian part of the population is already less than half if the number of mixed marriages and children opting to have Russian as the nationality entered in their passport is taken into consideration. This represents a major psychological turning point and emphasizes even more clearly the multinational character of the Soviet Union. The second largest group is the Ukrainians, with 42·3 million (16·2 per cent), and together with the Belorussians at 9·4 million (3·6 per cent) Slavs make up nearly three-quarters of the total population.

Russian nationalism takes many forms and merges from orthodoxy into unorthodoxy. On the right is a tendency that has been called National Bolshevism, derived from Nikolai Ustryalov, who in 1920 reversed the official slogan and argued that the new regime was 'socialist in form, nationalist in content'. Stalinism was imbued with a sense of militant nationalism, but Mussolini was mistaken when he argued that Bolshevism had disappeared in Russia and in its place a Slav form of fascism had emerged. Soviet nationalism on the whole had little in common with the fascist type, since it was not based on the militant projection of one ethnic group at the expense of others. The Russification that did occur was more of an administrative process than an attempt to glorify Russia proper. Modern national Bolsheviks praise the Soviet regime for having recreated the old Russian empire and restored Russia to great-power status. There is an element of truth in the assertion that Soviet patriotism is a veneer over Russian nationalism, if a particularly eviscerated form of nationalism is understood. The extreme right stress the racial purity of the Slavs in language couched in antisemitic allusions and imbued with militaristic patriotism. They are particularly harsh in warning against the Chinese threat.

The conservative nationalists, such as the group around the Molodaya Gvardiya publishing house of the Komsomol organization, can be characterized as Russites but not quite neo-slavophiles, since they lack a religious element. They worked within the establishment and were shielded by Polyanskii and allegedly by the KGB, since they served as a counterweight to unorthodox Russian nationalists who focused on religious or human rights issues. The semi-fascist and antisemitic features of this tendency represented morbid symptoms of the stifling immobility of the later Brezhnev years. The atmosphere was much refreshed by Gorbachev's opening of the windows, the restraint of the KGB, and a restoration of a sense of movement. Alexander Yakovlev had been 'exiled' to Canada for his struggle against Soviet Russophilism in 1973, and was brought back and made a member of the Politburo and the Secretariat with responsibility for ideology and propaganda. Under *glasnost* a number of 'historical-patriotic' groups among ethnic Russians have emerged such as Pamyat (Memory), Otechestvo (Fatherland) and Spasenie (Salvation). These groups find their support among intellectuals and, perhaps surprisingly, among scientists and seek to explore aspects of Russia's spiritual and historical identity. With the departure of their more moderate members to the mushrooming independent *neformaly*, groups such as Pamyat have taken on a distinctly antisemitic tone. Alexander Yanov has argued that the alleged erosion of Marxist-Leninist ideology will not automatically give way to the triumph of Western, rationalist, or liberal ideas but instead clears the space for a variety of nationalist ideas and permits a revival of the Slavophile *v.* Westernizers debate of the nineteenth century over the role and path of Russian development. A so-called Russian party, the fusion of unofficial and official Russian nationalism, might come together as the basis of an authoritarian but 'sanitized' (non-Marxist-Leninist) form of a new ruling ideology.[3]

The moderate orthodox nationalists are represented by the 'village school' of Russian writers such as Vladimir Soloukhin, the author of *Vladimir Back Roads*, and Valentin Rasputin, who has actively campaigned on ecological issues, joined by the painter Ilya Glazunov. They criticize the over-rapid pace of industrialization, which has caused great harm to the environment and village life. The Moscow headquarters of the All-Russian Society for the Preservation of Historical and Cultural Monuments is familiarly known as the 'Russian club' for its exposition of Russian nationalist sentiments. On certain issues this tendency has mobilized as a powerful lobby, notably to protest against the environmental degradation of Lake Baikal by cellulose plants. Similarly, the widespread anxieties aroused by the scheme to divert the flow of the Siberian rivers from north to south were acknowledged by Gorbachev to have contributed towards the plan's cancellation in August 1986. Major figures such as the Academician D.S. Likhachev have gained official approval to start a fund to preserve cultural artefacts in a Soviet Cultural Fund. In the union republics protests have helped prevent major projects, like the Daugavpils hydro-electric scheme in Latvia, and have provoked a major debate over building the Danube-Dneiper canal in the Ukraine.

Russian nationalism is coloured by the paradox that, while the Soviet state has ensured Russian political pre-eminence, in economic terms the Russian part of the republic is one of the most sluggish (see Table 11). Unorthodox Russian nationalists condemn the persecution of the Russian Orthodox church, the excessive internationalism whose burden is considered to fall excessively on Russian shoulders, the distortion of Russian history, and the imposition of socialist realism in place of Russian romanticism. National Bolshevism is condemned by more religious nationalists for espousing a Russian patriotism without a Christian foundation and being based purely on the great-power status of the Russian part of the Soviet Union. In other words, communism with a national face. Religious nationalists stress that Soviet nationalism is in fact antithetical to genuine Russian traditions. The Russian nationalism incorporated into Soviet patriotism serves to buttress the power system.

Solzhenitsyn argues that Russians must be permitted to play out their destiny without the burden of empire. Liberal nationalists would like to see the conversion of Russia from a military superpower to a spiritual great power which they insist would pose no threat to non-Russians or the outside world. The view is contemptuous of Western democracy but unsparing in its condemnation of Soviet totalitarianism. The authoritarian implications of such views derive from the sense of moral absolutism and the attempt to remove society from politics and instead bind it within an organic theocratic government of justice and order.[4] The All-Russian Social Christian Union for the Liberation of the People (VSKhSON) of the 1960s tried to sustain a uniquely Russian path, not democratic but benignly authoritarian, and endowed with a theocratic vision of Russian uniqueness. These themes were taken up by the journal *Veche*, edited by Vladimir Osipov, which between 1971 and 1974 proclaimed itself the voice of the 'loyal opposition'. It was marked by a liberal nationalism which condemned 'the bureaucracy' and was concerned with the regeneration of Russia based on the church and village traditions and focused on Siberia as the rampart of a reborn nation from which the threats from China and the West could be rebuffed.

If nationalism is strong in Russia itself, the issue is much more intractable in other republics. Non-Russian unorthodox nationalism also takes many forms and in its extreme shape takes on separatist demands. Issues range across cultural and linguistic concerns, job opportunities, and governmental priorities. The Baltic republics have protested against the regime's witting and unwitting Russification policies. Several trials have been staged in Latvia and Estonia of secessionist groups and of groups resisting assimilation. Only 53.7 per cent of the Latvian republic's population in 1979 were ethnic Latvians. During *perestroika* Estonia to a degree declared itself economically independent under the slogan 'regional self-accounting' and struck out in the direction of economic diversification from the old Soviet model. The Estonian 'popular front' in support of reform gained a degree of autonomy, and on the eve of the nineteenth party conference, in 1988, the new party leader stated that he would 'not rule out political pluralism' in his republic to defuse the wave of nationalist unrest. In Lithuania nationalist demands are buttressed by the strong Roman Catholic attachments of the population. The constitutional amendments of 1988 aroused unprecedented assertions of independence and forced Moscow to make concessions to preserve local autonomy.

In Moldavia there has also been much anti-Russian feeling, but the problems in Romania temper the desire to be associated with that country. Nationalist feelings in Belorussia have been weakened by the relative success of the Belorussian economy, and by the somewhat artificial nature of Belorussian nationalism, long divided between Russia and Poland. Ukrainian protest, on the other hand, has been frequent and voluble, especially in the western areas around Lvov taken from Poland in September 1939. Some Ukrainian aspirations have been covertly supported by their political leaders, like Shelest. The Uniate church of Orthodox converts to Catholicism has long been persecuted in the western Ukraine. In 1946 Stalin forcibly merged the Uniates, the Ukrainian Catholic Church, with the Russian Orthodox Church. In the Caucasus Georgian groups have condemned the persecution of the Georgian Orthodox church and the corruption of high officials. There has been some emigration of Armenians but the main effort is devoted to the preservation of their language and culture. Anti-Soviet Armenian nationalism is kept in check by memory of the horrendous massacres perpetrated against them by the Turks in 1915 and by the dispute with Azerbaidzhan over Nagorno-Karabakh (see p. 310). Far from all manifestations of nationalism challenge the regime.

The total population of the five Central Asian republics (Uzbekistan, Kazakhstan, Tadzhikistan, Turkmenistan, and Kirgizstan) in 1987 was 47.5 million, or one Soviet citizen in six. As noted, the area is witnessing major population growth at an average rate of 3 per cent per annum over the last fifteen years compared to the national average of 1 per cent. Single-child families are the norm in the European areas of the USSR, whereas in Central Asia four or five children are common. The birth rate of Uzbekistan in 1983, for example, was double that of the RSFSR, and by 1970 Central Asia provided 20 per cent of all births in the USSR. By 1979 the Turkic peoples as a whole, including Azerbaidzhan, Tatars, and so on, as a share of the total population of 262 million, had increased to 16 per cent and are projected to rise to a quarter by the end of the century. Turkic areas therefore contain a relatively high proportion of the nation's young, and their demographic weight may be reflected in greater assertiveness. The nationalism of the five Asian republics, however, is problematic. It is not clear whether religion (Sunni Islam), language (Turkic), ethnicity (Mongol), or some other factor would act as the unifying force to replace Soviet citizenship for these essentially artificially constructed republics, hewn out of an area marked by centuries of nomadic pastoral herding life.

The social and cultural dislocation engendered by intensive modernization creates opportunities for nationalist or religious appeals. As the only remaining large-scale labour reserve for the Soviet economy Central Asia faces Moscow with the dilemma of either increasing investment to absorb the growing population or to encourage more migration to the industrially developed areas in the western part of the country. The first option would see a further influx of Russian technicians, at least in the short term, and would anger areas deprived of the resources to modernize their ageing plant. The second option is barely viable, since the Turkic populations have been marked by a singular lack of desire to move from their homelands. The planned guidelines to the year 2000 indicate a faster rate of growth in Central Asia compared to the rest of the country (cf. Table 11).

Table 11 Comparative economic development of the union republics

	Per capita nominal income (1978: USSR = 100)	Per capita fixed capital (1975: USSR = 100)	Growth of industrial production (1970 = 100) 1980	1986	Persons having higher or secondary education (1984) per 1,000 aged 10 or over	per 1,000 employed population
USSR	100·0	100	178	224	686	868
RSFSR	100·9	115	174	216	691	863
Ukraine	95·9	90	172	212	681	877
Belorussia	97·9	80	232	323	653	839
Moldavia	89·9	69	205	276	620	811
Transcaucasia						
Azerbaidzhan	63·6	64	220	300	723	886
Georgia	93·6	75	194	264	743	902
Armenia	86·7	73	212	298	749	915
Central Asia						
Uzbekistan	71·6	54	192	256	684	907
Kazakhstan	88·4	102	168	211	678	869
Tadzhikistan	59·5	51	180	224	632	843
Kirgizstan	69·7	60	192	255	665	869
Turkmenistan	75·1	73	173	208	669	889
Baltic						
Lithuania	115·1	101	187	246	626	806
Latvia	113·7	117	164	201	696	855
Estonia	126·9	137	174	207	680	857

Sources: First two columns from Paul R. Gregory and R.C. Stuart, *Soviet Economic Structure and Performance* 3rd edn (Harper & Row, New York, 1986), p. 7; *SSSR v tsifrakh v 1986 godu* (Moscow, 1987), p. 94; last two columns from M. Ryan and R. Prentice, *Social Trends in the USSR from 1950* (Macmillan, London, 1987), p. 74.

Several cases of ethnic disturbances have been reported in Central Asia. In Uzbekistan the Tadzhik minority protested against changes in their internal passports which renamed them Uzbeks. The Bashkirs and Tatars have taken the lead in calling for a pan-Turkic movement to end discrimination by Russians in the economy, religion, education, and arts. The impact of the war in Afghanistan and the revival of Islamic fundamentalism in Iran and elsewhere is not clear, though Moslem Brotherhoods are known to exist. The government under Gorbachev initially responded with a renewed anti-religious campaign against Islam. Anti-Russian demonstrations took place in Tashkent in 1969 and in Alma Ata in 1986 but nationalist feelings are kept in check by the proximity of these areas to China. Mao Zedong's murderous attempts at Sinification of Chinese Turkic minorities and Tibet have enhanced the status of the Soviet model of nationality development. Literacy, health care, and industrialization have been promoted by the Soviet regime and are highly visible, whereas the losses, in terms of the destruction of the old cultural elite, religious freedoms, and old way of life are less obvious.

A major form of unorthodox nationalism is represented by the repatriatory movements, a kind of 'homeless nationalism' made up of various deported nationalities and the Jews. Their indeterminate status in society leads to poor integration into Soviet life (with the partial exception of the Jews), and hence their struggles are at the forefront of the nationality question. In the 1930s a Jewish autonomous region called Birobidzhan was established in the Soviet Far East, lying between two rivers in a sparse and rocky part of Siberia. According to the 1979 census the area contained 10,166 Jews and 170,000 Russians. Clearly the majority of the USSR's 2 million Jews do not consider Birobidzhan their homeland. Soviet authorities insist that Yiddish, and not Hebrew, is the language of Soviet Jews and thus hope to drive a wedge between Soviet Jews and those in Israel. The Jewish movement to leave for Israel (the *aliya* movement) received a massive boost after the Israeli victories in the Six Day War of June 1967. Between 1968 and 1985 265,657 Jews were able to emigrate, the number peaking at 51,330 in 1979 as Congress debated the SALT II accord and whether to grant the USSR most-favoured-nation trading status. Despite the sharp cutback in emigration since the invasion of Afghanistan the *aliya* movement continues. About 400,000 Jews have asked for invitations to Israel but have not formally applied. About 10,000 applied and were refused visas, known as 'refuseniks'; the refusal is usually accompanied by loss of job and by a myriad of petty and not so petty restrictions. Emigration increased and some of the better-known refuseniks were allowed to leave from 1987 in an attempt by Gorbachev to defuse the Jewish issue as part of the arms control process. It must be stressed, however, that the great majority of Soviet Jews are highly assimilated and, indeed, Russified.

The Crimean Tatars have waged a prolonged struggle to return from Uzbekistan and other areas to the Crimean peninsula, from which they were forcibly deported in 1944 for allegedly collaborating with the German invaders. Brezhnev 'rehabilitated' them but did not permit them to return to their homes, now occupied by Ukrainians. Individual Tatars who returned were forcibly removed and returned to Central Asia. They are one of the best organized unofficial groups in the USSR, as was revealed by a series of demonstrations in Red Square in July 1987. The fate of the Crimean Tatars remains one of the outstanding issues in Soviet nationality politics despite the lifting of all restrictions on their movement in 1988. Over a million Volga Germans were deported by Stalin to the East, and though 'rehabilitated' by Khrushchev are not allowed to return to their homes on the Volga. Out of 2 million some 75,000 by 1987 had emigrated, mainly to the Federal Republic of Germany. The Chechens,

Ingush, Balkars, and Karachai Moslem peoples were deported from the north Caucasus between 1944 and 1956. The fate of these nationalities is yet another of the 'blank pages' of Soviet history that is being revealed by *glasnost*. Other expulsions involved a sizeable group of Soviet Koreans, some deported Greeks who have been relatively successful in emigrating to Greece, and the Meskhetians, a Turkic national minority from the Georgian republic who were also deported at the end of the war.

Another manifestation of unorthodox nationalism is the problem of inter-ethnic conflicts, which often take the form of simple racism. In Sumgait in February 1988 such tensions erupted into a full-scale pogrom of Armenians by Azerbaidzhanis in which at least thirty people died. While strongly condemned by official policy, racism is seldom admitted and thus little is done to combat it. At times the regime itself is guilty of officially sponsored racism, as in the confused line drawn between anti-Zionism and antisemitism.

Inter-ethnic conflicts were revealed at their starkest in the struggle over the status of the autonomous region of Nagorno-Karabakh. In 1921 Lenin had promised the area to Armenia, but Stalin reversed the decision in favour of Azerbaidzhan, a region with which he had long been associated, even though the population was 90 per cent Armenian. Over the years the proportion of Armenians fell to 75 per cent and their language and culture were stifled. The onset of *glasnost* allowed the long-standing tensions to emerge, and from February 1988 the area demanded unification with Armenia, from which it is separated by only six kilometres at the closest point. The ensuing struggle represented the most serious challenge to Soviet nationality policy and, in Gorbachev's words, a 'sword at the throat of *perestroika*'. In the course of the struggle communist party authority effectively disintegrated in Nagorno-Karabakh as nationalist organizations, with the overwhelming support of the Armenian population, mounted the most sustained strikes in Soviet history. Since the constitution states that territorial changes can be made only with the agreement of all parties concerned, the conflict seems set to continue. The Supreme Soviet, afraid of setting a precedent, resolutely refused to redraw the country's internal borders.

Like other countries, the Soviet Union at its own peril underestimates the tenacity of nationalist sentiments. The roots of modern nationalism lie in the nineteenth century, but the sources of tension in such areas as the Caucasus reach back not merely centuries but millenia. Nationalism is fed by memories of greatness, of having survived successive invasions and deportations by clinging to religious and cultural traditions. In modern times the urge to autonomy and independence appears unquenchable, yet the social roots and psychological tenacity of nationalism are still little understood.

The politics of nationalism

Regime strategies to manage the multinational Soviet state reflect the Russian substance of Soviet nationalism. To a great extent the problem has been seen as one of managing the relationship between a Russian centre and a non-Russian periphery. The centre in Moscow is dominated by Slavs, and much of the republican machinery of government also. The overwhelmingly Russian leadership has been remarkably successful in managing the tensions inevitably engendered in a multi-national country. The conflict over Nagorno-Karabakh, however, demonstrated that the horizontal dimension in national relations is as important as the vertical relationship between the centre and minority ethnic groups. The government has applied a judicious balance of coercion and concessions to ethnic feelings, but in an era of economic restructuring the problems can only become more acute. The centrifugal tendencies unleashed by marketization and decentralization in Yugoslavia act as a stern warning to the Soviet leadership. Gorbachev frequently stressed that political decisions should be taken in the light of their impact on ethnic relations.

Unity above all is established through the mechanism of party rule. The party, as we have seen, is a unitary body, and although divided into republican parties it is not based on federal principles. The absence of a separate party organization for the RSFSR, and indeed the abolition of the bureau that used to manage its affairs after Khrushchev's ousting, only underline the administrative nature of the fourteen republican parties. In the Politburo Slavs have traditionally been greatly over-represented, although under Brezhnev there was significant minority representation, with the Turkic population represented by Kunaev from Kazakhstan, Rashidov from Uzbekistan and Aliev from Azerbaidzhan. The early Gorbachev Politburo strengthened Russian dominance, lacking a representative from Central Asia and with Shevardnadze the only non-Slav. The pattern underlined the principle that no nationality (or indeed post) has *ex officio* membership derived from holding a specific job. The stress has always been on individual merit, which in effect means suitability as seen from the point of view of the General Secretary. Certain patterns recur, like representation from the Ukraine, but this is convention rather than law.

Party recruitment tries to ensure adequate representation for the nationalities, although there are certain imbalances (see pp. 129–30). In his speech on the sixtieth anniversary of the USSR Andropov argued against mechanical or mathematical affirmative action. Recruitment was to be based on criteria of suitability and the individual qualities of the candidate, rather than by ethnic or other attributes. The over-representation of Russians and under-representation of the Baltic and Central Asian areas seems destined to continue.

The Soviet of Nationalities in the Congress of People's Deputies and the Supreme Soviet provides a ready-made forum for the resolution of nationality issues, yet its limited powers were revealed by the conflict over Nagorno-Karabakh. In response the nineteenth party conference resolved to create a new state body to oversee all aspects of the nationalities question. Greater independence is to be allowed to regions, but only within the federal structure. The management of national issues appears to be shifting from the party to state mechanisms.

A major aspect of nationality management is focused on investment policy and the state-sponsored modernization drive. Constant economic growth, albeit decreasing, has so far to some extent neutralized the sharp edge of the nationality question. The government tries to equalize levels of economic development between republics through the centralized allocation of resources. Economically the least developed regions have gained most from incorporation in the USSR. It has, as noted, created some tension in more advanced areas such as the Ukraine. The onset of economic reform has accelerated local responsibility for economic management, with Estonia advancing towards a form of regional economic accountability (*khozrazchët*).

Economic growth has given rise to rapid upward social mobility. Peasants leave the field, women leave the home (though in small numbers in Central Asia, owing to cultural resistance), and enter factories where they gain new skills and socialization to the demands of industrial life. Whole peoples have moved from yak-hide yurts to high-rise apartment blocks in the space of a generation. In the towns their children gain an education and training in modern skills. National students are a higher proportion in full-time courses than the minority in any republic, indicating a certain degree of preferential access. Expenditure on schools in Central Asia is higher than the national average. The aim is to iron out historic inequalities. While in Central Asia industrial jobs have tended to be taken by Russians, the long-term trend, as an indigenous working class develops, will be towards greater equality in this respect.

Education and language policy reveal a major problem in achieving social mobility in Soviet nationality areas. Advancement is more rapid for those who have adopted Soviet ideology and the Russian language learnt at a Russian school. The 'Khrushchev theses' of November 1958 increased the pressure to adopt Russian as the language of education and intellectual life. Russian is the *lingua franca* of the nation, but local elites are sharply divided over whether it should be used only for conversing with outsiders or for work and study within a non-Russian group. If a Russian was present in a party committee, then discussion was always conducted in Russian, in deference to the fact that it is unlikely that he or she would speak the local language. Estonia led the way in 1988 in rejecting this principle, and now party and soviet business is conducted in Estonian. An obligation for Russians to take courses in the local language acts as a disincentive against taking short-term jobs. Parents have the option of sending their children to elementary or high schools with instruction either in Russian or in the native language, and both are recognized as official languages in each republic. However, one of the major sources of conflict in Nagorno-Karabakh was the lack of provision for schooling in Armenian. In Belorussia the availability of Belorussian-language schools has declined, and in the Kirgizian capital, Frunze, there is only one Kirgiz-language school. In the 1950s republics were given the option of teaching higher education courses in the native language, although it is wasteful to conduct parallel courses in two languages. The concentration of the most prestigious institutes and universities in Moscow means that the most talented of elite offspring spend a period of effective socialization in the capital of the nation.

Economic development and upward social and educational mobility have led to the creation of thoroughly Sovietized local political elites. Russians largely rule the Soviet Union, but the indigenous ethnic elites to varying extents govern their own regions. Having been promoted by the existing system, they tend to have a strong commitment to maintaining it. In view of the careers of Stalin, Mikoyan, Kaganovich, Khrushchev, and Shevardnadze it is clear that non-Russians can rise high in the politics of the USSR. Within a national republic membership of the titular nationality usually confers a definite advantage in obtaining official positions and places in higher educational institutions. This helps explain the unsatisfactory position in leading echelons of national government of Tatars, Bashkirs, Jews, and other nationalities without their own republics. The political rights of non-indigenous nationalities in host republics remains a vexed issue.

The *nomenklatura* system of appointments provides a powerful lever for the centre to manage the nationality issue. Positive or negative discrimination in principle has no place, with allegiance to the Soviet system rather than ethnic identity being the crucial factor in advancement. The major exception is the Jews, who are subject to a range of restrictions and are now largely excluded from diplomatic, foreign trade, and some military posts. There is a conscious attempt to balance the proportion of nationalities but not in a 'mechanical' way. In the national republics Russians are found in many key posts but not usually at the expense of the local elite as a whole. There are great differences between republics, reflecting patterns of historical development, with the Georgians and Estonians, for example, dominating their own hierarchy to a much greater extent than the Central Asian peoples like the Kazakhs or Turkmens.

The influence of native political elites on policy-making also varies. Khrushchev appointed Russians to head the five Central Asian republics, whereas Brezhnev allowed the local elites to dominate to a degree that ultimately proved threatening to central control. Gorbachev reverted to Khrushchev's practice with the appointment of a Russian to head the Kazakh party organization. A Russian is usually appointed as second-in-command and is generally moved on to another posting before developing local allegiances or mastering the local language. An important channel of information for Moscow is provided through the republican KGBs, which are nearly always headed by Russians. Military forces are naturally part of a highly centralized command system. The two years of conscript service in the army act as one of the most effective tools in the creation of a multinational Soviet identity. The creation of a multinational elite whose members are responsible for their own republics acts as a tremendous force for stability, even though the republics have little power. Indeed, one of the republics' major functions is to provide a forum for local social mobility and a framework for local elites to express themselves. It is clear, however, that the latitude allowed under Brezhnev permitted widespread corruption. The crackdown since Andropov, especially in the Caucasus and Central Asia, and the attempt to reassert central control, represent a major political challenge to local elites.

In all the republics, native social elites have emerged whose degree of Sovietization is more uneven than that of their political counterparts. With the destruction of the old intelligentsia by Stalin, the new native intelligentsia and middle class owe their existence and privileges to Soviet power. However, the ability to Sovietize the cultural intelligentsia, who feel themselves the custodians of national traditions, is an ambiguous achievement. The fundamental problem for the Soviet leadership is how to maintain the vitality of the native political and social elites while preventing the emergence of undesirable forms of 'nationalism'.

The internal passport system, established in 1932, acts as a powerful instrument of nationality control. The fifth point on the passport specifies the national identity of the holder in addition to the general rubric of Soviet citizenship. The nationality registered in the passport is determined by either of the parents and is difficult to change. The system erects rigid boundaries between ethnic groups. If nationalism is above all subjective affiliation, then the fact of formal identification for life with a particular ethnic group decided by the parents at birth clearly causes much confusion as felt ethnic identification diverges from that inscribed in the passport. Mobility is always subject to the passport and registration (*propiska*) laws, though there is no evidence that they are used to tie people to their republics. Choice of place to live, like the place of work, is still largely a matter of personal preference, national temperament, or social class. While 96 per cent of all Georgians and 95 per cent of all Georgian graduates live in Georgia, only 51 per cent of Armenian graduates live in Armenia and 44 per cent of Armenians are scattered across the nation. Only 26 per cent of Tatars live in Tataria itself. The Baltic republics tend to retain most of their citizens, while the career patterns of Ukrainians and Belorussians are almost indistinguishable from those of Russians.

Coercive measures are always available to damp down unorthodox nationalist sentiments, and reports from released labour-camp prisoners in 1987 indicated that up to half of all political prisoners were nationalists of one sort or another. This sanction is tempered by its likely effect on international opinion, and in all respects the regime's ability to manage nationality policies is influenced by their effect on the world at large. Armenians have a broad range of links with their compatriots around the world. Relations with the Central Asian republics are watched by the Islamic nations of the Middle East. Central Asian developmental patterns are lauded in the Third World, and contrasted with the brutal policies of the earlier Chinese leadership. However, unresolved problems reflected in the repatriatory movements cannot be kept off the diplomatic agenda. Groups lobbying to emigrate, such as the Jews or Volga Germans, or to return to their homelands, such as the Crimean Tatars, influence the Soviet Union's image abroad and affect the success of its diplomatic initiatives. They are regarded as indices of its human rights violations. International lobbying on behalf of Jews seeking to emigrate, in particular, exerts a powerful hold on American policy-makers.

Soviet ideology provides a supranational rationale for the maintenance of the present structure of national relations. The impact of the ideology of Marxist-Leninist development and guided democracy is refracted through the prism of national political cultures. In the Baltic republics and the Caucasus anecdotal evidence suggests thoroughly Sovietized political elites riding hostile or indifferent populations, whereas in Central Asia the ideology is assimilated into indigenous social patterns. In the USSR even the smallest nationality can share pride in the great-power status and achievements of a mighty state. The Soviet pattern of development has improved standards of living, education, health care, and general social welfare. As long as comparisons are made only with their own past, then the achievements are tangible enough, though very different in Tadzhikistan from Estonia. If comparisons are made with other developing countries, then the successes look less impressive. This does not weigh so heavily, because few before *glasnost* were in a position to make such an evaluation. Comparisons are in any case balanced by a widespread conviction that the level of social justice, in terms of full employment and so on, compensates for the relatively slow rate of economic progress. The onset of economic reforms may disturb this equilibrium. Furthermore, creeping Russification may in the long run provoke a reaction. The Russian people are considered as the 'elder brother' of the republics: a viable proposition perhaps in Central Asia, but counterproductive when applied to the developed regions of the Baltic and the Ukraine. It is particularly galling when history is rewritten to emphasize the progressive role played by Russia in the past, and to highlight the backwardness of the incorporated regions.

One of the aspects of the 'psychological restructuring' under Gorbachev is the attempt to develop a new approach to national relations that eschews paternalistic attitudes in favour of a real fraternity of peoples based less on economic and more on social and cultural equality. The old Marxist reductionism that saw nationality conflict as a legacy of economic underdevelopment has begun to give way to a far more complex understanding of the sources of modern nationalism. The growth in national self-awareness is no longer automatically branded as dangerous. The very concept of a 'Soviet people' has been played down in favour of 'Soviet Russians', 'Soviet Uzbeks', and so on. In recent pronouncements the notion of *sblizhenie* leading to *sliyanie* has been notable by its absence.

Soviet federalism is national in form but supranational in content; but there is always the possibility that it will become national in content also. The dualism which grants the symbols of nationhood to republics while insisting on the supremacy of the central state and proclaiming the aim of transcending national separateness and ethnic identity is an inherently unstable compromise. The major consequence of the duality is that beneath the Sovietization effort there remains a powerful undercurrent strengthening the autonomy of the basic national groups. The institutions of this autonomy replicate almost the entire range of central cultural and economic institutions. They are administered by local indigenous elites on behalf of the central authorities, but there is always the tendency for this to be transformed into management on their own behalf.

The Soviet system is ideally built for crisis management, and the regime has been relatively effective in dealing with the problems arising in a multinational state. The major difficulty for would-be nationalists is that at the root of Soviet nationality policy there is no sustained economic exploitation. While some groups might well feel economically dissatisfied — and indeed few people did very well out of the unreformed economy — there is no systemic economic exploitative mechanism at work at the base of Soviet nationality policy. Furthermore, the process of Sovietization is very different from classical imperial policies such as Russification in the late nineteenth century. While Sovietization weakens traditional patterns, it does not deny a role for redefined national identities within the modernizing Soviet context. Nationalism has been co-opted, and hence the concept of empire to describe the Soviet multinational state is misleading, though for many nationalists subjectively accurate. The dynamics of Soviet nationality relations are between Moscow and the periphery ultimately political rather than ethnic. It is more difficult to build a nationalist movement on political expropriation alone, and this affects all nations equally, Russians included. The smaller nationalities have been able to articulate a sense of cultural grievance but have not been able to prove that they have suffered significantly more than Russians themselves. It is a balancing act, and the regime has been able so far to maintain its control through the mechanisms outlined above. The evidence from Nagorno-Karabakh, the Baltic republics, and elsewhere, however, suggests that it would be rash indeed to suggest that the nationality question has been 'solved'.

Notes

1 S. Bialer, *Stalin's Successors: Leadership, Stability, and Change in the Soviet Union* (Cambridge University Press, Cambridge, 1982), p. 210.
2 P. Rutland, 'The "Nationality Problem" and the Soviet State', in N. Harding (ed.), *The State in Socialist Society* (Macmillan, London, 1984), p. 151.
3 A. Yanov, *The Russian New Right* (Institute of International Studies, University of California Press, Berkeley, 1978).
4 The liberal nationalist view is advanced in the collection by A. Solzhenitsyn *et al*, *From under the Rubble* (Fontana, London, 1976).

Key texts

Carrère d'Encausse, H., *The Decline of an Empire* (Newsweek, New York, 1979)
Conquest, R. (ed.), *The Last Empire: Nationality and the Soviet Future* (Hoover Institution Press, Stanford, Cal., 1986)
Hammer, D.P., 'Russian Nationalism and Soviet Politics', in J.L. Nogee (ed.), *Soviet Politics* (Praeger, New York, 1985), pp. 122–49
Rakowska-Harmstone, T., 'The Dialectics of Nationalism in the USSR', *Problems of Communism*, 23, 3 (May–June 1974), pp. 1–22

Select Bibliography

Agursky, Mikhail, *The Third Rome: National Bolshevism in the USSR* (Westview, Boulder, Colo., 1987)
Allworth, E., *Ethnic Russia in the USSR* (Pergamon, New York, 1980)
Azrael, J.R. (ed.), *Soviet Nationality Policy and Practices* (Praeger, New York, 1978)
Azrael, J.R., 'The Nationality Problem in the USSR', in S. Bialer (ed.) *The Domestic*

Context of Soviet Foreign Policy (Westview, Boulder, Colo., 1981), pp. 139–53

Barghoorn, F., *Soviet Russian Nationalism* (Oxford University Press, New York, 1956)

Bennigson, A., 'Soviet Muslims and the World of Islam', *Problems of Communism*, 29, 2 (March–April 1980), pp. 38–51

Bennigson,A., and M. Broxup, *The Islamic Threat to the Soviet State* (Croom Helm, London, 1983)

Dunlop, John, *The Faces of Contemporary Russian Nationalism* (Princeton University Press, Princeton, N. J., 1983)

Dunlop, John, *The New Russian Nationalism* (Praeger, New York, 1985)

Dzyuba, I., *Internationalism or Russification? A Study in the Soviet Nationalities Problem* (Monad, New York, 1974)

Freedman, R.O., *Soviet Jewry in the Decisive Decade, 1971–1980* (Duke University Press, Durham, N.C., 1984)

Gitelman, Z., 'Are Nations Merging in the USSR?', *Problems of Communism*, 32, 5 (September–October 1983), pp. 35–47

Jacobs, D.N., and T.M. Hill, 'Soviet Ethnic Policy in the 1980s', in J.L. Nogee (ed.), *Soviet Politics* (Praeger, New York, 1985), pp. 150–82

Jones, Ellen, and Fred W. Grupp, 'Modernisation and Ethnic Equalisation in the USSR', *Soviet Studies*, 36, 2 (April 1984), pp. 159–84

Jowitt, Kenneth, *The Leninist Response to National Dependency* (Institute of International Studies, University of California Press, Berkeley, 1978)

Karklins, Rasma, *Ethnic Relations in the USSR: the Perspective from Below* (Unwin Hyman, London, 1988)

Katz, Z. et al. (eds.), *Handbook of Major Soviet Nationalities* (Free Press, New York, 1975)

Krawchenko, Bohdan, *Social Change and National Consciousness in Twentieth Century Ukraine* (Macmillan, London, 1985)

Lubin, Nancy, *Labour and Nationality in Soviet Central Asia* (Macmillan, London, 1984)

Mandel, Scott, *Soviet, but not Russian* (University of Alberta Press, Palo Alto, Alberta, 1985)

Olcott, Martha Brill, 'Yuri Andropov and the "National Question"', *Soviet Studies*, 37, 1 (January 1985), pp. 103–17

Olcott, Martha Brill, and L. Hajda (eds.), *The Soviet Multinational State* (Sharpe, London, 1987)

Pinkus, Benjamin, *The Jews of the Soviet Union: a History of a National Minority* (Cambridge University Press, Cambridge, 1988)

Pospielovsky, Dimitry, 'Russian Nationalism and the Orthdox Revival', *Religion in Communist Lands*, 15, 3 (winter 1987), pp. 291–309

Ramet, P. (ed.), *Religion and Nationalism in Soviet and East European Politics* (Duke University Press, Durham, N.C., 1985)

Rockett, Rocky L., *The Ethnic Nationalities in the Soviet Union: Sociological Perspectives on an Historical Problem* (Praeger, New York, 1981)

Rywkin, M., *Moscow's Muslim Challenge: Soviet Central Asia* (London, 1982)

Simmons, G. (ed.), *Nationalism in the USSR and Eastern Europe in the Era of Brezhnev and Kosygin* (University of Detroit Press, Detroit, 1977)

Ulam, Adam, 'Russian Nationalism' in S. Bialer (ed.), *The Domestic Context of Soviet Foreign Policy* (Westview, Boulder, Colo., 1981), pp. 3–17

Vardys, V.S., *The Catholic Church, Dissent and Nationality in Soviet Lithuania* (Columbia University Press, New York, 1978)

Wimbush, S. Enders (ed.), *Soviet Nationalities in Strategic Perspective* (Croom Helm, London, 1985)

Yanov, A., *The Russian New Right: Right-wing Ideologies in the Contemporary USSR*

(Institute of International Studies, University of California Press, Berkeley, 1978)
Yanov, Alexander, *The Russian Idea and the Year 2000* (Blackwell, Oxford, 1987)
Zaslavsky, Victor, 'The Ethnic Question in the USSR', *Telos*, 45 (fall 1980), pp. 45–76

Chapter fifteen

Resistance and dissent

Political dissent and the state

The emergence of overt dissent following Stalin's death illustrates that the Soviet Union is no longer an oppositionless state, even though it remains a one-party state. Political life is dominated by a single party which tries to monopolize institutional and ideological life, and yet the view of the Soviet Union as a sea of grey immobility and passivity can no longer be accepted. Soviet society is marked by many currents of autonomous activity, including those in favour of continuing destalinization, various trends of intellectual dissent, and elements of working-class resistance. The Soviet regime, as much as those in Eastern Europe, is faced with economic and social challenges which can less and less be contained within the bounds of economic reform alone. Dissent acts as a symbol or litmus test of the degree to which the Soviet Union has changed since the death of Stalin.

Barghoorn points out that dissent is endemic to political systems, but in the Soviet system it tends to be equated with opposition and under Stalin was treated as tantamount to treason.[1] Shtromas distinguishes between those who aim to change the system from within, and those who reject the system, and stresses the importance of the *overt* nature of dissent.[2] The evolution of terms used to describe the phenomenon reflects developments in the movement itself. The term dissent is rather restricted, covering a few thousand active protesters, and associated with disagreement only to certain of the regime's actions or policies. Another common term is opposition, the word used to describe the various tendencies that racked the party under Lenin. Medvedev has revived the term to talk of a 'loyal opposition'. Some of this is tolerated, and indeed some of the demands, since they coincide with the further rational development of the regime, have been taken up. Historically the Leninist form of organization has been authoritarian, but Medvedev argues that the participatory side of Leninism, the side represented by the debates of the early years, will permit the emergence of a modified Leninism, retaining its ambition to guide society but doing so by argument rather than by administrative order. *Dirigiste* commune democracy will give way to a participatory commune democracy. However, the term opposition is not adequate either, since the metaphor of a parliamentary system suggests a movement with an alternative programme wishing to replace the existing government or state. This exaggerates the ambitions of most dissenters.

The term preferred by some activists in the Soviet Union is 'other-thinker' (*inakomyslyashchii*), denoting being of a different mind or heterodox. The strength of this term is that it highlights the ideological challenge posed by such concerns as human rights and religious freedom. It undermines the attempt by officialdom to maintain ideological consensus to buttress its rule. Since the state is the universal employer, resistance has no autonomous socio-economic base. No rising class can couch its own demands in the language of universal truths: the demands of other-thinkers can only be cast in the language of intellectual and social demands. It is primarily cerebral. However, while illuminating an important aspect of regime-society relations, the term is too restrictive in excluding the influence of sociological factors in resistance and the play of social forces.

A far better term (though not without its drawbacks), which covers all groups in society and permits a more subtle gradation of oppositional activity, is the term resistance. The word refuses to accept the ghetto imposed by the term dissent. It suggests that resistance is a widespread phenomenon in Soviet society, taking many different forms, from mild criticism to outright rejection of the system. This definition of dissent encompasses small acts of resistance operating in the 'fifth column of social consciousness', the struggle for personal truth against the universal 'lie' sustained by the propaganda of success and the distortion of the past, to the societal struggle for the restoration of the public sphere, the area of life in which people behave as citizens engaged in free expression on matters of general interest (see p. 164). Resistance, of course, is not universal, but its boundary with the mass participation described in Chapter 8 is blurred. Just as many people participate without enthusiasm, so many resist without becoming dissenters.

Resistance includes all kinds of activities which challenge the prevailing norms and uncritical obedience. Resistance can be political, social, and economic. The second economy, for example, can be seen as a mark of resistance to the exclusivity and inefficiency of the command economy and as representing the emergence of the economic basis of civil society. Resistance can be found from the highest echelons of the party to the caretaker of a block of flats. Whereas overt dissent operates in the public sphere, personal resistance entails fewer risks, but by the same token its impact is less striking, if no less effective in the long run. Personal resistance takes on political significance very rapidly in the Soviet Union. The concept of resistance includes the concept of 'internal emigration', focusing on personal mental and spiritual concerns. It would be inaccurate to describe this as 'private', since much is shared with people of similar beliefs in sub-cultural ties of friendship and has an impact on society as a whole. It is for this reason that the word 'personal' is used in preference to the term 'private'. By putting the individual at the heart of the social project the dissenters seek to regain some of the advances of liberalism. They are re-enacting the centuries-long struggle for the creation of a public sphere.

While Stalin lived dissent was not only brave but suicidal. Under Khrushchev the secret police apparatus was partially dismantled, and the relaxation allowed the thaw to begin. The emergence of overt resistance revealed the strains generated by the command economy and *dirigiste* politics. Khrushchev's secret speech in February 1956 was only the most famous incident in a ferment that was questioning Stalinist orthodoxies. Gradually a cultural opposition emerged, consisting of small groups of students and writers who focused on artistic and intellectual issues rather than on political criticism of the regime. Khrushchev tolerated and to a degree even encouraged such activity as long as it was restricted to condemning Stalinist practices, hoping thereby to strengthen his position against the conservatives. Following the renewed anti-Stalinist campaign at the twenty-second party congress, Khrushchev in 1961 approved the publication of Solzhenitsyn's and Evtushenko's work. This was the high tide of officially tolerated literary opposition, called by Diane Spechler 'permitted dissent', especially in the pages of *Novy Mir*. By the early 1960s the concerns of the critical intelligentsia began to broaden from mainly literary issues to encompass political criticism encouraging genuine destalinization. This was accompanied by the emergence of *samizdat*, or the underground publication of materials bypassing the official censorship. The period saw the emergence of a democratic opposition which focused on political issues.

The last years of Khrushchev saw a clamp-down on dissent, including the trial of the poet Joseph Brodsky in 1964. The new Brezhnev leadership from October 1964 continued the trend towards stifling the opportunities for open criticism. Dozens of intellectuals were tried in the Ukraine in 1965. The attempt to suppress overt resistance culminated in the trials of the writers Andrei Sinyavskii and Yulii Daniel in the spring of 1966. The harsh sentence set the precedent of criminal prosecution for the publication of works abroad (a fate Boris Pasternak escaped for *Doctor Zhivago*). The trial stimulated a new wave of dissent, focused now on questioning the system that had allowed such a trial to take place in the first place. On a modest scale Ted Gurr's ideas on *Why Men Rebel* are applicable here, since the law of 'relative deprivation' ensured that resisters who had become accustomed to certain freedoms compared their status with conditions not under Stalin but under Khrushchev.

The high point of this phase came in 1968, when demonstrations against the Warsaw Pact invasion of Czechoslovakia were accompanied by petitions and the emergence of the *Chronicle of Current Events*. The unifying motif of this activity was the demand for legality, especially for the democratic freedoms of assembly and association, and for the Soviet regime to obey its own laws and constitution. The regime's response was uncompromising but now more subtle, masterminded by Yuri Andropov, who had become head of the KGB in 1967. The partial rehabilitation of Stalin was accompanied by the increased repression of active dissent. By 1972 organized opposition had largely been crushed through a combination of repression and by splits within the resistance. The regime stifled the aspirations of the democratic movement by imprisonment or exile to the West. In 1974 Alexander Solzhenitsyn was exiled and two years later Vladimir

Bukovsky was exchanged for the Chilean communist leader Luis Corvalan.

Repression against dissent only reflected the increasing rigidity of political structures under Brezhnev. In relative terms the years 1972–9 were a period of tolerance, with no large-scale arrests but steady pressure. By choice or by necessity the flower of a generation of Soviet intellectuals were forced out of the mainstream of Soviet life and into menial jobs such as caretakers and stokers. The Jackson-Vannik and Stevenson amendments of 1974 (to Congressional legislation on relations with the USSR) tried to exert pressure on the Soviet government to allow greater Jewish emigration, in part successfully for a time. However, a number of well publicised cases did the Soviet standing in the international community much harm. The arrest of Yuri Orlov in December 1976 was a signal to Washington of Moscow's refusal to be seen to alter domestic policies in response to external pressure. The replacement of the realist approach of Nixon and Kissinger by Carter's idealistic if inconsistent campaign for human rights in 1977 ultimately proved incompatible with the continuance of *détente*. The staging of trials as a snub to Carter's human rights campaign stretched the limits of toleration within the bounds of *détente* to the limit. In 1978 Anatoly Shcharanskii was tried and sentenced on a patently false charge. It showed more than anything the hazards of 'soft linkage', associated with the name of Marshal Shulman, to moderate Soviet behaviour not by direct pressure but by subtle influence, appealing to more 'progressive' elements in the Soviet hierarchy. The policy of 'hard linkage', as expressed through the amendments, however, fared little better.

The suppression or relative toleration of dissent and resistance in the Soviet Union is not a function of the Cold War, as many Western socialists have argued.[3] While the cycle may at times coincide with foreign policy cycles, the Soviet Union has always been careful to preserve its own autonomy and has rejected what it sees as interference in its domestic affairs. In the battle against nonconformity the authorities have been prepared to condone the breaking of their own laws and constitutional provisions. The inability of *détente* to be transformed in the Soviet Union into a genuine breakthrough into respect for Soviet legality and an acceptance of the right of criticism of the regime's actions was one of the major reasons not only for the failure but also for the widespread discrediting of *détente*. A strong case could be made for the proposition that *détente* was lost not, as Brzezinski put it, in the 'sands of the Ogaden' but in the KGB's Lefortovo prison in Moscow. Neither of the superpowers is likely to be willing to see a revival of *détente* in its old form. More than ever it provoked the Euro-communist challenge that democracy was an essential part of the socialist programme. Under Brezhnev the increased consultation of expert and interested opinion in policy-making and a certain tolerance of diversity of opinion on less sensitive issues were unable to offset the increasingly stifling atmosphere.

In mid-1979 the Soviet regime decided to eliminate dissent. Among the reasons for the new hard-line policy was the non-ratification by the US of SALT II, inner-party struggles for the Brezhnev succession, with Andropov above all bidding for power, and the traditional Soviet response of conducting a purge of potential opposition prior to a major international gathering, given the forthcoming Olympics in Moscow in summer 1980. The government clearly considered that it had nothing more to lose with the dissolution of *détente*. The invasion of Afghanistan in December 1979 and the onset of the second Cold War were accompanied by harsh repression, including the exile of the dissident physicist Andrei Sakharov to Gorky, which continued under Andropov and Chernenko.

Gorbachev's early years were marked by several major initiatives towards dissent which improved the international atmosphere and helped pave the way to arms control agreements. Shcharanskii was released in exchange for three Soviet spies early in 1986, and shortly afterwards the poet Irina Ratushinskaya was released from labour camp and allowed to emigrate. In December 1986 Andrei Sakharov was not only released but 'rehabilitated'. In 1987 329 out of 700 known political prisoners were 'pardoned' after pressure to recant and to sign documents stating that they would no longer participate in unofficial activities. The tempo of Jewish emigration significantly increased, including a number of leading refuseniks, which deprived the *aliya* movement of its leadership.

Under Gorbachev the trickle of overt dissent has become a flood which makes the term 'dissent' anachronistic, though still valid in certain cases. The inchoate resistance of earlier years is now beginning to take shape in the various *neformaly* organizations and in the publication by July 1988 of some 500 independent journals throughout the USSR. Some of these are reminiscent of the tradition of the 'thick journals' (*tolstye zhurnaly*) of the late Tsarist years. Much of this activity is what is now called the 'independent movement' (*nezavisimoe dvizhenie*), which seeks to defend a degree of autonomy from the ideological and political structures of the state. Even groups which declare themselves not only in support of *perestroika* but part of *perestroika* guard their independence.

The multi-faceted character of resistance is reflected in the absence of a single policy carried out by the state to control it in the post-Stalin years. The authorities have tried to isolate the most active dissenters, to split the movement, and to deal with various issues individually. Overt resisters are usually dismissed from their job and there is an attempt to turn them into social pariahs. Dissidents have been vilified more often than not for their individual moral failings, and an almost obsessive emphasis has been placed on their usually totally fabricated links with Western powers and the CIA. The more subtle tactic of the KGB is to intimidate potential resistance by calling people in for 'talks' (*besedy*) at KGB headquarters. The tone of these *besedy* is of a heavy-handed paternalism dealing with wayward children. If the individual proves obdurate there is a gradual escalation in the level of coercion. Some of the more active or isolated dissidents have been incarcerated in psychiatric institutions. Notable examples are Zhores Medvedev, Bukovskii, and Koryagin. Another method was the use of exile, applied against Solzhenitsyn. Medvedev had a taste of both, being held in a psychiatric hospital before being exiled to the West.

The varieties of resistance

The hopes raised by the Khrushchev thaw and their suffocation under Brezhnev once again raised the dilemma faced by the Polish resistance of the nineteenth-century: the choice between 'organic work', the steady devotion to the cause but working through the system; and insurrection. In the Soviet context insurrection is not a viable alternative, but, given the relatively impermeable nature of Soviet power, organic work for many resisters in the Soviet Union was felt not to be an option either, although some have chosen to try to effect changes from within. The third path lies amid a range of activities which as far as possible insulate themselves from official structures and begin to constitute an 'alternative society' which is not so much counterposed to the official world as ignores it.[4]

In the absence of an overriding national component, as in nineteenth century Poland, Soviet resistance can be categorized into three very broad tendencies. The first is the idea of genuine Marxism-Leninism, the belief that the present system has the capacity to be regenerated to provide a viable path of development, building on the achievements of the past. This is the 'organic work' view, which asserts that there is nothing fundamentally wrong with the system: all that is required are some adjustments to eliminate the distortions of the past and to return to Leninist ideals. This has something in common with Trotsky's idea of the degenerated workers' state, which held Stalin and the bureaucracy responsible. The view accepts the basic propositions of the Soviet system. Private property is seen as the source of exploitation and the establishment of collective or nationalized property is considered an achievement. The end of bourgeois parliamentarianism is regarded as progressive, although it is accepted that major distortions have taken place in Soviet legality which require only an act of political will to remedy. At the margin this is the view of some of the within-system reformers. This stance has been defended by Roy Medvedev in the Soviet Union, and earlier by Peter Grigorenko, and supported by Lev Kopelev. Medvedev argues that a neo-Stalinist formation has taken power in the USSR, and that once this is eliminated the basically correct system will emerge.

Medvedev's view of 'reformism' from above denies the need for a revolution or mass movement from below. Stalinism thus becomes a distinctive power system opposed to the correct principles of Leninism. Grigorenko, on the other hand, fought for the maximum political and organizational independence of the democratic movement from the ruling system. The leadership was characterized as a ruling caste. After enjoying some popularity in the 1950s and 1960s, especially when the belief in reform from above was stimulated by Khrushchev's denunciation of Stalin, this Marxist-Leninist tendency declined markedly. Its fundamental propositions on the internal reformability of Marxist-Leninist regimes was dealt a severe blow by the crushing after 1968 in Czechoslovakia not only of the reforms but of the ideas that had inspired them. Following the ban on Solidarity in Poland the tendency almost completely disappeared, although in both cases the attempts at reform were halted by outside influences which presumably do not apply in the Soviet context. In many respects the Brezhnev years saw the extinction of Marxism-Leninism as a meaningful political philosophy in the Soviet Union and Eastern Europe. It had become transformed, according to its critics, into a dogma supportive of the existing regimes. It no longer appeared to have any explanatory power. There are strict limits to the potential of a Leninist opposition to these regimes, since they share too many assumptions to be able to sustain an effective critique. It was a major achievement of Gorbachev's leadership to have restored some credibility to the philosophical base of the regime and to have revived the reformist current.

The second major strand in the resistance is the role of religion as a counter-ideology. A religious belief system acts as a filter, screening the attempts at political socialization by the regime. Of necessity under Soviet conditions this takes place mainly in the family. While Islam has been persecuted as much as any religion in the USSR, leaving few mosques still functioning, Islamic faith is widespread among Soviet Moslems and provides an effective alternative source of socialization and moral support. In Lithuania the Roman Catholic church is strong and is creating a situation somewhat analogous to that pertaining in Poland. The Baptists are particularly strong in the Ukraine. The Russian Orthodox church has recently been witnessing a revival in attendance but perhaps more importantly in its spiritual life. The notable figure in this respect is Dmitrii Dudko, who has tried to forge a link between Orthodoxy and intellectual criticism. While most religions do not directly equate belief and civil rights, emphasis on individual salvation implies some support for human rights. For this reason the independent movement is inspired and strengthened above all by the religious component.

The third major trend in the resistance is liberal ideology, or a belief in the values of liberal democracy in the broadest sense. The major representative of this tendency is Andrei Sakharov. These are the successors to the nineteenth-century Westernizers, especially in their support for a transition to a Western-style democracy. Sakharov himself rejects the division of ideas into Western or Slavophile as false: for him, there are only true or false ideas. Their cardinal principle is the rejection of views that place social justice above political liberty, the Marxist-Leninist view, but they would on the whole support the welfare state. They reject the view of some believers that religious community comes above individuality. They condemn the Soviet Union for having failed to achieve social justice, individual liberty, or community, and insist that economic development requires the liberation of individuals from state tutelage.

These three major trends are communicated to the Soviet public and the world by a number of different groups. *Glasnost* has permitted the emergence of relatively independent social movements and the exposure of religious, national, and class tensions. The groups include cultural associations, who have played a key role in the Gorbachev reforms. The Writers' Congress of 1986 heralded yet again a cultural thaw. Civil and human rights groups include the Helsinki Monitoring Group, established in the mid-1970s and broken up in the early 1980s. The group of the early 1980s to Establish Trust between the USA and the

USSR survives. An important feature of all these groups is universal opposition to the death penalty and the belief that change in the Soviet Union must come peacefully. This emerges not only because the regime itself has an almost complete monopoly of coercion, but also out of revulsion at the bloodthirsty past of Bolshevism, which set one group against another.

In almost all Soviet religions there is a mixture of belief and nationalism. This is particularly important among active Jews, where religion is the basis of ethnic identity. In Georgia and Armenia Christian churches of great antiquity bestow a spiritual element on to the proud nationalism. In Russia itself Solzhenitsyn represents a fusion of Orthodox belief and Russian nationalism. National dissent can be divided into linguistic, cultural, and other sub-groups. There are certain separatist movements, such as among the Polish population of Lvov. The Armenian groups of the 1970s were one of the few who resorted to terrorist acts. Ethnic politics is represented by the nationalist expatriate groups such as the Crimean Tatars. There are elements of militant Islam in Central Asia, taking on a radical nationalist hue. Jews make up a special group because of their concern with emigration and extra-national links with the state of Israel. They have provided one of the most consistent, vocal, sustained, and effective sources of resistance to the regime. The Volga Germans have achieved some of their aims, such as the ability to emigrate.

The 1980s have seen the increased importance of new social movements. These include groups concerned with sexual politics, especially feminists. They are an important tendency, especially in Leningrad, where a group revealed the structure of sexual exploitation in the Soviet Union (see p. 240). Many of them came from a dissident background but were disappointed to find that most dissidents failed to take their concerns seriously. Feminist dissent shifted attention from political to social oppression. Homosexuality is still illegal in the Soviet Union, and so it is well-nigh impossible to organize effectively to advance gay rights. Since lesbianism is not recognized as existing, it is not illegal. One of the most important movements is the wide variety of groups concerned with environmental issues. Ecologism might well come to replace socialism as the dominant idea of the twenty-first century. Resistance to the widespread despoliation of the Soviet environment has become a genuine mass movement. The problem here focuses on ensuring compliance with the impressive Soviet laws for the protection of the environment, and this requires a general improvement in the USSR's legal system. The ability to hold enterprises and ministries responsible for their actions in this field and others requires the development of a vigorous civil litigation system. One of the unwitting side effects of Andropov's peace campaign was the emergence of groups within the Soviet bloc itself asking provocative questions about the relationship of peace and human and civil rights.

Until the late 1980s the standard image of Soviet workers as divided, demoralized, and depoliticized was broadly accurate. The working class finds itself in a particularly difficult position, since the regime nominally rules in its name. Worker organizations have become institutionalized as the basis of the Soviet regime, and hence the working class finds its organizations and ideology colonized by the regime. Attempts at independent organizations have emerged, as in the attempt by V. Klebanov to form the Free Trade Union (SMOT). Workers' unrest appears to the widespread, usually over localized issues, though only seventy-five strikes were documented between 1953 and 1983. Most strikes are spontaneous occurrences provoked by exceptional circumstances, such as a cut in rations or increased work norms. The major incident of worker unrest took place in Novocherkassk in 1962, sparked off by food price increases and raised work norms. The strikers carried banners of Lenin, just as the demonstrators in 1905 carried pictures of the Tsar. The strike lasted three days before the authorities were able to crush it with tanks. National factors and level of development play their part in the incidence of strikes, with a disproportionate number in the Ukraine and the Baltic states, with a corresponding quiescence in the Russian republic. In Soviet circumstances a strike cannot remain economic for long and in the eyes of the authorities rapidly takes on the hues of a political challenge. A strike acts as a way of appealing for redress to a level above the local management or party authorities. Most strikes are fairly localized affairs, with the strikers usually remaining in the factories. The authorities usually concede immediate demands and then deal with the 'ringleaders' at leisure. With the onset of *perestroika* strikes grew in number though appear to have decreased in intensity. The revival of a workers' 'movement' is one of the challenges facing *perestroika*.

It is no longer true, as it might have been in the 1950s, that the resistance is made up overwhelmingly of the urban intelligentsia. The demands for cultural freedom are not purely selfish and of no concern to the rest of the population. The links with the workng class were at one time weak but the repression against many dissidents has forced them to manual work, if not into the larger industrial enterprises. In the Soviet Union there has always been fairly free movement between workers an intellectuals, and a large proportion of Soviet intellectuals are only a generation away from the working class. Barghoorn demonstrates that intellectuals have supported workers' demands, and Alexeyeva notes the lack of correlation in Soviet dissident activity between class identity and movement demands. In other words a social component has been added to the earlier concerns of the human rights movement. Now there is an equal emphasis on the right to strike, and against social injustices. At the same time, the belief in workerism, that the working class possesses certain innate virtues, has been thoroughly discredited by the experience of Stalinism. It would no longer be possible to repeat the Bolsheviks' own pattern of coming to power by agitation among workers under the guidance of intellectuals.

Glasnost has encouraged the emergence of a wide range of 'informal' (*neformaly*) groups (see p. 00), numbering several thousands. They were initially concerned with unofficial art or music but broadened out into ecological issues and finally into overt political concerns. In August 1987 a conference of about 600 independent left-wing groups was sanctioned by the authorities in an unprecedented break with tradition. The conference was co-ordinated by the Club of Social Initiatives (CSI), formed in late 1986 to transform the reforms from above into activism from below. The very fact that political clubs have been tolerated attests to the new atmosphere in which the authorities are willing to listen to some of the broad range of criticisms put forward by resisters and to learn about the true situation in the country. The conference formalized an umbrella organization, a Federation of Socialist Clubs, which in May 1988 encompassed forty clubs in seventy towns. The meeting called for the erection of a monument to Stalin's vctims and warned of the dangers of right-wing nationalist extremism. Toleration of such groups is part of the acceptance that society becomes more complex as it advances towards socialism and hence becomes more difficult to control from above. Internal dialogue and the rule of law will be expected regulate society, rather than administrative procedures and police coercion.

Resistance in perspective

The Soviet system is a guided system, but within it there is a great amount of social activity of one form or another. Resistance comes in many forms, from civil liberties groups, nationalist movements, religious believers, or simply individuals calling for greater truth in Soviet policy and an honest appraisal of the Stalin period. Increasingly these concerns have been joined by calls for social, political, and national justice. But the question remains of why resistance appears to be so much less widespread in the Soviet Union than in Eastern Europe. One major reason is that in the Soviet Union nationalism and the Soviet regime tend to be integrated, whereas in Eastern Europe nationalist tendencies run counter to regimes supported by the USSR. But that is only part of the answer. The reality in the Soviet Union is more complex, and the society that has emerged over seven decades of Soviet power has established a unique relationship with the regime which is based not only on opposition but also on a great degree of interaction.

Some of the weaknesses of Soviet dissent can be noted. While resistance may be widespread, it remains unfocused. There is no meta-dissent, like nationalism or religion in Poland, and the many national pressures to a degree cancel each other out. No mass movement has emerged as in Poland, and outright overt dissent is restricted to a small minority. The rest of the population are not so much passive as seeing no effective way of becoming involved. The resources available to the state to mould social consciousness are buttressed by the patrimonial relationship between a nation of employees and the state as the universal employer. It is also clear that the regime is more competent than the one in Poland in the 1970s. It has managed to avoid such acts of bravado, or ineptitude, as raising food prices on the eve of major holidays. The phasing out of food subsidies will take considerable political skill, since they provided a means of maintaining social peace, albeit at enormous cost.

Those who have specific grievances do complain, and there are channels to incorporate such complaints. The regime is always careful to keep its pulse on public opinion and is willing to pay almost any price to avoid having to use overt and widespread coercion. To some extent dissent is too bound up with single issues, and perhaps too introspective. The maximum expansion of overt dissent was concerned with the persecutions against dissidents themselves in the late 1960s. The concerns of many dissidents do not appeal to the mass of the Soviet people. In a larger perspective Soviet dissent even seems too parochial (with the exception of the issue of Jewish emigration) to make much of an impact on the rest of the world. The fate of Solzhenitsyn in the West appears to show that the issues that worry the alternative Russian society make little impact on Western public opinion. The absence of mass support clearly reflects the success of the regime in isolating dissent. Repression has been accompanied by the portrayal of dissenters in a wholly unfavourable light: as maladjusted people bearing some sort of grudge against society, threatening the achievements of the republic, and acting as conduits for foreign powers and influences.

Much overt dissent is concentrated among intellectuals. They are a small group divided among themselves. However, the whole movement of overt resistance cannot be dismissed as the demands of a section of the elite for the privileges of the bourgeois intelligentsia in the West. It is not necessarily true that the working class is concerned with bread-and-butter issues and not with the idea of political justice. The crisis of the late Brezhnev years appeared to confirm the dissident argument that social justice could not be achieved without political justice. A further weakness is that there is no clear alternative programme or idea of what might follow the Soviet regime. Effective resistance needs at least a minimum common programme around which to organize and mobilize. Socialist rhetoric is weakened by its identification with the regime, and the distinction between some purer socialism and the 'real socialism' practised by the government is too arcane to seize the popular imagination. Even such fundamental issues as support for basic civil rights and free elections are contested. Fortunately, the almost universal condemnation of violence inhibits the emergence of terroristic resistance groups.

A further weakness is that Soviet resistance has few international links: it is largely isolated within the Soviet Union (with the exception of the Jewish, Volga German, Armenian, and some other groups). Support in the West has been crucial for the success of any Soviet movement, and indeed for the physical survival of many of the individuals concerned. Some of the isolation has been transcended with the rise of transnational issues, such as feminism and ecological concerns, especially after the disaster at the Chernobyl nuclear power station. Furthermore, the rise of a Soviet peace movement established issues of common concern legitimated by the human rights groups and the Helsinki monitoring process. The extent to which these developments have internationalized Soviet dissent is not clear. One of the major weaknesses remains the poor links with Eastern European resistance movements.

A major problem of Soviet dissidents is that they have been unable to capitalize on splits within the bureaucracy itself. The deep conflicts within the Soviet political establishment under Khrushchev gave way to the bland facade of the Brezhnev leadership. The success of the Czechoslovak reform movement in 1968 was prepared by the emergence of a group of reformers within the party itself over a period of years who are willing to respond to the profound crisis in relations between the regime and society. Conditions in the Soviet Union are very different in that the pressures from society are far more diffuse and sometimes even neutralize each other. The group of reformers who have emerged around Gorbachev give the lie to the view that the leadership is populated only by cynics and careerists. But whether the new generation of reformers speak the same language as the majority of independent movement activists is very much doubted. The establishment of a common cause, as in Czechoslovakia in 1968, will be a long-term process. Nevertheless, certain dissidents have been shielded by patrons in the political establishment. It is noteworthy that some of the key dissenters came from elite families.

Resistance needs to establish some form of organizational identity to succeed, but in the Soviet Union such organizational achievement has traditionally been the signal for repression. In contrast, movements in Poland have not only been able to survive but are constantly growing in strength. Even Charter 77 in Czechoslovakia has been able to survive for several years. One factor explaining the difference is the widespread apathy in the Soviet Union: dissenters cannot operate quite like fish in the sea, as they can in Poland. The final reason for the weakness of resistance in the Soviet Union is the ferocious repression, managed for so many years by Andropov. The regime, especially after 1979, was committed to suppressing overt acts of resistance, and to a large extent it succeeded in its aim. However, the main result is that the regime has driven resistance deep into society, where it emerges in random acts of violent despair, poor work discipline, alcoholism, and in a profound popular distrust of the regime. Gorbachev's reforms have only begun to overcome some of this distrust.

Despite its drawbacks the achievements of resistance or dissent have not been negligible. The ferment of the post-Stalin years has left a permanent mark on Soviet society. It was the first major opposition since the elimination of Trotsky in the late 1920s. It has shown that apathy is not universal and that some people are willing to stand up for rights and truth. There is a broad political continuity between the concerns of the Bolshevik oppositions in the early years of Soviet power and the revived cultural and democratic opposition from the 1950s. They represent an undercurrent of resistance to the monopoly of political power that neither Stalin nor Andropov could wipe out entirely.

The resistance has provided an alternative source of information and ideas through underground printing (*samizdat*), sending material to be published abroad (*tamizdat*), and through audio cassettes of popular *chansonniers* such as Vladimir Vysotsky, Aleksander Galich, and Mikhail Zhvanetskii (*magnitizdat*). The increasing availability of video recorders has been accompanied by the emergence of *videoizdat*, and gradually *computizdat*, or *PCizdat*, is appearing. The resistance also provides an important source of information for the West, much of which is beamed back through Radio Liberty, the BBC, and Deutsche Welle. The magazine *Glasnost* tested the limits of Gorbachev's strategy of that name, yet the editor's (Sergei Grigoryants) contacts with the West exposed the magazine to the attention of the KGB. The case of this journal illustrates that the term *samizdat* is anachronistic, since like many other journals, it tried to get an official licence and to be distributed on a quasi-commercial basis.

These various means of communication have broken the regime's monopoly of information. Bolshevism as an idea in power ultimately can only be challenged in the realm of ideas as philosophy rationally debates with ideology. The Bolsheviks, as the fusion of ideology and organization, had no time, and indeed saw no need, for independent intellectual activity. The emergence of overt resistance has reconstituted the Enlightenment tradition of autonomy for intellectual endeavour, the search for the rational and the reasonable (however idealistic the project might be). Intellectual resistance lays down one of the essential foundations of a reconstituted public sphere, an arena of intellectual debate free of state tutelage. Whether this will lead to the reconstitution of civil society, an arena of free action and the interplay of social forces and groups, remains to be seen.

Resistance activity has been far more than simply an opposition to the regime. Its works have enriched Russian and national cultures with books, songs, and scholarly works, sometimes of a very high standard. It has given birth to a number of sub-cultures. They have kept the national memory alive, especially by revealing the undistorted history of the Soviet Union and its peoples. The outstanding works in this respect are Solzhenitsyn's *Gulag Archipelago* and Roy Medvedev's *Let History Judge*, both focusing on the hidden history of Stalinism and repression. Indeed, one of the major achievements of the resistance has been to prevent the rehabilitation of Stalin. In 1969 resistance to Brezhnev's plans expanded to include significant sections of the elite, joined by Eastern and Western European communist leaders. They have achieved an improved status for certain categories of political prisoners. Among the other successes of resistance currents have been the exoneration of the Crimean Tatars in 1967, the mass emigration of Jews in the 1970s, and the waiving of the education tax on emigrants.

Soviet and East European resistance in general has helped reformulate issues not only for the communist countries but for the intellectual life of the whole Western political tradition. In asking the most pertinent questions about its own society the resistance is raising issues of concern to all industrial societies. Among the cardinal questions are the restraint of authoritarianism, the possibilities of non-capitalist forms of democracy, and the relationship between political and social democracy. The latter issue is by no means resolved in the dissident movement, but the emerging answer that in the absence of political freedom there can be no social justice is of more than national significance. Soviet resistance points to the dangers of unrestrained social engineering, political *dirigisme*, ideological utopianism, and technocratic wilfulness.

Dissent can be seen as a conflict within the elite (though not within the leadership), since the intelligentsia (and the working class itself) are largely products of regime policies. The fundamental cleavage is between the communist party and other groups. In economic terms the Soviet Union is becoming an advanced industrial society, but the existence of informal resistance and dissent illustrates the slowness of the regime to undergo political modernization. The absence of effective formal means of conflict resolution and claims to a monopoly on deciding the parameters of legitimate intellectual debate create an underground market of ideas. In other countries many of the groups mentioned above, such as feminists and peace groups, would become interest or lobby groups. In the Soviet Union they have tended to become dissident groupings, hence dissent is a product of the system itself. By legitimating the concept of socialist pluralism Gorbachev recognized that such resistance does not pose a mortal threat to the Soviet regime but only to its most obscurantist features. Moroever, dissent is a sign that Soviet society is stirring and beginning to recognize its own strength. Ultimately the methods of early Bolshevism will become increasingly counterproductive. The regime has begun to accept that it can no longer mould society, but that it has to work within society and achieve its ends through patience and negotiation rather than confrontation and storming. Resistance has placed limits to the bureaucratic dream of remoulding society in its own image.

Granted that overt dissent has gained little support within the elite, it should nevertheless be stressed that resistance works at several levels, and while overt political dissent does not gain much sympathy, the fight, for example, for cultural integrity cuts across elite-society lines. A vivid demonstration of the democratizing capacity of cultural achievement was the common scene at the cramped Taganka Theatre under the director Yuri Lyubimov of a top party official sitting equally uncomfortably next to a dissident, flanked by an unofficial writer or poet, and all applauding the semi-official writer, singer, and actor Vladimir Vysotskii. Jeffrey Goldfarb has convincingly demonstrated that in communist societies cultural freedom is realized not simply as dissent in opposition to the prevailing order, but also within the official institutions of creative life.[5] The revival of Soviet cultural organizations during *perestroika* illustrates that the persistence of freedom in the aesthetic sphere, despite censorship and the whole vast apparatus of social control, survives in the interstices of *official* policy and institutions. This probably applies to the whole range of official Soviet institutions. The argument undermines not only the logic of totalitarian theory, but also ideas which stress the unified nature of the communist apparatus. As in granite, there are fault lines which can weaken under the glacial pressure of social and artistic forces.

Dissent and resistance in the Soviet Union have made a significant impact on Soviet politics. The resistance of a group of economists and sociologists under Brezhnev, for example, acted as the catalyst of change under Gorbachev. Many elements of the programme proposed by Sakharov are key features of the reform programme of Gorbachev, albeit in a controlled and limited form. The fundamental difference is that Gorbachev's reforms have come from above and can be reversed, whereas all the dissenters argue for the formalization of social initiative. Greater democratization is the essential condition for a successful economic reform. The existence of a vigilant public opinion expressed by dissenters ensures a modicum of lawfulness of the Soviet regime and restrains some of its arbitrariness. Dissenters act as the conduit to the West, which then acts as the loudspeaker, the substitute for an active society within the Soviet Union itself. The resistance ultimately has put limits to the power of the Politburo. The government can no longer push through genuinely unpopular legislation, since it would encounter too much resistance. Social resistance puts a limit to the powers of the government and represents the rebellion of society against the know-all paternalism of the Soviet state. The fundamental question is the extent to which the Soviet regime is restricted by traditional, contractual, or conventional elements in Soviet society. To put it another way, to what extent does the party's claim to dominance impede the futher development of Soviet democracy? Conversely, the changes in society can be expected to modify practices within the party itself.

Dissident activity and the state's response to it have kept the focus on Khrushchev's promises of establishing socialist legality to prevent the recurrence of Stalin's arbitrary and murderous rule. Socialist legality is the Soviet equivalent of a Bill of Rights without the backing of the force of law. Dissent of course is an artificial construct, since the boundary of permitted activity and thought is temporally and spatially defined: the 'healthy' criticism of a Novosibirsk academic becomes 'dissent' in the mouth of a Moscow intellectual. The resistance has broadened those limits and transformed them from bureaucratic departmental conflicts or social resistance to the level of political consciousness. The fundamental impact of the activities of dissenters was initially on society itself. It kept alive the memory of the past and hopes of other ways of living. Gradually society in the form of grass-roots pressure affected the state. Resistance represents an incipient pluralism, though with only indirect access to decision-making. Above all, overt dissent is a massive indictment of the authorities and challenges the moral authority of the government to govern in the old way. Dissidents have achieved something simply by continuing to exist. Dissent is ineradicable because it is an inalienable part of Soviet reality. It represents the struggle for the consolidation of a public sphere. As yet there are no guarantees of individual inviolability, no real restraints on state power, no irreversible process of democratization, so resistance will continue to exist. When the independent movement is transformed into a legal opposition, then dissent will disappear. Dissent is a reminder that, contrary to the arguments of modernization theories, there is no automatic link between socio-economic change and the political system. In this respect Gorbachev is in the Leninist tradition: political change requires conscious political intervention.

Notes

1 F.C. Barghoorn, 'Regime-Dissenter Relations after Khrushchev', in S. Solomon (ed.), *Pluralism in the Soviet Union* (Macmillan, London, 1983), p. 131
2 A.Y. Shtromas, 'Dissent and Political Change in the Soviet Union', *Studies in Comparative Communism* 12, 2–3 (summer/autumn 1979), p. 213.
3 E.g. E.P. Thompson, *The Heavy Dancers* (Merlin, Manchester, 1982), pp. 125–6.

4 For a discussion of these perspectives see Adam Michnik, *Letters from Prison and other Essays* (University of California Press, Berkeley, 1985), in particular the crucial essay of 1974, 'A New Evolutionism'; and V. Havel, *Power of the Powerless: Citizens against the State in Central Eastern Europe* (Hutchinson, London, 1985).

5 J. Goldfarb, *The Persistence of Freedom: the Sociological Implications of Polish Student Theater* (Westview, Boulder, Colo., 1980), p. 1.

Key texts

Barghoorn, Frederick C., 'Regime-Dissenter Relations after Khrushchev', in Susan Solomon (ed.), *Pluralism in the Soviet Union* (Macmillan, London, 1983), pp. 131–68

Medvedev, Roy, *On Soviet Dissent: Interviews with Piero Ostellino* (Columbia University Press, New York, 1980)

Reddaway, P., 'Dissent in the Soviet Union', *Problems of Communism*, 6 (November–December 1983), pp. 1–15

Shtromas, A.Y. 'Dissent and Political Change in the Soviet Union', *Studies in Comparative Communism*, 12, 2/3 (summer/autumn 1979), pp. 212–76

Select bibliography

Alexeyeva, L., *Soviet Dissent: Contemporary Movements for National, Religious and Human Rights*, trans. Carol Pearce and John Glad (Wesleyan University Press, Middletown, Conn., 1985)

Amalrik, A., *Will the Soviet Union survive until 1984?* (Penguin, London, 1970)

Barghoorn, F.C., *Detente and the Democratic Movement in the USSR* (Free Press, New York, 1976)

Bloch, S., and Peter Reddaway, *Psychiatric Terror: How Soviet Psychiatry is Used to Suppress Dissent* (Basic, New York, 1977)

Bukovsky, V., *To Build a Castle: my Life as a Dissenter* (Deutsch, London, 1978)

Bukovsky, Vladimir, *To Choose Freedom* (Hoover Institution Press, Stanford, Cal., 1987)

Chalidze, V., *To Defend these Rights* (Random House, New York, 1974)

Cohen, Stephen F. (ed.), *An End to Silence: Uncensored Opinion in the Soviet Union* (from Roy Medvedev's underground magazine *Political Diary*), trans. George Saunders (Norton, London, 1982)

Cutler, R.M. 'Soviet Dissent under Khrushchev: an Analytical Study', *Comparative Politics*, 13, 1 (October 1980), pp. 15–36

Dunlop, John, *The New Russian Revolutionaries* (Nordland, Belmont, Mass., 1976)

Gorbanevskaya, N., *The Demonstration in Red Square* (Deutsch, London, 1972)

Hopkins, Mark, *Russia's Underground Press: the Chronicle of Current Events* (Praeger, New York, 1983)

Kowalewski, D., 'Trends in the Human Rights Movement', in D.R. Kelley (ed.), *Soviet Politics in the Brezhnev Era* (Praeger, New York, 1980), pp. 150–81

Lane, D., 'Human Rights under State Socialism', in S. White and D. Nelson (eds.), *Communist Politics: a Reader* (Macmillan, London, 1986), p. 326–45

Litvinov, P., *The Demonstration in Pushkin Square* (Harvill, London, 1968)

Marchenko, A. *My Testimony* (Penguin, Harmondsworth, 1971)

Medvedev, Roy, *On Socialist Democracy* (Spokesman, Nottingham, 1975)

Medvedev, Roy, *Detente and Socialist Democracy: a Discussion with Roy Medvedev*, ed. Ken Coates (Spokesman, Nottingham, 1975)

Meerson-Aksenov, M., and B. Shragin (eds.), *The Political, Social and Religious Thought of Russian Samizdat: an Anthology* (Nordland, Belmont, Mass., 1977)

Michnik, Adam, *Letters from Prison and other Essays* (University of California Press, Berkeley, 1985)

Nahaylo, Bohdan, *Dissent and Opposition in the Soviet Union: a Concise History* (Croom Helm, London, 1987)

Reddaway, Peter, 'Policy towards Dissent since Khrushchev', in T.F. Rigby *et al.* (eds.), *Authority, Power and Policy in the USSR* (Macmillan, London, 1980), pp. 158–92

Reddaway, Peter, 'The Development of Dissent and Opposition', in Brown and Kaser (eds.), *The Soviet Union since the Fall of Khrushchev* (Macmillan, London, 1978), pp. 121–56

Reddaway, Peter (ed.), *Uncensored Russia: the Human Rights Movement in the Soviet Union: Documents* (Cape, London, 1972)

Rubenstein, J., *Soviet Dissidents: their Struggle for Human Rights*, 2nd edn (Beacon, Boston, Mass., 1985)

Sakharov, Andrei, *Progress, Coexistence and Intellectual Freedom* (Norton, New York, 1968)

Sakharov, A., *Sakharov Speaks* (Knopf, New York, 1974)

Sakharov, A., *My Country and the World* (Collins, London, 1975)

Saunders, George (ed.), *Samizdat: Voices of Soviet Opposition* (Monad, New York, 1974)

Schapiro, L. (ed.), *Political Opposition in One-party States* (Macmillan, London, 1972)

Shanov, D.R., *Behind the Lines: the Private War against Soviet Censorship* (St Martin's, New York, 1985)

Shatz, Marshall S., *Soviet Dissent in Historical Perspective* (Cambridge University Press, Cambridge, 1980)

Shtromas, Alexander, *Political Change and Social Development: the Case of the Soviet Union* (Lang, Frankfurt am Main, 1981)

Solzhenitsyn, A., *Letter to Soviet Leaders* (Collins Harvill, London, 1974)

Spechler, D.R., *Permitted Dissent in the USSR* (Praeger, New York, 1982)

Tokes, Rudolf L. (ed.), *Dissent in the USSR: Politics, Ideology, and People* (Johns Hopkins University Press, Baltimore, Md, and London, 1975)

Ulam, Adam, *Russia's Failed Revolutions: from the Decembrists to the Dissidents* (Weidenfeld & Nicolson, London, 1981)

Well, Josephine, *Soviet Dissident Literature: a Critical Guide* (Hall, 1983)

Afterword

After seventy years of change and consolidation the Soviet political system under Gorbachev entered an unprecedented phase of experimentation and innovation. The whole polity was examined anew and the legacy of the past was found wanting. The exaggerated *dirigisme* of war communism, the unstable compromise during the New Economic Policy between economic liberalization and political authoritarianism, the horrors of the Stalin period which raised the powers of the state to unprecedented levels, Khrushchev's muddled reforms, the stagnation of the Brezhnev years followed by an interregnum of rule by the gerontocrats Andropov and Chernenko, all seemed to exhaust the possibilities of the old approach to socialist development. Answers were sought which could imbue the moribund economy with a new dynamism and free society from the shackles of the old 'command and administer' socialism. While he has been careful to present his radical solutions as true to the old ideological prescriptions, Gorbachev's reforms represent a fundamental reconsideration of the type of socialism that the Soviet Union will build.

The system is at present in a state of considerable flux. The nineteenth party conference in June–July 1988 was the scene of debate the like of which had not been since the 1920s. The conference sanctioned the reorganization of the institutions of the communist polity on the basis of the proclamation of a 'socialist legal state'. The Soviet regime is reaching back to its roots to find solutions to current problems, endowing the reform process with an air of *déjà vu*. Not for the first time in Soviet history has the role of the soviets been debated, or the proper role of the leading party in a communist society been discussed. But in politics, as in life, there is never precise repetition — some of the same themes may recur but not in the same way.

It would be misleading to call the present economic reforms a type of second NEP, since the circumstances have changed so radically since the 1920s. There is no longer an independent peasantry, in terms of output Soviet industry ranks second in the world, and the balance between town and country has dramatically altered in favour of an urbanized and educated population. Nevertheless, some of the old themes of Russian and Soviet debates have recurred. At the Central Committee meeting of 29 July 1988 Gorbachev sought a solution to the country's chronic agricultural crisis in the reconstitution of personal farming through the long-term leasing of land to farmers. As in the past, the reinvigoration of the economy and society must begin in the villages.

In political life, while some of the same questions are being raised as in the early years of Soviet power, the global context and the meaning of words have changed. In the early years communism was an ascendant force, the party and sections of the population were arrogant with enthusiasm for the construction of a propertyless utopia on earth, and were willing to break a few eggs to make the socialist omelette. In the present debate the huge economic, moral, and political costs of the radical eschatology of human liberation from capitalist exploitation, religion, and private property which culminated in Stalin's rule of terror have now to be reckoned with. Although its actual features under Stalin were not inevitable, Stalinism itself was the product of political and social processes that had been gestating for at least a century in the heart of the revolutionary movement. This is why at present the re-examination of Soviet socialism is accompanied not only by renewed destalinization but also by attempts to understand the roots of the Stalin phenomenon in socialist political ideology and practice.

In her book *Poland's Self-limiting Revolution*, on the Solidarity trade union movement of 1980–1, Jadwiga Staniszkis argued that 'post-totalitarian' communist regimes are forced to find a means of transforming totalitarian domination into some sort of pluralist authoritarianism. Otherwise, she argues, society itself will seek to sweep away the remains of an outdated and ineffective style of government in a revolution that can no longer be restrained. In one-party states like the USSR, rather than policy-making becoming simpler, the dream of the early commune democrats, the policy process became clogged. It became increasingly difficult to take rational decisions. The solution of problems tended to become more difficult in face of the complexity of adjudicating between conflicting interests and priorities. From this perspective the Gorbachevite reforms are a rational and much-postponed response to the accumulating problems of the Soviet polity and society. Better to reform from above, could be the unspoken assumption of the reformers, than face unrest or stagnation from below.

Gorbachev has revived the reformist option of regenerating communist systems from within. Rather than relying only on the party machinery and its *apparatchiki*, internal party debate and the political activism of the mass of the party membership have begun to be restored. In its relations with society, the party in 1985 was faced with the choice of continuing the neo-Stalinist path of suffocating individual and social autonomy, or of finding a way of allowing the transformation of the political structure to permit exchange between its constituent elements and society as a whole. This is the purpose of *glasnost*. *Perestroika* is not a once-and-for-all measure but part of a long-term *process* of change and adaptation in which consensus and hegemony gradually take the place of traditional Soviet *dirigisme*. Elements of instrumentality remain in the processes of *perestroika* and *glasnost* in the insistence that they are intended to serve certain purposes, such as reviving the economy or strengthening socialism, rather than being good in and for themselves. However, there is increasingly an understanding that the reform process must be open ended. The more that limits are placed on the scope and nature of change, the more difficult it is for even limited changes to succeed.

All political writing is an attempt to impose a rational pattern on complex reality, and in the service of brevity and comprehensiveness some of the sharp contours of controversies in Soviet studies have perhaps been unduly flattened in this book. If the analysis outlined in the preceding chapters proves anything, it is that no single theory can hope to capture the multi-faceted reality of the country's politics. The text has tried to convey something of the element of transformation in Soviet politics, while providing a sense of the continuities proclaimed by its leaders and found in reality. The Soviet political system, as befits any dynamic system, is in a constant process of change, but this occurs in the context of certain stable principles and practices which are subject only to slow modification. Writing at a time of profound internal renewal precipitated by the leadership under Gorbachev, it would be rash to speculate unduly about the future. The changes have been radical, but the reform process is still in its infancy. There is still a degree of arbitrariness in that the announcement of the creation of a 'socialist legal state' at the nineteenth party conference was accompanied by the harassment and arrest of activists in the independent movement.

The debate over the development and reform of the Russian lands that began in the nineteenth century has still not been resolved. The crisis in Russian self-identity and the solutions that have been applied have profoundly affected the course of world history in the twentieth century., The attempt continues to find answers to questions of economic development, the relationship of the individual to authority, and of the state to society. On the answers found depends the fate of the Soviet peoples and the world. It is for this reason that we can all share the concern voiced by the radical reformers under Gorbachev that the reform process must be made irreversible.

Select bibliography of general works

Acton, Edward, *Russia* (Longman, Harlow, 1986)

Armstrong, John A., *Ideology, Politics, and Government in the Soviet Union: an Introduction*, 4th edn (University Press of America, Lanham, Md, 1978/1986)

Barghoorn, Frederick C., and Thomas F. Remington, *Politics in the USSR*, 3rd edn (Little Brown, Boston and Toronto, 1986)

Barry, Donald D., and Carol Barner-Barry, *Contemporary Soviet Politics: an Introduction*, 3rd edn (Prentice-Hall, Englewood Cliffs, N.J., 1987)

Basily, N. de, *Russia under Soviet Rule: Twenty Years of Bolshevik Experiment* (Allen & Unwin, London, 1938)

Bialer, Seweryn, *Stalin's Successors: Leadership, Stability, and Change in the Soviet Union* (Cambridge University Press, Cambridge, 1980)

Bialer, Seweryn (ed.), *The Domestic Context of Soviet Foreign Policy*, 2nd edn (Westview, Boulder, Colo., 1988)

Brown, Archie, *et al.* (eds.), *The Cambridge Encyclopedia of Russia and the Soviet Union* (Cambridge University Press, Cambridge, 1982)

Brown, Archie, and Michael Kaser (eds.), *The Soviet Union since the Fall of Khrushchev*, 2nd edn (Macmillan, London, 1978)

Brown, Archie, and Michael Kaser (eds.), *Soviet Policy for the 1980s* (Macmillan, London, 1982)

Brzezinski, Z. (ed.), *Dilemmas of Change in Soviet Politics* (Columbia University Press, New York, 1969)

Brzezinski, Z., and S.P. Huntington, *Political Power USA/USSR* (Penguin, Harmondsworth, 1977)

Bunce, V., and J.M. Echols III, 'From Soviet Studies to Comparative Politics: the Unfinished Revolution', in S. White and D. Nelson (eds.), *Communist Politics: a Reader* (Macmillan, London, 1986), pp. 317–25

Byrnes, Robert (ed.), *After Brezhnev: Sources of Soviet Conduct in the 1980s* (Indiana University Press, Bloomington, 1983)

Churchward, L.G., *Contemporary Soviet Government*, 2nd edn (Routledge & Kegan Paul, London, 1975)

Churchward, L.G., *Soviet Socialism: Social and Political Essays* (Routledge, London, 1987)

Cocks, Paul, R.V. Daniels, and Nancy Whittier Heer (eds.), *The Dynamics of Soviet Politics* (Harvard University Press, London and Cambridge, Mass., 1976)

Cohen, Stephen F., Alexander Rabinowitch, and Robert Sharlet (eds.), *The Soviet Union since Stalin* (Macmillan, London, 1980)

Cohen, Stephen F., *Rethinking the Soviet Experience: Politics and History since 1917* (Oxford University Press, Oxford, 1986)

Colton, Timothy J., *The Dilemma of Reform in the Soviet Union*, revised and expanded edition (Council on Foreign Relations, New York, 1986)

Cornel, R. (ed.), *The Soviet Political System* (Prentice-Hall, Englewood Cliffs, N.J., 1970)

Dallin, Alexander, and Condoleeza Rice (eds.), *The Gorbachev Era* (Stanford Alumni Association, Stanford, Cal., 1986)

Daniels, R.V. (ed.), *A Documentary History of Communism*, 1, *Communism in Russia* (Tauris, London, 1985)

Davies, R.W., and D.J.B. Shaw (eds.), *The Soviet Union* (Allen & Unwin, London, 1978)

Deutscher, Isaac, *The Unfinished Revolution: Russia, 1917–1967* (Oxford University Press, Oxford, 1967)

Field, Mark G. (ed.), *Social Consequences of Modernisation in Communist Societies* (Johns Hopkins University Press, Baltimore, Md, 1976)

Fainsod, Merle, *How Russia is Ruled* (Oxford University Press, London, 1963)

Fitzpatrick, S., *The Russian Revolution, 1917–1932* (Oxford University Press, Oxford, 1982)

Hammer, Darrell P., *USSR: the Politics of Oligarchy*, 2nd edn (Westview, Boulder, Colo., 1986)

Harding, N. (ed.), *The State in Socialist Society* (Macmillan, London, 1984)

Hazard, J.N., *The Soviet System of Government*, 5th edn (University of Chicago Press, Chicago and London, 1980)

Heller, Mikhail, and Aleksandr Nekrich, *Utopia in Power: the History of the Soviet Union from 1917 to the Present* (Summit, New York, 1986)

Hill, Ron, *Soviet Union: Politics, Economics and Society* (Pinter, London, 1985)

Hill, Ron, *Governing Soviet Society* (Harvester, Brighton, 1987)

Hoffmann, E.P., and Laird, R.F. (eds.), *The Soviet Polity in the Modern Era* (Aldine, New York, 1984)

Hosking, Geoffrey, *A History of the Soviet Union* (Fontana, London, 1985)

Hough, J.F., *The Soviet Union and Social Science Theory* (Harvard University Press, Cambridge, Mass., 1977)

Hough, J.F., and Fainsod, M., *How the Soviet Union is Governed* (Harvard University Press, London and Cambridge, Mass., 1979)

Huntington, Samuel P., and Clement H. Moore (eds.), *Authoritarian Politics in Modern Society: the Dynamics of Established One-party Systems* (Basic, New York and London, 1970)

Janos, A. (ed.), *Authoritarian Politics in Communist Europe* (University of California Press, Berkeley, 1976)

Johnson, Chalmers (ed.), *Change in Communist Systems* (Stanford University Press, Stanford, Cal., 1970)

Juviler, Peter H., and Henry W. Morton, *Soviet Policy-making: Studies of Communism in Transition* (Praeger, New York, 1967)

Keeble, Curtis, (ed.), *The Soviet State: the Domestic Roots of Soviet Foreign Policy* (Gower, Aldershot, 1985)

Kelley, D.R., *Soviet Politics in the Brezhnev Era* (Praeger, New York, 1980)

Lane, David, *State and Politics in the USSR* (Blackwell, Oxford, 1985)

Lane, David, *Soviet Economy and Society* (Blackwell, Oxford, 1985).

Lane, David, *The Socialist Industrial State: towards a Political Sociology of State Socialism* (Allen & Unwin, London, 1976)

Mackenzie, David, and M.W. Curran, *A History of Russia and the Soviet Union*, 3rd edn (Dorsey, Chicago, 1987)

McAuley, Mary, *Politics and the Soviet Union* (Penguin, Harmondsworth, 1977)

McCauley, Martin, *The Soviet Union since 1917* (Longman, London, 1981)

Medish, V., *The Soviet Union* (Prentice-Hall, Englewood Cliffs, N.J. 1984)

Millar, James R., *Politics, Work and Daily Life in the USSR: a Survey of Former Soviet*

Citizens (Cambridge University Press, Cambridge, 1988)

Morton, Henry W., and Rudolf L. Tokes (eds.), *Soviet Politics and Society in the 1970s* (Free Press, London, 1974)

Nogee, Joseph L., *Soviet Politics: Russia after Brezhnev* (Praeger, New York 1985)

Potichnyj, Peter J. (ed.), *Soviet Union: Party and Society* (Cambridge University Press, Cambridge, 1988)

Reshetar, John S., *The Soviet Polity* (Dodd Mead, New York, 1971)

Rakowska, T. (ed.), *Perspectives for Change in Communist Societies* (Westview, Boulder, Colo., 1979)

Rigby, T.H., Archie Brown, and Peter Reddaway (eds.), *Authority, Power and Policy in the USSR* (Macmillan, London, 1980)

Rosenberg, W., and M. Young, *Transforming Russia and China: Revolutionary Struggle in the Twentieth Century* (Oxford University Press, Oxford, 1982)

Rothman, S., and G.W. Breslauer, *Soviet Politics and Society* (West, St Paul, Minn, 1978)

Ryavec, Karl W. (ed.), *Soviet Society and the Communist Party* (University of Massachusetts Press, Amherst, 1978)

Schapiro, Leonard, *The Government and Politics of the Soviet Union*, 2nd edn (Hutchinson, London, 1978)

Shtromas, Alexander, and Morton A. Kaplan (eds.), *The Soviet Union and the Challenge of the Future*, I, *The Soviet System: Stasis and Change*; II, *Economy and Society*; III, *Ideology, Culture and Nationality*; IV, *Russia and the World* (Paragon, New York, 1987)

Skocpol, Theda, *States and Social Revolutions* (Cambridge University Press, Cambridge, 1979)

Smith, Gordon B., *Soviet Politics: Continuity and Tradition* (Macmillan, London, 1988)

Smith, Hedrick, *The Russians* (Sphere, London, 1976)

Soviet Union, 1984/85: Events, Problems, Perspectives (Westview, Boulder, Colo., and London, 1986)

Treadgold, Donald W., *Twentieth Century Russia*, 4th edn (Rand McNally, Chicago, 1976)

Tucker, R.C. (ed.), *The Marx-Engels Reader* (Norton, New York, 1978)

Ulam, Adam, *A History of Soviet Russia* (Praeger, New York, 1976)

Ulam, Adam, *The Unfinished Revolution*, revised edn (Longman, London, 1979)

Walker, Martin, *The Waking Giant: the Soviet Union under Gorbachev* (Abacus, London, 1987)

Wesson, Robert (ed.), *The Soviet Union: Looking to the 1980s* (Hoover Institution Press, Stanford, Cal., 1980)

Zaslavsky, Viktor, *The neo-Stalinist State: Class, Ethnicity and Consensus in Soviet Society* (Harvester, Brighton, 1982)

Zaslavsky, Viktor, 'The Soviet World System: Origins, Evolution, Prospects for Reform', *Telos* 65 (fall 1985), pp. 3–22

Index

Note: page numbers in **bold** *denote the key passages*

Index

SS20 missiles 94, 283
stability of cadres 84-5, 89, 180
stagnation era 84, 88-91, 99, 109, 146, 211,
    251-6, 263
Stakhanov, Alexei 98
Stalin, Joseph V. 4, 30, **37-59**, 64-5, 75-8,
    80-1, 85, 87, 98-9, 102, 108, 112, 118,
    135-6, 139, 145-6, 151-2, 155, 161, 167,
    170, 175-6, 178, 183-5, 187, 204, 206,
    208-9, 218-19, 228-30, 233, 237, 241,
    249, 252, 254, 303, 309-10, 313, 319,
    321, 328; foreign policy 273-81, 285-6;
    nationality policy 297-300; and
    participation 64, 163; pattern of
    industrialization 6, 43-7, 64, 257-8; and
    purges 50-5, 77, 118, 273-4; as
    revolutionary 14, 22; succession struggle
    38-43; see also destalinization
Stalingrad 95, 276-7
Stalinism 30, 38, 40, 49, 55-9, 64, 68, 71,
    81-2, 84, 88, 143, 179-80, 189, 206-7,
    213, 215-16, 331, 337
standard of living 7, 49, 75, 78, 86, 88, 251,
    253-4, 257, 267
standing commissions 109, 152, 155-6
Staniszkis, Jadwiga 337
START (Strategic Arms Reduction Talks)
    284, 289
Star Wars (Strategic Defence Initiative, SDI)
    115, 283, 289
state, the 1-4, 6-8, 25, 27-8, 30, 31, 33, 58,
    120, 140, 184, 195, **197, 216-17**, 253,
    328; withering away 78, 87, 106, 120,
    145, 162, 285
state capitalism 27, 37, 229-30
state committees 74, 110, 165
state of the whole people 77-8, 87, 106, 121,
    128, 132, 145, 151, 163, 191, 213
Stavropol *krai* 96
Stevenson amendment 322
Stewart, Philip 190
Stolypin, Peter A. 13, 42
storming 49, 116, 249
STR, *see* scientific-technological revolution
strikes 7, 14, 268, 310, **327**
Struve, Peter 11
students 48-9
subbotniki (unpaid Saturday work) 170
subculture 196, 320, 331
subsidies 260, 328
substitutionism, *see podmena*
succession 37-40, 46-7, 57, 64-6, 90-2,
    176-8, 283, 293
Suez 70
Suleimenov, Olzhas 302
Sumgait 310
superministries 110, 257, 259
Supereme Council of the National Economy,

see Vesenkha
Supreme Court of USSR 98, 109, 121
Supreme Soviet 102-3, **103-10**, 112, 140,
    152, 155, 159, 168-9, 239, 262, 299,
    310; presidium, 109, 112; *see also*
    Congress of People's Deputies,
    presidency, and standing commissions
Suslov, Mikhail A. 80, 85, 92, 96, 178, 215
Sverdlov, Ya. M. 30
Syrtsov, S.I. 50
Szelenyi, Ivan 232
Szklarska Poreba 280

Table of Ranks 3
Tadzhikistan 307-8, 315
Taganka theatre 332
Tallinn 185
Talyzin, Nikolai V. 258
Tambov peasant uprising 32
Tashkent 308
Tatars 130, 300, 307-8, 313-14
Taubman, William 156-7
taxes 155; *see also* finances
tax in kind 32, 37
Taylorism 27
technocracy 86, 89, 93, 97, 129, 147, 163,
    207, 230, 234, 263, 268
technological innovation 59, 72-3, 87, 89,94,
    114-16, 251, 255, 260-1, 283-4, 293
Teheran conference (1943) 277
teleology 57, 207-8, 214
Tereshkova, V. 136
terror 52, 184, 186, 189, 219, 221; *see also*
    purges
terrorism 4, 9, 10
Thatcher, Margaret 283
thaw 65, 71, 321
Third Phase 273
Third Rome 1
Third World 5, 8, 97, 235, 281, 287, 290-1,
    314
Tibet 309
Tikhonov, N.S. 85, 93, 112
Timashev, Nicholas 46
Tito, Josip Broz 69, 279, 281
Tkachev, Peter 10, 11
Tocqueville, Alexis de 3
Toffler, Alvin and Heidi 252
Togliatti, Palmiro 68-9
tolstye zhurnaly 4, 323
totalitarianism 30, 55, 57-8, 157, 163, **183-7**,
    189, 192-7, 216, 230, 234, 286, 332, 337
trade union debate 32
trade unions 3, 7, 13, 29, 76, 78, 138, 147,
    159, 163, **165-6**, 167, 185, 194, 210,
    239, 263, 273, 327
transitional society 195
transmission belts 58, 163-5, 169, 193

354

3